The Educational Thought
and Influence of
MATTHEW ARNOLD

The Educational Thought and Influence of
MATTHEW ARNOLD

by

W. F. CONNELL

*Ph.D. (London), M.A., M.Ed. (Melbourne),
A.M. (Illinois). Lecturer in Education,
University of Melbourne.*

With an Introduction by
SIR FRED CLARKE, M.A.

GREENWOOD PRESS, PUBLISHERS
WESTPORT, CONNECTICUT

TO
MARGARET

Originally published in 1950
by Routledge & Kegan Paul, Ltd., London

Reprinted with the permission
of Routledge & Kegan Paul, Ltd.

First Greenwood Reprinting 1971

Library of Congress Catalogue Card Number 74-109305

SBN 8371-3580-X

Printed in the United States of America

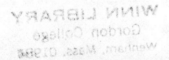

CONTENTS

ACKNOWLEDGEMENTS

The author wishes to acknowledge the guidance and assistance he has received both from Sir Fred Clarke, at whose initial suggestion the study was undertaken and whose invaluable insights into and understanding of the English tradition of education have proved to be a constant source of inspiration, and from Dr. R. W. Greaves, of Bedford College, London, whose friendly support, professional advice and critical judgment have been of the greatest value and encouragement.

The following have generously given permission to quote from and make use of unpublished material in their care: Miss Dorothy Ward, Professor Arnold Whitridge, Rear Admiral F. D. Arnold Forster, Lord Lansdowne, The Librarian, Oriel College, Oxford, and The Librarian, Sheffield University. My thanks are due to the Oxford University Press for permission to quote from Lowry's *Letters of Matthew Arnold to Arthur Hugh Clough*.

THE LIFE OF MATTHEW ARNOLD

1822 Born at Laleham, Surrey (December 24th), son of Rev. Thomas Arnold and Mary Penrose.

1828 Father became Headmaster of Rugby.

1832 Father bought Fox How, Ambleside.

1836 Sent to Winchester College.

1837 Removed to Rugby School.

1841 Scholar at Balliol College, Oxford, under the tutorship of R. Lingen.

1842 Father died.

1843 Newdigate prize poem on "Cromwell".

1844 Second Class in Literae Humaniores.

1845 Taught at Rugby. Fellowship at Oriel College, Oxford.

1846 Journey to France and Swiss Oberland.

1847 Private secretary to Marquis of Lansdowne, President of the Council.

1849 "The Strayed Reveller, and Other Poems," Arnold's first volume of poetry.

1851 Appointed one of Her Majesty's Inspectors of Schools. Married Frances Lucy Wightman, daughter of Judge Wightman. Arnold henceforth spent much time in travel, both on circuit with the Judge and on inspectorial duties.

1857 Professor of Poetry at Oxford. Inaugural Lecture on "The Modern Element in Literature".

1859 Foreign Assistant Commissioner to Newcastle Commission. France, Holland, Switzerland. "England and the Italian Question".

1861 "The Popular Education of France".

1862 "The Twice Revised Code".

1864 "A French Eton".

1865 France, Italy, Germany, Switzerland for Taunton Commission. "Essays in Criticism" (First Series).

1866 "Thyrsis".

1867 Professorship ended.

1868 "Schools and Universities on the Continent".

1869 "Culture and Anarchy".

1870 D.C.L., Oxford, "St. Paul and Protestantism." Senior Inspector of Schools.

1871 "Friendship's Garland."

1872 "A Bible Reading for Schools: The Great Prophecy of Israel's Restoration."

1873 "Literature and Dogma."

1875 "God and the Bible."

1877 "Last Essays on Church and Religion." Declined nomination to Lord Rectorship of University of St. Andrew's.

1879 "Mixed Essays."

1882 "Irish Essays."

1883 Civil List Pension of £250. Visit to America. "Isaiah of Jerusalem".

1884 Chief Inspector of Schools.

1885 Declined re-nomination for Oxford Professorship. "Discourses in America."

1886 Resigned Inspectorship. "Report on Certain Points Connected with Elementary Education in Germany, Switzerland, and France."

1888 Died. "Essays in Criticism" (Second Series).

1889 "Reports on Elementary Schools (1852–82)", ed. Sir Francis Sandford.

INTRODUCTION
by Sir Fred Clarke, M.A.

Much good work has been done, and is being done, on the history
of English education in the nineteenth century. We shall understand ourselves and our situation better when that work has been
carried nearer completion. It cannot yet be called "adequate"
(if we may use the term that was one of Arnold's favourite criteria).
The educational story needs to be brought into closer relation
with the accelerating pace of social and economic change which
became so marked after the turn of the century. Particularly
does it need to be told in the light of an analysis of that ferment of
conflicting ideas which presaged the new era. For such an
analysis a study of Arnold's life and work is indispensable, for he
was himself a powerful fermenting agent.

Some of the ideas were new and disturbing, others were old and
not always obstructive. But some were endowed with a traditional
authority to which they had no real claim. An example is the
notion of the "Poor" as a fixed institution, even held by some to
be divinely ordained.* How revealing, for instance, is Robert
Lowe's remark about his Revised Code for the elementary schools,
with its rigorous insistence upon the Three R's, and financial
penalties for deficiencies in teaching them! He confessed that the
Three R's were "more a financial than a literary preference".

A further feature of the time, of which historians of education
will need to take notice is the steady, if slow, weakening of national
insularity. Doubts were creeping in, there was less of Palmerston-
ian insolence and Podsnap had already become a fit subject for
caricature.

So an interest in comparative education could arise, a study
which in England has had no greater pioneer and illuminator
than Arnold. Through it our sense of the need to study education
and the history of education in their social and cultural setting
has been awakened and strengthened. It is not too much to say
that Arnold was the creator in this country of what may be
called, as a study, the "politics" of education.

*It was at this time that the final clause of My Duty Towards My Neighbour came
to be so generally misquoted by those who should have known better. It runs, o
course, "and to do my duty in that state of life into which it *shall please* God to call
me"; not "*hath pleased*".

ix

How fortunate it is then that we should have had, in such an age, that sensitive and forward-looking mind contemplating with high moral sense and acuteness of judgment those critical years of transition! That for him the times were decisive and right action urgent he makes clear again and again, sometimes even with a touch of anguish. For instance, in *Friendship's Garland* he makes Arminius remark in a farewell letter, "your country, where I have lived so long and seen so much, is on its way either to a great transformation or a great disaster".

Again, how fortunate it is for us, uncongenial as it may have been at times for Arnold, that he held the post of Her Majesty's Inspector of Schools! So his judgments upon the changing contemporary scene carried with them so often their educational implications, forcibly and penetratingly expressed. It is in this respect that his work and thought have such value and relevance for our own times. Indeed, his mode of approach to the tasks of education might well be taken as a model to-day by those who feel themselves capable of it. In his sensitiveness to the impact of current ideas, in the subtlety and force of his social and cultural analyses, in his insistence upon *values* (for that is what culture seems to mean for him), in his awareness of the value of comparative studies to bring defects and virtues into relief and to give definition to axioms and standards, and in his high conception of the functions of the State: in all these respects the force of his example has gained rather than lost with the lapse of years. Something will have to be said presently of the striking vindication of his prophetic vision that has been afforded by he course of events since his death.

There is another respect in which we can cc. t ourselves fortunate, that is, in finding a man of Dr. Connell's powers and qualifications to undertake the comprehensive review of Arnold's work and influence that is now so clearly due.

I had long been feeling that the time had arrived for such a review. When Dr. Connell called on me at the University of London Institute of Education while the war was still in progress in order to discuss possible work for the University degree of Ph.D, it needed no more than a brief conversation for me to decide that here was the man. I can safely leave the question whether I was right to be answered by readers of the book itself, published now with the University's approval as a thesis presented for the degree of Ph.D. (Education).

Although I was in contact with the writer while the work was in process and had several discussions with him, the book is very definitely his own. It is worthy of note too that the author is Australian, a graduate of the University of Melbourne. Arnold, in his somewhat acid comments on the America of his day showed that he never appreciated the possibilities of the "new" countries. Such a book as this, by an Australian, is, one can feel, precisely the kind of retort that he would have appreciated.

It would be uncalled for here to offer any kind of summary of Dr. Connell's work and I have no intention of doing so. But there are certain points of particular interest in Arnold's efforts to reform education which need to be emphasized as they are not without relevance at the present time. They reveal, too, the almost uncanny sureness of Arnold's foresight. He was a prophet in both senses of the word. What was the inspiring purpose that informed and directed his lifelong effort? No better answer can be found than the sentence from *Irish Essays* which Dr. Connell prefixes to Chapter XI:

"English civilization—the humanizing, the bringing into one harmonious and truly humane life of the whole body of English society,—that is what interests me."

There can be no greater tribute to Arnold's work and influence than the fact that so many more would re-echo this sentiment in our own day than would have been prepared to do so in his. One can imagine him contemplating the Education Act of 1944 with its generous presuppositions and saying, "Yes, something like that". But would he be quite at ease? Would he feel that the battle was won? It is to be doubted. We may hazard the guess that he would measure the extent of the *moral* commitment and decide that the fight had still to go on. Moreover, would he feel that the battle was quite won with that "religion of inequality" which in his view worked such vast mischief in the social and cultural life of the England of his day, "materializing the upper class, vulgarizing the middle class and brutalizing the lower class"?

We can be assured, I think, that admitting so much achieved, he would still find himself beset with doubts and anxieties. One can almost hear his sharp comments on some current interpretations of the phrase "standard of life". And how would he regard the religious prospect, particularly from the point of view of his preoccupation with morals? Would he think that *Aberglaube* was still re-invading, and what would be his estimate of Agreed Syllabuses of religious instruction?

It may be permissible to particularize a little in acknowledging our debt to him. It is possible to quarrel with his conception of Culture and to find contradictory elements in it. We need not go into detail here. Mr. T. S. Eliot, perhaps the nearest parallel to Arnold that we have with us to-day, has apparently a somewhat different conception. Possibly he would agree that anything which is calculated, in Arnold's phrase, "to animate and ennoble" is covered by the term.

What Dr. Connell has to say of Arnold's conception is of particular interest. There is so much more in it than just "knowledge of the best that has been thought and said". The transformation that has come over what was the elementary school may illustrate Arnold's meaning, though he would not be entirely satisfied with it. As for culture as an educational objective, we may suppose that, in practice, this would imply a certain sustained "severity", a rigorous application of standards to achievements in respect of quality and motive. There may be something here that we have still to learn to apply in its full significance.

Arnold's conception of the cultural and educational functions of the State must have startled his contemporaries and he never tired of insisting upon it. But is it so much a commonplace among us to-day as we may imagine it to be? Contemplating the British State as it now is he might agree that it is nearer to his ideal than the state upon which he himself looked out and which he served so well. But, seeing it as the acknowledged Welfare State, might he not feel that its moral and intellectual currency was not quite up to standard, and so be led to define anew the purposes of national education? And that, be it noted, in the conditions of industrial democracy, certainly somewhat novel to him and perhaps a little alarming.

He sees the State as succeeding to the functions of a displaced aristocracy, chief among its benefits being "an ideal of high reason and right feeling, representing its best self, commanding general respect and forming a rallying-point for the intelligence and for the worthiest instincts of the community, which will herein find a true bond of union". We are reminded of Burke's great summary: "A partnership in all science; a partnership in all art; a partnership in every virtue and in all perfection".

We could feel like that in the high moments of the war, but

what of the strains and stresses of industrial democracy in the midst of economic struggle? So once more the purposes of education call for re-definition.

One more point: Arnold, with his penetrating insight into influences at work in English society, might well have foreseen, had he thought about it, the marked cleavage of attitude towards the State in education which is now to be observed between two sections of the people. On the one hand there are those, a minority, still influential, for whom the State is, traditionally, that which they *serve*, though often at a price for their service. On the other hand there are those, the great majority, for whom, traditionally, the State is that which serves *them*. Strong and penetrating as are the effects of the sharp difference of attitude, all too little account is taken of it. For the minority the "independent" schools are the stronghold of faith and any encroachment by the State upon the freedom of such schools is sure to evoke tenacious resistance. The majority have learned from experience to look to the State as the source of their educational good and are disposed to look with favour upon every extension of its power and authority.

There is still danger here. To transcend this cleavage with no loss to enshrined values and fine traditions will be a test of capacity to rise to the heights of Arnold's conception of the State.

We have already noted Arnold's overwhelming sense of the school as a civilizing agent. In the technical "office" sense he was probably not a highly efficient inspector and, as Dr. Connell shows, his suggestions concerning teaching were not always well-considered. But, as the Americans would say, he had the right idea. So he fought relentlessly, and at some risks to himself, the application of Lowe's Revised Code, not because it was in itself de-civilizing but because it diverted resources and energies from the proper civilizing function of the school, in this case the elementary school. The lesson has been learned now, at least in principle, and many a primary and secondary school to-day demonstrates how generously and skilfully this civilizing function of the school is being recognized and discharged. But not only is there much more yet to be done, it is also becoming clear that there are limits to what even the best school can do.

The general life of society is also a "school", and, uninspired by similar values, can quickly undo what the regular school, with so much labour, achieves. Arnold, Greek-inspired as he was, was well aware of this and the time has come when we need to be more aware of it too.

Even those who know little of Arnold's work will have heard of his famous slogan: "Organize your secondary education!" What he had in mind was the needs of the middle class, and he might well have regarded the Act of 1902 as, in principle, meeting his demand. For the State then, for the first time, accepted the responsibility of providing for secondary education. It was to urge the taking of just this step that Arnold, influenced by Continental example, expounded his view of the proper functions of the State in education. His most pointed shafts were reserved for what he took to be the failings and weaknesses of the middle class of his own time, and the very vigour of his criticism was itself an expression of his sense of the importance of the class whose faults he so scarified. "They want culture and dignity; they want ideas"; and he was convinced that the State could do far better for them than the unsatisfactory private schools whose deficiencies are so ruthlessly laid bare in the reports of the Taunton Commission.

In the light of later developments it would be a bold thing to say he was wrong. The middle class of to-day is somewhat differently constituted and certainly larger as compared with that of Arnold's time. Nor can its upper and lower boundaries be clearly defined. It would be extravagant to suggest that the effect of Secondary Education For All, imaginatively and consistently carried out, will result in the whole nation becoming middle class! That might not be a desirable consummation. However, Arnold's idea of equality is relevant here. In emphasizing it he was clearly not thinking so much of economic condition as of culture, conceiving of a *common culture* in which all alike genuinely shared, and to which each, in the measure of his capacity, made his contribution.

For a social democracy this would not seem to be an undesirable ideal and there are signs that we have already made some progress towards it. What kind of class-structure will issue from it all no one can say. But much will depend on the qualities we single out as distinguishing those whom we look upon as *élite* types, and on the capacity of the schools to discover and cultivate those who possess such qualities.

In summing up all these illustrations of the debt we owe to Arnold it may be sufficient to suggest a close reading of the concluding pages of Chapter VIII of this book where the essence of his philosophy of education is set forth. Then look at the brief sketch on p. 88 where he gives in outline his plan for national education and compare it with what has now been achieved.

Of Arnold's weaknesses and deficiencies little need be said here. They are obvious enough and Dr. Connell deals faithfully with them. We have already noted his failure, excusable enough, to appreciate the true significance of the "new" countries. More serious was his failure to realize that science was a necessary ingredient, growing in importance, of any conception of culture that could even then be called "adequate". He would have understood it better to-day, but the limitations of training and experience were too strong then. In the debate with Huxley the honours were not with Arnold. Indeed, he does not seem to have grasped the issue in its full cultural bearing. Perhaps he can be excused, as even to-day there are those in positions of influence who have not grasped it yet.

For his writings on religion he may well have deserved what critics like F. H. Bradley meted out to him. But here again, let it be remembered that his dominant interest throughout was in morals; he was concerned supremely with securing for the England that was taking shape the moral basis that he knew to be indispensable. If he is accused of drawing religion too exclusively into morals, are we not equally open to accusation in the converse sense, that we have failed to keep close, as the nineteenth century did, the effective relation between religion and conduct, and become too tolerant of the hiatus between profession and actual behaviour? There may have been, after all, an element of integrity in Arnold that is less strong with us than it was with him.

Although, in his reports as Inspector, he had much to say about the work of the schools, it can be doubted whether he ever fully understood the difficulties of the elementary teacher's job. Sympathy there was in abundance, but the gulf set by training and social experience was too wide to be completely bridged. The same gulf, though now much narrowed, is still with us; we have still to overcome imperfections of communication between the various sections of the people. The schools, by generous interpretation of the essentials of a common culture, and by imaginative and humane methods of communicating them, can do much towards closing the gap. But they cannot do all that is necessary. We must trust to the slow movements of social and cultural change to complete the process.

Finally Arnold is accused of vagueness, of imprecision in the handling of ideas, and of failure to examine critically his own presuppositions. There is substance in the charge and Dr. Connell deals with it adequately. But there is this to be said. Arnold was no speculative thinker, he was rather prophet and poet, preacher and, above all, moralist. He was not concerned to convince men of the truth of a theory but to move them to right action. In the light of all the facts, can it be said that his methods were ineffective, whatever weakness the logician may detect in his mode of argument? The truth is that he *cared*, and cared intensely, and gave himself to his chosen task with a completeness of commitment that is not easily equalled.

Always present to his consciousness was a sure insight into the elements that constituted true greatness in a people. As an arch-enemy to greatness he singled out Vulgarity. What would he say on the matter if he were with us to-day? Possibly he would say that while culture had extended farther downwards in the social scale, Vulgarity would appear to have moved upwards. Thus we have been told that Britain continues to be great because a few years ago she built two very big ships and has just built a very big aeroplane. So too, the Pharaohs built some very big piles of stones. Can we not almost hear Arnold exclaiming that that is precisely what he meant by Vulgarity? And we can imagine him adding that Britain will continue to be great precisely in so far as she refuses to regard such criteria as the measure of greatness.

In any case, the coming years can be counted upon to apply the true test, severe as it is likely to be. So far as education is concerned the task before us is clear enough. It is to seize the opportunity afforded by the "adequate" legislation that has come at last, and by patient endeavour in the nearest we can approach to Arnold's spirit to ensure that

> ". . . tasks in hours of insight will'd
> Can be through hours of gloom fulfill'd."

F. Clarke.

13/10/49.

CHAPTER I

SOCIAL AND EDUCATIONAL TRENDS OF THE MID-NINETEENTH CENTURY

"To understand the early Victorian Age it is necessary to enter into the emotions of 1851".—*Early Victorian England* (ed. G. M. Young, vol. i, p. 212).

WHEN Matthew Arnold was gazetted Her Majesty's Inspector of Schools on 15th April, 1851,[1] not only was he entering upon a new and very promising career of social usefulness, but English education also was at a critical stage of development. Roused by the ferment of the period, it too was beginning a new career, tentatively taking its first footsteps along the uncertain path of National Education that was to become clearer and more-defined as the century wore on.

The year 1851 saw the opening of a new era in English history, and was made especially significant to contemporary Victorians, if not to the whole world, by the impressive spectacle of the Great Exhibition. Disgruntled cynics such as Colonel Sibthorp might sneer at the "unwieldy, ill-devised unwholesome castle of glass", but the six million visitors who thronged the Crystal Palace between 1st May and 11th October were more likely to endorse the sentiments of the Earl of Derby. He was inspired to refer in more than usual Victorian fulsomeness to "that enchanted pile which the sagacious taste, and the prescient philanthropy of an accomplished and enlightened Prince have raised for the glory of England, and the delight and instruction of two hemispheres".[2] The Hallelujah chorus into which the massed choirs burst as overture to the Queen's inspection of the Exhibition harmonised with her own paean in praise of "the greatest triumph of peace

[1] The following entry occurs in the *List Book of Orders in Council* 1846–52, Privy Council Office, under the date 14th April, 1851:

"Education Inspector {Reception of Education Comtee (sic) recommending Matthew Arnold Esq. to be appointed one of H.M.'s Inspectors of Schools, Appd. (gazd. 15th.)"

[2] Monypenny and Buckle, *Life of Disraeli*, ii, 1119. Charles de L. W. Sibthorp (1783–1855), an ultra-Tory M.P., who had served in the Peninsular Wars, gained notoriety by his uncompromising opposition to Catholic Emancipation, The Reform Bill, and Free Trade. His dislike of foreign influence led him in 1840 to propose successfully the reduction of the proposed allowance of £40,000 for the Prince Consort to the sum of £30,000.

I

which the world has ever seen"[1]; and the fanfare of trumpets
that echoed through the great glass nave and eddied past the
leafy branches of the tall elms, still standing, enclosed, away to
the upper galleries, when Her Majesty at length declared the
Exhibition open, seemed a fitting prelude to the great age of
boundless progress that was beginning.

England was in fact entering upon an era of unexampled
economic prosperity. It was just at the beginning of a period of
a steady upward swing in prices which lasted from 1849 to 1873.
Concurrently with the beginning of this upward trend came the
gold discoveries of 1849 and 1851 in California and Victoria
which stimulated the price movement and the increasing volume
of investments associated with it. United Kingdom exports
expanded rapidly and trade flourished.[2] English capital and
English enterprise were at work in every quarter of the globe
reaping to the full the benefits of the new freedom that the advocates of *laissez-faire* had achieved with the break-up of the traditional system of Protection after the downfall of the Corn Laws
in 1846. Already in 1851[3] *The Economist* was writing, "As a rule
England gives credit to all the world and takes none". The laying
of the underseas cable between Calais and Dover in 1851, and
the subsequent world-wide development of cable and telegraph
systems increased the sensitivity of the market and strengthened
the position of London as the commercial centre of the world.
Even the financial crisis of 1857 which temporarily checked the
upward swing of prices and investment, served to demonstrate
both the dominant position of the United Kingdom and the new
interconnectedness of commerce throughout the world.[4]

[1] T. Martin, *Prince Consort*, ii, 405. A comprehensive description of the Great Exhibition and its effect on contemporary England is to be found in G. M. Young (ed.),
Early Victorian England, i, 212–23.
[2] The growth of the export trade can be gauged from the following table:—

					Exports of U.K. produce million £
1849–54	..	..	..	..	67
1855–59	..	..	..	..	116
1860–64	..	..	..	..	133
1865–69	..	..	..	..	181
1870–74	..	..	..	..	235

Fiscal Blue Book, 1909, Cmd. 4954, quoted in L. C. A. Knowles, *The Industrial and
Commercial Revolutions of Great Britain during the Nineteenth Century*, Routledge, London,
1937, p. 18.
[3] *The Economist*, ix, 30, 11th January, 1851.
[4] This upset was the first world-wide financial crisis of modern times. Starting
with the failure in mid-September of the Ohio Life and Trust Company it quickly
spread throughout the London market and the European world. By January of the
new year the Bank of England had it judiciously under control and world trade was
once more on the upward grade. J. H. Clapham, *An Economic History of Modern
Britain*, vol. ii, pp. 368–9.

Just as she led the world of finance and trade, so the United Kingdom also had an indisputable lead in industry. In cotton, coal, woollens, worsted, and steel, the lead she had obtained by her early industrial start was fully maintained. Her world importance is well summed up by the following striking passage by a well-known economic historian: "In the twenty-three years from 1850 to 1873 Great Britain was the forge of the world, the world's carrier, the world's shipbuilder, the world's banker, the world's workshop, the world's clearing-house, the world's entrepôt. The trade of the world during this period pivoted on Great Britain."[1] It is to be noted that the emphasis is placed on world trade. The modern era of worldwide interdependence had begun. The transactions of the Liverpool cotton exchange, a drought in New South Wales, the failure of a *Crédit mobilier* in Paris, the building of a railway in the Argentine or India were no longer merely of local concern but were reflected through an increasingly sensitive commercial system to all quarters of the globe. "British mechanical deputations to the United States, continentals besieging Gilchrist Thomas before breakfast for licences to work his invention, Rathenau founding his Edisongesellschaft; or the careers of the brothers Siemens planted in two countries yet working together are symbolic of the new age. Engines are toiling indifferently for all."[2]

Unemployment in England was generally low throughout the whole period except for special instances, such as the Lancashire cotton famine during the American Civil War of 1861–5, and the declining silk industry, which had little effect on the general level of employment throughout the country. At the same time there was a steady rise in wages outstripping the rise in prices, and leaving the working classes better off. The fear of social revolution that seemed to haunt all social legislation from the beginning of the century was no longer apparent. It had died with the Chartist fiasco on 10th April, 1848. The population of England was increasing rapidly, and its geographical distribution steadily altering. An important factor in upsetting the old balance was the Poor Law of 1834. By prohibiting outdoor relief, in so far as it could be implemented, it increased the mobility of labour by forcing distressed agricultural workers into the towns and on to

---

[1] L. A. C. Knowles, *The Industrial and Commercial Revolutions in Great Britain during the Nineteenth Century*, p. 139.
[2] J. H. Clapham, *An Economic History of Modern Britain*, vol. ii, "Free Trade and Steel", p. 113.

the industrial labour market. One of the conditions of expanding capitalism is just such a mobility of labour, which in turn was further stimulated by the increasing popularity of the weekly wage system. Hence it is found that the increase in population was confined to industrial areas. The agricultural population remained fairly constant as its natural increase migrated city-wards. By 1851 the general pattern of present-day England had taken shape. The industrial areas were already clearly marked. With the main exceptions of the Middlesborough and Cardiff areas, few new regions were developed. The development that did take place was in the extension and linking-up of established areas, encroaching more and more on to agricultural lands and growing into the seemingly endless manufacturing centres and sprawling conurbations of the present day.

The main characteristic of the period under consideration was that of mobility. The new railways made for mobility of goods, ease of distribution and mobility of persons; rapidly developing capitalism brought with it mobility of capital and mobility of labour; and new developments in industry or trade introduced new occupations and accelerated the movement of persons from class to class or among the several gradations of the ever-expanding middle classes.

The tempo of life was increasing as the old era of tradition, privilege and status was vanishing in the middle class solvent of utility and *laissez-faire*.

It is not surprising therefore to find this mid-century instability reflected in contemporary politics. Seldom has such confusion existed in English politics as was apparent in the decade that followed the abolition of the Corn Laws in 1846.

By the passage of that legislation Peel split his own Tory party from top to bottom, and by a combination of vengeful Protec-tionists and ambitious Whigs was removed from office in the same month that the Corn Bill became law. Lord John Russell then, failing to entice the breakaway Tories into a more permanent union, formed a ministry from the Whig minority which survived a general election in 1847 and although discredited on many counts did not lose office until early in 1852. The year 1851 opened with Russell's uneasy Whig ministry endeavouring to rally popular support by raising a "No Popery" protest against the recent establishment of a Roman Catholic hierarchy in England, but succeeding only in alienating the Irish members on whose support it had hitherto leaned in some small measure, and in intensifying sectarian feeling throughout the country. Russell's fall was delayed only by the difficulty of finding another leader who, in the confused state of politics, could command not a majority but only sufficient support in the House to enable essential legislation to be passed from time to time.

At the close of the year, Palmerston, who twelve months earlier had electrified the country with his celebrated "civis Romanus sum" oration was dismissed from his Foreign Secretary-ship for his tactless expression of opinion on Louis Napoleon's *coup d'état*, and within two months had had his "tit-for-tat with John Russell"[1] by organising his defeat on a Militia Bill in mid-February of 1852. A government of half-hearted protectionist Tories followed under Derby in the Lords and Disraeli in the Commons, and managed to remain intact until the general election in July. The parliament which re-assembled in September was virtually the same medley of Peelites, anti-Peelites, Manchester radicals, Irish members, and Whigs of diverse beliefs and loyalties. The Derby-Disraeli coalition, which "had neither political principles nor administrative experience",[2] failed to carry its budget in December and was succeeded before the New Year by a Whig-Peelite combination under the Earl of Aberdeen, which, despite a multitude of conflicting counsels that led to the unedifying policy out of which the Crimean War issued, managed to retain the confidence of the House until January 1855.

Trevelyan has well summed up this period when he spoke of it as "one of parliamentary confusion, of weak governments, of rapid combinations and dissolutions of political partnerships."[3]

Amid this confusion of political loyalties and economic change, one would hardly expect to find in contemporary England any widely agreed and consistently held policy on educational matters.

Until 1833, all funds for the support of schools had been raised by voluntary subscription, endowment, or the payment of school fees. In that year, for the first time, the central government voted a grant to assist in the building of new schools erected either by the Anglican National Society for promoting the Education of the Poor in the Principles of the Established Church, or by the un-

[1] Palmerston to his brother, quoted S. Low and L. C. Sanders, *The Reign of Queen Victoria* (1837–1901), p. 94.
[2] J. Morley, *Life of Cobden*, vol. ii, p. 97.
[3] G. M. Trevelyan, *Life of J. Bright*, p. 178.

denominational, British and Foreign School Society.[1] This practice was maintained until 1846. Meanwhile, in 1839, parliament had appointed a Committee of the Privy Council to supervise the disbursement of the grant, and the Committee in its turn, appointed the first batch of Her Majesty's Inspectors to do the necessary fieldwork for them.

The Minutes of the Committee of Council issued in August and December of 1846 made a decisive change in the relationship of the state to the schools. By these minutes a pupil-teacher system was established under which selected pupils during the course of their apprenticeship to their schoolmasters and their subsequent training as Queen's Scholars in normal schools were paid a small stipend by the State, and their teachers received also an augmentation of their salaries from the same source. These payments were conditional upon the due certification of Her Majesty's Inspectors that a prescribed course of study had been successfully followed, that the schools in which they were trained were suitably organised, and the schoolmaster "competent to conduct the apprentice through the course of instruction to be required".[2] This meant that the State which had hitherto confined its efforts to assistance in the erection of school buildings, had decided to take a hand in supervising, through its inspectorate, what went on inside those school buildings. In those minutes were contained the germ of much of the State's future development in the educational field. It had, thereby, declared itself vitally interested in the qualifications of schoolmasters, the selection and training of teachers, the school curriculum, and the method of classroom organisation.

It is not too much to describe the Minutes of 1846 as the beginning of a period of renascence in English Education. By tackling the problem of the production of efficient teachers they went to the very core of all educational reconstruction, and the stimulus given to the better training of teachers was soon relayed throughout the whole educational system. With the foundation of the two great educational societies at the beginning of the century, a start had been made with a systematic training of teachers. The British and Foreign Society founded the Borough Road Training College, and the National Society followed suit

---

[1] Other societies, also, later were made eligible for assistance. For a list of them *vide* J. W. Adamson, *English Education* 1789–1902, p. 127.
[2] *Minutes of the Committee of Council*, 1, 2-3, 21st December, 1846, "General Preliminary Conditions".

with a number of small training establishments and model schools. But the courses in each case lasted only a few months and were, for the most part, confined to the acquirement of the mechanical technique of school management that the monitorial system required. What Kay-Shuttleworth called the first genuine training institution in the country was established by David Stow in 1836 as the Glasgow Normal Seminary. In 1839 there were in England only three organised Training Colleges: the Borough Road, the Central Schools of the National Society at Westminster, and the Home and Colonial Society's school for training infant teachers.[1] In that year the Committee of Council tried unsuccessfully to establish a State Normal School but denominational opposition to the project proved too strong. Kay-Shuttleworth, however, founded privately, in 1840, a college which later became Battersea Training College, and after three years handed it over to the National Society which meanwhile, together with the British and Foreign School Society, had slowly increased the number of their training establishments.

The Minutes of 1846 led to a speedy increase in the number of normal schools. Six years after the Minutes, 39 had received building grants from the Committee of Council, and 30 were under regular inspection as against 13 in 1846.[2] This resulted in an increased output of certificated teachers even before the first of the Queen's Scholars had completed their training in 1853.[3] It is probably to this sudden outpouring of trained teachers that Dickens' "attention was drawn when he satirised the new product in the person of Mr. McChoakumchild who "had worked his stony way into Her Majesty's most Honourable Privy Council's Schedule B" and with "some one hundred and forty other schoolmasters had been lately turned at the same time, in the same factory, on the same principles, like so many pianoforte legs."[4] Whatever their faults, the new elementary teachers, had they been, everyone of them, McChoakumchilds, would, unlike the majority of their predecessors, be entering at least upon a deliberately chosen profession for which they had been carefully

[1] R. W. Rich, *The Training of Teachers in England and Wales during the Nineteenth Century*, p. 81.
[2] J. K. Shuttleworth, *Public Education as affected by the Minutes of the Committee of Council from 1846–52*, pp. 64–66.
[3] id., p. 78. On 31st December there were 1,173 certificated teachers in Great Britain (845 men and 328 women), and 5,607 pupil-teachers (3,657 boys and 1,950 girls), id., pp. 79–80.
[4] *Hard Times*, chap. I. This was first published in 1854.

prepared by the best methods of contemporary pedagogy. The Minutes had the effect of "planting, in every part of the country a class of still imperfectly developed model schools, under the charge of teachers who have obtained certificates of merit, assisted by pupil-teachers in various stages of their apprentice-ship".[1] The stimulating effect of these "model schools" is diffi-cult to estimate. As, however, Her Majesty's Inspectors' reports for the next fifteen years are full of praise for the system, it may be assumed that they endeavoured to spread the influence of such schools by recommending their example to the managers and teachers of others. Mr. Morell in 1850 said, "The system of pupil-teachers still remains one of the most interesting and im-portant features in your Lordships' Minutes, and none, I believe, has had as great effect in raising the general tone of primary education throughout the country. . . . A single effective school, held up as a model to a district, is a *realized idea*, which places the entire problem of education to the minds of observers in a new light. To bring the mass of our population under such influences is seen at once to be an object worth all the effort and the sacrifice that can be directed towards it."[2] A further way in which the Minutes reacted favourably upon elementary schools in general was by the encouragement to study and improvement of those masters who had not passed through Training Schools. Both a fear of being "pushed from their stools by Queen's Scholars",[3] and a desire to increase their salaries by qualifying as suitable persons to be entrusted with the education of pupil teachers, appears to have led many to renew their studies and improve their school-keeping.

This new system also broke up the monitorial system of in-struction which had been in vogue since Bell and Lancaster had introduced it into England at the beginning of the century.[4] The Minutes of 1846 required that schools in which pupil-teachers were employed should be divided into classes and that the apprentices should have experience of teaching the various classes, and this proviso appears to have been actually carried out with great resultant benefit. "In the schools where pupil-

---

[1] J. K. Shuttleworth, op. cit., 99–100.
[2] *Minutes of Committee of Council* 1850–1, II, p. 627.
[3] J. K. Shuttleworth, op. cit., p. 79.
[4] It is interesting to note that A. N. Basu in his recently published *Education in Modern India*, Orient Book Coy., Calcutta, 1947, p. 7, refers to the system as having "been in use in the village Pathshalas from time immemorial" before Bell wrote his celebrated description of the Madras System in 1797.

teachers are employed, the monitorial system has generally been given up"; "Every one who has had opportunities of comparing schools so organised with schools conducted on the old monitorial system, must have recognised the improved aspect . . ." are the opinions of two of Her Majesty's Inspectors in 1850.[1] This change in organisation was a necessary pre-requisite to the development of any curriculum that purported to be much more than a mere mechanical course in the 3 Rs, and therefore must be considered as a move of considerable significance in modern English education.

Lastly, the influence of the inspectorate, which was almost entirely "absorbed by the administration of the Minutes of 1846",[2] the leaven of improved teachers and enthusiastic pupil-teachers, and the zealous response of normal school masters, led to a diffusion of new books on methods and improved school text books. The Committee of Council in 1848 even went so far as to publish a list of the best school books used in Great Britain, made grants for their purchase, and entered into arrangements with the publishers for their sale at reduced prices to schools under inspection. So far had its position moved in less than ten years from that of a mere approving authority of parliamentary grants for the erection of new school buildings.[3]

The consequences of these Minutes in the actual schoolroom are well summarised in the report of one of the inspectors for 1851. "I have taken pains to compare schools very carefully which have been instructed by young monitors on the one hand, and by pupil-teachers on the other, under the superintendence of masters nearly equal in mental power and force of character, and, with scarcely an exception, I have arrived at one uniform result. The quantity of work done throughout the school has increased and is still increasing at an accelerating rate of progress. . . . The elder pupils learn much that was scarcely attempted in former years, and understand much better what was formerly taught upon a superficial and mechanical system. . . . It is, however, in the middle part of the schools, in those classes which contain the mass of children in regular attendance,

---

[1] Rev. H. Moseley, *Minutes of Committee of Council* 1850–51, II, p. 2, and Rev. J. P. Norris, ibid, p. 489; C. Birchenough, *History of Elementary Education*, pp. 238–93 analyses the development of school organisation in the first 60 years of the nineteenth century.
[2] J. K. Shuttleworth, op. cit., p. 87.
[3] id., p. 89.

that I have observed with pleasure the most striking improvement, owing to the employment of pupil-teachers. . . . This is a fact of immense importance. A vast number of children leave school without rising to the first division, and, in that case, formerly left without having acquired so much knowledge of the elements of reading, writing, and cyphering as would enable them to discharge the duties of any station where such qualifications are needed. At present a fair proportion of these same children would write neatly, and not incorrectly, from dictation, read the Holy Scriptures and common secular books with tolerable ease, work elementary rules in arithmetic with facility, and have some acquaintance with geography, the history of their own country, and not infrequently with the rudiments of natural history."[1]

Such comments were re-echoed and reinforced by the statements of many of the witnesses before the Select Committee on the Manchester and Salford Education Bill in 1853, such as the remark of Rev. W. McKerrow, a leading promotor of the Bill: "I find that the improvement that has been made in education has depended very much upon the grants which have been given under the Minutes in Council, and the appointment of pupil-teachers."[2]

The years 1850-1 are significant for the introduction of a series of Bills which began the long campaign for the establishment of a national system based on the authority of an Act of Parliament. The first was the Secular Education Bill, 1850, of W. J. Fox[3] based on three main principles; that the means of education should be supplied by local rates; that education should be free; and that pupils should not be obliged to accept any religious instruction whatever. The Bill was defeated on the second reading in the House of Commons, but not before its advocacy of secular education had roused Lord Arundel to exclaim: "The two armies were drawing up their forces and the battle was now between religion and irreligion—the Church and Infidelity—God and

---

[1] Mr. Cook's Report, *Minutes of Committee of Council* 1851-2, II, pp. 39–41 (J. K. Shuttleworth, op. cit., pp. 93–4).
[2] *Parliamentary Papers*, 1852–3, xxiv, Report from the Select Committee on Education (Manchester and Salford, etc.) (1853), p. 53, Q. 363.
[3] W. J. Fox (1786–1864), Unitarian minister, M.P. for Oldham (1847–63), a celebrated radical orator made his reputation as a leading member of the Anti-Corn Law League. Bright wrote to his son in 1883, "Your father was the *orator* of the League". Trevelyan writes of the three leading speakers: "Cobden was argument, Bright was passion, Fox was rhetoric". G. M. Trevelyan, *The Life of John Bright*, p. 98.

the Devil—and the reward for which they must contend was
Heaven or Hell."[1] Nothing daunted, in the following May, Fox
returned to the attack by proposing a resolution "that it is
expedient to promote the Education of the People in England
and Wales, by the establishment of Free schools for secular
instruction, to be supported by local rates, and managed by
Committees, elected specifically for that purpose by the ratepayers".[2] This was again overwhelmingly rejected. It was
followed toward the close of the year by the Manchester and
Salford Education Bill.[3] This proposed to provide free education[4] for the poor inhabitants of Manchester and Salford from
funds raised by local rates administered by the district school
committees elected from among the members of the respective
town councils.[5] Existing schools which wished to avail themselves of assistance from the rates or any new ones that might be
established by the school committee must provide for "the reading of the Holy Scriptures in the authorised version",[6] but must
not require any child "to learn therein or elsewhere any distinctive religious creed, catechism or formulary"[7] to which the parents
of the child might object. This, according to Mr. Brotherton
who moved the second reading, was an attempt to carry out the
Queen's express wish "that the youth of this country should be
religiously brought up, the rights of conscience being respected."[8]
It also meant, however, as Gladstone pointed out, "the adoption
of a system of education involving principles of the greatest
novelty and the greatest importance . . . the principle of supporting out of the rates the existing schools subject to certain
limitations, and to apply to a new system of education a new
and specific religious basis as yet unknown to the country, for
schools that might hereafter be built out of the rates. It was,
in fact, a full, perfect, and consummate system of popular education for one district".[9] Before accepting responsibility for such
innovations mature deliberation was necessary. The debate was
therefore adjourned for three weeks. Two days before the

[1] *Parliamentary Debates*, 3rd Ser., cx, 450.
[2] *Parliamentary Debates*, cxvi, 1255.
[3] The Bill is printed in full in Kay-Shuttleworth, op. cit., p. 477, Appendix G.
[4] Para. 29.
[5] Para. 2.
[6] Para. 86.
[7] Para. 31.
[8] *Parliamentary Debates*, cxix, 379.
[9] id., 388.

scheduled resumption of the debate Lord John Russell's ministry resigned, and Lord Derby took office. In the next month, March 1852, the Bill was again brought forward, and was referred to a Select Committee. The committee, described by Wilson Patten as "so largely constituted of opponents that" the promoters "were almost inclined to withdraw the Bill",[1] collected from witnesses of all shades of opinion throughout the country, two volumes of evidence which form a most important first-hand source of the state of contemporary educational opinion, but they were so divided among themselves that they could eventually agree only "That the evidence be reported, without any opinion thereon, to the House".[2] This they did in June 1853. Meanwhile Lord John Russell who had returned to office had asked leave of the House to introduce another Education Bill for the support of existing schools by a system of local rating.[3] Three months later the Earl of Aberdeen announced that the Government would not proceed with the Bill.[4] In February 1854, the Manchester and Salford Bill was re-presented, and, after a lengthy debate, defeated and finally scrapped.[5]

The debates on this series of abortive education bills, and the select committee report occasioned by them provide an abundance of evidence of the various shades of opinion currently held on the question of National Education, and of the inability of the parties to reach a working agreement that would permit the adoption of any comprehensive scheme by Parliament. Sir James Kay-Shuttleworth had ventured the remark to Lord John Russell in 1851 that "the education question is ripe for solution"[6] It was certainly in need of solution but the possibility of attaining that desired object seemed as far off as ever. For it was so closely linked with religious questions that its discussion immediately raised seemingly irreconcilable antagonisms, with the result that inflexible and frequently over-sensitive consciences would rather see the complete failure of all educational ventures than have any tittle of their own privileges and beliefs in any way subject to compromise. *Punch* summed up the situation in a dialogue in

---

[1] id., cxx, 342.
[2] *Parliamentary Papers*, 1852–3, xxiv, Report from the Select Committee on Education (Manchester and Salford, etc.), 6th June, 1853, motion of Mr. Peto, id., p. vii.
[3] *Parliamentary Debates*, cxxv, 522.
[4] id., cxxix, 973.
[5] id., cxxx, 1045–1111.
[6] F. Smith, *The Life and Work of Sir James Kay-Shuttleworth*, Murray, London, 1923, p. 239.

which a father explained painstakingly to his small son that "Parliament is made up of gentlemen who belong to different religions, and not one of them except a few will vote for a school unless his own religion is taught in it. So the poor little boys and girls can't be taught anything because the sects can't settle their differences."[1]

[1] Quoted A. Woods, *Educational Experiments in England*, Methuen & Co., London, 1920, p. 9.

CHAPTER II

MATTHEW ARNOLD'S THOUGHT IN 1851

"Sink, O Youth, in thy soul!
Yearn to the greatness of Nature!
Rally the good in the depths of thyself!"
—M. Arnold, *The Youth of Man*, ll. 116–118.

UNLIKE his admired Marcus Aurelius, Matthew Arnold left to the world no comprehensive notice of the debt he owed to each of his teachers, and of the sources from which he derived his main ideas in life; but he did leave a number of note-books, a small portion of which refer to his early development, a considerable volume of correspondence of which a large proportion, referring to the years before his marriage, appears to have been destroyed, and most importantly, two volumes of poetry composed while he was still in his twenties and revealing in some detail the state of mind in which the young inspector found himself at the outset of his new career.[1] From these sources it is possible to construct, not a philosophy of education nor even any ideas directly bearing on education, but simply the chief problems and the main lines of thought which interested Arnold at that time and which were instrumental in determining the direction of his subsequent thought on educational matters.

His qualifications for the post of one of Her Majesty's Inspectors sound, to modern ears, very meagre indeed. He had been educated for the most part at Rugby under his father's eye, had had a distinguished, but not outstanding, undergraduate career at Balliol, finishing with second class honours in classics, spent a few months teaching the Lower Fifth at Rugby, and had returned to Oxford as a Fellow of Oriel College.[2] After a year in residence there, he became in 1847 private secretary to Lord Lansdowne, Lord President of the Privy Council and head of the Committee of Council on Education. Four years later, to enable the young

---

[1] In a letter to Clough, dated 14th December, 1852, referring to the volume just published, *Empedocles on Etna and Other Poems*, M. A. referred specifically to the revealing nature of his recent poems: "woe was upon me if I analysed not my situation" (H. F. Lowry, ed., *The Letters of Matthew Arnold to Arthur Hugh Clough*, O.U.P., 1932, letter 41, p. 126). A selection of M. A.'s notebooks was published by his daughter in 1902. A complete edition of them is now in the press under the editorship of H. F. Lowry.

[2] Lowry, ed., op. cit., Letter 1, 28th March, 1845.

man to marry with a sense of some security, Lansdowne had Arnold appointed Inspector of Schools.

He thus came to his work not only devoid of all professional training, and with only a very minimum of teaching experience, but even without any particular desire for, or interest in educational work. He could not, of course, at that time, have had any professional preparation, even if he had so wished, since the normal schools in existence did not cater for university graduates, and courses in education within the universities at post-graduate level were things of the distant future. Of his Rugby experience, there is only his testimony in a letter to Clough that, "I hear a large form, the Lower Fifth", and the confused recollection[1] of the later headmaster of Haileybury who wrote a novel on his own school-days at Rugby. In it Matthew Arnold appeared to be "not the stuff to make a Master of . . . Fancy him teaching little chaps τύπτω, and the verbs in μι! How could he? There's not a bit of the Dominie about him. He's much too great a swell. . . ."[2]

One of the chief impressions recorded by his friends at this time was of a rather flippant young man affecting a general air of nonchalance and fashionable sophistication. Even as early as 1842 his elder sister Jane wrote in the family *Fox How Magazine* of the "fine young Oxford gentleman" with the eyeglass.[3] At Oxford his lack of concentration worried his more earnest friend Clough,[4] and his irresponsible behaviour and apparent refusal to take life seriously was a source of misunderstanding and

[1] A. G. Butler, *The Three Friends: A Story of Rugby in the Forties*, H. Frowde, London, 1900. The author probably retained a correct general impression of Arnold's attitude to his work, as his remarks tally with those in contemporary letters referring to M. A.'s sophisticated demeanour, but in other details he was sadly astray. He placed M. A. at Rugby sometime after the 1848 mutiny, and referred to him as "the poet", when in fact at the time of his brief Rugby career, he had not yet published anything. He had of course won the Newdigate prize at Oxford but that would scarcely qualify him for the sobriquet. The author furthermore managed to have him visited by Clough who produced for M. A.'s edification Tennyson's *In Memoriam* "just out" (published 1850). The poem elicited such ecstatic comments as "Beautiful! Luminous! . . . A masterpiece!" (p. 105), and "Immortal!" (p. 106), than which it is difficult to imagine anything less likely to have been uttered by M. A. whose contempt for Tennyson went to such lengths that he requested a correspondent to mark whatever places in Sohrab and Rustum reminded him of Tennyson "for I would wish to alter such". (E. H. Coleridge, *Life and Correspondence of John Duke Lord Coleridge*, London, 1904, i, p. 211, Letter dated 22nd November, 1853.)

[2] id., pp. 100–101.

[3] Fox How was the Arnolds' house at Ambleside in the Lake District. Unpublished copies of several numbers of the Magazine are in the possession of Miss D. Ward, M. A.'s grand-niece. *Vide* also *The Nineteenth Century*, cxiii, April, 1933, art. A. Harris, Matthew Arnold: "The Unknown Years".

[4] Lowry, ed., op. cit., p. 29, Letter of A. H. Clough to J. P. Gill, 2nd April, 1845.

irritation to other friends who did not appreciate his bantering humour. He appears to have been trying out on them the weapon that he employed so delightfully and devastatingly upon his opponents in later life. "Our friend Matt utters as many absurdities as ever, with as grave a face, and I am afraid wastes his time considerably, which I deeply regret . . ." wrote J. M. Hawker,[1] and a little later again showed himself an unwilling but apparently irresistible butt for Arnold's witticisms when the two were holidaying together in Hawker's native Devon. "It is certainly most trying to hear a man say of a country which you have for years been accustomed to admire in every shape and under every aspect, 'This is nice, *when* it has the sun upon it,' in a sort of patronizing concession to me".[2] Arnold's "frivolous criticism" of affairs seemed to his acquaintances to betoken a want of interest in them and led several times to a marked criticism of his behaviour and to a cooling of their friendship towards him. "It is an old subject" he said when J. D. Coleridge upbraided him, "which I need not discuss over again with you. The accusation, as you say, is not true. I laugh too much, and they make one's laughter mean too much."[3]

In 1846 he became a "fan" of the celebrated French actress Rachel whom he followed to Paris "and for two months never missed one of her presentations".[4] He returned "with a chanson of Béranger's on his lips—for the sake of French words almost conscious of tune", and with his hair "guiltless of English scissors".[5]

When therefore he entered the polite circle of Lansdowne House and mingled with the wealth of talent and sophistication with which that peer was accustomed to surround himself it is no wonder that his brother and Clough were a little anxious about the effect of the appointment on his character.[6]   His

[1] E. H. Coleridge, op. cit., i, 125, Letter to John Duke Coleridge, Oxford, 11th March, 1843. John Duke Coleridge (1820–94) was later solicitor general, attorney-general, and Lord Chief Justice. He became the first Baron Coleridge in 1874.
[2] id., i, 129, Letter to J. D. Coleridge, 12th April, 1843, cf. id., Letter of 3rd July, 1843, in which M. A. is described as pretending to a coachful of people "that I (Hawker) was a poor mad gentleman and he was my keeper".
[3] id., Letter of M. A. to J. D. Coleridge, 28th July (1844).
[4] *Irish Essays*, "The French Play in London," p. 151.
[5] Lowry, ed., op. cit., p. 25, Letter of A. H. Clough to J. C. Shairp. For other instances of M. A.'s dandyism *vide* A. Harris, *The Nineteenth Century*, April, 1933; C. A. Tinker and H. F. Lowry, *The Poetry of Matthew Arnold*, O.U.P., 1940, 138 ff; L. Trilling, *Matthew Arnold*, Norton, New York, 1939, pp. 15–36; E. K. Chambers, *Matthew Arnold: A Study*, Clarendon Press, 1947, pp. 1–12; Mrs. Humphrey Ward (M. A.'s niece), *A Writer's Recollections*, Collins, London, 1918, pp. 32–52.
[6] Chambers, op. cit., p. 10.

mother appeared greatly relieved therefore to be able to record in 1850 that she found him "so unspoiled by his being so much sought after in a kind of society entirely different from anything we can enter into".[1] Arnold, later in a letter to Lord Shelburne on the occasion of Lord Lansdowne's death considered that the greatest advantage of his private secretaryship was the "comparative leisure for reading at a time of my life when such leisure was of the greatest value to me."[2] Nevertheless, despite such studious habits, he still gave the outward appearance of "a very gentlemanly young man with a slight tinge of the fop".[3]

It is not to be wondered at therefore that the hard-headed old Judge Wightman insisted upon the young poet acquiring a secure and substantial position before entrusting his daughter Lucy to his care. Nor is it a matter for surprise that the same young man should not have thought with much enthusiasm of what was to prove to be his life's work.

When Clough thought of applying for an inspectorship to enable him to marry too, Arnold put him off by giving him the fruit of his first two months experience: "Hard dull work, low salary, stationariness, and London to be stationary in under such circumstances, do not please me.   However, I myself should gladly have married under any circumstances, . . ."[4] Several times he tried to change his position. In 1866 he "wasted a week in applying for a vacant Charity Commissionership",[5] and in the following year tried for the Librarianship of the House of Commons.[6]   Finally in 1869 he applied for one of the three Commissionerships formed under the new Endowed Schools Act only to find "Gladstone stopping the way".[7] And so he remained an Inspector of Schools for 35 years, being promoted to a Senior Inspectorship in 1870.   In 1884 he became a Chief Inspector. One year before he had been granted a civil pension of £250, not, however, for his educational services but "expressly for literary and poetic performances".[8] He seems never to have taken

---

[1] Mrs. H. Ward, op. cit., p. 46.

[2] Unpublished letter in the *Bowood Papers*, dated 2nd February, 1863.

[3] E. J. Morley, ed., *Correspondence of Henry Crabb Robinson with the Wordsworth Circle* 2 vols., Oxford, 1927, ii, p. 743.

[4] Lowry, ed., op. cit., p. 118, Letter 36, 19th December, 1851.

[5] G. W. E. Russell, ed., *Letters of Matthew Arnold*, 1848–88, 2 vols., Macmillan, 1895, i, 320, 10th March, 1866.

[6] id., i, 360, 362, Letters to Lady de Rothschild, 29th April, 1867, and to his Mother, 17th May, 1867.

[7] id., ii, 9, 12, Letters to his Mother, 5th June, 1869 and 18th June, 1869.

[8] *vide infra*, Appendix, p. 285, Letter to A. J. Mundella, 26th November, 1886.

very kindly to his connection with the schoolmastering profession "that common but most·perfidious refuge of men of letters",[1] but merely to have resigned himself for the sake of security and livelihood to do his duty "whatever that may be"[2] in a sphere in which, as he says, "I have no special interest".[3] Even at the end of his life he still referred to his career as "routine work", and felt, a little sadly, that his talents had not been used to their best advantage.[4] His work, however, had some redeeming features. He does seem to have enjoyed the numerous contacts that his travels brought him, even though the life at times might be "cold and uncomfortable"[5] and more than usually migratory.[6] His chief objection was to the "incessant grind"[7] of routine work which did not appear to contribute to the enlargement of his mind. But the wider issues of educational thought and controversy he was ready and eager to examine and argue. His somewhat naïve observation at the very beginning of his work, "I think I shall get interested in the schools after a little time; their effects on the children are so immense . . .",[8] was amply fulfilled. The young man whose manner in 1850 had displeased the critical eye of Miss Emily Brontë "from its seeming foppery"[9] became the earnest and untiring exponent of the necessity for clearer thought on and fundamental re-organisation in the educational system of the country. For behind his youthful mask of dandyism there lay as Miss Brontë divined, "some genuine intellectual aspirations".[10]

The first impression that one is likely to get on reading the volumes of poems published in 1849 and 1852 is of a mind that has great difficulty in coping with the problem of living. It is a little overwhelmed by the immensity of the problem and, not possessing the buoyancy and optimism that enabled a Samuel Smiles to go forth and conquer all, is inclined to sink beneath the weight of the world's cares into a state of passive resignation. It was the young poet's fate to pass his youth in the midst of the

[1] *Essays in Criticism*, First Series, Maurice de Guerin, p. 103.
[2] Russell, ed., op. cit., i, p. 40, Letter to his Mother, 9th December, 1854.
[3] id., i, 78, Letter to Mrs. Forster, 16th February, 1859.
[4] *vide infra*, Appendix, p. 285, Letter to A. J. Mundella, 26th November, 1886.
[5] id., i, 38, Letter to his Wife, 21st October, 1854.
[6] In 1858 he wrote (Russell, ed., op. cit., i, 61): "We have taken a house in Chester Square. It is a very small one, but it will be something to unpack one's portmanteau for the first time since I married, now nearly seven years ago."
[7] id., i, 26, Letter to his Wife, 8th March, 1853.
[8] id., i, 17, Letter to his Wife, 15th October, 1851.
[9] Mrs. Humphrey Ward, op. cit., p. 32.
[10] ibid.

theological questionings and speculation brought to a head in the 30's and 40's by his godfather, Keble, and the Oxford movement, and by Lyell and the geologists, the clink of whose "dreadful hammers" Ruskin heard "at the end of every cadence of the Bible phrases".[1] The usual instability of adolescence was thus accentuated for Arnold, the more so as his father played a leading role in the current controversies, and Matthew was constantly in a position to know that old faiths and beliefs religious and political, were no longer accepted without question, but were by many admirable people being subjected to an informed and critical examination.

In the first year of his residence in Oxford his father died. The loss was expressed by Matthew in a remark contained in a letter written by A. P. Stanley that "the first thing which struck him when he saw the body was the thought that their sole source of *information* was gone, that all they had ever known was contained in that lifeless head. They had consulted him so entirely on everything and the strange feeling of their being cut off for ever one can well imagine".[2]

There is no exact way of judging the effect of the loss of such a forceful character, from the direction of the Arnold family, just at the moment when his elder sons stood most in need of intellectual guidance. The moral earnestness that was their heritage from Rugby they carried with them to the university and it never left them throughout their lives, but they did lose the sense of certainty as to the direction of their efforts. Dr. Arnold had believed in expelling from his school a boy whose moral sense seemed to be unequal to the task of living in Rugby society. His three elder sons, bereft of his helping hand, appear to have applied the same drastic treatment in their own difficulties. Matthew concealed his inner struggles behind a mask of foppishness. Thomas expelled himself to New Zealand, and Tasmania, and, subsequently was twice converted to the Roman Catholic church. William left Oxford and went off to join the Indian army at the age of twenty, and five years later wrote a semi-autobiographical novel, *Oakfield or Fellowship in the East*. This book expressed admirably the conflict taking place in the mind of a conscientious and intelligent youth at that time. *Oakfield*, says the author, was "perhaps an old mind—a mind forced into growth by education and circum-

[1] Quoted by Trilling, op. cit., p. 308.
[2] Quoted in Lowry, ed., op. cit., p. 5.

stances, struggling with a body for supremacy",[1]—a very good description of the Rugbeian product who had been submitted to Dr. Arnold's process of hastening "the change from childhood to manhood".[2] The struggle between the increasing forces making for social change and "the bonds of old belief" made it increasingly difficult for the immature and thoughtful to arrive at a satisfying and reasonably stable philosophy of life. Either one must "quit society altogether or mix in it on its own terms".[3] *Oakfield* chose to quit. The plight of those who remained he analysed thus: "or which is every day becoming more and more common, (they) seeing on the one hand, the dominion of the world so strong that they cannot but believe it to be half-divine, and on the other disgusted with the pettiness of one party (the Tractarians) and the ignorant folly of the other (Exeter Hall), they think that the faith over which the two profess to be wrangling is itself a narrowness and a folly; and shake off, as they suppose, all bonds of old belief; and believe in what they see,—the world; or in what they feel,—their own intellectual powers; and so pass on into a wretched jumble of epicureanism and self worship,—"[4]

William Arnold's brother Matthew experienced these doubts and depressions to the full during his period at Oxford. With Theodore Walrond, and his brother Thomas they would breakfast every Sunday in Clough's rooms and discuss the more serious issues of life.[5] Supplementing these meetings between 1843 and 1845 "there was a society called the Decade in those days (a Balliol scout long since gone to his rest persisted in embodying the external world's judgment on it by always calling it the Decayed) which I think did a good deal for the mental education of those who belonged to it". There Arnold could discuss "all things, human and divine", fighting and wrangling "to the very stumps of their intellects",[6] among friends of the calibre of Temple,

---

[1] W. D. Arnold, *Oakfield or Fellowship in the East*, 2nd ed., Ticknor & Fields, Boston 1855, p. 61.
[2] *Sermons*, vol. iv, ii; *vide* J. J. Findlay, *Arnold of Rugby*, Cambridge U.P., 1925, pp. 58, 148–55.
[3] W. D. Arnold, op. cit., p. 18.
[4] id., p. 21.
[5] *Nineteenth Century*, xviii, p. 107, January 1898, T. Arnold, art. "Arthur Hugh Clough: A Sketch".
[6] E. H. Coleridge, op. cit., p. 76, extract from "Principal Shairp and his Friends", W. Knight, 1888, pp. 411–12. The emphasis was of course on theology, cf. *Goldwin Smith's Correspondence*, ed. A. Haultain, London, p. 269, quoted Lowry, ed., op. cit., p. 16. "If it had not been for the Class List which kept a certain number of us working at classics and mathematics, the University would have become a mere battlefield of theologians".

the future Archbishop of Canterbury, John Duke Coleridge, later
Lord Chief Justice, Church, Lake, and Stanley, all three to
become Deans of the Church of England, Jowett then tutor and
subsequently master of Balliol, and Shairp, like Arnold, a winner
of the Newdigate Prize and later Professor of Poetry at Oxford.

Closely following this mental stimulation came the revolutionary events of 1848. "What a time of boundless excitement for
the young and unsteady was that year 1848!"[1] Clough went off
to Paris to stay with Emerson and to study the revolution there
at first hand, and Matthew Arnold could not resist the opportunity
to address a letter to Citizen Clough, Oriel Lyceum, Oxford,[2]
and to compose a trio of sonnets to his "Republican Friend".
At the same time Arnold was to be found mingling with the
Chartists "in the great mob in Trafalgar Square"[3] on 6th March,
and later "at the Chartist convention" where he was "much
struck with the ability of the speakers".[4] These events heightened
in Arnold's mind the sense of misgiving, that haunted him, about
the destiny of English society. He wrote to his sister Jane, upon
the prospects of a revolution in England "and such is the state of
our masses that their movements now *can* only be brutal plunder-
ing and destroying". Moreover, if they postponed their rising the
future prospects were equally discouraging since, as a result of
"the deep ignorance of the middle and upper classes, and their
feebleness of vision" there is no one who can train the masses in
right action.[5] To Clough he spoke of "this *wide and deepspread
intelligence* that makes the French seem to themselves in the van
of Europe", and gave the product of his own reflection on the
current English mental crisis. "Our weakness", he wrote, "is
that in an age where all tends to the triumph of the logical
absolute reason we neither courageously have thrown ourselves
into the solid ground of our individuality as spiritual, poetic,
profound, *persons*. Instead of this we have stood *up* hesitating:
seeming to refuse the first line on the ground that the second is
our *natural* one—yet not taking this. How long shall ye halt
between two opinions: woe to the modern nation, which will
neither be philosophe nor philosopher. . . . Yet it is something

[1] This is Thomas Arnold's reaction recorded by him fifty years later in *Nineteenth
Century*, xviii, p. 110.
[2] *Yale Papers*, cited C. B. Tinker and H. F. Lowry, op. cit., p. 33.
[3] G. W. E. Russell, op. cit., i, 4, Letter to his Mother, 7th March, 1848.
[4] id., i, 7, Letter to his Mother, April 1848.
[5] Russell, op. cit., i, 5, 10th March, 1848.

for a nation to feel that the only true line is its natural one?"[1]

In these reflections we can find the germ of his later thoughts and efforts in the educational field.

, There is, initially, his tendency to despair of the future, which passes into a resolve to understand and analyse society and the Zeitgeist. There, too, is his perception of the deep divisions of English society which are to be healed only by an adequate education of which the middle class stands most in need. Above all, there is the example of the fundamental cultural unity of the French, of whom Arnold was an immense but not unqualified admirer, pointing to the necessity for the greater use of intelligence, "geist", or common-sense in dealing with problems of English society. Especially, one should find out what one's "nature" is, in what sphere each person or society has a special talent, and resolve to follow that line intelligently and thoroughly. This is the way to achieve unity amid the present multitudinousness, and a worthwhile existence in place of aimless and sometimes painful wandering.

In this same year Arnold made a literary pilgrimage to the Bernese Oberland and the delightful Swiss town of Thun, then a leading holiday resort. His primary object was to explore the countryside which had concealed Senancour, the author of Obermann, from the world. He appears to have heard of Obermann first from the lips of George Sand, his first love in French literature, whom he had visited at Nohant in 1846. She had edited Obermann in 1840, and, in her Lelia, had been powerfully affected by him. Now she recommended his study to the "young Milton on his travels".[2] Forthwith the impressionable youth acquired a copy of the book and found that it fitted his current mood so perfectly that he could in later life apostrophize the author as "thou master of my wandering youth".[3] Obermann was a collection of letters written from the solitude of the Bernese Oberland by a French recluse, Etienne Pivert de Senancour. They are romantic, melancholy reflections upon the passing bustle of the world. George Sand spoke of them as "a complaint of powerlessness, ineffectiveness" showing a "lack of courage to take the plunge to

---

[1] Lowry, ed., op. cit., pp. 72–3, Letter 10, 6th March, 1848.
[2] M. A. describes his visit to Nohant in Mixed Essays, pp. 315–20, "George Sand" (1877).
[3] Obermann Once More, l. 39. The edition of M. A.'s poems used throughout is: The Poetical Works of Matthew Arnold, with an Introduction by Sir A. T. Quiller-Couch, Oxford University Press, 1942.

see whether he can swim".[1] *Obermann* is, in effect, the epic of youth which cannot make up its mind, and, while searching for maturity, is constantly fearful of committing itself to any one mode of con- duct or system of belief, yearning for stability, yet regretting the fancied lost opportunities which other chosen paths might have afforded.[2] Obermann shunned society but remained sufficiently in touch with civilization to have the benefits of its simpler ameni- ties. He was not the type who would seek a Robinson Crusoe exist- ence on a Pacific Island—that would involve hard work, and Obermann was as ill-equipped with energy as he was with will- power.

He produced on Arnold "an extraordinary impression",[3] which he was steadily outgrowing when he wrote his poem "Obermann" in 1849,[4] but from which he was never entirely to free himself. In 1866 he felt again the charm of Obermann's melancholy sufficiently to compose "Obermann Once More", and to write two years later an analysis of Senancour's thought for *The Academy*. His articles on Maurice de Guerin in 1863, Joubert, 1864, and Amiel, 1887, reflect his continued suscepti- bility to the influences emanating from or similar in character to the letters of Obermann.[5]

The characteristics which impressed themselves on Arnold were "the writer's profound inwardness, his austere and sad sincerity and his delicate feeling for nature", together with "a passion for order and harmony".[6] The first and the last of these, Obermann's inwardness and desire for harmony, were to be of great importance in Arnold's subsequent thought. Obermann's self-examination displayed what was for him a conflict between emotion and intellect resolvable only by removing as far as possible from the excitements of life in society. This conflict Arnold made much of in "The New Sirens" whose life was a continuous alterna- tion of periods of sensual enjoyment and of jaded appetite and

---

[1] *Pivert de Senancour, Obermann*, ed. G. Sand, Charpentier, Paris, 1882, préface.

[2] "Chez Obermann, la sensibilité seule est active, l'intelligence est paresseuse et insuffisante", G. Sand, ed., op. cit., p. 4. She makes an interesting distinction between the threnody of Obermann the impotent, of René who made the plunge and hurt himself, and of Werther who struggled against a cramping environment.

[3] Letter to Henry Dunn, 12th November, 1867, quoted C. B. Tinker and H. F. Lowry, op. cit., p. 271.

[4] "C'est un Obermann transfiguré", said Sainte-Beuve, "Chateaubriand et son Groupe littéraire", 1861, i, 356.

[5] I. E. Sells, *Matthew Arnold and France*, Cambridge U.P., 1935, has given the most complete analysis of Obermann's influence on Arnold.

[6] Art. on Obermann, *The Academy* (9th October, 1869), reproduced in Sells, op. cit., pp. 260–1.

disillusion. This surely is not what life is meant to be. It is a mere expenditure of energy. And, like Obermann, Arnold thought "that in the absence of any real inward basis life was weariness and vanity".[1] We therefore need calm to enable us to think out our purposes aright. "Calm's not life's crown though calm is well",[2] and is a necessary preliminary to the understanding of our aims in this "Modern life, with its sick hurry, its divided aims".[3] We can achieve it by a withdrawal from active life.

> He who hath watch'd, not shar'd, the strife
> Knows how the day hath gone;[4]

This is Obermann's method. But it is not for Arnold:

> I go; Fate drives me . . .
> I in the world must live.[5]

And in that world he finds more perplexing than ever the need on the one hand to stand aside from "the strife of men",[6] in order to take a comprehensive view, to study the direction of events, to become a Sophocles "who saw life steadily and saw it whole",[7] and the necessity, on the other hand, to garner knowledge which comes only through experience. "Only what we feel we know".[8] None was more keenly aware than Arnold of the intimate connection of experience and knowledge. On his very pilgrimage to Obermann's country in 1848 he encountered at Thun the "Marguerite" who in that year and the next, inspired him to compose some of the finest lyric poetry of the Victorian age. The feelings he had hitherto paid but lip-service to, he then experienced poignantly. His equipment was apparently unequal to the task of gaining the lasting affection of the young lady and he eventually betook himself in a "not altogether comfortable state" with an "aching head to the mountains",[9] and further contemplation on Obermann.[10]   Nevertheless he did learn to

---

[1] ibid.
[2] "Youth and Calm," l. 23.
[3] "The Scholar Gipsy," ll. 203–4.
[4] "Obermann," ll. 101–2.
[5] id., ll. 131, 137.
[6] id., ll. 99–100.
[7] "To a Friend," l. 11.
[8] "The New Sirens," l. 84.
[9] Lowry, ed., op. cit., Letter 32, p. 110, Thun, 23rd September, 1849.
[10] Obermann was hardly the type of reading that would cure a weakness of will that appears to have been the prime cause of his loss of "Marguerite", and his resultant outburst against the world in general, "My Dearest Clough, these are damned times, etc.," *vide* Lowry, ed., op. cit., Letter 32, p. 111.

value experience, and to see the need for action as well as observation. This was the very point that astonished his observant
younger sister when she read his book of poems in 1849: "it
showed a knowledge of life and conflict which was *strangely like
experience*, if it was not the thing itself".[1]

Just as he never quite released himself from Obermann's
influence so he was never quite able to harmonise completely
these two views.

> Ah! Two desires toss about
> The poet's feverish blood
> One drives him to the world without
> The one to solititude.[2]

And although he was never to achieve a synthesis satisfying enough
to transcend this almost Hegelian conflict, he remained profoundly convinced of the necessity for paying regard to the knowledge which comes from experience whose foundation lay "below
the surface stream".

> Below the surface-stream, shallow and light
> Of what we *say* we feel—below the stream,
> As light, of what we *think* we feel—there flows
> With noiseless current strong, obscure and deep,
> The central stream of what we feel indeed.[3]

This central core of experience was becoming for Arnold the
most important factor in life. He was beginning to feel that life
meant just the expression of some such essential self. The way
to achieve satisfaction was to discover our own nature and to
live in accordance with its promptings. His "Nature" or "self"
was never rigorously and philosophically defined, but his general

---

[1] Mrs. Humphry Ward, op. cit., p. 44. Letter from Mary Twining. In 1849
Mary was 23, already a widow, living in London, and much interested in F. D.
Maurice.

[2] "Obermann," ll. 93–6.

[3] "Below the Surface-stream," first published in "S. Paul and Protestantism II",
Cornhill Magazine, November 1869. A short treatise could be written on M. A.'s
treatment of water both in his poetry and in his letters. Two features stand out.
First in his almost fanatical desire for clear running water in streams—perhaps
originating from an "economic" motive in enabling him to see clearly the trout in
his own mountain streams for the better pursuit of his favourite pastime!—he frequently displays his distaste for the murky yellow rivers of Italy and his pleasure in
the clear blue waters of the Swiss Alps. This can be equated with his desire for
clarity of thought, for seeing to the essence of things, and bringing to bear upon
social problems "a fresh stream of ideas". Secondly, there is his constant preoccupation with the metaphor of the "surface and buried stream". The uppermost,
his observation told him, ran faster and narrower, the lower was really the main
body of the stream moving slowly and surely onward.

concept of the matter was of great value to him in all his thought. His "one natural craving" he wrote in 1849, "is not for profound thoughts, mighty spiritual workings, etc., but a distinct seeing of my way as far as my own nature is concerned."[1] This led him to look always for the nature or central tendency in other persons, in social and political problems, and the literary works that he read and reviewed. It resulted at times in an over-simplification of the issues involved, and, in his literary criticism, in a lack of the subtilty that distinguished his contemporaries, Newman and Pater. It was, in fact, a dangerous weapon, for in tending to reduce all his subjects to a single driving force, he could by a slight error or preconception in selection, distort their significance considerably. His later treatment of religion as "morality touched with emotion" was to many of his contemporaries the supreme example of this feature of his thought.

Nevertheless in a period of *laissez-faire*, expansion and rapid change, it was a valuable guiding principle, and in implementing it throughout his published writings Arnold performed an important function for contemporary society. To delve to the essence, to see the object as it really is, required a continued effort to clarify one's thought, and its successful achievement produced a unity among the current multitudinousness.[2]

The search for unity was in keeping with the other trait in Obermann, the passion for order and harmony, that made an indelible impression on Arnold. But it led him also beyond the chill, depressing sage of the Bernese Oberland to the study of an older and nobler philosophy that was enshrined in the Bhagavadgita. In these formative years Arnold appears to have read with delight and considerable profit what Wilhelm von Humboldt described as "the most beautiful, perhaps the only true philosophical song existing in any known tongue."[3] He tried to induce Clough to appreciate its significance; but Clough could see in it, and in Arnold's poetry that was influenced by it, only "the dismal cycle of his rehabilitated Hindoo-Greek theosophy".[4] Similarly his sister, Jane, thought that his interest in the Bhagavadgita to be to his detriment. "Surely language

[1] Lowry, ed., op. cit., Letter 32, p. 110.
[2] Lowry, ed., op. cit., Letter 24, p. 97, "begin with an Idea of the world in order not to be prevailed over by the world's multitudinousness."
[3] Quoted in S. Radhakrishnan, *Indian Philosophy*, vol. i, Allen & Unwin, London, 1923, p. 519.
[4] *North American Review*, vol. lxxvii, Boston, July 1853, art. "Recent English Poetry," A. H. Clough.

which tells . . . of a dumb unalterable order of the universe, and of the vanity of the labours in which they are mixing, will seem too unreal and far too hopeless to listen to. Dear Matt has a good deal of the Eastern Philosopher about him at present which does not suit the European mind."[1] But Matthew appeared to think his new study to be beneficial and was not dissuaded from it by his friends' disapproval. "I am disappointed", he wrote to Clough, "the Oriental wisdom, God grant it were mine, pleased you not."[2]

It was, in fact, a healthy aid to him in stepping beyond the dreary bounds of Senancourism. The "Celestial Song" is set not in solitude and retreat, but in action. It is a discussion of ethics for the practical man of affairs. Arjuna, the practical soldier and a representative man, is overcome with dejection on the eve of a great battle, which is taken to represent a crisis or period of transition and reconstruction in human society. In his dilemma he is instructed on the problems of human life and human destiny by Krishna, an incarnation of Divinity. The appositeness of the Gita to the situation of cultural crisis in which Arnold found himself in early Victorian England is easily apparent. It is applicable also to the critical period of adolescence from which Arnold was emerging at this time. Like Arjuna he was troubled and dispirited by the difficulties and confusion of the world. He had not yet matured sufficiently to have formed within himself a central core or body of ideas that would give him a consistency and confidence in facing up to the tasks that lay before him. He had not yet, in effect, constructed his "self".

From the Bhagavadgita, he absorbed three leading ideas, the necessity for a unity, the urge for perfection, and the desirability of acting in accordance with one's own nature.

In man's quest for satisfaction, he cannot rest until he has subsumed all the fragments of his experiences under one all-embracing principle, "until", as the Gita says, "he perceives the diversified existence of beings abiding in the one eternal Being."[3] In a world of uncertainty, amid the "thousand discords",[4] much of Arnold's poetry became "a plangent threnody for a lost whole-

[1] Unpublished letter in the possession of Miss D. Ward; Jane Arnold to Tom Arnold, Fox How, 27th October, 1848. Jane was commenting to her brother in New Zealand, on M. A.'s recently published book of poems.
[2] Lowry, ed., op. cit., Letter 8, 1st March, 1848.
[3] *Bhagavadgita*, xiii, 31.
[4] Sonnet, "Quiet Work," l. 9.

ness and peace."[1] The quest for unity was to be one of Arnold's lifelong tasks and was to be constantly in the forefront of his thinking. His later advocacy, both of increased State participation in education, and of an improved middle class education through which all sections of the community might be linked together, was its chief manifestation in the field of education.

The central theme of Hindu philosophy, constantly enlarged upon throughout the Bhagavadgita, is man's urge towards perfection. The round of births and rebirths is aimed at man's spiritual perfection, and ceases when this object is attained by a perfect understanding of the oneness of the universe.[2] This became for Arnold the essence of his chief dogma of culture. Culture is "a study of perfection and of harmonious perfection, general perfection, and perfection which consists in becoming something rather than in having something, in an inward condition of the mind and spirit, not in an outward set of circumstances."[3] It was hinted at in his early poems, such as "Quiet Work", and enlarged upon in his emphasis upon the need for poetry to "elevate the mind".[4] Perfection, for the Gita and for Arnold, was not an isolated affair but a kind of social grace through which the individual is "continually doing all he can to enlarge and increase the volume of the human stream. . . ."[5] This concept links up with the parallel doctrine making for unity amid existing diversity, and issued in similar thoughts on social and educational problems. There was also at the same time a second aspect, an emphasis upon "perfection in an *internal* condition."[6] "A man who is intent on his own natural work", said the Gita, "attains perfection".[7] The secure basis of all action lies in discovering your own true self and living in accordance not with some outer standard but with the truth of your own highest and inmost existence.[8] This harmonized with similar views expressed by Obermann,[9] and strengthened Arnold's feeling

[1] Trilling, op. cit., p. 79, cf. the sonnet, "Written in Butler's Sermons".
[2] *Bhagavadgita*, vii, 19.
[3] *Culture and Anarchy*, ed. J. Dover Wilson, Cambridge U.P., 1946, p. 48.
[4] Lowry, ed., op. cit., Letter 26, p. 100, c. 1st March, 1849, and Letter 51, p. 146, 30th November (1853). cf. M. A.'s reasons given in his Preface to his 1853 Poems for omitting "Empedocles on Etna" from that edition.
[5] *Culture and Anarchy*, p. 48.
[6] id., p. 47.
[7] *Bhagavadgita*, xviii, 45.
[8] id., *vide* especially chap. xvii and xviii, and Sri Aurobindo's summary on p. 259.
[9] *vide* supra pp. 25–26.

that the only satisfactory way, through the cares and distresses of "the old unquiet breast",[1] towards perfection was to

> Resolve to be thyself; and know, that he
> Who finds himself, loses his misery.[2]

For this process both knowledge and action are necessary. The Greek sage's "know thyself" is good advice but it must be supplemented by the resolve to "be thyself". To self-knowledge must be joined right conduct in accordance with that knowledge. In this Arnold with the help of the Bhagavadgita stepped beyond the passivity of Obermann. "Do thou do controlled action, for action is greater than inaction,"[3] and again, in acting, "Better is one's own law of works, though in itself faulty, than an alien law well wrought out".[4] In Arnold's words:

> . . . be true
> To our own only true, deep-buried selves,
> Being one with which we are one with the whole world.[5]

Right action, however, according to the Gita is the doing of one's duty in a spirit of non-attachment by "abandoning the fruits of action".[6] In "Resignation", Arnold wished the poet, whom he described to be one who "bears to admire uncravingly",[7] to set out "in the search for a kind of amor intellectualis Dei, the poet's loving, non-personal vision of the world".[8]

In this feeling Arnold drew also upon his affection for the Stoics whose way of thinking had much in common with the Bhagavadgita. Epictetus, in particular, seemed to be the chosen one to "prop" his mind "in these bad days".[9] From him Arnold would obtain support for his desire to seek out his own nature and live in accordance with it, for "being instructed consists in this very point to learn what things are our own, and what belongs to others".[10] The object of life is to live in accor-

---

[1] "A Summer Night," l. 27.
[2] "Self-dependence," l. 31–2.
[3] *Bhagavadgita*, iii, 8.
[4] id., iii, 35, and xviii, 47.
[5] "Empedocles on Etna," l. 370–3.
[6] Lowry, ed., op. cit., Letter 9, p. 71, 4th March, 1848.
[7] l. 161.
[8] Trilling, op. cit., p. 100.
[9] Sonnet, "To a Friend," l. 1, *vide* also Lowry, ed., op. cit., Letter 21, p. 89 (August ?, 1848), where Arnold mentions his reading "with equal surprise and profit", Epictetus' "Enchiridion".
[10] Epictetus, *Discourses*, iv, v, i.

dance with our own powers. We discharge our functions wrongly and lose our happiness when we allow our desires to rule our lives. This Arnold made the theme of "Empedocles on Etna"[1] who, after advising his companion "not to fly to dreams but moderate desire",[2] committed suicide in what one feels is a fashion a little too flamboyant to be approved by a Cato.

At the same time, however, as this Hindu-Stoic influence was apparent in Arnold's thought, he was noting down a direction to himself to "Chew Lucretius",[3] and throughout his life he returned again and again to the construction of a Roman tragedy centering round Lucretius, without ever completing it.[4] Much of his reading of Lucretius appears to have found its way into "Empedocles on Etna"; but he was more concerned with the revolt of Epicureanism against a cramping religious sentiment than with its ethical system. He was even writing at this time to Clough that he was reading Béranger, but felt that "there is something 'fade' about Béranger's Epicureanism."[5]

The critical attitude of this school to received religious opinions, however, harmonised with the doctrine of one whom Arnold had "been studying lately with profit",[6] and who was to be his religious guide from that time forth. From Spinoza, who "stands out from the multitude of philosophers",[7] he must have gained support for the tolerance and broad churchmanship that he had inherited from his father, and which enabled him to stand above the narrowness of the sectarian squabbles that beset the contemporary educational scene. He found also in Spinoza support for "a stoicism not passive, but active"[8] that believed in following out the law of one's own nature to the improvement of the common weal, and for a positive doctrine of the State as an agent of enlightenment that Arnold was to develop in much of his

---

[1] *vide* Tinker and Lowry, op. cit., pp. 297–9. J. C. Shairp wrote to Clough in 1849 (p. 287), "He (M. A.) is working at an 'Empedocles'—which seemed to be not so much about the man who lept in the crater—but his name and outward circumstances are used for the drapery of his own thoughts".

[2] l. 386.

[3] In a notebook referred to by Tinker and Lowry, op. cit., p. 8 ff, as the Yale mss. This entry refers to a list of poems headed "Comp. 1849".

[4] Tinker and Lowry, op. cit., pp. 340–7. The unpublished fragments are reproduced at pp. 345–7. Ruskin, *Praeterita*, p. 613, says: "I have ever since (1839) held it the most hopeless sign of a man's mind being made of flint-shingle if he liked Lucretius."

[5] Lowry, op. cit., Letter 22, p. 92, Baths of Leuk, 29th September, 1848.

[6] id., Letter 35, p. 117, 23rd October, 1850.

[7] *Essays in Criticism*, 1st Series, p. 341, "Spinoza and the Bible".

[8] id., p. 333.

educational writing.[1] But what immediately caught Arnold's attention was not the imposing geometric edifice of Spinoza's thought, but the fertility of one of his much-used expressions. "What a remarkable philosopher really does for human thought", Arnold later wrote, "is to throw into circulation a certain number of new and striking ideas and expressions, and to stimulate with them the thought and imagination of his century or of after-times. So Spinoza has made his distinction between adequate and inadequate ideas a current notion for educated Europe."[2] Facility of phraseology, the knack of producing a telling expression, was much to Arnold's liking. He wrote later, evidently with some relish, to his sister Jane during one of his American visits, concerning one of his own successful coinings, "I understand what Dizzy meant when he said that I performed a 'great achievement' by launching phrases".[3] He was therefore appreciative of Spinoza's happy invention and speedily incorporated it into his own language and thought.

Spinoza in using the word "adequate" appears to mean "not partial", complete and sufficient without addition. Thus an idea which is adequate is a true idea since it represents complete knowledge; an adequate cause is one whose effect can clearly be perceived through it alone.[4] Hence Arnold spoke of Pope's poetry as "*adequate* (to use a term I am always using) to Pope's age—that is, it reflected completely the best general culture and intelligence of that age."[5] So important was this concept to him that he made it the subject of his Inaugural Lecture for the Chair of Poetry at Oxford in 1857, and he was to devote the whole of his professional life to the effort to secure that English education should be "adequate" for the times. The word in fact contained in itself much of Arnold's philosophy of life. For an action or a thought to be adequate, one had first to bring to bear a certain clarity of thought to see the problem or object as it really was; one had then to study it in its setting to see what was required for it to be adequate to that setting; and lastly when a proposal had been thought out and implemented it was necessary to see

---

[1] id., p. 326, cf. F. Pollock, *Spinoza, His Life and Philosophy*, Duckworth, London, 2nd ed., 1912, pp. 31–2, 289 ff.
[2] id., p. 341.
[3] Unpublished letter in the possession of Miss D. Ward, written Hartford, Connecticut, 13th November, 18—.
[4] *Ethics*, ii, Prop. 34; iii, Defs. i, ii.
[5] Unpublished letter in the possession of Miss D. Ward, to Tom Arnold, 28th December, 1857(?).

if it did, in actual practice, work adequately. There was a tendency here towards pragmatism, towards judging adequacy by practical effects, later accentuated by his life as a school inspector, that was to become an important part of his approach to all social problems. There was present also a strong feeling for the need to study current tendencies with care, to judge aright what the actual situation was and how it might develop, in effect, to investigate the Zeitgeist.

"To few men . . . was the Zeitgeist a stronger or more dis-spiriting force."[1] There was continual reference in his early letters to "the sickening consciousness of our difficulties"[2] in this "modern situation in its true *blankness* and *barrenness*, and unpoetrylessness."[3] It was with this feeling that he "took up Obermann and refuged myself with him in his forest against your Zeit Geist".[4] Yet the age was "not unprofound, not ungrand, not unmoving—but unpoetical".[5] The meaning of his expression is rather obscure. He spoke in the same tone in his essay on Gray and in a letter written to his sister Jane in 1858, but his words seem to mean no more than that a poetical age is one in which poetry is written and a poetryless one, the reverse—a not very helpful or profound observation. He was concerned, however, with other aspects of a diagnosis of his age and with the remedial treatment adequate to it. The age was an "iron"[6] one, "fer-ruginous", as Ruskin called it, in spirit, and an age of iron in the field of commerce. Just as the iron of industry brought with it an abundance of bustling and directionless energy, so the same spirit was affecting every other department of life.[7] It was an age in need of direction, an age of expansion rather than con-centration. If poetry be conceived as a "criticism of life" it must be informed by a sense of direction before it could adequately

---

[1] Lowry, ed., op. cit., Introduction, p. 32.
[2] id., Letter 32, p. 111, 23rd September, 1849.
[3] id., Letter 41, p. 126, 14th December, 1852.
[4] id., Letter 23, p. 95, November, 1848.
[5] id., Letter 25, p. 99, February, 1849.
[6] "Memorial Verses," 1850, l. 43.
[7] cf. "The Future", 1852, ll. 50–57:
> "This tract which the River of Time
> Now flows through with us, is the Plain,
> Gone is the calm of its earlier shore,
> Border'd by cities and hoarse
> With a thousand cries is its stream,
> And we on its breast, our minds
> Are confus'd as the cries which we hear,
> Changing and short as the sights which we see."

perform its function. The lack of this very sense from Arnold's age made it, in his opinion, poetryless. The task, therefore, of the thinkers of his age, was to probe the meaning of current life to discover the Time-Spirit, to clarify it, show its direction, and thereby "create a current of true and fresh ideas."[1] Duly impregnated with these ideas, a poetry might be born, in the fulness of time, sure in its message to the world and free of the fragmentariness that results from living in a disjointed age.

In his early sonnet "To a Friend", Arnold spoke of three men as the props of his mind, Homer, Epictetus, and Sophocles. In his American lecture on Emerson, he referred to the four voices that were heard in the Oxford of his undergraduate years as Newman, Carlyle, Goethe, and Emerson. In 1872 he wrote to Newman to the effect that "There are four people, in especial, from whom I am conscious of having learnt—a very different thing from merely receiving a strong impression—learnt habits, methods, ruling ideas, which are constantly with me, and the four are—Goethe, Wordsworth, Sainte-Beuve, and yourself."[2]

The thread which holds such a diverse lot together is their concern with the problems of establishing some acceptable values and standards amid the flux of a changing society.

Carlyle was an early favourite, and Arnold's gradual change of opinion concerning the Sage of Chelsea is a good indication of his growing maturity. Sartor in a state of hopelessness, his Everlasting No passing into Indifference, was a kindred spirit in Arnold's early uncertainty. The advice to lessen his denominator accorded with his tendency to Stoicism, and evoked an appreciative reference in 1848 "to the style and feeling by which the beloved man appears."[3] Eighteen months later he was referring to "moral desperadoes like Carlyle" as one of the trials with which the times were afflicted.[4] The stormy, muddling Sage had, as Clough said, "led us all out into the desert, and he has left us there."[5] The pessimism and lack of positive guidance to be found in Carlyle yielded place to the optimism of the North

[1] *Essays in Criticism*, 1st Series, "The Function of Criticism at the Present Time," pp. 18-19.
[2] *Times Literary Supplement*, 31st March, 1921, p. 211. Letter dated 28th May, 1872.
[3] Lowry, ed., op. cit., Letter 11, p. 75 (8th March, 1848), cf. Russell, ed., op. cit., i, 4.
[4] id., Letter 32, p. 111, 23rd September, 1849.
[5] Whereupon the story goes, Emerson to whom the words were addressed put his hand on Clough's head and said, "Clough I consecrate you Bishop of all England" id., Introduction, p. 47.

American philosopher. Though there was never at any time any likelihood that Arnold would "hitch his wagon to a star", at least he could agree that "happiness was a desirable aim," and that "in the life of the spirit is happiness".[1]

By 1859 Arnold was writing of "that regular Carlylean strain which we all know by heart, and which the clear-headed among us have so utter a contempt for,"[2] and he considered Carlyle's greatest service to him to have been his introduction to Goethe especially through the translation of Wilhelm Meister's Apprenticeship.[3] The youthful trials of Wilhelm Meister, and the opposing views of life depicted in his conflict with Werner, perhaps the union of bourgeoisie and nobility, by Wilhelm's marriage to Natalia, in a common striving for the progress of humanity, appealed to Arnold's mind. But above all he found in Goethe the "Physician of the Iron Age" and "the clearest, the largest, the most helpful thinker of modern times."[4] Goethe is such a complex force that one can get from him whatever one wants. For Arnold he supplied "a large, liberal view of life",[5] which came from "the width, depth, and richness of his criticism of life" and made him stand forth as "by far our greatest modern man."[6]

The essence of Goethe, Arnold found in his words, " '*The fashion of this world passeth away;* and I would fain occupy myself with the abiding'. There is the true Goethe", and there, as H. F. Lowry has remarked, "is the true Arnold, from his early youth to his final hour".[7]

Arnold's turning from Carlyle to Carlyle's greater master, Goethe, represented the gradual assertion in him of the ascendancy of the spirit of Hellenism. Nurtured among the classics by his father and his Oxford environment, Arnold throughout his years of doubt and conflict never lost this classical framework, though at times he seemed to turn aside in melancholy and despair towards other guides. Carlyle, despite his contempt for the Philistines, was in his unregulated moralistic energy, a force

---

[1] *Discourses in America*, "Emerson", p. 203.
[2] Lowry, ed., op. cit., Letter 54, p. 151, 29th September, 1859.
[3] *Discourses in America*, "Emerson", p. 143. *Mixed Essays*, "A French Critic on Goethe", p. 283.
[4] "Memorial Verses," 1850, l. 17. *Mixed Essays*, "A French Critic on Goethe", p. 311.
[5] "Emerson," p. 143.
[6] "A French Critic on Goethe", pp. 311–2.
[7] Lowry, ed., op. cit., Introd., p. 36. Arnold's translation is in "A French Critic on Goethe," p. 313.

of the same nature, Hebraist not Hellenic. This Arnold saw to
be a movement in the wrong direction, a superfluity of the
wrong force, an inadequacy, and a misjudgment of the Zeitgeist.
What Victorian England required was not more morality, not
even more religion, but more culture, the culture of the "clearest
soul'd of men" who "saw the Wide Prospect", and of him "who
saw life steadily, and saw it whole".[1]

It was Arnold's chosen task to be for England the prophet of
this culture.

In dedicating himself to this task the young Inspector of Schools
was acting in the spirit of his schoolmaster father. Although he
appears never to have taken kindly to the profession of schoolmastering, Arnold was too close in nature to his father ever to
cease to act the pedagogue. It is impossible to disentangle the
particular instances in which Dr. Arnold's influence determined
his son's thoughts and actions. The resemblances become more
and more striking, the more Matthew's contribution to educational thought is examined. But overriding all his work is the
clear force of Dr. Arnold's spirit which

> upraisest with zeal
> The humble good from the ground,

and

> woulds't not *alone*
> Be saved.[2]

From this came Matthew's zeal for "elevation". The test of a
classic, of poetry in the "grand style" is whether it elevates the
mind by a sustained tone.[3] This was the chief ground of his
criticism of one of his most popular poems, the "Gipsy Scholar".
"Homer *animates*—Shakespeare *animates*, in its poor way I think
Sohrab and Rustum *animates*—the 'Gipsy Scholar' at best
awakens a pleasing melancholy. But this is not what we want.

> The complaining millions of men
> Darken in labour and pain—

what they want is something to *animate* and *ennoble* them—not
merely to add zest to their melancholy or grace to their dreams—

---

[1] "To a Friend," ll. 2–3, 12. The references are to Homer and Sophocles.
[2] "Rugby Chapel," ll. 49–50, 124–5. Arnold Whitridge, M. A.'s grandson, in his
study, *Dr. Arnold of Rugby*, p. 204, was even of the opinion that Dr. Arnold was "the
determining factor in all Matthew Arnold's social philosophy".
[3] Lowry, ed., op. cit., Letter 26, p. 100, c. 1st March, 1849.

I believe a feeling of this kind is the basis of my nature—and of my poetics".[1]

Animated himself by this improving zeal, striving continually to point the way towards perfection, and inspired with a clarity of vision that saw both the essence of a problem and its reference in its widest setting, Arnold, for all his initial inexperience, was destined to become in English education, as in English literature, a critical force of great power, sketching out the true direction of future progress, and indicating the developments necessary to secure education adequate to such an age of expansion.

[1] Lowry, ed., op. cit., Letter 51, p. 146, 30th November (1853).

CHAPTER III

THE CONFLICT OF OPINION ON NATIONAL EDUCATION

"Nil sine magno
Vita labore dedit mortalibus".
Life has given nothing to mortals
without great labour.

Horace, *Sat.* i, 9, 59.

IT APPEARED to many men that a new era in English education had begun in 1846.[1] But the new era brought with it greatly increased governmental grants to the educational societies. And from this fact the Minutes proved fruitful not merely of educational progress, but also of a less auspicious future of intensified party rivalries and increasingly embittered sectarian strife. Richard Cobden thought in 1848 that education was the main cause of the split in his own party.[2] For there was at stake a double issue about which there was as little concord in educational circles as there was agreement on any matter in the confused parliamentary politics of the time.

In the first place, the role of the State in education was by no means clear. It was a comparatively recent problem in England, and, being faced in the heyday of economic *laissez-faire*, was productive of sharply conflicting opinion. Complicating the question was the second source of controversy, the religious issue. The Church of England was the religious denomination "by law established", and as such might be expected to score a considerable advantage over its rivals by the increase of State authority in education. This, in actual fact, it did, in procuring the great bulk of the increased governmental grant under the 1846 Minutes, by reason of the much wider diffusion of the activities of the National Society in comparison with the activities of all the other societies then existing.[3] Even if this situation did not obtain, was it still right for the State to interfere in

---

[1] *vide* supra, pp. 6 ff.
[2] Morley, *Life of Cobden,* i, p. 528, Letter to E. Baines.
[3] The accompanying table taken from the *Educational Census of* 1851 compiled by H. Mann, shows clearly the preponderant position held by the National Society in the provision of elementary education. It is also a convenient summary of the position generally in that year.

EXTRACT FROM CENSUS OF GT. BRITAIN, 1851, EDUCATION, REPORT AND TABLES, P.P. 1852–3, XC.

Description of Schools	Number of Schools	Number of Scholars	Number of Schools making return of Income	Permanent Endowment £s	Voluntary Contributions £s	Grants from Government £s	Payments by Scholars £s	Other Sources £s	TOTAL £s
Total Day Schools	44,836	2,108,592	—	—	—	—	—	—	—
Private Day Schools	29,425	695,422	—	—	—	—	—	—	—
Public Day Schools	15,411	1,413,170	7,842	212,654	303,898	27,643	227,901	66,212	838,308
Supported by general or local taxation	610	48,826	—	—	—	—	—	—	—
Supported by endowments	3,125	206,279	1,911	188,878	26,048	1,539	58,293	14,228	288,986
Supported by: Religious bodies — C. of E.—National Schools	10,595	1,048,851	5,761	15,586	227,535	25,432	156,672	34,402	459,627
—Others	3,720	464,975	2,397	8,342	104,614	15,262	59,594	16,434	204,246
Independents	4,851	336,532	2,149	4,898	75,151	2,870	43,670	10,917	137,506
Baptists	431	47,406	282	142	9,742	89	10,567	924	21,464
R.C.	115	8,665	59	4	1,230	—	1,145	111	2,470
	311	38,583	108	220	5,104	626	4,495	447	10,892
Jews	10	1,234	6	50	917	—	308	386	1,661
Undenom. (British)	514	82,597	382	728	16,124	3,901	16,589	2,020	39,362
—Others	4	1,062	1	—	407	—	110	—	517
Other Public Schools (Non-Religious)	1,081	109,214	170	8,190	50,315	672	12,936	17,582	89,695
Ragged Schools	123	22,337	79	25	9,815	130	91	1,004	11,065
Factory Schools	115	17,834	15	—	823	215	917	52	2,007
Total British Schools (whether connected with religious bodies or not)	852	123,015	628	829	24,150	4,455	26,590	3,108	59,132

matters that were the particular concern of religious congregations?

Such were the questions that provoked the Voluntaryists to organise a very vocal opposition to all plans made by the Committee of Council. A concerted movement was first made by them in successfully combating the Factory Bill of 1843 wherein Sir James Graham proposed to reorganise factory schools in which, while the diversities of religious beliefs would be safeguarded by a conscience clause, the schoolmaster and a majority of the managers would be members of the Established Church.

In 1846 the Minutes served to re-arouse their zeal. These they stigmatized on the ground that "though certainly proceeding from sincere friends of education, they were founded on false principles, and involved danger to liberty and a corruption of the public sense of independence, as well as grievous injustice to Dissenters".[1]

The core of the Voluntaryist opposition was the Congregational Board of Education which steadfastly refused to accept governmental assistance for its schools. Leader of the crusade was Edward Baines, Jun., Esq., the prominent editor of the *Leeds Mercury*. Educated at a dissenters' grammar school in Manchester where the celebrated chemist, John Dalton, was mathematics master, Baines early applied himself to the cause of non-conformist education and spent many years as a Sunday School promoter and teacher. He entered parliament in 1859 as member for Leeds which he represented until 1874. On his defeat in that year Gladstone sent to him a letter in testimony of "the single-minded devotion, courage of purpose, perfect integrity, and ability" with which he had always acted. From 1864–7 he served as a member of the Schools Inquiry (Taunton) Commission, and was knighted in 1880. Almost equally prominent was Edward Miall, the son of a merchant who had opened a school in London and relapsed into a state of poverty. Miall had been an assistant in his father's school, and an usher in several country schools before he joined the Independent ministry in 1831. He became a figure of note for his vehement and continued

---

[1] *The Eclectic Review*, April 1851. M. Arnold wrote in 1887 (*Reign of Queen Victoria*, T. H. Ward, ed., vol. ii, "Schools", p. 252): "Mr. Henry Dunn, the acute and accomplished secretary of the British and Foreign School Society, who took part with great energy in that agitation, told me himself that what he had seen of tempers and motives while prosecuting it had so shocked him that he had registered a vow never to be induced to take part in a religious agitation again."

attacks on the Establishment, to further which he founded the "Nonconformist" newspaper with the motto "the Dissidence of Dissent and the Protestantism of the Protestant religion", and established the British Anti-State Church Association in 1844.[1] In 1858 he served as a member of the Newcastle Commission, and, with Goldwin Smith and Senior, formed the minority deprecating state influence on education. He served as member of parliament on two occasions, for Rochdale 1852–7, and Bradford 1868–74, where his fellow-representative was W. E. Forster, the author of the 1870 Education Act to which Miall duly objected. From then until the end of his life in 1881 he spent the main efforts upon what had been the chief object of his life, the Disestablishment of the Church of England.

The most complete statement of the Voluntaryists' position was made at the Crosby Hall Lectures, a series of seven lectures organised by the Congregational Board of Education, and delivered in 1848 by seven leading men of the party, including Baines and Miall. These arguments were supplemented in 1851 by a lengthy article in *The Eclectic Review*, entitled "The Rival Educational Projects", which examined current literature on National Education as a background to a presentation of the Voluntaryist case.

Taken together these two publications present a comprehensive exposé of this party's thoughts on the leading problems of contemporary education. They were repeated with much rhetoric and force by the party's representatives in Parliament in the highly contentious debates of the early fifties.

It was on a religious basis that the Voluntaryists chiefly made their claim that all provision for education should come from voluntary effort, and that education was no concern of the government in any respect.

Their argument, like a good sermon, fell under three main heads.

First came the religious aspect of the case. Education and religion are and should be indissolubly united. "The *fact* is undeniable, that the combination of religious with secular instruction is *the rule of English Education*, and is practised by all the societies hitherto formed for the educating of the poor."[2] This

---

[1] Both his paper's motto and his "Liberation Society" were the subject of criticism by M. A. in *Culture and Anarchy* (1869), pp. 87 ff, and 170.
[2] *The Eclectic Review*, April, 1851, p. 481.

combination is in accordance with the conscientious convictions of the religious-minded people of the country. This is the result of the accepted opinion that the leading function of education is the training of character, which means that it is of unspeakably higher importance that they (the children) should grow up with sound moral and religious principles than that they should possess the mere elements of secular knowledge.[1] The secularists who supported W. J. Fox's Bill considered that the desirable moral training could be given without the inclusion of religion. "But," said the voluntarists, "if there is to be moral training, we ask, first, why should the lower part of morals be taught, and the higher part be excluded? Why should children be taught their duty to man and not be taught their duty to God? Again, we ask, *Can* any such severance be made without taking away from morals their only real authority and effective sanction, namely, the Divine command contained in the Holy Scriptures?" It is unthinkable that the people of England would "allow the living system of God's truth to be cut asunder, as with the executioner's sword, and one bleeding half given to the schoolmaster, and the other to the Minister."[2]   If then, religion and education are inseparable,[3] whenever the Government makes a grant to a denominational school it is automatically endowing the religious sect that upholds that particular school. This is "the greatest objection to the Minutes of Council, that they held out a perpetual bribe to the abandonment of sacred principles and gently insinuated through a measure of education, the system of universal religious endow-

---

[1] ibid. cf. *The Economist*, ix, 142–4, 8th February, 1851: "No Education without religion will satisfy the public demands or be agreeable to the public feelings."

[2] id., 482.

[3] The finest statement of the position was given in an inspiring address to his graduating students in 1851 by Rev. W. J. Unwin, Principal of the Congregational Homerton College. It is quoted in Appendix No. 4 to the *Select Committee Report on the Manchester and Salford Education Bill* (1853), pp. 249–50:

"Besides the direct religious teaching of the School, you have large opportunities of influencing the minds of your youthful charges by indirect means. The value of this cannot be exaggerated, and a faithful teacher will, in connection with all pursuits, keep in view the culture of the moral affections and religious susceptibilities. . . . Now in the schoolroom and in the playground, character is perpetually forming for good or evil; at all times and in connection with all duties manifold occasions occur for exercising the moral faculties by the presentation of proper motives and, therefore, secular and religious education, like the warp and the woof, must go together and no opportunity of appealing to the conscience of a child be neglected. Our youth, thus trained, will grow up with a conviction that religion is not a thing of places and times, but a life, a character, which should underlie all the powers of the mind, mingle with the pursuits of everyday life, and be exhibited, not only in the sanctuary and in the closet, but by the poor man in his daily toil and by the rich man amid the activities of business, or the dazzling scenes of human greatness."

ment."[1]   This indiscriminate endowment of all religions by the State "tends to destroy, in popular estimation, the difference between truth and error, and to degrade religion into a mere engine of popular government."[2]   In this point, the leading members of all communions were agreed, even if there was little else about which they were unanimous.   It aroused also among Nonconformists a conscientious objection to contributing to public funds which were used for such purposes.   "They demur to pay for the teaching of the Church Catechism, and the Roman Missal—of John Wesley's System, and the Improved Version; and, were equity to be fully carried out, of the Jewish Ritual and the Deists' maxims."[3]

"They believe it (the Government grant) will, in the end, impede, deaden, restrict, and injure this sacred cause (of education). . . . State power in religion, State power in education, State power in money, State power in inspections, State power in Whitehall reaching over England; these all as kindred influences, are against Dissent, against liberty, against national spirit,— and, therefore, against every allied interest of a self-governed, self-acting people."[4]

The religious argument thus passed by an easy transition into an examination of the proper sphere for the activities of the State.   The keynote of the argument was struck by Baines when he exclaimed: "And we have scarcely emancipated industry from Government control, under the name of 'protection', when the same control, under nearly the same misnomer, lays its grasp on the more sacred interests of education."[5]   The prevalent philosophy was that of *laissez-faire*.   It had been accepted in the field of commerce, why should not its arguments *mutatis mutandis* be applied also in the sphere of education?   It was a mode of thought that appealed particularly to the Dissenters who had played such an important part in the building of England's industrial and commercial supremacy.   The question, "Is it for the interest either of individuals or of society, that the great work of education should be taken out of the general law of *individual*

[1] *The Eclectic Review*, op. cit., p. 474.
[2] ibid.   The Congregational Union in 1843 passed a resolution refusing to accept money raised by taxation for the teaching of religion "and considering that the education given by the Congregational Churches must be religious education, advises most respectfully, but most earnestly, that no government aid be received by them for schools established in their own connection."
[3] *Crosby Hall Lectures*, speech of Rev. A. Wells, p. 66.
[4] id., p. 67.
[5] *Crosby Hall Lectures*, p. 5, cf. *The Eclectic Review*, April 1851, p. 473.

action and free competition, and put under a system of *public super-intendence and compulsory support?"* [1] could surely admit of only a decisive negative from the men who had just succeeded in having the Corn Laws abolished. Neither Cobden nor Bright, however, the leaders of the Anti-Corn Law League, were convinced of the logic of the position. They both supported the Secularist party. The reasons, however, by which they should have been convinced were set forth briefly and pointedly by Miall. "The truth is that the proposal put before us is that to an immense extent we should shift the axis of social morality," [2] . . . "from the self-moving power of moral obligation to the external power of legal author-ity." [3] Now there is no doubt that voluntary benevolence is a force of a higher order than legal compulsion. The change, therefore, to the latter would be a retrogression and one of unfore-seen consequences as yet ill-studied and little understood. Once commence with such compulsion, and it will stultify all innova-tion and spontaneity on which progress depends until inevitably it will affect the whole spirit of the nation. State interference in education in fact is a continental importation, "creeping in among us", that "will impair the noble self-reliance" [4] on which the greatness of our nation has been built.

[1] *The Eclectic Review,* April 1851, p. 492–3.
[2] *Crosby Hall Lectures,* p. 150.
[3] id., p. 149.
[4] id., p. 47. Such innuendoes would appeal quickly to contemporary Englishmen who were entering, under Palmerston's guidance, a period of nationalistic self-importance. Plausibility was lent to the statement by the fact that in inducing the Committee of Council to accept the pupil-teacher plan of 1846, Kay-Shuttleworth had laid great stress on the successful working of a similar plan in Holland (*vide* Kay-Shuttleworth, *Public Education,* p. 58 ff.). The examples of Prussia and France, with state-centralized education systems, as "more generally educated countries than England" was also familiar at the time (*vide Crosby Hall Lectures,* p. 55).
The most extreme form of the Voluntaryists case was put in a series of articles in *The Economist* during 1851. The following extracts indicate the stand taken:
1st February. "Our impression is and we have attempted to justify it by some reasons, that NATIONAL education and societies to promote it are founded on an erroneous principle. To be successful, education must be sought from self-interest and obtained from self-exertion. With the question of the poverty of the people, which precludes them from getting education, we have now no concern; but it may be feared that supplying them with education may help to keep them in poverty and dependence. Putting out of view their pecuniary condition, we think they should be left to provide education as they provide food for themselves. National institutions to provide the latter for the people are justly Mr. Cobden's abhorrence, and national institutions to educate them are hardly wiser. The error consists in attempting to make them *national,* because it is beneficient, which can only be accomplished, like successful trade by self-interest and private enterprise. We have a high respect for the motives of the Manchester gentlemen, and believe them to be generous and desirous to be just; but they have taken a wrong course in proposing a law on the subject and in applying the contrivances of Government, which are necessarily national and

The third contention on which the Voluntaryists rested their case was the fact that their principles were not merely right in theory but that they were working successfully in practice. Voluntary effort in education was increasing in effectiveness and was sufficient for the needs of the country. "Looking at the mighty progress that has been made, at the velocity with which the great engine of education is now travelling on its magnificent way, at the unexhausted force of the motives which are impelling it, at the momentum which the brute mass of society has acquired, I no more expect to see it brought to a stand, than to see our planet halt in its revolution round the source of light," said Mr. Baines.[1] This was a theme that lent itself easily to much sentimental and platitudinous nonsense such as the panegyric pronounced in justification of the extraction of school pence from the struggling parents of pauper children: "They (the weekly pence) are the exponents of the affection of the parents, and of their desire to promote the best interests of their children. They express their sympathy with the work of the teachers, and are pledges that they will diligently second his labours at home. . . ."[2] It was sufficient answer to such expressions for his more matter-of-fact opponents merely to refer him to the latest grim reports of the newly formed Board of Health on the living conditions of the poorer classes in the industrial cities. In defence of their claim of progress in education the Voluntaryists could point to the vast increase in the number of day scholars attending the schools of the various educational societies. This Baines did, and showed how the numbers had risen from half a million in 1803 to two millions in 1846, triumphantly pointing out that the proportion of scholars to the total population had increased over the same period from 1 : 17½ to 1 : 8½, a figure which compared favourably

have a common object, to the purposes of education which is and must be individual."

22nd February. "To all these foregoing schemes of education there remains the decided objection that they nourish into life a degree of intellectual activity which finds no corresponding object for its exertion and makes its possessors more the instruments for corrupting than improving society. They are bounties on a species of production not at the moment in demand."

13th December. "The scheme (of the Secularists) is opposed to the principles generally adopted for the government of society. It interferes by a tax with the application of individual resources; it directs some capital and some labour in a particular manner; as society is now composed, it will tax some, and this seems to be intended, to bestow advantages on others; and it is equally opposed to respect for property and to the important principle of *laissez-faire*."

[1] *Crosby Hall Lectures*, p. 39.
[2] Quoted from the *Edinburgh Review* by a witness before the Select Committee on the Manchester and Salford Education Bill (29th April, 1853), Q. 1639.

with that of any country on the continent.[1] Again it was sufficient answer, without a careful analysis of the meaning of his figures,[2] merely to inquire what was happening to the other two million children between the ages of 5—15 years that were abroad in England in 1846 but not appearing on the registers of any schools.   Voluntaryist lecturers constantly appealed to figures showing the progress of their efforts, but it was the weakest link of their argument.   Such figures alone could not be used to forecast the future progress of their activities, and, they were, at the same time, being controverted not merely by opponents who pointed to the patent inadequacy of existing educational provision, but also by themselves when on a different platform they were appealing for funds in support of their schools.   For Baines, himself, in an editorial in the *Leeds Mercury* of 12th April, 1851, in an appeal for Rotherhithe Chapel confessed that "it has partaken of the common lot of voluntarily supported institutions, and has often struggled for existence. . . . Just a year ago it seemed as if it must be abandoned."[3]

The Voluntaryists, in fact, were fighting for a losing cause, and one by one their numbers left them for the other side.   Even Edward Miall, in another decade, was to join forces with the advocates of State intervention.   Such desertions were a source of deep regret and sorrowful resignation at a fellow-creatures failings, on the part of the staunch, unbending leader of another school of Voluntaryists, G. A. Denison, Archdeacon of Taunton.

This forthright high churchman was first moved to protest against governmental influence on education in respect of the Management Clauses of 1847 that formed a corollary to the 1846 Minutes of the Committee of Council.   By these clauses the government prescribed for the National Society what would be the acceptable terms of management and composition of managing committees of those schools which wished to avail themselves of grants under the Minutes of the Committee of Council.   This, according to Denison, was an unjustifiable intrusion of govern-

---

[1] *Crosby Hall Lectures*, p. 33.
[2] Such an analysis was made by Matthew Arnold in his report *Schools and Universities on the Continent*, vi–xi, written in 1867.
[3] H. Mann in his report on the census of 1851 stated: "The numerical strength of this party is probably not inconsiderable.   It comprises nearly the whole of the Congregational and Baptist bodies (which together possess 6,033 chapels and 1,820,103 sittings) and many members of the small sections of Wesleyan Methodists.   The Friends, too, for the most part, adhere to this standard." *Parliamentary Papers*, 1852–3, xc, p. lxxxiii.

mental power into the sphere properly belonging to the church.
"That it is the duty of the state to annexe conditions to its
assistance, I have never disputed," he said, "The whole question
is *what conditions?*

"There are two necessary and legitimate conditions, and two
only:—

1. That the site be legally secured.
2. That it be ascertained, from time to time, as the State may
   appoint, that the school built with its assistance is used for
   the purposes stated at the time when the application for assistance was made."[1]

The State, in fact, may legitimately be a moneylender but not
an educator. The process of education is a religious one, since
"the system of Education is that of training childhood and youth
to do their duty in that station of life to which God has called
them." The mind of the child must be trained "to begin with
the assumption, and to abide and rest in it, that the highest use
of reason is to submit reason to Revelation, as delivered and
interpreted by the Church." This provides a sure, fundamental
basis on which can be built the various knowledges and skills
necessary for particular callings, and "so founded, prepared and
encouraged (the mind) proceeds to educate itself throughout
this life for heaven."[2] Education must be sharply distinguished
from Instruction, which "is not only a different, but an opposite
thing," not laying its basis in authority derived from Holy
Scripture but merely in the authority of the individual will which
of its very nature excludes an unquestioning obedience to the
Book of God, "as committed to, delivered, and interpreted by
the Church." In short, one is "educated" for the heavenly life,
through the earthly life; but "instructed" for the earthly life
only. "Religion is the beginning, the middle, and the end of
'Education'." It is the chance, and not very welcome companion
of "Instruction".[3]

It is therefore the province of the Church to exercise unimpaired

---

[1] G. A. Denison, *Notes of My Life*, p. 145.
[2] id., pp. 17–18.
[3] cf. id., p. 109: "Religion is the beginning, middle, and the end of all Christian
teaching; the golden thread that runs through it all." The insidious growth of
"instruction" of late, tending to promote a democratic disrespect and lack of
reverence for those put in authority over us, led the Archdeacon to quote with approval
a remark: "There have been priest-ridden ages, and king-ridden ages; ours is a child-
ridden age," and to express his reverent thanks to God that "the system of 'Education'
is that upon which I was brought up", id., pp. 19–20.

control over education. The Government has "no Creed", and is so constituted "of divers interests and influences" that "it is not bound by the principles of the Church."[1] It is therefore a secular intrusion that, with a kind of reversed Midas-touch, turns whatever "Education" it contacts into a mere "Instruction", a leading, perhaps *the* leading . . . and the most unhappy characteristic of our time."[2]

Denison, therefore, severed his connection with the Committee of Council as soon as the insidiousness of State influence on "education" was brought home to him through the 1847 Management Clauses.[3] He further considered it his duty to expose and to counter to the utmost of his ability what he was convinced was "the Whig plot, concocted for Whig purposes; concocted to please Nonconformists, religious and political, at the expense of the Church."[4] Looking back in later life he outlined the course of the plot as follows:

1. Minutes of Council, 1846.
2. Management Clauses, 1847.
3. Abolition of exclusive character of Church schools, in respect of admission of children, and teaching, 1847 to 1870.
4. "Education" Rate attempted. Manchester and Salford Scheme, 1851–3.
5. "Conscience Clause", 1850 to 1870.
6. "Time Table Conscience Clause", 1870.
7. Education Rate completed, with School Board, 1870.[5]

These successive steps he opposed as best he could, and, for a while, he was able to organise such a formidable resistance composed chiefly of the clergy who had been most influenced by the Oxford Movement,[6] that in 1849 there was much talk of forming a breakaway society in opposition to the National Society.

[1] id., pp. 150–1, extracts from a letter by Denison to Canon Wordsworth in 1853 describing at length the history of the controversy that he waged over the six preceding years.

[2] id., 14.

[3] id., 100. His final renunciation was made in conversation with the local inspector. "I said to Bellairs thereupon—'My dear Bellairs, I love you very much; but if you ever come here again to inspect, I lock the door of the school, and tell the boys to put you in the pond'." It appears that muscular Christianity was not wholly the invention of the Christian Socialists and Charles Kingsley.

[4] id., 118.

[5] id., 136.

[6] John Keble gave his blessing and encouragement to Denison's cause, *vide Notes of My Life*, pp. 171–6. It is not, however, possible to associate any particular educational programme with the Tractarians. The conflict in the National Society during this period is briefly reviewed in C. K. F. Brown, *The Church's Part in Education*, 1833–1941, pp. 23–5.

Denison's agitation came to a head in 1853 when he organised the opposition to Gladstone's re-election as Member of Parliament for the University of Oxford. The grounds of his campaign were that Gladstone was a member of the same cabinet and sat in the same Committee of Council as Lord John Russell and Lord Lansdowne who were pledged to a scheme of "education" whose "starting point is religious Indifferentism, and whose end will be finally to destroy by law the Parochial System of the Church of England." Gladstone's success in the contest broke up Denison's party and thenceforward, though his voice was frequently heard, it was little heeded.[1]

The supporters of State influence in education were of many shades of opinion, approving of varying degrees of State control and divers means of exercising it. They may, however, be generally divided into three broad parties, the Secularists, the Denominationalists,[2] and those who supported the current policy of the Committee of Council.

Most prominent of the Secularists was George Combe, well-known for his championship of the budding science of phrenology. From this study he was led into an intimate connection with the work of education on which both he and his brother, Dr. Andrew Combe, wrote numerous articles and pamphlets. He aided Wilderspin in establishing his Infants Schools in Scotland, and later, in 1848, was the chief promoter of Williams' Secular School in Edinburgh which, with the Birkbeck Schools of William Ellis, started at the same time, formed the model for a number of similar experimental ventures throughout the United Kingdom.[3] His efforts on behalf of education were summed up by his admiring biographer, a well-known inspector of schools in the 1870s as follows: "There is no doubt that to George Combe personally,

---

[1] "The battle was virtually lost in 1852, though it continued against hope for some sixteen years after," *Notes of My Life*, p. 168. It is interesting to note that at this time, Denison's brother William who was Lieut.-Governor of Van Dieman's Land, and later Governor of New South Wales, was denouncing the educational system there for leaning too heavily on the state's finances. Matthew Arnold's brother Thomas, was Inspector of Schools during Denison's regime in Van Dieman's Land.

[2] The terminology is that of C. B. Adderley in introducing the Manchester and Salford Education Bill for the last time in February 1854, *Parliamentary Debates*, cxxx, 1047.

[3] In evidence before the Select Committee on the Manchester and Salford Bill, in 1853, Dr. Watts stated that the following Secular Schools were then functioning: British and Foreign School at Camberwell, five Birkbeck Schools in London, National Hall School at Holborn, Mr. Brooks' School in John Street, Mr. Shields' School in Peckham, Odd Fellows School in Manchester, Williams' School in Edinburgh, and two Glasgow Secular Schools.

the country is more indebted than to any other single individual for the development of National Education as now greatly accomplished and for the prevalence of broader views regarding the function of Government in the education of the people."[1] He travelled widely in the United States, and on the continent of Europe studying and lecturing on education, and became particularly attracted by the Massachusetts System which contained the essence of the Secularists' proposals.

The Massachusetts System was a popular source of inspiration, misrepresentation, and vilification on English educational controversies of the 1840s and 50s, and aroused a degree of mixed feelings not unlike that occasioned by a somewhat similar use at the present day of the Soviet Russian system. Interest in Massachusetts was stimulated by the visit in 1844 of Horace Mann, the first Secretary to its Board of Education. Mann at that time was a great force in American Education, and together with Henry Barnard, his Connecticut counter-part, was one of the chief instruments in organising a major revival in education throughout the United States.

Before taking office in 1837 in Massachusetts he had studied the works of George Combe, was in constant correspondence with the author and looked on his acquaintance with Mr. Combe and his works as an important epoch in his life.[2] It is not surprising, therefore, that there was a considerable degree of similarity in the views of the two men on what they considered to be the most desirable system of education, nor that, with such an eminent educator of their persuasion guiding the educational destinies of the leading American state, the Secularists should try to make the most of the Massachusetts System in the interests of their own case. Yet, in advocating the introduction of the Massachusetts System, they did not mean that all the provisions of the law of 1789, or all the details of district organization, or even the important recent secondary high school developments, should be applied to the United Kingdom. They selected, in fact, a few vital principles that in their opinion accorded with the requirements of the current situation of English elementary education. When Richard Cobden, after fifteen years of fruitless hoping for a system of national education that would couple "the education

---

[1] W. Jolly, ed., *Education*, G. Combe, lxviii.
[2] Jolly, op. cit., lxxiii. Cf. G. H. Martin, *The Evolution of the Massachusetts Public School System*, p. 168.

of the country with the religious communities which exist," turned from the idea in despair of ever finding a reconciliation amid the flurry of sectarian strife,[1] and declared in 1850, "I have made up my mind to go for the Massachusetts System as nearly as we can get it," he meant a system of education provided from the local rates, free, and admitting to its schools no book or teaching "which favours the doctrines of any particular religious sect."[2]

The Secularists challenged the leading tenet of the Voluntaryists that education and religion are inseparable. They pointed out that in actual practice the two were separated in schools, and that it was possible to refer to a body of secular knowledge that could be taught without any reference to religious beliefs. Arithmetic, writing, geography and many other subjects had no necessary connection with religion, and when they were forced into it, one found absurdities produced such as were to be found in the Rev. J. C. Wigram's Elementary Arithmetic: "The Children of Israel were sadly given to idolatry, notwithstanding all they knew of God. Moses was obliged to have three thousand men put to death for this grievous sin. What digits would you use to express this number?"[3] Furthermore, "in the schools of the middle classes, the separation of religious from secular education is more marked and decided than in eleemosynary schools. Take, for example, an orthodox boarding-school. The pupils are taken to Church twice on Sundays, and they are assembled for prayers morning and evening, before and after school hours, but the real school business is conducted through the medium of separate masters, who attend each to a separate department and never dream of including in it the exposition of creeds."[4] There is surely no legitimate reason why one philosophy of education should apply to the middle classes, and another, quite different, to the working classes just because the latter happen to be the recipients of charitable activities.

Not only is this distinction between secular and religious education well-known and constantly in use, but it is also in the interests of improved religious teaching. The main complaint of Sunday School Teachers is that their progress is constantly

---

[1] Morley, *Life of R. Cobden*, i, p. 520.
[2] id., p. 53 (letter to G. Combe). "These gentlemen measured everything by the American model; if it fitted that model any proposition was good," C. B. Adderley complained in a debate on the Manchester and Salford Education Bill, *Parliamentary Debates*, cxxx, 1049–50.
[3] *Westminster Review*, July 1851, vol. lv, p. 463.
[4] id., p. 462. Cf. *Parliamentary Debates*, cxvi (1851), 1252, W. J. Fox.

impeded by the ignorance of the fundamentals of reading and writing on the part of their pupils. If, then, the whole time in day schools were concentrated simply on secular education, the pupils would come better prepared for the instruction they are to receive at their Sunday Schools, and thus both secular and religious education would profit by the separation. This type of argument then led to an investigation of the proportions of Day School pupils who attended Sunday Schools, which it would be fruitless to pursue. The upshot generally was that their opponents, like the diehard Sir Robert Inglis, Member for Oxford, would declare the Secularists' plans to be nothing more than a gigantic system of Godless education,[1] while the Secularists retorted that such an effect could not be further from their thoughts, and that they, in fact, numbered among their supporters many clergymen of the Established Church, and a considerable number of Dissenting ministers.[2] They could point also to the published preamble to their 1847 manifesto: "None will deny the value of religious instruction, but the most effectual barriers should be provided against the introduction of Sectarian teaching." In the words of the Honourable Horace Mann, United States, "Our aim obviously is, to secure as much of religious instruction as is compatible with religious freedom."[3]

Not only, therefore, is it possible to separate religious from secular education, and desirable on educational grounds and acceptable to many religious-minded people, but it is also essential, at the present moment, if a national system is to be established. "The best of all reasons, in our opinion, why Secular education should be separated from Religious Instruction is, that it is *impossible*, in the present state of opinion, to unite them in a manner that will satisfy the *whole* people; or what is practically the same thing, an overwhelming majority of them. And *this* is an indispensable condition in any efficient system of National Education."[4]

Once having decided that national education should be secular,

---

[1] *Parliamentary Debates*, cxvi (1851), 1289–92.
[2] For the details of this argument *vide* Rev. W. McKerrow's evidence (a leading Secularist in Manchester) before the Select Committee on the Manchester and Salford Education Bill, (1853), Questions 229 ff.
[3] Jolly, op. cit., p. 720.
[4] id., p. 573, taken from G. Combe's article on "Secular Education", *Westminster Review*, July 1852. These arguments are identical with those which 20–30 years later persuaded the governments of each of the Australian States in facing the self-same controversy to establish a state system of education that should be "free, secular and compulsory".

it was necessary to consider by what agency education should be carried on.

Should it be left in the hands of the churches? Now the very elements of which any one church is composed are those in which it differs from all others. Church education cannot by its very nature be secular, and must tend to divide society. The churches therefore are not fit vehicles for national secular education.

Can voluntary effort be entrusted with the task? Voluntary Schools are almost exclusively sectarian, but even if this were not the case, there are unanswerable objections to them.

First, after a trial of about fifty years they have shown that their efforts are inadequate to the demand.[1] At the present moment "one half the female adult population, and one-third the adult male population of England and Wales, cannot, according to the returns of the Registrar-General, sign their names to a marriage certificate."[2]

Secondly, voluntaryism operates in a capricious fashion, as is evidenced by the fact that while one half of the adult population of the United Kingdom are unable to read or write, our school and university corporations are, some of them, among the richest in the world![3]

Thirdly, its efforts are fitful. Schools, for example, that were founded in Manchester from the stimulus given by the 1846 controversies have in some cases been abandoned as enthusiasm has waned.[4] Voluntaryism often fails just when it is most needed, for example, "in times of Bad Trade". Subscriptions may cease upon the death of the subscriber or his removal to another district.[5]

Fourthly, there is little evidence that voluntary contributions really spring from a proper sense of self-denial and kind-heartedness for less fortunate fellow creatures; they are more likely to have been caused by the dictates of mere good form. "Look down

[1] Cf. Sir John Pakington's downright statement of the insufficiency of Voluntary education, *Parliamentary Debates*, cxxx, 1076.
[2] *Westminster Review*, January 1851, vol. liv, p. 390.   Horner, the well-known factory inspector, stated that he had frequently seen attendance certificates signed by schoolmasters with a cross. This was before the 1844 amendment which declared specifically that "no certificate shall be valid unless the schoolmaster shall in his own handwriting subscribe to it his Christian and surname in full," Select Committee, Manchester and Salford Education Bill, (1853), Q. 1425.
[3] *Westminster Review*, July 1851, vol. lv, p. 457.
[4] Stated by Rev. W. McKerrow in evidence before the Select Committee on the Manchester and Salford Bill, (1853), p. 39.
[5] id., evidence of Dr. J. Watts, p. 79 ff.

the subscription list. . . . How many have cared to inconvenience themselves, or have measured the aid they afforded by their own ability to render it? Mark the long array of guineas in single file. Why this uniformity where no such uniformity of worldly circumstances can be pretended?"[1]

Lastly, "another defect in the principle of voluntary associations as applied to public objects, is their irresponsibility."[2] There is no guarantee that their duties are being efficiently discharged, or, if they are, that they will continue to be so. As the duties of a school association are such as vitally to affect the public, it is necessary for the public to exercise some supervision over them which is incompatible with a voluntary status on their part.

It becomes increasingly clear that education must be undertaken as a public function by a public body, that education, in short, is a sphere over which the State can properly exercise control. Combe supports this conclusion by an analysis of the nature of society. Man is inherently a social animal. From his social faculties, Government springs. But man subsists primarily as an individual; it is, therefore, the function of government to see that each individual is able to pursue his own happiness, but also, that in doing so, he does not invade that of his neighbours. When an individual chooses to live in society and to claim his rights, he becomes bound to perform his duty to it in return. His duties to society are, first, to preserve physical health, and secondly "to qualify himself . . . for acting well his part in that society." These duties society has a right to enforce. It has therefore a right "to train and instruct him and his children to that degree which shall render him and them moral and intelligent agents, fit to play their parts in the society of which they claim to be members."[3]

But how is this right of society to be exercised? Through the agency of the central government or through local authorities. This issue was not carefully argued. It was largely assumed that it was "inadvisable for a central Government . . . to undertake to educate the people." Increased centralization meant automatically increased bureaucracy and over-government.[4]   A

---

[1] ibid.
[2] *Westminster Review*, July 1851, vol. lv, p. 457.
[3] Jolly, op. cit., p. 555, and Part v for the general argument.
[4] Evidently John Austin's lengthy article of January 1847 in the *Edinburgh Review*, lxxxv, 221, showing that centralization has no necessary connection with bureaucracy was as neglected by his contemporaries as his subsequently celebrated volume on "Jurisprudence".

further factor contributing to a dislike of central government administration was the fact that it would almost certainly mean an extension of the power of the Committee of Council which had been too closely associated with the development of sectarian feuds to have the full confidence of all Secularist supporters however its functions and powers might be altered in the future.

At all events the Secularist party stood for education supported by a system of local rating. This meant also that their schools would be free. The Voluntaryists might claim that the public provision of free schools would dry up the sources of their contributions, and that free education would not be appreciated by its recipients, and was not the best "suited to the independent feelings of the lower orders."[1] The Secularists however insisted that by the payment of rates a citizen had automatically paid the necessary school fees. It was, furthermore, anomalous that while payers of poor-rates in a rural district found themselves rated to provide a gratuitous education for pauper children in the workhouses superior to that which their own children were able to obtain, they could not freely avail themselves of the same means to improve the instruction of their own children.[2]

A number of the Secularists, including Cobden, thought also that education should be made compulsory. Combe did not go so far, but it was a logical corollary of his argument concerning the rights of society and the individual.

The place largely occupied by religion was filled in the secular schools by the introduction of instruction in social and political science. This course in "social studies" included the principles of morals, the laws of production, distribution and exchange, and the principles and practice of civic duties and affairs. The leading promoters of these activities were the ex-Chartist William Lovett, and William Ellis who worked together for the promotion of secular education in London. This was the first major extension that had been accomplished in the elementary school curriculum beyond the 3 Rs and a little geography and history, in a background of religion, that constituted their staple.[3]

The Secularists first became an organized body in the year after the publication of the Minutes of 1846 which had done so much to arouse an educational ferment throughout the land. At

[1] *Parliamentary Debates*, cxvi (1851), 1269, Loftus Wigram, Member for the University of Cambridge.
[2] *Parliamentary Debates*, cxvi (1851), 1246, W. J. Fox.
[2] R. Dawes, Dean of Hereford, and founder of the King's Somborne Schools, also introduced Social Science at about the same time.

a meeting held in Manchester in August 1847, "The Lancashire Public School Association for Promoting the Establishment of a General System of Secular Education in the County of Lancaster" was formed. The chief object of the members was to use the methods and goodwill of the Anti-Corn Law League, many of whose members immediately joined the new association, to promote the introduction of a Bill, embodying their principles, before Parliament. For three years it carried on an increasingly successful agitation until in 1850 it changed its name to "The National Public School Association". The object of the Secularist movement was neatly summed up in the official announcement of its new title and aim: "The National Public Schools Association, formed to promote the establishment, by law, in England and Wales, of a system of Free Schools; which, supported by local rates, and managed by local committees, specially selected for that purpose by the ratepayers, shall impart *secular* instruction only; leaving to parents, guardians, and religious teachers, the inculcation of doctrinal religion, to afford opportunities for which, it is proposed that the schools shall be closed at stated times in each week."[1] It organized meetings throughout England and was able to call on the services of men of such prominence as Bright, Cobden, W. J. Fox, Milner Gibson, Hickson, editor of the *Westminster Review*, and W. E. Forster, later to be the author of the Education Act of 1870.[2] The year 1850 also saw the presentation of an unsuccessful Secular Education Bill by W. J. Fox. A Select Committee investigating both the Secular Bill and the Manchester and Salford Education Bill put forward by the Denominationalists of Manchester, kept up a lively interest in education for the next few years. The Association subsequently dwindled in enthusiasm, although Milner Gibson sponsored a further bill on secular education in 1855, and its remnants appear to have joined hands with the Denominationalists in forming a new Manchester Education Aid Society formed in 1864. This, in turn, gave rise to the Manchester Education Bill Committee which was instrumental in presenting to Parliament the unsuccessful Bills of 1867 and 1868, and in preparing for the eventually acceptable Act of 1870.[3]

[1] *Westminster Review*, January 1851, liv, p. 411.
[2] In 1850 he also became Matthew Arnold's brother-in-law by marrying Matthew's elder sister Jane.
[3] The history of these movements is given in S. E. Maltby, *Manchester and the Movement for National Elementary Education*, pp. 67–105; F. Adams, *The Elementary School Contest*, pp. 151–93; Jolly, op. cit., pp. 237–47.

The Denominationalists agreed with the Secular party, in principle, on administrative matters in the educational controversy, but parted company in their treatment of the religious question. In their opinion, the local rate should be raised for the benefit of the schools of every denomination which was willing to accept the grant. Education was considered to be essentially the concern of religious denominations who, however, must respect their pupils' rights of conscience by permitting those who so desired, to absent themselves from instruction in a specific church creed. The Secularists would hand over the rates only to the schools which taught no religion, while the Denominationalists would aid only those who did. In the actual classroom it might be very difficult to see any difference, for the Secularists were quite willing to have the Bible read in their schools, and to have religious instruction as a sort of extra-curricular activity. The Denominationalists insisted on Bible reading in the Authorised Version, and the giving of religious instruction at certain specific hours so that objectors could exempt themselves from it. The essential point of difference was that the one group left schools undisturbed in the hands of the existing religious management, the other insisted upon the renunciation of any sectarian allegiance.

The 1851 Manchester and Salford Education Bill[1] gives a complete picture of the Denominationalist position. The objections urged against this scheme were chiefly two. First, it meant the disbursement of public money for religious education. Those who objected to it, such as the Quakers, or the Roman Catholics who could not accept the Authorised Version, would have to pay twice over—once for their own separate education, and again, by the local rate, for the education of others. There was secondly no acceptable security for the rights of conscience. Teachers could teach the distinctive doctrines of their sect at any time without specifically calling it religious instruction. And in an age when teachers were chosen to a very large extent for the enthusiasm that they showed for their particular faith, this was a very valid objection. The only remedy, outside Secularism, lay in the growth of indifferentism in religion among the teaching body.

In so far as there can be said to be an orthodox body of opinion on education in the mid-nineteenth century, it was to be found in the policy of the Committee of the Privy Council on Education.

[1] *Vide* supra, p. 11 ff.

But its actions and its pronouncements were not always clear, and sometimes far from consistent,—sometimes a move taken one year, a minute promulgated in one session, an instruction issued in one circular, would be rescinded in the next. It could not be said to have formed a particular educational party. At times even the very members of the Committee of Council spoke with divergent voices.[1]

The Committee of Council, established in 1839, administered the parliamentary grant, that had been voted since 1833, and had the power to affect education through requiring certain conditions to be fulfilled by the recipients of its bounty. It did not directly control any schools or teachers and even found that the fields of education over which the government exercised direct control were not all entrusted to its care but were the responsibility of quite a number of other government departments. Thus the Union schools for paupers came under the supervision of the Poor Law Commissioners, Penitentiary and Factory schools under the Home Secretary, the Naval and Military Colleges under their respective service heads in the cabinet, and finally the lone Woods and Forest School under the Commissioner of Her Majesty's Woods and Forests. Two other fields of education also came within the scope of central government influence in the 50s, but were excluded from the purview of the Committee of Council by the creation of the Charity Commission in 1853, and the Universities Statutory Commissions in 1854 and 1856.

[1] The fullest exposition of their policy is to be found in the works of Kay-Shuttleworth, in particular, in his *Four Periods of Public Education*, and his *Public Education*. Shuttleworth occupies in English education a position very similar to that of Horace Mann in American education, and the two had much in common. Both had an upbringing amongst Unitarians though Shuttleworth later became a "pillar to the Establishment" (*Westminster Review*, January 1851, liv, p. 413. For a discussion of his religious belief *vide* F. Smith, *The Life of Sir James Kay-Shuttleworth*, pp. 82, 331. J. W. Adamson, *English Education* 1789–1902, p. 146, wrongly refers to him as a Nonconformist,) and both undertook their first educational work in "special" fields, the one among pauper children, the other on behalf of defectives. Both were the chief instruments of an educational renascence in their respective countries, and in undertaking this work singled out teacher-training and the establishment of Normal Schools as their primary task. Lastly, they both proved to be indefatigable workers, immensely patient and painstaking, willing to travel and learn from other countries, and prolific pamphleteers and public speakers in the interests of their chosen cause. Mann was elected Secretary of the Massachusetts School Board in 1837 and resigned in 1848 to enter the United States Senate; Shuttleworth was chosen first secretary to the Committee of Council in 1839, resigned ten years later, and was knighted in the same year. His duties were not dissimilar to those of Mann. For the Committee of Council and the Massachusetts Board of Education were both similar in composition and in function. Horace Mann of Massachusetts should not be confused with his English contemporary Horace Mann of Lincoln's Inn, Barrister at Law, who conducted the Educational Census of 1851.

The Committee of Council was therefore not a ministry of education and bore little resemblance to one. It was an extra-parliamentary Committee, whose members invariably also sat in parliament, formed for the purpose of supervising the distribution of a grant voted annually by parliament in aid of the education of the "poorer classes". In administering this grant the Committee, without formulating any theory of education or attempting to analyse the over-all educational requirements of the country, did build up a simple policy that with small additions, and alterations from time to time, characterised its work during the greater part of its existence.

First, grants were made only for the construction or improvement of buildings and for teacher training purposes to schools concerned with the education of the poorer classes.[1] With few exceptions these schools were in connection with an education society, and the great majority were controlled through the National Society of the Church of England.

Secondly, it was made a condition of the grant, that the schools accepting it should be open to an annual inspection by the Committee of Council's representatives, known as Her Majesty's Inspectors. The Committee thus achieved the right to prescribe certain requirements and to see that the schools carried them out. Their Lordships' circular letters to Her Majesty's Inspectors are full of the details requiring examination by them to accord with a proper interpretation of Their Lordships' Minutes. Any infringement of the freedom of the various societies to conduct their schools as they thought fit was mitigated by the proviso that the appointment of each inspector must be previously approved by the Society to whose schools he was allotted. It thus happened that all inspectors appointed to National Society schools were in holy orders, and, under a Minute of 1840, were removable at the pleasure of the Archbishops of Canterbury and York.

Thirdly, it was a fixed principle of the Committee that schools supported by it must impart religious instruction. Thus the

---

[1] Later, in 1853, the "capitation" minutes provided grants to schools in rural areas on the basis of attendance and the successful passing of examinations by three-quarters of the pupils. It was extended in 1856 to the whole of England and Wales. These Minutes were important forerunners of the Revised Code. The 1853 Minute owed its inception to a suggestion by Kay-Shuttleworth who disapproved of its extension in 1856. How far he countenanced the principle of payment by results incorporated in it is not known, *vide* F. Smith, *The Life and Work of Sir James Kay-Shuttleworth*, p. 246; *vide infra*, pp. 208–9.

Birkbeck and other Secular schools could not claim any assistance from them.[1]

And fourthly, the aim of the Committee of Council was essentially to act as a stimulus to voluntary effort. Money was granted only as a supplement to local subscriptions. Kay-Shuttleworth, in answer to Baines' complaint that the 1846 Minutes would raise the annual education grant to the region of £2,000,000, replied, that before this amount could be voted, two millions would have to be raised by voluntary efforts.[2]

This last principle was especially the object of criticism on the ground that by helping areas which could best help themselves the Committee of Council was distributing the money where it was least required. The objection was unanswerable. It could be contended that the policy encouraged voluntary effort by rewarding it, and stimulated its development where it might otherwise be absent, but it was still incontestable that the most necessitous areas of, for example, Ancoats or Wapping, where there was no prospect of raising voluntary subscriptions, remained unaided by any grant from the Committee. This provision had the further effect of distributing most of the grant to the schools of the Established Church which controlled the vast majority of voluntary schools. It could therefore be argued with some plausibility that the vaunted impartiality of the Committee of Council was a fiction, since they distributed to one denomination four-fifths of the nation's taxes, although half of the amount had been collected from members of other denominations. This led in turn to the objection, of which the Voluntaryists and Secularists both made much, that the State was subsidising religious teaching and thus violating the consciences of those who were unwilling to subscribe money for the propagation of the doctrines of a sect of which they did not approve.[3] Finally, the point was raised that the position of the Committee of Council, if not actually uncon-

---

[1] On the formation of the National Public School Association in 1850, Kay-Shuttleworth wrote to the secretary: "I cannot conscientiously concur with them (the founders of the association) in seeking to establish a system of daily schools separate from the superintendence of the great religious bodies of the country". He actively supported the Denominationalists' Manchester and Salford Education Bill, the principles of which were not objectionable to the Committee of Council. Lord John Russell, for years a leading member of the Committee, gave notice of the introduction of a Bill in 1853 that closely resembled the Manchester and Salford Education Bill, *vide supra* p. 12.

[2] F. Smith, op. cit., p. 185.

[3] Select Committee, Manchester and Salford Education Bill, McKerrow's evidence, (1853), p. 37. Cf. *Westminster Review*, January 1851, liv, pp. 403 ff.

stitutional, was at any rate undesirable on two very good grounds. First as a central administrative board it represented an undesirable tendency towards centralization in government with its "fancied danger". Secondly, in its capacity as a non-elective, extra-parliamentary body it was subject to no effective control by the representatives of the nation. Its actions could be called into question once a year when its annual grant was voted, mixed with a multitude of other items in the budget, but, except for this occasion, it was an irresponsible body spending public money on its own terms promulgated not as laws duly sanctioned by parliament, but as minutes "subject to arbitrary change without notice."[1]

In the educational census report of 1854 the outline of the essential features of the Committee of Council as controlling a "fund derived from *general* taxation—administered by a *central* board—in *aid* of voluntary contributions—to *all* religious bodies,"[2] was both a concise and an accurate picture of that body, and also a precise outline of the main points of contention not only in the organization of the Committee of Council but even in the very question of National Education itself. It points once more to the current confusion and lack of unanimity in educational thought.

This is the period of the formation of the "Victorian compromise", the period in which "English society was poised on a double paradox. . . . Its practical ideals were at odds with its religious professions, and its religious belief was at issue with its intelligence."[3] Utilitarianism was "the philosophy in office", but it was not unchallenged. It ruled in Manchester, but existed on sufferance in Chelsea. It guided the economic destinies of the United Kingdom, it swept cleanly through the legal apparatus of the State, it provided the increasing middle-class with a justification for their new-won prestige; and in doing so it was a strong factor in precipitating a crisis, a cultural crisis that the twentieth century is still experiencing. It was the solvent in which Burke's world of privilege, and status, and the matchless constitution threatened to melt away with a bewildering rapidity. It seemed

---

[1] These arguments may be found throughout the *Minutes of Evidence of the Select Committee on the Manchester and Salford Education Bill*, especially the evidence of Dr. J. Watts, (1853), p. 109. *Vide* also H. Mann's Report pp. (lxxxiii–lxxxv), *Parliamentary Papers*, 1852–3, xc, Census of Great Britain, Education, 1854.
[2] Mann, op. cit., lxxxv.
[3] *Early Victorian England*, ed. G. M. Young, vol. ii, p. 426.

as if the English tradition, whatever it might be, was powerless to resist the rising unregenerate tide of disbelievers. At this juncture, however, at the moment of its most noted triumphs, Benthamite individualism was being entrusted to the hands of one who although destined to be Utilitarianism's leading philosopher, would yet end his days by writing "Chapters on Socialism". John Stuart Mill, though never losing his sense of the importance of individualism, showed the necessity for some measure of control over its behabiour. The stabilising agent that he found, was not the "tradition" of Burke, but the State acting at the service of society. The social service State of the future was dimly foreshadowed. Yet it was significant that this aspect of Bentham's philosophy was at this time receiving even some small attention. For it is at this point in its development that Utilitarianism first seriously concerned itself with education. The education reports of a number of Select Committees, followed by the institution of an inspectorate in 1839, acting on behalf of a central board were typical of utilitarian technique; but progress was slow, and utilitarian influence was quite overshadowed by that of the churches. It is therefore not until the 50s that it is possible to see with any distinctness a definite and growing utilitarian influence. This was marked by the beginning in 1850 of persistent attempts to regulate education by Act of Parliament, for it was one of Bentham's central tenets that the administrative and law-making activities of government should be brought under the direct control of the people's representatives through parliamentary legislation. Criticism, therefore, of the extra-parliamentary position of the Committee of Council, and of its Minute-making power, and the succession of Parliamentary Bills on education that were presented for debate from 1850 until the successful passage of the 1870 Act were overt signs that utilitarian influence had penetrated into the field of educational thought, and had come to stay.

The popular justification for the development of the State's interest in education was that given in defence of the 1846 Minutes by Macaulay who was then a member of the Committee of Council. In respect to "the great fundamental principle that at this moment divides the country—whether the education of the common people be or be not something to which it is the duty of the State to attend.... I hold," he said, "that it is the right and duty of the State to provide for the education of the common people." [1]

[1] *Parliamentary Debates*, xci, 1006–7, 19th April, 1847.

The ground for this belief was the one that had been stated seventy years before by Adam Smith who compares ignorance spread through the lower classes, neglected by the State, to a leprosy or some other fearful disease, and says that where this duty is neglected, the State is in danger of falling into the most terrible disorder.[1] Now, it is commonly agreed that it is the duty of the government "to take effectual measures for securing the persons and property of the community; . . . can it be denied that the education of the common people is the most effective means of protecting persons and property?" Take away education, and what are your means?—military force, prisons, transportation, and "all the other apparatus of the penal laws."[2] The State is bound to punish its subjects for not knowing their duty, but at the same time it should take steps to let them know what their duty is by helping to provide means for their education.

On this view the State is a police State, in which education is one of the weapons of the governmental armoury for the prevention of crime. This led to many discussions on the efficacy of education in performing such a function, and the fruitless production of columns of inconclusive figures on juvenile delinquency and opinions of police officers, now in support of one side, and now another. The question became more urgent in the 40s and 50s with the increasing difficulty of finding an easy solution of the criminal problem by disposing of them in large numbers throughout the British Empire. There was a growing reluctance on the part of the colonies to the continuance of this one-way traffic. In 1840 transportation to New South Wales was stopped. From that time, it was continually curtailed and excluded by various colonies until it was eventually abolished in 1857.[3] "Now that they had put an end to the transportation of convicts" said Hume, a little inaccurately, in 1853, "they must provide some means either of taking care of them in this country or of reducing their

---

[1] ibid. Macaulay might have added from the same section an even clearer statement of A. Smith's conception of the state's relation to education: "The more they (the common people) are instructed, the less liable they are to the delusions of enthusiasm and superstition which among ignorant nations, frequently occasion the most dreadful disorders. An instructed and intelligent people, besides, are always more decent and orderly than an ignorant and stupid one." *Wealth of Nations*, Bk. V, chap. I, pt. iii, art. ii. Apart from such internal disorders, the external security of the nation is threatened if the martial spirit of the people declines as it must do through want of attention to education. This argument is developed at considerable length by A. Smith and considered to be the chief justification for a limited attention by the State to educational matters.

[2] ibid.

[3] The convict system lingered on till 1866 in Western Australia.

number." This latter could be done by "a really national instruction."[1]

The civil disturbances and disorders that had worried the country since the beginning of the century without ever reaching the proportions of an organized revolution had kept in the forefront of the minds of the governing classes the concept of the police function of the State. There is good ground for thinking that all the social legislation of the first half of the century up till 1848 was conceived in fear of the outbreak of revolution that was periodically shattering the peace of the nearby continent at this time. This fear appears to have died away rapidly after the fiasco of 10th April, 1848. Thenceforth the way was open for the growth of a more generous concept of the State's function as an agent of social service, but the police function lingered on and was an important factor in educational discussion for many years.

The new tendency received authoritative expression in Mill's *Political Economy*, which he published in 1848. There are cases, he said, "in which the interest and judgment of the consumer" are not "a sufficient security for the goodness of the commodity," in which "the demand of the market is by no means a test" of the worth of the product. Education is one of these cases. "The uncultivated cannot be judges of cultivation". It is idle, therefore, to expect the poorer classes to have a desire for education sufficient to cause an adequate supply of it through voluntary means. "Education, therefore, is one of those things which it is admirable in principle that a government should provide for the people."

In England education cannot be paid for from the common wages of unskilled labour, yet, if their children are not provided with "certain primary elements and means of knowledge which it is in the highest degree desirable that all human beings born into the community should acquire during childhood," there is a breach of duty towards the children themselves and towards the community in general. On this ground, therefore, the State is justified in taking measures to insure that instruction shall be accessible to them. It is justified also in providing it gratuitously if it is not sufficiently well done already by individual liberality. For "this is not one of the cases in which the tender of help perpetuates the state of things which renders help necessary." Education, on the contrary, "is help towards doing without help."[2]

[1] *Parliamentary Debates*, cxxv, 550.
[2] J. S. Mill, *Political Economy*, Bk. V, chap. xe, pp. 8–9.

This modification in attitude had its counterpart in a re-direction of the energies of the working classes. After the Chartist failure, attempts at drastic political solutions by revolutionary means were superseded by efforts for social betterment and reform through co-operative and friendly societies and orders, and the trade union movement. The new trend was given the blessings of the newly formed group of Christian Socialists whose leader dedicated one of his most successful books, *Alton Locke*, to its cause.[1]

This attitude of greater seriousness and responsibility in word and deed on the part of the working classes was accompanied by a more serious consideration by the government of the question of the extension of the franchise. Inevitably, it became linked with the problem of National Education. Lowe's comment in the debate on the 1867 Reform Act, "I believe it will be absolutely necessary that you should prevail on our future masters to learn their letters," later popularized as "we must educate our masters,"[2] was preceded by a similar sentiment expressed by Lord John Russell in 1852 when he announced his intention of making some extension of the franchise. "In my mind this question of the franchise is not alien from that other one of providing that the instruction and education of the people should be in a better condition than it now is."[3] This consideration served somewhat to modify the starkly police function of education that was widely canvassed and to blend it by imperceptible degrees into the later broader concept of it as an agency of social service.

"National Education" was one of the most popular phrases of the period. It constantly recurred in parliamentary debate, was featured on the title page of numerous pamphlets, was preached from a multitude of pulpits, and was seldom absent for long from the columns of the newspapers or the pages of contemporary reviews and periodicals. Nevertheless there was as yet no plan or concept of education that could be called a national one. One of the most zealous workers in the cause of national education, and a man who might generally be considered to be in the vanguard of the educational thinkers was the secretary of the Committee of Council, Kay-Shuttleworth. After his retirement he issued a volume entitled *Public Education* in which, amongst other matters,

---

[1] *Vide* in particular Tom Hughes' Introduction describing Kingsley's mental development in the late 40's.
[2] *Parliamentary Debates*, clxxxviii, 1549, 15th July, 1867.
[3] *Parliamentary Debates*, cxix, 268, 9th February, 1852.

he summed up his views on the function of the State in education.
His principle argument is like that of Macaulay. "Government must, within a certain sphere, be even a moral teacher."[1]
Responsibility for educating children rests primarily with their
parents, but where they fail education devolves upon the Christian
sympathies of their neighbours and the Christian congregation.
If the deficiency still exists it is the task of the government to step
into the breach with educational measures to prevent the increase
of crime and disorder. "The School is a more salutary agent than
the reformatory prison."[2] But, like Mill, he considers that government provision of educational facilities has a further justification
in enabling "the unfortunates" to improve themselves for their
own sakes. A Christian State professing the morality of the Sermon
on the Mount, has "certain grave and high responsibilities, as to
the spiritual welfare of these unfortunates,"[3] and cannot let them
perish for want of a helping hand. "But, in fulfilling this duty it
has peculiar functions."[4] It must not take upon itself functions
that can be adequately discharged by voluntary effort, but act
always as a promoter of such efforts. There are, however, "objects
of a purely economical and commercial nature, essential to the
material prosperity of the country, of which the Religious Communions are not discriminating judges."[5] These are the industrial
arts, mechanical and physical instruction, health education, and
simple principles of economics. Provided that it does not act in
such a way as to shackle individual enterprise, the Government is
justified in giving its special encouragement to these educational
fields.[6]

There, in the utterance of the chief educational administrator
of the State, we look in vain for any hint of a comprehensive or
well-rounded scheme of education of the nation as a whole.
National education meant for him the education of the poorer
classes, and so it did also in all contemporary discussions on the
topic. The legislature of the land was concerned only with the
instruction of the children of those who were unable to secure it
out of their own resources. It is not necessary that a scheme of
National Education should be one provided by or even regulated

[1] Kay-Shuttleworth, *Public Education*, p. 286.
[2] id., p. 287.
[3] id., p. 281.
[4] id., p. 288.
[5] id., p. 291.
[6] id., p. 292.

by the State. But the use of the term does imply a reference to some form of educational provision common to the whole of the community. This concept, however, had not yet arrived in mid-Victorian England. Education was of two types, one for the upper classes through endowed or public schools leading in some cases to the university, and the other, "national education", for the children of the poor with the object of inculcating moral and religious knowledge and a smattering of the three Rs.

The efforts already made, however, showed several signs, barely perceptible though they were, of the tendency, that became more and more apparent as the century progressed, to think of the educational problem as one which concerned the nation as a whole and required a single educational system of some coherence. Richard Dawes, discussing the policy of the Committee of Council, asked in the expectation of a negative reply, "Are we then only aiming at a charity system after all?"[1] and he was able to show in his schools at King's Somborne how to combine the labouring poor with the sons of farmers in one school system. The broadening of the curriculum apparent in Secular schools was an attempt to raise the standard of "national education" above the minimum required for literacy and elementary bookkeeping. And, above all, the persistent efforts to bring education within the sphere of direct parliamentary legislation, and, in particular, to make it a charge on local rates directly affecting all persons and classes, though it might be initially concerned with a limited field, was pregnant with future unforeseen possibilities.

These efforts, however, of themselves could not develop far. Before the semblance of a national system could be formed three developments independent of the educational structure were necessary: the widespread growth of the middle classes, the articulation and stimulation of local government, and the growth of indifferentism in religion which rendered sectarian differences no longer a factor of importance in the provision of education.

Cavour has said that anyone can govern in a state of siege. Such had largely been the state of England in the first half of the nineteenth century, and the educational policy had been drafted accordingly. But by the mid-century the atmosphere had cleared, the era of progress had been signalled by the Great Exhibition, and the age of mobility was under way. It was

[1] R. Dawes, *Remarks on Committee of Council on Education*, p. 45.

becoming necessary to govern, not merely regulate, to play the part of statesmen rather than policemen. The attempted educational legislation of the early 50s was a sign of a growing consciousness that a new age was dawning, in which the old ways and practices were inadequate, and stood in urgent need of reconsideration.

It was a moment that offered splendid opportunities to the man who could grasp the direction of events, who could enter into the Zeitgeist, and interpret it aright.

Such was the age, and such the educational situation when Matthew Arnold obtained his appointment in 1851.

CHAPTER IV

THE STATE AND EDUCATION

"Das wenige verschwindet leicht dem Blicke
Der vorwärts sieht, wie viel noch übrig bleibt—"
says Goethe: "the little that is done seems nothing when we look
forward and see how much we have yet to do."—*Essays in
Criticism*, 1st Series, p. 22.

FROM his earliest adult years Arnold displayed a spirited aversion
to what he termed "Americanism".

"I see a wave of more than American *vulgarity*, moral, intellectual, and social, preparing to break over us," he wrote in
1848[1]. A little later he spoke of "the absence of any culture in
America, where everybody knows that the Earth is an oblate
spheroid, and nobody knows anything worth knowing."[2] America
stood for the exaggeration of everything that was objectionable
in the newly-developing industrial, middle-class culture of
England. Self-importance, the want of great natures, the lack of
beauty, the uninteresting pursuit of "das Gemeine", restlessness,
and multifariousness, were the traits of this culture that Arnold
never ceased to impugn.[3] From his earliest letters through all
his literary and social writings, up to his last essay on "Civilisation
in the United States," written in 1888, the year of his death, there
is a constant refrain of anti-Americanism. It was not directed
against the United States as a nation, it was a campaign against
a way of life towards which Arnold considered England to be
drifting and which he imagined to be exemplified in America
more clearly than anywhere else. The root fault of Americanism
was a distressing fragmentariness, an absence of any great
principle, that would "elevate" and give meaning and coherence
to life.

[1] Russell, ed., op. cit., vol. i, p. 4. Letter to mother dated 7th March, 1848.
[2] Lowry, ed., op. cit., p. 132, Letter 43, 21st March, 1853.
[3] Goethe's "was uns alle bändigt, das Gemeine—that which holds us all in bondage
the common and ignoble" was a favourite quotation with M. A., *vide Essays in
Criticism*, 1st series, Preface xi, "Literary Influence of Acadamies," p. 47; "Civilisation in the United States," *Nineteenth Century*, April, p. 487. For other expressions
on "Americanism", *vide* Lowry, ed., op. cit., pp. 69, 70, 126, 130, 132–3; Russell,
ed., op. cit., vol. i, pp. 4, 6, 130. But after finding a favourable article on his writings
in the *North American Review*, July 1865, he temporarily modified his views and wrote
to his sister that he had recently been struck "with their intellectual liveliness and
ardour"! For American reactions to M. A. and his impact on American education,
vide S. G. Link, *Matthew Arnold's "Sweetness and Light" in America, 1848–1938*.

His own early years had given him an experience of this state of mind that impressed ineffaceably upon him the mental dangers of "the sick hurry, the divided mind" that threatened contemporary British civilization. In 1853 he had written to his sister Jane concerning the lack of philosophical unity in his poems, "The true reason why parts suit you while others do not is that my poems are fragments—i.e. that I am fragments while you are a whole."[1] And he had before him constantly in the person of his closest friend, Arthur Hugh Clough, the outstanding example, in the Victorian era, of this feature of Americanism. Clough did not display the more superficial traits of "vulgarity" that his early upbringing in South Carolina might have inclined him to, but, despite his six years' schooling and continuous association with Dr. Arnold's household at Rugby he succumbed to the restlessness of the age. Though considered one of the most brilliant products of his school, and an outstanding student at Balliol, he failed to reach the First Class. His failure initiated a short run of four years, 1841–4, which the historian of the college records as the "one break in the continuous series of Firsts" from 1830 to the end of the century.[2] Arnold repeated his friend's failure in 1844. The tragedy of Clough's life was that although he had absorbed the moral earnestness of Dr. Arnold and his conscientiousness to an almost morbid degree, he was never able to make up his mind to a definite and consistent line of action. This weakness in Clough's character was a constant source of anxiety and exasperation to his friend who wrote in 1853, "You ask me in what I think or have thought you going wrong: in this: that you would never take your assiette as something determined final and unchangeable for you and proceed to work away on the basis of that; but were always looking for this and that experience, and doubting whether you ought not to adopt this or that mode of being of persons *qui ne vous valaient pas* because it might possibly be nearer the truth than your own: you had no reason for thinking it *was*, but it *might* be—and so you would try to adapt yourself to it. You have, I am convinced, lost infinite time in this way. . . . There—but now we will have done with this: we are each very near to the other—"[3]

[1] A. Whitridge, *Unpublished Letters of Matthew Arnold*, p. 17, Letter to Mrs. Forster, *vide infra*, Appendix, p. 285.
[2] H. W. C. Davis, *Balliol College*, Robinson & Co., London, 1899, p. 222. A letter reprinted in the *Life of John Duke Coleridge*, p. 93, referred to a contemporary report that Clough "has the reputation of being the best head Balliol has had for years."
[3] Lowry, ed., op. cit., Letter 42, 12th February, 1853.

Associated with this defect Arnold had felt always in Clough's work, as in contemporary American society, a certain lack of beauty. Clough could express the "stormy note of men contention—tost . . .",[1] "but consider", wrote Arnold, "whether you attain the *beautiful*, and whether your production gives PLEASURE, not excites curiosity and reflection."[2]   Clough's example was so striking and so close to Arnold that it could not fail to leave a deep and lasting impression.

Years after his friend's death, when he composed his celebrated elegy, "Thyrsis", the leading impression that he gave of Clough was still that of a man who "could not rest" and a poet whose "piping took a troubled sound".[3]

Severest of all the critics of contemporary Americanism were the French, and it was their criticisms and opinions that Arnold heeded most. Tocqueville's *Democracy in America*, which Arnold read in his early years[4] was an excellent analysis of the fundamentals of democracy whose progress the author considered to be inevitable and irresistible; but it painted, at the same time, in impressive colours, and made clear to Arnold "the disadvantage of having social equality before there has been any such high standard of social life and manners formed."[5]   From time to time his favourite journal the *Revue des Deux Mondes* published opinions that reinforced Tocqueville's work. Such were the eight articles by Ampère, son of the famous physicist, entitled "Promenade en Amerique" which Arnold found "so cool clear désabusé and true".[6] Renan, too, "between whose line of endeavour and my own", wrote Arnold, "I imagine there is considerable resemblance",[7] was moved to remark: "The countries which, like the United States, have created a considerable popular instruction without any serious higher instruction, will long have to expiate this fault by their intellectual mediocrity, their vulgarity of manners, their superficial spirit, their lack of general intelligence."[8]

[1] "Thyrsis," ll. 223-4.
[2] Lowry, ed., op. cit., Letter 25, February 1849.
[3] "Thyrsis," ll. 41, 48. Cf. Lowell's comment, "Clough will be thought a hundred years hence to have been the truest expression in verse of the moral and intellectual tendencies, the doubt and struggle towards settled conviction of the period in which he lived"; quoted p. 26, *The Eighteen-Sixties*, ed. J. Drinkwater, which contains an interesting analysis of Clough's outlook on life.
[4] "A Word More about America," *Nineteenth Century*, February 1885, p. 219.
[5] *Mixed Essays*, "Equality." p. 68.
[6] Ampère's articles appeared during 1853. Matthew Arnold's comment was made in a letter to Clough, Lowry, ed., op. cit., Letter 43, 21st March, 1853.
[7] Russell, ed., op. cit., i, p. 111, Letter to Mrs. Forster, 24th December, 1859.
[8] Renan, Pref. to *Questions Contemporaines*, Paris, 1868, p. vii, quoted by M. A. in *Culture and Anarchy*, p. 17 ff.

In his preface to *Culture and Anarchy*, published in 1869, Arnold used Renan's observation as the text for a sermon on the need to rescue man's life "from thraldom to the passing moment"[1] which was the bane of the Hebraising middle-classes of America and England. The narrowness of thought engendered by enslavement to each passing whim gave to society a provinciality that prevented it from seeing and grasping things in their totality. The most telling example of the growth of this tendency in England was to be seen in her foreign policy from the Crimean war to the Franco-Prussian war. The multitudinous shifts and alterations of plans, ever accompanied by self-righteous and censorious declarations and empty warnings to the other powers, which earned her the title of "perfidious Albion", were satirized by Arnold in his delightfully written *Friendship's Garland*. The policy was indicative of the inability of the middle-classes controlling England's government to see matters in their totality.

The period when her rulers "saw life steadily and saw it whole" had passed with the coming of the new industrial era. The epoch of concentration had passed into one of expansion in which all things were held in doubt, and old standards shared in the general mobility and restlessness of the age. It was, however, more than ever necessary, then, to exercise a critical intelligence that could judge events and thoughts by reference to a standard elevated above temporary advantage and passing interest in order to set humanity upon its rightful path.

In his first political essay, "England and the Italian Question", written in 1859, Arnold showed how the era of concentration, characterised by an established order of things and dominated by an aristocracy, had served England well in the immediate past. But the Zeitgeist of the nineteenth century required fresh ideas to accord with its era of expansion. No longer could it trust to the practical managing ability of aristocracies adept at preserving the *status quo* and setting the tone for a society of fixed habits. Taking his cue from Tocqueville, he showed the insufficiency of aristocracy in the face of the contemporary situation which required not prudence and a flair for the practical ordering and solution of simple straightforward problems, but an openness of mind and receptivity to ideas . . . "an aristocracy has naturally a great respect for the established order of things, for the *fait*

[1] *Culture and Anarchy*, p. 37.

accompli. It is itself a *fait accompli*, it is satisfied with things as they are. . . .

"In general an aristocracy is not sympathetic to ideas; it regards them as visionary, because it has not experienced them, and as dangerous, because they are independent of existing facts. It regards them, therefore, at once with some contempt as illusory, and with some apprehension as subversive. . . .

"With this want of sympathy for ideas, aristocracies have generally been most successful in times when force and firmness and vigour of character were of more account than ideas, in the stages when society is forming. They have generally been unfortunate in times of advanced civilization; in times when a complicated society has arisen; in times which imperiously demand the comprehension of ideas and the application of them."[1]

Just as Arnold was considerably influenced by French views upon Americanism, so also were his thoughts on political and social organisation deeply affected by his experience of French life and government, and contemporary French literature on the subject. His Italian pamphlet was written on the basis of his reflections arising out of his tour of France, Holland and Switzerland as a special commissioner inspecting primary schools in those countries on behalf of the Newcastle Commission in 1859.

By the time that he presented in 1861, his official report of this tour of inspection, he had formed the main outlines of his thought in the political and social field, and on the part to be played by the State, particularly in education. From that time right through to his very last magazine article, over a period of three decades, he pursued the same line of argument with remarkable consistency, expressing it clearly and pungently in smooth-flowing and simple, yet effectively repetitive, prose.

The Introduction to Arnold's *The Popular Education of France, with notices of that of Holland and Switzerland,* he later reprinted in a collection of *Mixed Essays,* under the title "Democracy".

It is his most explicit and straightforward exposition of the function of the State in education. In many later essays he elaborated various aspects of his views but in this Introduction he first put forward simply and coherently the principal lines of his argument.

[1] *England and the Italian Question,* pp. 27–8.

The English aristocracy, Arnold regarded, "as the worthiest, as it certainly has been the most successful, aristocracy of which history makes record."[1] But the break up of the old aristocratic political parties had long been apparent through the growth of democratic ideas throughout the nation. ". . . signs not to be mistaken show that its headship and leadership of the nation, by virtue of the substantial acquiescence of the body of the nation in its predominance and right to lead, is nearly over."[2] Now the great virtue of aristocratic government is that it fosters in people it governs "a greatness of spirit, the natural growth of the condition of magnates and rulers, but not the natural growth of the condition of the common people". This spirit comes from "that elevation of character that noble way of thinking and behaving, which is an eminent gift of nature to some individuals, (and which) is often generated in whole classes of men (at least when they came of strong and good race) by the possession of power, by the importance and responsibility of high station, by habitually dealing in great things, by being placed above the necessity of struggling for little things". Thus, a nation led by such a class can become a nation, like the poetry of Homer, "*in the grand style*".[3]

Take away this leadership, however, and what is likely to become of the nation? It is bereft of the force that has given it coherence, and inspired it to rise above its petty multifarious desires and distractions by the example of a "lofty spirit, commanding character, and exquisite culture".[4] Is it not then likely to become Americanised, unless some fresh unifying and guiding power can be found and willingly adopted?

This is the kernel of Arnold's argument. He summed up his position in the following paragraph:

"On what action may we rely, to replace, for some time at any rate, that action of the aristocracy upon the people of this country, which we have seen exercise an influence in many respects elevating and beneficial, but which is rapidly, and from inevitable causes, ceasing? In other words, and to use a short and significant modern expression which everyone understands;— what influence may help us to prevent the English people from becoming, with the growth of democracy, *Americanised?* I confess

[1] *Popular Education*, p. xxvii; *Democracy*, p. 19.
[2] *Popular Education*, p. xvii; *Democracy*, pp. 7–8.
[3] *Popular Education*, p. xvi; *Democracy*, pp. 6–7.
[4] *Popular Education*, p. xxvii; *Democracy*, p. 20.

I am disposed to answer:—*Nothing but the influence of the State.*"[1]

The State then is the *deus ex machina* that will save society from a seemingly inevitable relapse into vulgarity. Arnold was aware that his proposal would not be popular.

He introduced his essay almost with a note of apology for having to make known these truths which were unpalatable to the many Englishmen with whom "it is a maxim that the State, the executive power, ought to be entrusted with no more means of action than those which it is impossible to withhold from it."[2] His misgivings were speedily justified, for the *Edinburgh Review* in July 1861, immediately after the publication of Arnold's report, contained a sorrowing but uncompromising indictment of the position taken up by the eminent poet and critic.

"We are unwilling", said its contributor, "to speak with any harshness of the opinions of Mr. Matthew Arnold, whose name, whose talents, and whose character entitle him to our regard and respect. But we must say that the whole tone of his Report on the popular education of France betokens a propensity to adopt the bureaucratic spirit of continental administration to a degree which is painful and repugnant to the mind of every liberal Englishman. God forbid that public spirit in this country should be so dead, or the upper classes of this country so dull to their duties and their true interests (as Mr. Arnold appears to think they are beginning to be), that we should consign our first social concerns to the paid officials of the State, and make State administration the panacea of social evils! It is a lamentable proof of the effect of official mechanism on the mind, that a man of Mr. Arnold's broad and liberal disposition should have narrowed his judgment to this single principle."[3]

The reviewer need not have been surprised at what seemed to him to be back-sliding on Arnold's part. Had he read Stanley's Life of the great Doctor, a book in great vogue some fifteen years earlier, he would have found abundant evidence that Matthew's father had also had a marked aversion to disunity and a belief in the growing inadequacy of England's aristocracy, and had proposed, as a remedy, to increase the sphere of action of the State. His concept of the State as a creative force for social betterment

---

[1] *Popular Education*, pp. xxix–xxx; in *Democracy*, p. 23, the punctuation of this passage was slightly altered, and the final phrase, "Nothing . . . State" reads "On the action of the State".

[2] *Popular Education*, p. xii; *Democracy*, p. 2.

[3] *Edinburgh Review*, cxiv, July 1861, pp. 10–11.

was the central feature of his thought, and appears to have left a deep impression on the mind of his son.[1] Dr. Arnold's correspondent, Carlyle, who was as deeply conscious of the increasing fragmentariness of the times, turned more and more for his solution to the dominating influence of Great Men, "the few rise to take command of the innumerable foolish".[2] Both Arnolds, however, while greatly interested in and affected by Carlyle's writings, were yet able to retain their faith in liberalism and a steadily increasing enlightenment of mankind through the influence of its collective wisdom embodied in the State.

The Edinburgh reviewer might also have consulted the back files of his own publication for the contribution on "Centralization" by John Austin in 1847. In it the celebrated jurist pointed out the various fallacies that had become attached to the idea of centralization but which, in reality, were either not peculiar to a centralized government or were symptoms of a misuse of centralization. He argued, in particular, that over-government, restriction of freedom, suppression of local initiative, and bureaucratic control of lesser officials by the higher, were not of the essence of centralization, and concluded, that, provided the government confined its activites to its legitimate province, which included the sphere of public education, "we may say that centralized government is synonymous with regular administration."[3]

Like most of Austin's work, however, this plea fell on deaf ears, and was not appreciated during his lifetime.

Arnold sought to turn the flank of his opponents' objections by approaching the question of the function of the State on grounds that might be expected to have a natural appeal to them. The bulk of the opposition came from the middle-class manufacturing population of whom a large proportion were Dissenters. It was not without profit that he had spent the last decade in the inspection of schools run solely by dissenting congregations, rubbed shoulders with innumerable managing committees of the same class, stayed in their houses absorbed their conversation and their habits, and explored the civilization of the chief manufacturing

[1] L. Trilling, *Matthew Arnold*, p. 53 ff, makes a close analysis of Dr. Arnold's concept of the State. "He speaks of it," says Trilling, "in language as glowing as that of Burke for whom the State was God-ordained mystical, sacred, in words as passionate as those of Coleridge."
[2] "Shooting Niagara: and After?" *Macmillan's Magazine*, August 1867.
[3] *Edinburgh Review*, lxxxv, January 1847, p. 258. It is interesting to note that Austin while writing his article was, like Arnold twelve years later, temporarily residing in France, and much influenced by French ideas on administration.

towns of England. He knew that in their minds State-action had become inextricably identified in the past with restrictions on their development, "with the idea of a Conventicle Act, a Five-Mile Act, an Act of Uniformity" and that as they had "never known a beneficient and just State-power, they enlarged their hatred of a cruel and partial State-power, the only one they had ever known, into a maxim that no State-power was to be trusted, that the least action, in certain provinces, was rigorously to be denied to the State, whenever this denial was possible."[1] To argue for an extension of State power, just when they had thrust aside the Corn-laws, the Navigation Acts, and other restraints on trade, on the press, and on religious liberty, and were flexing their muscles preparatory to a wholesale plunge into the profitable delights of unregulated liberty, was seemingly the counsel of an impractical visionary out of touch with the realities of the situation.

But Arnold was neither impractical nor visionary.

His approach was not on the basis of a philosophical theory of the State, but on a practical assessment of the current situation. He struck this note from the beginning of his Report.

"I desire", he wrote, "to lead them to consider with me, whether, in the present altered conjuncture, that State-action, which was once dangerous, may not become, not only without danger in itself, but the means of helping us against dangers from another quarter."[2]

Examples of State action restrictive to the middle-classes came from a time when State power was in the hands of the aristocracy. That era had come to an end. It was true that though they no longer dominated the legislature they did still influence the administration, and that while they administered, they did, as Montesquieu had long since pointed out, in fact also govern, but the administration was being increasingly leavened by the recruitment of members of the middle-class. Arnold might have mentioned as an additional safeguard that just recently the civil service had been committed to the anti-patronage principle of the Arbuthnot-Trevelyan reforms. In these circumstances, then, with the middle classes controlling the mechanism of the State, they need not be apprehensive of its exercising a repressive influence upon them. Those in power do not oppress themselves. "So it is not State-action in itself which the middle and lower

[1] *Popular Education*, p. xxxvii; *Democracy*, p. 31.
[2] *Popular Education*, p. xiii; *Democracy*, p. 3.

classes of a nation ought to deprecate; it is State-action exercised by a hostile class, and for their oppression."[1]

To what use should this power be put? What are the important advantages that might be expected to accrue to the middle classes from their support and extension of State-action? There was, Arnold pointed out, one important general advantage, and there might also be innumerable particular applications, of which he was concerned to point out only one.

"The State can bestow certain broad collective benefits which are indeed not much if compared with the advantages already possessed by individual grandeur, but which are rich and valuable if compared with the makeshifts of mediocrity and poverty."[2] Chief of these general benefits is "an ideal of high reason and right feeling, representing its best self, commanding general respect, and forming a rallying-point for the intelligence and for the worthiest instincts of the community, which will herein find a true bond of union."[3]

The middle class "want culture and dignity; they want ideas";[4] their energy and worship of liberty will not by themselves make a great nation. These attributes need to be combined with "a high reason and a fine culture", and this combination can come about only by the elevation of the middle classes through the influence of the State. Such a combination is in the interests also of the lower classes, since "their natural educators and initiators are those immediately above them, the middle classes."[5]

But how are the middle classes to be "elevated" by contact with State-action? In his answer to this, Arnold is not very convincing.

Those who administer the State, he said, have two great advantages from their position; "access to almost boundless means of information, and the enlargement of mind which the habit of dealing with great affairs tends to produce."[6] Their position, therefore, is such that they have greater possibility of doing good and improving their breadth of outlook, than if they remained in their private station. Of this there is no doubt. Every educationalist from Plato onwards would agree that increased know-

[1] *Popular Education*, p. xli; *Democracy*, p. 36.
[2] *Popular Education*, p. xxxviii; *Democracy*, p. 32.
[3] *Popular Education*, p. xxxv; *Democracy*, pp. 28–9.
[4] *Popular Education*, p. xlii; *Democracy*, p. 37.
[5] *Popular Education*, p. xlv; *Democracy*, p. 41.
[6] *Popular Education*, p. xlvii; *Democracy*, p. 43.

ledge and the habit of exercising it in problems of widespread significance should tend to increase one's ability to appreciate the broader significance of other problems that might be encountered in life. But it is also notorious that the possessors of power have not always shown such a desirable development. Arnold's contemporary, the historian Acton, who was accustomed to move in high administrative circles and had served a term in Parliament, lent the weight of his authority to the view that power corrupts. The arguments raised by contemporaries against centralization, that Austin had attempted to answer, were indicative of a distrust of the "elevating" influence of participation in the affairs of State.

Arnold, however, pointed to the example of France. There he admired "the coherence, rationality, and efficaciousness which characterize the strong State-action of France."[1] This was an example that might well be imitated, just as Frenchmen might examine with profit the independent and local habits of action in England. For "strengthen in England the action of the State as one may, it will always find itself sufficiently controlled."[2] The *Morning Star* loses its labour when it inveighs against the despotism of centralization such as may be seen across the Channel. Any exaggeration of the action of the State in France "furnishes no reason for absolutely refusing to enlarge the action of the State in England; because the genius and temper of the people of this country are such as to render impossible the exaggeration which the genius and temper of the French rendered easy."[3]

Such was Arnold's plea for State-action on general grounds. It was not couched in terms of first principles, or based on the arguments of "any philosophical school". His main approach was on a purely practical basis. It was simply desirable for the improvement of contemporary English civilisation to increase the sphere of State-action at that juncture. Without such action there was a danger that that civilization might waste its efforts in energetic pursuit of unco-ordinated activities and thus might never achieve the greatness that comes from the possession of "a high reason and fine culture". The thesis was easy to grasp and undoubtedly one which invited very thoughtful consideration

[1] *Popular Education*, p. xxxi, *Democracy*, p. 25.
[2] ibid.
[3] ibid.

and attention by his contemporaries. It must be admitted, also, however, that it was just sufficiently vague in its use of terms such as "high reason", "enlargement of mind", "the worthiest instincts of the community", to remain unconvincing to a public which had just acclaimed and enthusiastically bought out the stocks of the eight editions through which Samuel Smiles' *Self-Help* had passed in the two years since its first publication in November 1859.

To his general examination of the advantage of State-action Arnold added a consideration of "a matter of practical institution, designed to meet new social exigencies, the intervention of the State in public education."[1]

Before the establishment of public secondary schools in France under the Consulate, the middle classes were poorly provided with schools for their children. Now, however, "through the intervention of the State this class enjoys better schools for its children, not than the great and rich enjoy (that is not the question), but than the same class enjoys in any country where the State has not interfered to found them".[2]

Similarly, in England, the aristocracy has its Eton and Harrow, but the middle classes have only their unsatisfactory private schools. "The State can do a great deal better for them,"[3] by providing them with public schools. Such schools could be an improvement over existing private schools in two ways.

First, State provision would make the schools subject to "a criticism which the stock of knowledge and judgment in our middle classes is not of itself at present able to provide". Secondly, "by giving to them a national character, it can confer on them a greatness and a noble spirit, which the tone of these classes is not of itself adequate to impart". In short, State intervention in middle-class education would both improve it from a pedagogical standpoint and be at the same time a means of bringing about the "elevation" of the middle classes which the nation so sorely needed.

"Thus the middle classes might, by the aid of the State, better their instruction, while still keeping its cost moderate. This in itself would be a gain; but this gain would be slight in comparison with that of acquiring the sense of belonging to great and honour-

---

[1] *Popular Education*, p. xxxix; *Democracy*, p. 33.
[2] *Popular Education*, pp. xxxix–xl; *Democracy*, p. 34.
[3] ibid.

able seats of learning, and, of breathing in their youth the air of the best culture of the nation."[1]

It appears that "the ideal of high reason and right feeling" which the middle classes lack and which is the general benefit that State action can confer, is to be absorbed by them through the improved and public character of their schools.

Arnold's argument was consistently held and expounded also in the field of literature, whenever his subject provided him with a suitable opportunity. The function of literary criticism in his age was like the function of the State, to knit together the diverse strands that the epoch of expansion put forth, to range widely over the field in order "to know the best that is known and thought in the world, and by in its turn making this known, to create a current of true and fresh ideas."[2] Literature, like the body politic, had lost its greatness. Before another period of greatness could ensue, a vast critical effort was required to get it into order and make current the best ideas that could be produced. On the sure foundations laid by such criticism a new creative epoch of literature could be built.

In laying these foundations the aim of criticism must constantly be directed towards improvement, towards selecting the best "to keep man from a self-satisfaction which is retarding and vulgarising, to lead him towards perfection."[3] Criticism, therefore, like the State, should have an "elevating" influence. The similarity in function was brought out by Arnold's comparison of certain contemporary writings with the garish edifice which housed the British College of Health in the New Road. "In England, where we hate public interference and love individual enterprise, we have a whole crop of places like the British College of Health; the grand name without the grand thing. Unluckily, creditable to individual enterprise as they are, they tend to impair our taste by making us forget what more grandiose, noble, or beautiful character properly belongs to a public institution."[4]

Arnold's feeling was constantly directed towards what was improving, towards whatever would lead to perfection, and in his mind the institutions of the State should embody the degree of advancement that had been made and serve as an ennobling

---

[1] *Popular Education*, p. xli; *Democracy*, p. 36; *vide infra*, pp. 263 f.
[2] *Essays in Criticism*, 1st Series, p. 18, "The Function of Criticism at the Present Time" (1864).
[3] *Essays in Criticism*, 1st Series, p. 21.
[4] id., p. 33.

inspiration for its citizens. It was in conformity with this thought that he turned to the examination of the achievements of the French Academy.

"I say," he wrote, "that in the bulk of the intellectual work of a nation which has no centre, no intellectual metropolis like an academy, like M. Sainte-Beuve's 'sovereign organ of opinion', like M. Renan's 'recognised authority in matters of tone and taste',— there is observable *a note of provinciality*".[1] An academy, such as that which exists in France, may commit errors, but it does establish a general level of excellence to which all writers can aspire. It is the embodiment, in tangible and effective form, of Arnold's ideal of criticism.

The effect of the French Academy was summed up thus: "Well, an institution like the French Academy . . . sets standards in a number of directions, and creates in all these directions, a force of educated opinion, checking and rebuking those who fall below these standards, or who set them at nought. Educated opinion exists here as in France; but in France the Academy serves as a sort of centre and rallying-point to it, and gives it a force which it has not got here."[2]

Is it too much to suggest that the State Arnold desired to see in England was really an Academy not merely of literature, but of life, an Academy whose chief function was educative, which would set ever-advancing standards, not to bring about a mere uniformity or meticulous conformity, but to give to society a unity and to act as an inspiration towards that perfection which is the goal of all endeavour which can rightly be called human?

But what is the State? "The State is properly just what Burke called it: *the nation in its collective and corporate character*. The State is the representative acting-power of the nation; the action of the State is the representative action of the nation."[3] Such phraseology is reminiscent of the idealist theory of the State that had been built up by the German schools of the early nineteenth century, and which Arnold's near-contemporary, T. H. Green,

---

[1] *Essays in Criticism*, 1st Series, "The Literary Influence of Academies," p. 60. In his General Report for 1876, Arnold suggested a modified academy in the shape of a permanent Royal Commission "with the function of watching our language", for the purpose of eliminating from it "evident anomalies" of spelling. *Reports on Elementary Schools*, 1852–82, M. Arnold, ed. F. S. Marvin.

[2] *Essays in Criticism*, First Series, p. 56.

[3] *Popular Education*, p. xlvi; *Democracy*, p. 42. Burke's phrase was not mentioned in *Popular Education*. Trilling, op. cit., has made a comprehensive analysis of Matthew Arnold's concept of the State and its philosophical pre-suppositions.

and his successor, Bosanquet, made an important force in English political thought. But Arnold cared as little as their critic Hobhouse about metaphysics.[1] He even gloried a little in his inability to form a "philosophy with coherent, interdependent, subordinate and derivative principles".[2] He contended that he was a plain man with a few simple notions. He did not pretend to "philosophical completeness",[3] and it is therefore useless to try to place him within any school of philosophy or to expect a logical consistency throughout all his statements. His method was "the free spontaneous play of consciousness" about "stock habits of thinking and acting"[4] in the contemporary community, with the object of arriving at "the firm intelligible law of things and thus to get a basis for a less confused action and a more complete perfection than we have at present."[5] He did not seek a philosophical justification for his ideas, but merely a knowledge of the principles which should guide the activities of contemporary society.

He professed himself to be a Liberal, but a liberal with a difference. Deeply influenced by Burke, whose Irish speeches he edited in 1881, he declared against the principle of abstract right. "So far as I can sound human consciousness I cannot, as I have often said, perceive that man is really conscious of any abstract natural rights at all. . . . If it is the sound English doctrine that all rights are created by law and based on expediency, and are alterable as the public advantage may require, certainly that orthodox doctrine is mine".[6] Expediency, which had become in Burke's hands an anti-revolutionary doctrine, was equated by Arnold with the Zeitgeist, a force which, in his conception of it, was quite as revolutionary as that of "natural right". One of the main ingredients of the Zeitgeist was the influence of the French Revolution, and Arnold considered himself to be one of its continuators. This influence he summed up in his essay on "My Countrymen". "It is the great glory of the French Revolution . . . passionately to have embraced the idea: the work of making human life, hampered by a past which it has outgrown, natural and rational."[7]   And again, "What is the modern problem? to

[1] E.g. Hobhouse's criticism of Bosanquet in *The Metaphysical Theory of the State*.
[2] This was Frederic Harrison's criticism, in *Culture: a dialogue*, of Matthew Arnold's essay "Sweetness and Light", *vide Culture and Anarchy*, ed. J. D. Wilson, Camb. Univ. Press, 1946, pp. 73, 85.
[3] *Culture and Anarchy*, p. 98.
[4] id., p. 198.
[5] id., p. 163 *et passim*.
[6] *Mixed Essays*, "Equality," pp. 61–62.
[7] *Celtic Literature*, "My Countrymen", p. 205.

make human life, the life of society, all through, more natural and rational; to have the greatest possible number of one's nation happy."[1] Bentham could not have stated his own principle more happily. But the Liberals of Arnold's generation thought the road to the greatest happiness lay through a freedom that consisted in absence of regulation. "You seem to think", Arnold exclaimed, "that you have only to get on the back of your horse Freedom, or your horse Industry, and to ride away as hard as you can, to be sure of coming to the right destination."[2] The prime necessity, however, of a natural and rational life was not freedom as the Liberals conceived it, but Equality. The Revolution which, early, ran riot in liberty, ended by laying its chief emphasis on equality. It is this lesson that England most needs to take to heart, for she has made almost a religion of inequality.[3] "Mr. Lowe", for example, "declared that 'no concession should be made to the cry for equality, unless it appears that the State is menaced with more danger by its refusal than by its admission', and Mr. Gladstone averred that 'There is no broad political idea which has entered less into the formation of the political system of this country than the love of equality.' And he adds, 'It is not the love of equality which has carried into every corner of the country the distinct undeniable popular preference, wherever other things are equal, for a man who is a lord over a man who is not. The love of freedom itself is hardly stronger in England than the love of aristocracy'."[4]

Contrast this love of inequality, said Arnold with the injunction of that "consummate critic of life," Menander, "Choose equality and flee greed."[5]

Is it possible that our English civilisation might be on the wrong track? One of the most "gifted spirits" of France, George Sand, "asserts that France is the most civilised of nations, and that its pre-eminence in civilisation it owes to equality."[6] This point was for Arnold the crux of the matter, "Well, it is in its effects upon *civilisation* that equality interests me".[7]

But, what is civilisation? "Civilisation is the humanisation of man in society. Man is civilised, when the whole body of society

[1] id., p. 209.
[2] id., p. 213.
[3] *Mixed Essays*, "Equality", pp. 52–3.
[4] id., p. 51.
[5] id., p. 49.
[6] id., p. 52.
[7] id., p. 60.

comes to life with a life worthy to be called *human*, and correspond-ing to man's true aspirations and powers."[1] These powers are fourfold, the power of social life and manners, the power of con-duct, the power of intellect and knowledge, and the power of beauty, and are characteristic, respectively, of the four European nations of France, England, Germany, and Italy. But the characteristic in which France is pre-eminent, the power of social life and manners, is precisely that which enables one to judge of the degree of civilisation of a whole nation. As one travels through France one cannot but be struck by "the profoundly democratic spirit which exists among the lower orders, even among the Breton peasants. Not a spirit which will necessarily be turbulent or over-throw the Government, but a spirit which has irrevocably broken with the past. . . ."[2] "The Revolution has cleared out the feudal ages from the minds of the country people to an extent incredible with us."[3]

It is, however, precisely in this power of social life that England is most lacking. She is, therefore, so much the less a civilised community. "But a community having humane manners is a community of equals. . . . A community with a spirit of society is eminently, therefore, a community with a spirit of equality."[4] Arnold summed up his argument in two effective paragraphs: "And to him who will use his mind as the wise man recommends, surely it is easy to see that our shortcomings in civilisation are due to our inequality; or in other words, to that great inequality of classes and property which came to us from the Middle Age and which we maintain because we have the religion of inequality that this constitution of things, I say, has the natural and necessary effect, under present circumstances, of materialising our upper class, vulgarising our middle class, and brutalising our lower class. And this is to fail in civilisation."[5]

The manner in which this anti-civilising effect takes place was explained. "What the middle class sees is that splendid piece of materialism, the aristocratic class, with a wealth and luxury utterly out of their reach, with a standard of social life and manners, the offspring of that wealth and luxury, seeming utterly out of their reach also. And thus they are thrown back upon

---

[1] *Mixed Essays*, Preface, p. vi.
[2] Russell, ed., pp. 86–7, Letter from Paris, 8th May, 1859.
[3] id., Letter from Bordeaux, 14th May, 1859.
[4] *Mixed Essays*, "Equality", p. 69.
[5] id., p. 87.

themselves,—upon a defective type of religion, a narrow range of intellect and knowledge, a stunted sense of beauty, a low standard of manners. And the lower class see before them the aristocratic class, and its civilisation, such as it is, even infinitely more out of *their* reach than that of the middle class; while the life of the middle class, with its unlovely types of religion, thought, beauty, and manners, has naturally, in general, no great attractions for them either. And so they are thrown back upon themselves; upon their beer, their gin, and their *fun*. Now, then, you will understand what I meant by saying that our inequality materialises our upper class, vulgarises our middle class, brutalises our lower.

"And the greater the inequality the more marked is its bad action upon the middle and lower classes."[1]

In stressing equality rather than freedom Arnold was in advance of his fellow-liberals. Freedom of a kind there was in plenty in contemporary English society. Arnold did not underestimate its importance. But he criticised its lack of direction, and held the opinion that his contemporaries were apt to over-emphasise it to its own detriment, at the expense of equality.

He was never tired of referring to his times as an age of expansion, and, despite the difficulties which it created, to welcome it as such. For "first and foremost of the necessary means towards man's civilisation we must name *expansion*. The need of expansion is as genuine an instinct in man as the need in plants for the light, or the need in man himself for going upright."[2]

The two manifestations of "expansion" are the love of liberty and the love of equality. Both are vital for the humanisation of man in society which is civilisation, but the latter has so far received insufficient emphasis in this country. "From such a defeat of our instinct of expansion, political liberty saves us Englishmen; and Liberal statesmen have worked for political liberty. But the need of expansion suffers a defeat, also, wherever there is an immense inequality of conditions and property; such inequality inevitably depresses and degrades the inferior masses."[3]

It was Arnold's attitude towards the problem of equality that

[1] id., pp. 91–2; *vide infra*, p. 266f. Cf. H. J. Laski, *The Danger of Being a Gentleman*, Allen & Unwin, London, 1939, p. 27: "A people, in brief, which has been ruled by gentlemen is more timid in affirming its own essence than one which has been accustomed to the self-exercise of power. That is why there is so much less servility in France and America than in England."

[2] *Mixed Essays*, Preface, p. vii.

[3] *Irish Essays*, "The Future of Liberalism", p. 127.

justified his claim to be considered "a Liberal of the future rather than a Liberal of the present".[1]

Future Liberal political theory, summed up for example by Hobhouse, in 1911, took as its central core the idea of growth which Arnold had called "the instinct of expansion". "The foundation of liberty," said Hobhouse, "is growth",[2] and liberty is "not so much a right of the individual as a necessity of society," which, in its turn, rests upon the idea of equality. "This sense of ultimate oneness is the real meaning of equality, as it is the foundation of social solidarity and the bond which, if genuinely experienced, resists the disruptive force of all conflict, intellectual, religious, and ethical."[3] Hobhouse's sentiments would have been warmly endorsed by Arnold, who would also have appreciated the examination of Equality made two decades later by R. H. Tawney who took Arnold's phrase, "the religion of inequality", as the text of his argument for environmental equality. After pointing to the fact that Arnold, had he been writing then, in 1930, would have placed a different emphasis on the various effects of inequality, and would have used different illustrations for his theme, Tawney concluded: "Observing the heightened tension between political democracy and a social system marked by sharp disparities of circumstances and education, and of the opportunities which circumstance and education confer, he would find, it may be suspected, in the history of the two generations since his essay appeared, and, in particular, in that of the last decade, a more impressive proof of the justice of his diagnosis than it falls to the lot of most prophets to receive. 'A system founded on inequality is against nature, and, in the long run, breaks down.' "[4]

When Tawney wrote "because men are men, social institutions—property rights, and the organisation of industry, and the system of public health and education—should be planned, as far as is possible to emphasise and strengthen, not the class differences which divide, but the common humanity which unites them,"[5] he was directly in the Arnoldian tradition.

So also was the analysis of equality made by Laski in his

---

[1] id., p. 103.
[2] L. T. Hobhouse, *Liberalism*, O.U.P., 1911, p. 122.
[3] id., p. 121. Cf. Pollard, *The Evolution of Parliament*, p. 183: "There is only one solution of the problem of liberty, and it lies in equality. . . ."
[4] R. H. Tawney, *Equality*, Allen & Unwin, London, 1931, pp. 26–7.
[5] id., p. 50.

monumental *Grammar of Politics*. "The meaning, ultimately, of equality surely lies in the fact that the very differences in the nature of men require mechanisms for the expression of their wills that give to each its due hearing."[1] One of the basic mechanisms or "basic conditions of equality" is "the provision of adequate opportunity, . . . and it is mainly founded upon the training we offer to citizens. For the power that ultimately counts in society is the power to utilise knowledge; and disparities of education result, above all, in disparities in the ability to use that power."[2] The importance of equality for freedom and an enlightened society, he summed up as follows:

"But if the individual is thus, in concert with his fellows, the author of his own freedom, he cannot exert himself to build it save as he is prepared for that constructiveness. He must know what it means to find himself before he seeks the adventure. That is no easy task in a world encumbered by its traditions. There is never likely to be an enlightened State until there is respect for individuality; but, also, there will not be respect for individuality until there is an enlightened State. It is only the emphasis upon equality which will break this vicious circle. When the source of power is found outside of property, authority is balanced upon a principle which bases prestige on service. At that stage, the effort of statesmanship is the elevation of the common man".[3]

In the thought of these later liberal and radical thinkers we may discern the prime elements of Arnold's argument. An individual whose life is worthy to be called human, must seek to know himself, and to expand by expressing his "aspirations and powers". This he can do only in so far as his society is an enlightened one which seeks the "elevation" of all the individuals which compose it. The foundation on which this liberating and elevating process is based is the general permeation of society by a belief in equality.

By what means is this desired aim to be achieved? Surely, by none other than the expansion and improvement of educational facilities through the instrumentality of the State.

[1] Laski, *A Grammar of Politics*, Allen & Unwin, London, 1928, p. 153.
[2] id., p. 156.
[3] id., p. 172. Laski, p. 539, referred to Matthew Arnold with approval: "Half a century has passed since Matthew Arnold warned the English people to choose equality and abjure greed. The warning has a universal significance. . . ."

CHAPTER V

NATIONAL EDUCATION

"The proctor for a nation is the national government".—M.
Arnold, *Higher Schools and Universities in Germany*, 1874, Preface,
p. xlix.

"Modern states cannot either do without free institutions, or
do without a rationally planned and effective civil organisation".
—*Schools and Universities on the Continent*, p. 272.

IN ALMOST his last article on education, written in 1886, Arnold at
its conclusion outlined what he considered to be a desirable system
of education for the England of his day. In doing so, he summarised the scheme that he had suggested twenty years earlier in his
report to the Taunton Commission, a scheme whose merits he
had consistently advocated over the intervening two decades.

"May we live to see the coming of a state of things more
promising. Throughout the country good elementary schools
taking the child to the age of thirteen; then good secondary
schools, taking him to sixteen, with good classical high schools and
commercial high schools, taking him on further to eighteen or
nineteen; with good technical and special schools, for those who
require them, parallel with the secondary and high schools—this
is what is to be aimed at. Without system, and concert and
thought, it cannot be attained: and these, again, are impossible
without a Minister of Education as a centre in which to fix
responsibility, and an Educational Council to advise the Minister
and keep him in touch with the tendencies, needs, and school-
movement of the time. May the founding of such a system
signalise the latter years of Her Majesty's reign, as the founding
of public elementary instruction has signalised its earlier years!"[1]

In this summary of his thoughts on an educational system for
England, Arnold made clear what to him were the two things
most necessary, first greater provision of schools of various grades
and types, and secondly, "an organic connection between all
our schools, primary, intermediate, and higher."[2] It was to the

[1] T. H. Ward, *The Reign of Queen Victoria*, ed., vol. ii, p. 279.
[2] id., p. 270.

achievement of a general acceptance of the latter necessity that Arnold devoted much of his educational efforts.

In his report Schools and Universities on the Continent made for the Taunton Commission and published in 1868 he recalled a conversation with Cardinal Antonelli in which he had expressed his consciousness of the similarity of the schools in Rome with those of England. "I meant", said Arnold, "in real truth, that there was the same easy going and absence of system on all sides, the same powerlessness and indifference of the State, the same independence of single institutions, the same free course for abuses, the same confusion, the same lack of all idea of *co-ordering* things, as the French say—that is, of making them work fitly to a fit end; the same waste of power therefore the same extravagance, and the same poverty of result, of which the civil organisation of England offers so many instances." He went on to cite the statement of a contemporary French publicist to the effect that the modern spirit required "des libres institutions populaires et des organisations administratives positives et strictement controlées." Upon this Arnold commented: "Modern States cannot either do without free institutions or do without a rationally planned and effective civil organisation."[1]

Essential to a "rationally planned and effective civil organisation" of education, that might enable England to rise above the waste and confusion of her existing absence of system, was the establishment of a Ministry of Education.[2]

But there were disadvantages in the employment of such an agency. In France, for example, "political considerations are in my opinion too much suffered to influence the whole working of the system of public education."[3] The most notorious example of this was to be seen in the recent changes enacted concerning normal schools for primary teachers. Carnot's famous circular during the course of the 1848 revolution exhorted the primary teachers to rally to the republican standard, and, as a reward for their ready support, the State grant for primary education was doubled, the addition being intended to go entirely to the increase of their salaries. But "the Revolution fell; and its conquerors did not forget that it had made the schoolmasters its missionaries."[4]

---

[1] *Schools and Universities on the Continent*, p. 272.
[2] "I cannot but think an Education Minister a necessity for modern States", id., p. 196.
[3] ibid.
[4] *Popular Education in France*, p. 61.

A subsequent commission appointed by the monarchist majority in the Legislative Assembly reported unfavourably upon the pretentiousness and subversive tendencies of the primary teachers, which they attributed in large measure to the over-ambitious programmes of the normal schools. The curriculum was therefore reorganised and restricted by an order of July, 1851, to bring it more into line with the political ideas of the prevailing party in the Assembly.[1]

In Prussia, however, in Arnold's opinion, political influence had no effect, or next to none, upon the schools. His informants told him that, despite the recent great political pressures throughout Prussia, "the State administration of the schools and universities was in practice fair and right; that public opinion would not suffer it to be governed by political regards. . . ."[2] This was written in 1867. Arnold appears to have been strangely unaware of the history of Prussian education under Raumer, the predecessor of Mühler, the Minister during the period of Arnold's visit. School legislation during this period followed a reactionary course almost identical with that of France. "High politics", wrote Paulsen, referring to the period 1840-70 of the ministries of Eichhorn, Raumer, and Mühler, "by which elementary education had so far been hardly affected at all, were now also introduced into the domain of training colleges and primary schools. The educational administration was marked by a profound distrust of the teachers and a profound aversion to 'over-education'."[3] This was the period of the Regulations of 1854, and the banning of the works of Fr. Fröbel lest they should exercise a subversive influence.

A danger that Arnold saw demonstrated in Prussia was the assumption of dictatorial powers by the central authority, which might regulate in detail the conduct of local authorities and arrogate to itself a position beyond its due, by requiring "that schoolmasters should be men who will train up their scholars in notions of obedience towards the sovereign and the State". This, however, is not a danger to which England might be liable. "It

---

[1] A detailed analysis of the educational legislation of this period in France is to be found in E. H. Reisner, *Nationalism and Education since 1789*, Macmillan, New York, 1927, p. 63 ff.

[2] *Schools and Universities on the Continent*, p. 197.

[3] F. Paulsen, *German Education, Past and Present*, T. F. Unwin, London, 1908, p. 245. There is a more comprehensive treatment in Paulsen, *Geschichte des Gelehrten Unterrichts*, Leipzig, 1919, Band ii, p. 491 ff. R. H. Quick, *Life and Remains*, C.U.P., 1899, p. 182, wrote: "M. Arnold must have shut his eyes and ears to everything that went against his governmental theories. He is specially absurd about the absence of political influence (in Germany) on appointments".

is not, indeed, at all likely that in England, with the forces watching and controlling him here, a minister would use language such as I have quoted; and even if it were, I am not at all sure that to have a minister using such language . . . which I cordially dislike, is in itself so much more lamentable and baneful a thing than that anarchy and ignorance in educational matters, under which we contentedly suffer."[1]

England could not hope to progress towards an organic system of education, towards a system that could rightly be called "national" until she had some "centre in which to fix responsibility" for its promotion. "I need hardly point out," wrote Arnold, "that at present, with our Lord President, Vice-President, and Committee of Council on Education, we entirely fail to get, for primary instruction, this distinct centre of responsibility".[2]

In 1856 it had been felt that some closer link was desirable between the Committee of Council and the people's representatives assembled in the House of Commons, and Earl Granville, the Lord President, had accordingly introduced a Bill to appoint a Vice-President who should sit in the House of Commons.[3] The purpose of the new appointment was to accord with the suggestion made in the previous session by Sir John Pakington, "that, considering the large grants of money now made for the purpose of promoting education, it would be desirable that some Minister should be appointed who should be responsible to the House of Commons for the proper distribution of these grants and who could answer any question that might be put upon the subject."[4]

Hitherto, as Sir James Graham pointed out, the Home Secretary was responsible for answering "the three or four questions" that were put on the subject of education in the course of a session.[5] Although the Home Secretary was a member of the Committee of the Privy Council on Education, he could scarcely be regarded as the minister responsible to the House of Commons for its activities. Lord Derby, in the course of the debate, suggested that perhaps the time had come to supersede the Committee of Council by "a Minister as the head of a Department who should have no other duties to perform, and who should be, in fact, responsible

[1] *Schools and Universities on the Continent*, p. 196.
[2] id., p. 282 n.
[3] The concluding line of this one-clause Bill read, "and such Vice-President shall be capable of being elected and sitting and voting as a member of the House of Commons."
[4] *Parliamentary Debates*, 1856, cxl, 814–5 (cf. 1855, cxxxvii, 644).
[5] id., cxliii, 991, 1218.

for the education of the people."[1] His proposal, however, was
not followed up, and a Vice-President was duly appointed to act
not as an independent minister controlling a fully-fledged department of State, but "to act under the orders of the President and
for him in his absence, and . . .(to be) . . . subordinate to the
head of the department."[2]

The Vice-President thus became a minister of State, but was
seldom considered of sufficient importance to be ranked as a
member of cabinet. The biographers of the two most prominent
Vice-Presidents of the nineteenth century, Robert Lowe and
W. E. Forster, refer to them as Ministers of Education,[3] but such
a title was both technically incorrect before the Education Act of
1944, and also misleading in its implication that its holder might
be considered the responsible head of the Education Department.
The Vice-President's duties were in fact not entirely confined to
education. For some curious reason he was also responsible for
the health of the cattle of the country! Forster's biographer
related how, during a particularly busy period, questions concerning the code, inspectors' reports, and the details of the Scotch
Education Bill "were for ever jostling questions about the vaccination laws and the importation of foreign cattle."[4] This Gilbertian
situation gave all the more point to Arnold's plea, some twelve
years after the creation of the office for a real centre of responsibility through the establishment of an Education Minister.

With the amalgamation of the offices of the Committee of
Council and the Science and Art department into an Education

[1] id., cxl, 815.
[2] id., cxl, 825. The Vice-Presidents during the course of the nineteenth century,
and the secretaries to the department were as follows:—

Vice-Presidents

1857–8	W. F. Cowper (afterwards Mr. Cowper-Temple, and Lord Mount-Temple)	1878–80	G. F. Hamilton
		1880–85	A. J. Mundella
		1885	E. Stanhope
1858	C. B. Adderley (Lord Norton)	1885	H. T. Holland
1859–64	R. Lowe (Lord Sherbrooke)		(Viscount Knutsford)
1864–66	H. A. Bruce (Lord Aberdare)	1886	Lyon Playfair
1866	H. T. L. Corry	1886	H. T. Holland
1867–68	R. Montagu		(Viscount Knutsford)
1868–74	W. E. Forster	1887–92	W. Hart-Dyke
1874–78	D. F. S. Ryder (Earl of Harrowby and Viscount Sandon)	1892–95	A. H. D. Acland
		1895–1902	J. E. Gorst

Secretaries

1839–49	J. Kay-Shuttleworth	1884–90	P. Cumin
1849–69	R. Lingen	1890–1903	G. Kekewich
1870–84	F. R. Sandford	1902–11	R. L. Morant

[3] A. P. Martin, *Life and Letters of Viscount Sherbrooke*, Longmans, London, 1893.
T. Wemyss Reid, *Life of the Rt. Hon. W. E. Forster*, Chapman & Hall, London, 1888.
[4] Reid, op. cit., pp. 533–4, 458.

Department in 1856, a step was taken towards a more unified direction of the educational functions then in the hands of the central government. At the same time, the Education Department still remained a department of the Privy Council[1] and continued as such until the Board of Education Act of 1899 established the rather anomalous body that, though never meeting, officially directed the fortunes of English education for the next 44 years. The administrative confusion that surrounded the Education Department throughout the latter half of the nineteenth century was well illustrated by the story told of the Duke of Devonshire, Lord President in 1899. When asked why the new body was to be a Board he replied that the point had been fully considered, though for the life of him he could not remember why the decision had been taken, but he could assure their Lordships that there were good reasons for it![2]

The fact that the office of Vice-President was occupied by a man who, unlike the Lord President, had essentially one duty to perform, that of attending to the Education Department, did lead to his being regarded as the leading authority in Parliament on educational questions. Thus the Revised Code of 1862 was associated with the name of Robert Lowe rather than that of Granville the Lord President, and the important Education Acts of 1870, 1876, and 1880 are still familiarly known as the Forster, Sandon, and Mundella Acts. In 1864 the Education Department came under parliamentary criticism in regard to the practice instituted under Lowe's direction in 1860 of editing the reports of Her Majesty's Inspectors before their publication. A vote of censure was passed which Lowe construed as the House's disapproval of his conduct of the Department, and accordingly, he resigned and demanded a Select Committee of investigation.[3] His interpretation of the vote was that of a responsible minister whose policy no longer had the confidence of the House. This view, however, was not accepted as a precedent by his successors, and was not felt at the time to reflect the actual status of the office of the Vice-President. Sir Charles Wood, then at the India Office, expressed the general view of Lowe's resignation in a letter to him: "I do not think, as I think you would have seen was

---

[1] Earl Granville pointed out (*Parliamentary Debates*, 1856, cxl, 816) it had been "founded on the analogy of the Board of Trade".

[2] W. I. Jennings, *Cabinet Government*, Camb. Univ. Press, 1936, pp. 89–90.

[3] *Vide* A. P. Martin, op. cit., vol. ii, pp. 221 ff. The Select Committee subsequently exonerated Lowe, and the House of Commons rescinded its motion.

the general opinion of the Cabinet, that it was necessary for you to do so." Ministerial responsibility, as a contemporary reviewer pointed out, rested with the Lord President who, however, was too affable and inoffensive a peer to have such responsibility fastened upon him. [1] In these circumstances, with a Lord President considered as a mere benign figurehead, a Vice-President, active in the conduct of affairs but subordinate in official position, and a Committee of Council, the elusive "My Lords" of official memoranda, an extra-parliamentary body, technically referred to as the determiners of educational policy, there was no little justification for Arnold's earnest plea for "a centre in which to fix responsibility".

In 1865, the year after Lowe's resignation, the House of Commons became so far aware of the existing administrative confusion as to appoint a Select Committee to investigate the situation. The Draft Report of Sir John Pakington, the chairman, was quite outspoken. "This system is peculiar; there is no precedent for it in any other part of our Government. The Board of Trade is similar only in name, as the Board never meets. The Poor Law business is practically conducted by the President of the Poor Law Board.

"The Admiralty is managed by a Board, but the members of it are connected exclusively with that office, and their whole time and attention are given to its duties; and the same may be said of the Indian Council.

"It appears to your committee to be more than doubtful whether any advantage is derived from the different practice which has been established in the Education Department."

Several witnesses professed to see a value in the existing system, but the Secretary of the Department pointed out that the Committee of Council met only to consider drafts of minutes or similar business of importance, and not being experts had to have every detail explained by the Vice-President. The Select Committee may therefore well have been excused for thinking that the

[1] id., p. 231. When, later, P. Cumin became Secretary of the Education Department in 1884, his appointment was a bone of contention between the Vice-President and the Lord President. By then it had become tacitly accepted that the Lord President's functions should be limited to the exercise of patronage within the Department. A. J. Mundella, the Vice-President, however, by threatening to resign if Cumin was not appointed, asserted his influence even in this last remaining stronghold of the Lord President. Vide G. W. Kekewich, The Education Department and After, pp. 20–1. The inner administrative history of the Committee of Council on Education is to be found in the evidence of F. R. Sandford (QQ. 1–369) before the Select Committee of 1884, Parliamentary Papers, 1884, xiii, 501.

Committee of Council on Education "is anomalous and unnecessary".[1]

The system was originally established as a temporary device with the expectation that "after no long period" it would be superseded by a general system.[2] The appointment of a Vice-President was a step in this direction, but his existence so far had led to greater administrative confusion as "the question arises who is the Education Minister?"[3]

Lowe in his evidence tried to show the difference in function between the Vice-President and the Lord President.

"First I must state, I suppose, what was my own business. There was a particular department of the business of the office as to which the practice was that it should be transacted by the Vice-President, namely, the sanctioning of the money granted for building or repairing new schools. Then there was besides that, anything of any importance that occurred in the management of the office, either internally or externally; and any question arising out of correspondence on the annual grants to schools, or on any subject indeed which the Secretary considered of sufficient importance to consult the Vice-President upon. Those may be described as being the duties, speaking roughly, of the Vice-President. Then, as regards the Lord President, my duty, I considered, was to bring before him any of those matters brought before me which appeared to me to be of sufficient consequence to deserve his attention; or I brought before him any case, which was very rarely, in which the secretary did not agree with me in opinion, and anything that was likely to be mentioned in Parliament, or which concerned the general policy of the office. It was my duty to bring before the Lord President, and take his opinion on these subjects. In fact, the practice of the office may be described as a succession of sieves, getting larger and larger; I was the last sieve, and what did not pass through that was reserved for the consideration of the Lord President."[4]

[1] *Parliamentary Papers*, 1866, vii, 115, Select Committee on Committee of Council, p. vii, § 11. This Draft Report was not agreed to by the Select Committee who reported officially only the evidence given before them. It is therefore only Sir J. Pakington's personal view but is well substantiated by the evidence of the prominent witnesses that he quotes. Where the term "Select Committee" is used it should be interpreted as the Chairman's opinion expressed in the Draft Report.
[2] id., p. xiv, § 35.
[3] id., p. vii, § 11.
[4] *Parliamentary Papers*, 1865, vi, Q.586. Cf. *Parliamentary Papers*, 1864, ix, pp. 55–6, Select Committee on Education (Inspectors' Reports), Q.679–80, evidence of Lord Granville: "I presume that your Lordship considers yourself responsible for the whole

"But," said the Select Committee, "the merits or defects of the Education Department as representing the action of the State on National Education, must be judged, not so much by the duties they now have to discharge, as with reference to a much extended and more complete system."[1]

It appeared from the latest Report of the Committee of Council that there were more than 11,000 parishes representing a population of 6 millions which received no assistance "from what is called our education system."[2]

Such neglect seemed to be inherent in a "provisional" system without initiative power in education. As Ralph Lingen stated, it does not lie in it "ever to become complete and national", and to that the then Vice-President, H. A. Bruce, added the testimony that "the system is an imperfect system beyond all doubt", while Robert Lowe stated also that it was not "on the right basis".[3]

Three changes were therefore proposed by the Select Committee:

First, "one of the first requisites in an Education Department is, that it should be suggestive; that it is through the agency of that Department that the public have a right to expect the establishment of an effective system that shall penetrate every part of the country."[4]

Secondly, it followed "with this view there should be placed at the head of that Department a Minister of Public Instruction, whose duty it should be to regulate and control the whole subject of national education, and to propose to Parliament and with the concurrence of Cabinet, of which he should be a member, such measures as the extension of education might require." The Minister of Public Instruction would supersede the Committee of Council on Education with its machinery of Lord President and Vice-President. This recommendation had the support of the Duke of Marlborough who, as the Lord President, in 1868, introduced a short-lived Bill proposing the appointment of a

action of the department?" "Yes."—". . . but since the appointment of the Vice-President . . . a general understanding existed, between the Vice-President and myself, that no new rule should be established, and no new alteration in the old rules should be made without my sanction; but of course it was a matter of discretion with the Vice-President what matter he brought before me. We were in constant communication."

[1] *Parliamentary Papers*, 1866, vii, id., p. xi, § 16.
[2] id., § 17.
[3] id., § 18.
[4] id., § 21.

Secretary of State for Education.[1] In 1884 a further Select
Committee presided over by H. C. E. Childers recommended
that primary education in England and Scotland should be under
the control of a minister. They saw "no sufficient reason why
there should be any more real connection between the Education
Department and the Privy Council than between the Board of
Trade and the Privy Council."[2]

And, thirdly, the Select Committee of 1865 recommended
that the adoption of some system of local organisation was
necessary.[3]

Lingen, Lowe, Lord Granville, Lord Russell, and several
of the Inspectors all gave their approval to some form of local
rating in aid of education.[4] However, "the differences of religious
opinion which unhappily exist have long been considered to be a
serious impediment to a rate for education". The use of the
Conscience Clause put forward in the 1853 Minutes of the Committee of Council should be the solution of this difficulty.[5]

With each of these three suggestions Arnold was in complete
agreement.

The centre of responsibility, in a Minister of Public Instruction,
was, of course, quite to his taste. The conception of the Ministry
as a "suggestive" centre struck a new note in official or semi-
official views on National Education, and again was in accord
with Arnold's concept of the State as the organ of the "high
reason" of the nation, the directive and uplifting stimulus towards
national betterment. The third suggestion, that of the development of local organisations on a scale wider than the individual
management committees for each school, was also approved by
him.[6] But his concern was chiefly with the reorganisation of the
central machinery as being of the most immediate concern.

The establishment of a responsible minister was vitally important, but, in order to express adequately the nation's "best self",
his views needed supplementing by the expert advice of the
nation's educational élite.

The men who occupied the position of Vice-President could

[1] *Vide infra*, p. 113.
[2] *Parliamentary Papers*, 1884, xiii, p. 501, Select Committee of Education, Science and
Art (Administration), p. iii, § 3. They came to no decision as to whether the Minister
of Education should have a seat in Cabinet.
[3] *Parliamentary Papers*, 1886, vii; id., § 32.
[4] id., § 37.
[5] id., § 40.
[6] *Vide infra*, p. 106 ff.

compare favourably in scholastic attainment and intellectual acumen with the Ministers of Education of most other countries. But, as Arnold pointed out, the ministers in France and Italy, at least, had an inestimable advantage over English educational authorities, in the existence in their countries of a Council of Public Instruction. This council was selected to represent the State, the Church, the Protestants, the Jews, the law, the Institute, and schools both public and private. It numbered among its ranks, at least in France, men of world-wide repute "whose opinion on matters of instruction may with propriety and advantage be asked."[1] Contrast with this the English establishment. "The secretary of our Education Department is almost invited to settle of his own authority education-questions which M. Duruy, though a minister, would not settle without referring them to a Council composed as we have seen. Nay, and even supposing our secretary refers them to his chiefs and they refer them to the Committee of Council—how is this Committee of Council composed? Of three or four Cabinet Ministers, with no special acquaintance with educational matters."[2]

For efficient national education, therefore, in addition to a duly constituted Minister of Education, England requires also "a High Council of Education, such as exists in France and Italy, comprising without regard to politics the personages most proper to be heard on questions of public education, a consultative body only, but whose opinion the minister should be obliged to take on all important measures not purely administrative."[3] It is interesting to note Arnold's suggestion of an obligation on the part of the minister to take the advice of a consultative committee. This was in line with his belief that the organs of the State should represent the "high reason" and "best self" of the nation, and be an example that would elevate and ennoble the people. The nearest examples to such a proposed body, offered by contemporary practice, were the numerous Royal Commissions that were established, from 1858 to the end of the century, to consider various aspects of English Education. Their personnel was suitably distinguished, and their reports comprehensive and often enlightening, but they were, nevertheless, an inadequate realisation of Arnold's suggestion. The terms of reference, for example, of the

[1] *Schools and Universities on the Continent*, pp. 28–9.
[2] id., p. 62.
[3] id., p. 282.

first, the Newcastle Commission, 1858–61, were "to consider and report what Measures, if any, are required for the Extension of sound and cheap elementary instruction to all classes of the People," a sentiment that Arnold could scarcely have classified as "elevating". The Taunton Commission (1864–7) on middle-class education made a number of progressive recommendations, including one for the establishment of a consultative education committee attached to the Charity Commission, but its advice was for the most part unheeded by the educational authorities of the day. It was not until 1899 that an expert committee was set up for the purpose of "advising the Board of Education on any matter referred to the committee by the Board."[1] The position was further improved in 1944 by the introduction of two Central Advisory Councils, one for England and the other for Wales and Monmouthshire, whose duty is "to advise the Minister upon such matters connected with education theory and practice as they think fit, and upon any questions referred to them by him."[2] "For the first time," said a member of the House of Commons, "in the history of education there is going to be some kind of integration of the best national experience with education administration."[3] In this way Arnold's desire has come closer to fulfilment. The Consultative and Central Advisory Committees have consisted of men whose outlook and attainments would have met with his approval, and their reports have had a widespread influence throughout the British Commonwealth. They have, nevertheless, not yet become the organic part of educational

[1] Board of Education Act, 1899, § 4b (62 and 63 Vict., c. 33). The Consultative Committee had the duty also of "framing regulations for a register of teachers, but it required a further Act eight years later, Education (Administrative Provisions) Act, 1907, before a system of partial registration was instituted. H. C. Barnard, *A Short History of English Education from 1760 to 1944*, pp. 223–5, neatly summarises this development.

[2] Education Act, 1944, § 4 (7 and 8 Geo. 6, c. 31).

[3] Professor Gruffydd, 8th February, 1944. *Parliamentary Debates.* Another member was so impressed with the importance of making the Advisory Councils effective parts of the educational framework that he proposed an amendment to the Bill to the effect "that when the Minister makes his annual report to the House, the report shall include four things: first, a statement as to the matters which the Minister has referred to the Councils; second, a report upon the advice tended to him by the Councils on these matters; third, a report on the matters on which the Councils of their own volition have tended advice; and, fourth, an account of what the Minister has done in answer to the advice tendered." "This," he pointed out, "is the only way in which the House can ensure that the Council is not only properly constituted and has a proper sphere of jurisdiction, but is actually in operation and working. It is the only way in which we can put flesh upon the bones of the Clause 4 and in which the House can see that the Councils are what the Minister has promised they shall be, an effective part of the new set-up of education."

administration that he wished. They may keep the general public, and the minister and his staff informed of "the tendencies, needs, and school-movement of the time,"[1] but they are not directly responsible for the formulation of the educational policy of the Ministry of Education within the limits allowed by statute.

An educational administration headed by a Minister of Education acting on the advice of a High Council of Education was essential to the organisation of an organic system of national education. This term for Arnold meant not the minimum partially provided through the assistance of the national government to those who could afford no more generous provision,[2] but the education of the nation as a whole. To speak of National Education as "now greatly accomplished",[3] as one of Her Majesty's Inspectors did soon after the passing of the Education Act of 1870 was in Arnold's opinion to fall far short of an adequate idea of what National Education meant. It made National Education but one segment of the nation's education and thereby tended to perpetuate the religion of inequality, that bane of English society. The idea of education, as one, in character, for the nation as a whole, but differing with various types of schools, supervised but not necessarily directly administered by a central organ of the nation, was present in all Arnold's writing on the subject. He saw the State as a unity, and its education as a means of building and cementing that unity. The functions that he would have his High Council of Education perform illustrated this viewpoint. "It would be its function to advise on the propriety of subjecting children under a certain age to competitive examination, in order to determine their admission to public foundations. It would be its function to advise on the employment of the examination test for the public service; whether this security should, as at present, be relied on exclusively, or whether it should not be preceded by securities for the applicant having previously passed a certain time under training and teachers of a certain character, and stood certain examinations in connection with that training. It would be its function to advise on the organisation of school and university examinations, and their adjustment to one another. It would be its function to advise on the graduation of schools in proper stages, from the elementary

[1] Ward, ed., op. cit., vol. ii, p. 279.
[2] Vide supra, p. 65.
[3] Vide supra, p. 49.

to the highest school; it would be its function to advise on school books, and above all, on studies and on the plan of work for schools. . . ."[1] There we find its function embracing the planning of all grades of education up to the university, and even taking into consideration the question of admission to universities and the public service.

Although Arnold was well ahead of public opinion in his views on national education, he was by no means unique among his contemporaries. Ruskin, in his Appendix vii to the third volume of the *Stones of Venice*, had written in 1852 that "every man in a Christian Kingdom ought to be equally well educated". He held it to be "indisputable, that the first duty of a State is to see that every child born therein shall be well housed, clothed, fed, and educated, till it attain years of discretion. But in order to the effecting this, the government must have an authority over the people of which we now do not so much as dream. . . ."[2] From time to time also Her Majesty's Inspectors discussed the limits of national education in their official reports. The most striking and comprehensive passage occurred in J. D. Morell's General Report for the year 1857. Morell was one of the most accomplished of all H.M.I.'s, a congregational minister who shared with Arnold the inspection of Nonconformist schools, and a philosopher whose works were held in considerable respect in contemporary academic circles. He was first appointed to the inspectorate in 1848 and finally retired in 1876. His educational viewpoint was in many ways similar to that of Arnold with whom he shared the leadership in the attack launched on the Revised Code. His carefully considered and well-written reports are among the finest of those published by the Committee of Council.

Morell began his reflections upon National Education with a truly Arnoldian observation that "Every country's history is bound up with its educational development". Furthermore, *"middle-class education* is as important as *Primary education*, and the state of the community in point of national advancement will depend upon its being vigorously carried out more perhaps than upon any other single assignable cause.

"These considerations naturally lead us to form *an ideal* of national education which, though only a work of the imagination,

[1] *Schools and Universities on the Continent*, p. 283.
[2] *Stones of Venice*, vol. iii, Appendix vii, George Allen, London, 1898, pp. 231–2.

yet is necessary in order to estimate the actual state of *things as they are*, by the light of what they *ought to be*. The first great requisite for every country is, that the means of mental enlightenment and moral training should be placed upon easy conditions in the hands of every individual in the community; the second is, that professional training should likewise be provided on similar terms *to all*, whatever their position may be in the social scale. Looking first to the lowest strata of society, every country requires a complete system of *primary* schools, which may carry the most important elements of human culture into every village, and hamlet, and suburb in the kingdom; for every human being that grows up ignorant and undisciplined is so far a savage, and detracts in his proportion from the general civilisation of the whole country. These primary schools require to be of various grades, some *perfectly free*, for the poorest and most needy; some with a moderate fee, adapted to the circumstances of the working classes generally, and some of a still superior character, which may combine with elementary instruction such professional teaching as is adapted to artisans of a more skilled description. Next to these, *commercial* schools are required for the larger towns, in which the arts and sciences, the elements of mathematics, and the study of modern languages, are introduced. These schools may be termed *professional*, in relation to the trading community, and should aim at giving exactly that kind of instruction and that kind of mental training which is necessary to fit a man for commercial life in its present prodigious development. Then next to these come *the high schools*, in which a complete classical and scientific education should be afforded, more particularly as a preparation for the advanced studies of the University. Such schools are required and ought to exist in all the larger towns of the kingdom. Lastly, the national universities should be open *to all* without religious distinctions, as being properly *scientific* and not *dogmatic* institutions; and should afford the highest culture which the country can supply at a cost which brings it within the resources of the whole mass of the *middle* as well as the *higher* classes.

"With the whole country divided into educational districts, the wants of each district thoroughly investigated and supplied, the proper gradation of schools established, and the whole under such management and inspection as gives no room for indolence, neglect, or inefficiency, we should come at length to something approaching *the ideal* we might form of what a practical system of national education, in its main provisions, ought to be."[1]

It is interesting to see such enlightened opinions upon the sphere of national education being expressed by members of the central administration. But they cannot be said to have had any noticeable effect upon official policy during the 50s and 60s of the nineteenth century.

The scope of national education remained officially the same as it had been when Richard Dawes had exclaimed in 1850: "Are we then only aiming at a charity system after all?"[2] The Committee of Council confined its activities to the administration of the parliamentary grant for national education and defined its scope, in Article 4 of the Revised Code of 1862, as being "to promote the education of children belonging to the classes who support themselves by manual labour."[3] The interpretation of this article appears to have given trouble in the next few years, for in 1865 the Committee of Council found it necessary to issue "Supplementary Rule No. 10" defining its scope more closely. It stated there that "Article 4 does not exclude children from the grant whose parents, though not supporting themselves by manual labour, yet are of *the same means and social level* as those who do so; such as shop-keepers who have only petty stocks, and employ no one but members of their own family.

"Cases of doubt are to be determined according to the answers to one or more of the following inquiries:—

"(a) Does A. B. work for himself or for a master? If for himself, does he employ apprentices, or journeymen? This will apply to masons, carpenters, tailors, blacksmiths, mariners, fishermen, etc.

"The class denoted by Article 4 supports itself by its own manual labour only, and not by profit on the labour of others.

"(b) Would it be unreasonable to expect him to pay 9d. per week for the schooling of each of his children?

"The payment equals about 30s. per annum, the estimated cost (*Royal Commissioners' Report*, p. 345) of elementary instruction in a day school.

"(c) Does he rank and associate with the working men or with the tradesmen of the place?

[1] Minutes of Committee of Council, 1857–8, pp. 512–513.
[2] *Vide supra*, p. 66.
[3] Minutes of Committee of Council, 1861–2, p. xvi, Revised Code, etc., Preliminary Chapter, § 4.

"Simple policemen, coast-guards, and dock and railway porters may commonly be regarded as labouring men. But petty officers in those services, excisemen, pilots, and clerks of various kinds, present more difficulty, and must be judged of according to the answers to the preceding inquiries."[1]

There, in the Committee of Council's official instructions, was set forth with the precision of a census-taker's questionnaire the exact class of persons who came within the orbit of the parliamentary grant. It was considered that an adequate education could be provided for such persons by persevering along existing lines. "By the encouragement", said the official report, in justifying the Revised Code, "which we have given to the instruction of infants, as a foundation, and to the instruction of evening scholars, as a continuance, of the elementary day school, we trust that a road has been marked out for the solid and suitable education of the classes who support themselves in independence by manual labour."[2]

Blakiston, an experienced H.M.I., might venture to report that the general consensus of opinion in 1867 held that "in this island as on the continent and in the United States, means of passing from an elementary to a university education ought to be more generally available."[3] But official opinion frowned upon any extension of State influence to bring about such a desired end. The State was interested neither in promoting nor in regulating any form of education other than that for the children of manual labourers. To venture further afield would be an infringement of parental duty.

Such a view was endorsed by Rev. E. P. Arnold, Matthew Arnold's brother, and also one of Her Majesty's Inspectors. "There is no regulation which under the present system of public grants it is more necessary to insist upon, if we would not pauperise half the middle classes, and destroy in them the feeling of responsibility. . . ."[4] A similar opinion was expressed by a

[1] id., 1864–5, p. lxxiv.
[2] Minutes of Committee of Council, 1861–2, p. xii; The Code of 1871 abolished the restriction of grants to "education of children belonging to classes who support themselves by manual labour". Yet the alteration indicated little real change in the destination of the grant, since a new condition nearly equivalent, though not quite so stringent, prescribed in the definition of a public elementary school by the Act of 1870, was embodied in this Code, viz. that "no grant should be made to a school in which the ordinary fee exceeded ninepence a week". *Parliamentary Papers*, 1888, xxxv, 61 Cross Commission, Final Report [Cmd. 5845], p. 37.
[3] id., 1867–8, p. 95.
[4] id., 1865–6, p. 29.

minority of the Newcastle Commissioners[1]: "if the State proceeds further in its present course, and adopts as definitive the system which has hitherto been provisional, it will be difficult hereafter to induce parental and social duty to undertake the burden which it ought to bear."[2]

The view that the State's connection with National Education should be carefully watched lest it become excessive and lead to the deterioration of the nation's character was endorsed also by the leading economist of the time, Nassau W. Senior. From 1858–60 he served as a member of the Newcastle Commission, and in 1861 was moved to publish independently his reflections upon the existing educational situation. His position was based upon his proposition made near the commencement of his essay: "I hold that the main, almost the sole, duty of Government is to give protection."[3] From this it followed that the government must assure itself that the nation's children receive an adequate education, but it should not necessarily be called upon to contribute to the maintenance of that education. In existing circumstances, however, it would be folly not to continue with the "Privy Council system" at present in operation. Its justification lay in regarding the State as a sort of trustee for the labouring classes who were insufficiently well educated to realise the necessity for improved education which would thus be denied to their children but for the intervention of State "protective" influence. This is an intermediate and by no means a permanent condition of affairs. Government "assistance and superintendence" we may treat "as only a means of preparing the labouring classes for a better, but remote state of things, when that assistance and superintendence shall no longer be necessary,"[4] so that "we may look forward . . . to the time when the labouring population may be safely intrusted with the education of their children."[5]

It is somewhat surprising, therefore, to find that the municipal council of the city which gave its name to the economic school to which Senior adhered, had early expressed its belief in the desirability of state supervision of elementary education, not

[1] The names of the dissenting minority were not mentioned in the Report, and no separate minority Report was made. As there were only seven commissioners the dissentients must have been either two or three and included Nassau Senior, the redoubtable Edward Miall and perhaps also Goldwin Smith.
[2] *Parliamentary Papers*, 1861, xxi, Pt. i, 299.
[3] N. W. Senior, *Suggestions on Popular Education*, Murray, London, 1861, p. 6.
[4] id., p. 9.
[5] id., p. 5.

merely as a matter of expediency but of principle also. "Schools which give an early direction to the intelligence and character of a people are fit objects of national care, inasmuch as the interests involved are too important to be dependent upon the precarious action of spontaneous zeal, and demand a scale and constancy of expenditure for which public resources and organisation ought to be made available."[1] The Manchester Borough Council was, therefore, sympathetic with proposals to extend facilities for elementary education by authorising the raising of a school rate by municipal authorities. They objected to the Manchester and Salford Bill of 1852 because of its sectarian and local character, but were favourably disposed towards Lord John Russell's unsuccessful Bill of the following year which intended to give the municipal authorities power to impose a school rate.

With this movement for the control of schools by local government authorities Arnold was in complete sympathy. His experience during two tours of inspection, for the Newcastle and Taunton Commissions, on the Continent, had impressed on him the desirability of an effective municipal organisation to alleviate a possible over-centralisation of State control, and to further the spread of a spirit of equality throughout the community.[2] National education was inconceivable apart from public control exercised through a developed system of local government.

"But what," he wrote in 1867, "is the capital difficulty in the way of obligatory instruction, or indeed any national system of instruction, in this country? It is this: that the moment the working class of this country have this question of instruction really brought home to them, their self-respect will make them demand, like the working classes on the Continent, *public* schools, and not schools which the clergyman, or the squire, or the mill-owner, calls "my school". And what is the capital difficulty in the way of giving them public schools? It is this: that the public school for the people must rest upon the municipal organisation of the country. In France, Germany, Italy, Switzerland, the public elementary school has, and exists by having, the commune and the municipal government of the commune, as its foundations, and it could not exist without them. But we in England have our municipal organisation still to get; the country districts, with us,

---

[1] A. Redford, *The History of Local Government in Manchester*, Longmans, London, 1940, vol. ii, p. 236.
[2] *Schools and Universities*, pp. 165, 243.

have at present only the feudal and ecclesiastical organisation of the Middle Ages, or of France before the Revolution. This is what the people who talk so glibly about obligatory instruction, and the Conscience Clause, and our present abundant supply of schools, never think of. The real preliminary to an effective system of popular education is, in fact, to provide the country with an effective municipal organisation; and here, then, is at the outset an illustration of what I said, that modern societies need a civil organisation which is modern."[1]

It was no wonder that Arnold spoke feelingly upon the lack of efficient organisation in England. The Municipal Corporations Act of 1835 gave to a limited number of municipal boroughs a form of self-government suitable to urban areas. The number and powers of these local councils were increased throughout the century, but outside these "oases of comparative order there grew up an increasing chaos of areas and authorities."[2] Beyond their boundaries the chief authorities were the non-elected Justices of the Peace of whom Blackstone had said in 1765, "that few care to undertake and fewer understand the office", such was the multiplicity of their business.[3] Throughout the country the Parishes with their vestries were also charged with certain items of local administration into which Turnpike Trusts, and Improvement Commissioners also thrust themselves. After 1834 Poor Law Unions were established, cutting across all the already established districts to make a pattern of their own throughout the length and breadth of the country. And as the nineteenth century wore on, and the needs of a modern civilisation became more evident, Parliament set up special *ad hoc* authorities, such as the Local Boards of Health with their urban and rural sanitary districts, related only in small part to the structure already in existence.

It must have been painfully clear to a man fresh from the investigation of educational administration in the continental countries how confused and ill-adapted to such a purpose were the local authorities in England. It was manifestly impossible to use such a system, if system it could be called, to implement a coherent and comprehensive scheme of national education such as Arnold desired. Three choices lay before those who wished to introduce municipal government into the field of education. One

---

[1] id., p. 274.
[2] K. B. Smellie, *A History of Local Government*, Allen & Unwin, London, 1946, p. 40.
[3] id., p. 18.

set of the existing authorities could be used, such as the borough councils; but this would not provide a universal coverage. Special *ad hoc* authorities could be newly set up. This would, of course, add to the confusion, but would be in line with the prevailing administrative trend. Or, thirdly, a wholesale reorganisation and simplification of local government could be taken in hand, and education could be added to the functions of whatever re-organised bodies emerged from such an Augean cleansing.

The campaign for local government participation in education which had commenced in earnest in Parliament with the introduction of W. J. Fox's Secular Bill of 1850, initially followed the lines of the first choice. The Manchester and Salford Education Bill, and the Promotion of Education (Cities and Boroughs) Bill sponsored by Lord John Russell[1] proposed the introduction of local rating for education in the municipal boroughs only.

A renewed attempt upon the problem was made in 1855. In that year Parliament was regaled with the prospect of three separate schemes of national education for its due consideration. A Promotion of Education Bill[2] was again introduced by Lord John Russell of a nature similar to his earlier one. The council of any borough was to be empowered to submit a scheme of education to the Committee of Council for the support of existing schools or the establishment of new ones, to be paid for by raising a local education rate. Parishes might also adopt the Act and pay for their schemes through an increase in the poor rate. The other two bills adopted the second choice of those mentioned above. The Promotion of Education (No. 2) Bill,[3] promoted by Sir John Pakington, suggested the creation of new *ad hoc* authorities. In each borough, union, or parish, there might be elected school committees who could support existing schools or establish new schools, which should be free, subject to the approval of the Committee of Council. Expenditure incurred should be met in equal proportions out of consolidated revenue administered by the Committee of Council, and the product of a special education rate.[4] The third proposal was a Free Schools Bill[5] sponsored by

---

[1] *Parliamentary Papers* (Bills), 1852–3, iii, 235.
[2] *Parliamentary Papers* (Bills), 1854–5, ii, 235.
[3] id., 245.
[4] "I propose that there shall be an education rate levied by these boards, under the provisions of the Act, and I likewise propose that the boards shall act under the general supervising authority of the Central Education Department as boards of guardians act under the Poor Law Commission," Sir J. Pakington, *Parliamentary Debates*, 1855, cxxxvii, 659.
[5] id., 461.

Milner Gibson and Cobden. This envisaged the more ambitious scheme of the establishment of a Board of Public Instruction for England and Wales with a President who would be a member of parliament. The country was to be divided into school districts under school committees elected by the ratepayers with the task of supporting existing schools, and establishing new free, secular ones. The school committees were to have the power to levy their own education rate. One member, speaking to the motion for leave to introduce this bill, remarked that "he thought that with so many schemes before the House, there was danger of something like a triangular duel on the subject of education."[1] His expectations, however, were not realised, for after a few desultory and short debates all three bills were withdrawn on the same day before the end of the session.

In 1857, Pakington returned once more with an Education (Cities and Boroughs) Bill[2] suggesting school committees to be elected in every borough by persons assessed for the poor rate, for the support of schools charging fees within the range of 1d.— 4d. per week. The school committee's expenses were to be paid by an increased poor rate payable on demand to them by the Overseers of the Poor. The bill was dropped without debate at its second reading.

The reason for the failure of all these proposals in the 50s was succinctly expressed by Sir J. Kay-Shuttleworth in a letter to Lord Granville in 1861: "the ratepayers would not accept a transference of the charge of public education, in whole or in part, from the assessment of 550,000,000 L. of annual value to the local assessment of 86,000,000 L. without so substantial transference of authority in the management of the schools as would be subversive of that of the religious communions."[3]

The abortive bills, however, of Parkington and Milner Gibson set the fashion for future proposals, and, with the exception of that of the Newcastle Commission, all subsequent schemes considered by parliament envisaged *ad hoc* education boards independent of existing local government bodies.

The Newcastle Commission carefully considered the position and were favourably disposed towards a rate-supported system

[1] *Parliamentary Debates*, 1855, cxxxvii, 1372. Mr. Henley, conservative M.P. for Oxfordshire.
[2] *Parliamentary Papers*, 1857 (Sess. i), i, 95.
[3] *Parliamentary Papers*, 1861, xlviii, 295. Copy of a letter to Earl Granville . . . on the Report of the Commissioners appointed to enquire into the state of National Education, dated 2nd April, 1861.

on the ground that it would lead to greater economy, thus according well with their terms of reference, that it would carry the means of education into every part of the country, and that it should arouse and sustain local interest, a defect which was noticeably lacking in the existing system. They felt that "the economy and local interest which some amount of local payment and management secures" were "essential elements in a system of national education."[1] But the establishment of such a system at that juncture was impracticable as the fate of the various Bills showed, because of the difficulties which "arise as to the religious teaching to be given in them, and as to the authority which the clergy of different denominations should exercise over them."[2]

The commissioners therefore proposed a compromise. All assistance to schools should be "reduced to grants of two kinds". The first was to be paid by the Committee of Council if schools fulfilled certain conditions as to the adequate provision of educational facilities. The second was to be paid on the results of the examination of each child over seven years in the school by inspectors of a County or Borough Board of Education. This board was to be elected by the Court of Quarter Sessions, or, in the case of boroughs by the town council. The sole function of this body would be the distribution of funds from the county or borough rate to schools in accordance with the findings of their examiners.

A similar leaning towards devolution was expressed by the Taunton Commission.[3] Endowed schools should be subject to supervision by an enlarged Charity Commission acting through and on the advice of District Commissioners whose area should be that of the Registrar-General's districts. There should be an Official District Commissioner paid by the central government, serving on a Board of whom the other six or eight members should be appointed by the Crown from among local residents. In any county or large town in which the chairman of the Board of Guardians wished to unite for the purpose of forming their own board they should have added to their numbers a few Crown nominees and the Official District Commissioner. They would then constitute the local Board for their particular area and would act independently of the larger District Board.

In his report to this commission Arnold proposed an inter-

[1] *Parliamentary Papers*, 1861, xxi, Pt. i, 307.
[2] id., 304.
[3] *Parliamentary Papers*, 1867–8, xxviii, Pt. i.

mediate authority between the central government and the municipal organisation. The institution of these Provincial School Boards suggested by his experiences in Prussia, "supplies a basis for local action, and preserves one from the inconveniences of an over-centralised system like that of France. Eight or ten Provincial School Boards should be formed not too large, five or six members being the outside number for each Board, and one member being paid." The board was to be both advisory and administrative, "superintending the execution of all public regulations' concerning the schools, and "keeping the Education Minister informed of local requirements".[1]

What the relationship was to be between these boards and the municipal organisation was not made clear. The proposal was, in fact, put forward in connection with the examination and inspection of secondary schools and is nowhere applied generally to the educational system. The composition of the boards and their functions are also left quite vague, so that it is impossible to assess the value of Arnold's proposal. It may at least be said that as industrialisation increased interdependence and tended to form units larger than accepted traditional ones, the need for establishing governmental units on a regional scale became more appreciated.

In his earlier report to the Newcastle Commission Arnold suggested a different intermediate authority and defined a little more closely the sphere of parochial committees. "Perhaps in England a well-chosen county committee might safely be intrusted with the functions which in France, under the law of 1833, the district (arrondissement) committee performed so unsatisfactorily; but to give them to the more narrowly local body, to the communal committee, to the parish vestry, would be to destroy your school-system, however promising. . . . To superintend the actual expenditure of money voted, to inspect, and to report to a higher authority, is the proper province of the parochial committee. It cannot safely be trusted with full powers over the teacher."[2] Arnold's county committee is to a certain degree an anticipation of the modern L.E.A.

After the lull occasioned by the sittings of these various Royal Commissions on education, a further attempt was made in 1867 along lines similar to Pakington's proposals. Two names came

[1] *Schools and Universities*, p. 283.
[2] *Popular Education*, p. 151.

into prominence in parliamentary debates on education, and formed an association which led to the successful Act of 1870. The proposer of The Education of the Poorer Classes Bill[1] was H. A. Bruce, later Lord Aberdare, Vice-President of the Committee of Council, 1864-6, a liberal from Merthyr Tydvil, who, after a long life largely devoted to the cause of education finally crowned his efforts by being elected the first chancellor of the university of his native Wales. In 1867 he was keenly interested in the work of the Manchester Education Bill Committee, which had grown out of a Manchester Education Aid Society formed in 1864 through an amalgamation of the remnants of the two earlier associations, the secularists of the National Public School Association and the denominationalists of the Manchester and Salford Committee on Education.[2] This new committee was responsible for the bill which Bruce proposed to Parliament. He was supported by W. E. Forster, who in the next year also became Vice-President of the Committee of Council and piloted through the House the Endowed Schools Bill of 1869, and the Elementary Education Bill of the following year. Forster was Arnold's brother-in-law, and through his wife, Jane, kept in very close touch with Arnold's family. Mrs. Humphrey Ward, Matthew Arnold's niece, was of the opinion that "the scheme of the Bill (1870) was largely influenced by William Forster's wife, and through her, by the convictions and beliefs of her father".[3] But there is no extant tangible evidence of the nature of Jane Forster's influence, nor of the effect either her father or her brother may have had upon her educational outlook, and upon that of her husband. That Matthew Arnold was sympathetic to Forster's Bills of 1869 and 1870 is apparent from his desire for a commissionership "under William's Bill" in the former year, and his expression of relief at Forster's success with the Elementary Education Bill,[4] which he had seen privately a few months before it had been presented to Parliament.[5] What Arnold's comments

---

[1] *Parliamentary Papers* (Bills), 1867, ii, 683.
[2] *Vide supra*, p. 55, and T. Wemyss Reid, *Life of the Rt. Hon. W. E. Forster*, vol. i, p. 445; F. Adams, *The Elementary School Contest*, p. 191.
[3] *A Writer's Recollections*, p. 35.
[4] Russell, ed., vol. ii, p. 9. Letter to his mother, 5th June, 1869, and p. 36, Letter to same, 25th June, 1870. Rear Admiral F. D. Arnold-Forster has written privately (4th February, 1948) describing the close link between the Matthew Arnolds and his adopted Grand-parents, the Forsters, at Burley-in-Wharfedale, Yorkshire, but knows of no extant correspondence between W. E. Forster and M. A. As a boy he personally welcomed his great-uncle Matt's visits as he was in the habit of tipping with 5s. instead of the usual 2s. 6d.!
[5] Russell, ed., vol. ii, p. 27, letter to his mother, 21st February, 1870.

were at this preview, whether he was responsible for the redrafting of any of its provisions or what other influence he may have had upon the educational views of his then official superior, are quite uncertain. All that can be done is to show how current educational policy was or was not consonant with Arnold's expressed ideas, and conjecture that the similarities may have been the result of his close personal link with the Vice-President.

At all events, the Bill of 1867 was a further attempt to bring local government authorities into the sphere of national education that would have had Arnold's approval at least in principle. School districts were to be formed in which school committees elected by the ratepayers of the metropolis, or municipal boroughs, or poor law unions, should assist existing schools provided that they were free or charged a fee less than 9d. per week. The committees should not ineterfere with existing managers, but might open schools of their own where necessary, and should in all their activities be subject to the supervision of the Committee of Council. They should also have the power to require the local government body of their area to defray their expenses by means of a school rate if necessary. This measure was withdrawn without explanation after a short debate.

In the following year, however, with Forster's help once more, Bruce introduced the Elementary Education Bill, 1868,[1] framed along very similar lines. The school districts of this bill might be either boroughs or some specially created districts with the power of demanding their expenses from whatever local government body was appropriate. In the same session the Lord President, the Duke of Marlborough, introduced a bill into the House of Lords proposing a reform of the central government administration,[2] by the establishment of a Secretary of State for Education[3] who, amongst other things, might initiate elementary education where it was defective. The bill also incorporated the provisions of the Revised Code, then enforced as Minutes of the Committee of the Privy Council on Education, in order to "give a greater permanence and a greater degree of security to those conditions on which the Parliamentary Grant is distributed."[4] Again, after short debates these bills were withdrawn.

In the House of Lords a further attempt was made in 1869 by

___
[1] *Parliamentary Papers* (Bills), 1867–8, ii, 359.
[2] *House of Lords Sessional Papers* (Bills), 1867–8, iv, 227.
[3] *Parliamentary Debates*, 1868, cxci, 120.
[4] id., cxcii, 1984.

114 EDUCATIONAL THOUGHT AND INFLUENCE OF MATTHEW ARNOLD

Lord Campbell along the lines of Lord John Russell's 1853 Bill. This Borough Education Bill, 1869,[1] proposed the election by borough councils of school committees of whom half should be councillors. The committees should support from the rates the day schools approved by the Committee of Council, and also all the evening, industrial, reformatory and ragged schools within their districts. They should also have the power of enforcing attendance at day schools of children from 6–10, and at evening schools of those from 10–14 years. The following year, he tried again, presenting the same bill, but for one interesting alteration which introduced a new local authority into educational thought, the sanitary district, and illustrated by its cumbrous wording the lack of clear-cut municipal organisation that hindered would-be educational reformers. The authorities proposed in this short-lived Borough Education Bill, 1870,[2] were the borough councils, and "the local board of every district formed under 'The Health of Towns Act, or the Local Government Act' (1858)."

In the meantime Rev. James Fraser, who had served as assistant commissioner to the Newcastle and Taunton Commissions, and was later to become a distinguished Bishop of Manchester, had begun a lengthy correspondence in the pages of *The Times* in the course of which he made a comprehensive analysis of the contemporary educational situation. Fraser remarked, "At this moment we are beset with theories propounded with much earnestness, though somewhat deficient in distinctness; all of them, too, or almost all penetrated with the same idea—that it is hopeless to expect a complete or sufficient system of national education till we abandon the voluntary principle, and adopt the principle of local rating in its stead."[3] He himself added to the number yet another scheme of local control. These should be County Boards of Education appointed by the Committee of Council to superintend the local Committees of Education established in each Poor Law Union District, of which there were about 600, and elected from among the Guardians. These committees should have the power to levy a rate to supplement the efforts of existing voluntary schools and to establish new ones where necessary.

Of all these schemes that were aired in the two decades before

---

[1] *House of Lords Sessional Papers* (Bills), 1868–9, iv, 479.
[2] id. (Bills), 1870, iv, 151.
[3] *The Times*, 18th April, 1867, p. 4, c.d.

the Act of 1870 none obtained to a widespread popularity. In fact, J. Flint, the registrar for the Newcastle Commission, was moved to write to *The Times* in 1867: "A rate-supported system of schools we can never have in England, even if many persons desired it." He added also that "the idea of the American system of 'common schools' is as Utopian as that of the Prussian compulsory system. Both are equally repugnant to English feelings and the habits of thought on which our countrymen have been reared."[1] It would perhaps be difficult to find a more striking example of false prophecy based upon the still all too common platitudinous generalisations apt to be made about the English character.

There were, however, several weaknesses and difficulties in implementing a scheme of local educational authorities that were brought out in these proposals.

First there was the difficulty of deciding which was the appropriate authority to be used, or, if none seemed suitable, what was to be the relationship between the new body created and the already existing authorities. Bruce's schemes, and Pakington's 1857 Bill proposed *ad hoc* authorities who should command the borough councils or the overseers to tax their districts and deliver to them the amount demanded without having any control over the manner of its expenditure. This procedure was incorporated into Forster's 1870 Act and became an important bone of contention for the next 32 years until the abolition of school boards. For efficient working the new *ad hoc* bodies should have been entrusted with independent financial powers, or their functions should have been exercised by authorities which had such power. In the controversy which raged over Clause 25 of the 1870 Act[2] the Birmingham town council under the spirited leadership of Joseph Chamberlain was able to hamstring the local school board with which it disagreed until it secured a majority on the school board of like mind with itself. Other local authorities were not slow to follow Birmingham's lead, and in the ensuing contest school boards, armed with the authority of parliament and the Queen's Bench, were forced to distrain upon the goods and chattels of the conscientious objectors who refused to contribute to their upkeep.[3]

---

[1] *The Times*, 1st May, 1867, p. 5, d-f.
[2] *Vide infra*, p. 140.
[3] The story of this contest is told in J. L. Garvin, *Life of Joseph Chamberlain*, vol. i, p. 125 ff, and in greater detail in F. Adams, op. cit., p. 254 ff, and J. Morley, *The Struggle for National Education*.

It was on this ground of irresponsibility and detachment from the local government rating authority that Arnold criticised the working of the school boards after some 7 years experience of them.[1] He considered them to be acting too ambitiously and expensively. Concerning the London School Board he said, "I am quite sure that their conception of what is requisite in the way of accommodation, studies, salaries, administration, is pitched too high."[2] For this tendency there were two reasons. Abroad a sense of scale and proportion is supplied by having education treated on the same basis as other local government expenditures. "Public elementary education is properly a municipal charge, and abroad it is treated as such. It is co-ordered with the other branches of municipal expenditure. A measure and a check are thus obtained."[3] Unless the school boards of England can be made an integral part of the municipal organisation they will continue to function in an inexpert impractical manner. "True, it was not practicable to give to the school boards a municipal constitution, because in England we have no proper or complete municipal system. But here is only another reason for getting a proper and complete municipal system; our school boards are 'in the air' without it. They have not, and cannot well have, a due sense of scale and proportion; they proceed as if they were educationalists in Utopia."[4]

There Arnold pointed to a very important principle of administrative planning. The effective implementing of any planned activity depends to a large extent on the degree of agreement that those implementing the plan have with its purposes and proposals. Such agreement is most readily achieved by including their representatives among the personnel of the planning authority. It is the division of authority between a planning and an executing body that leads to the faults of remoteness, unpracticalness, and red-tape, with which the word bureaucracy is associated. Arnold's lengthy experience as a civil servant had made him acquainted with this fault, and in his administrative suggestions he was careful to unite advisory and executive functions in the same body. He was not concerned with the problems of central

---

[1] In his General Report for 1878.
[2] *Reports on Elementary Schools*, 1852–82, ed. F. S. Marvin, p. 197.
[3] id., p. 198. Cf. M. A.'s speech before the University of Pennsylvania, reported in the *Century Magazine*, 1886, "Common Schools Abroad," p. 898. "The popular school is naturally and properly a municipal thing."
[4] id., p. 199.

planning on the scale that the twentieth century has experienced, but the bent of his thought was not alien from such a development. He would have endorsed the viewpoint of a present-day analyst of the existing situation. "This type of central planning only works if those who are involved in the decision feel bound by it and convinced by rational considerations that what is proposed is as fair and reasonable as can be in the circumstances. . . . It is necessary that the principal agents should acknowledge a commitment to the decision."[1]

It became apparent through the School Board—Local Council contest that the solution of the problem of establishing effective local authorities for education lay along the lines of Arnold's pronouncement upon the question: "The real preliminary to an effective system of popular education is, in fact, to provide the country with an effective municipal organisation."[2] Neither the use of one of the existing forms of local government, nor the creation of *ad hoc* authorities could provide a universal and workable system of local control for education.

The third remaining choice, that pointed to by Arnold, the reorganisation of local government, was the feasible and eventual solution.

When, therefore, the Local Government Act of 1888 created an effective system of elective County Councils to supplement the urban organisation that had come into being in 1835,[3] the way was clear for the establishment through them of a local education system that would be both effective and national. A start was made in the following year by the Technical Instruction Act[4] which gave the councils of counties and county boroughs power to aid technical instruction out of the rates. Finally, in 1902, by the Balfour Act[5] a system of national education was placed securely in the hands of the remodelled local government authorities. "Our reform", said Balfour, "if it is to be adequate, must, in

---

[1] O. Franks, *Central Planning and Control in War and Peace*, London School of Economics, Longmans, 1947, p. 12.

[2] *Schools and Universities*, p. 274; *vide supra*, p. 106. S. Maccoby, *English Radicalism 1853–1886*, Allen & Unwin, London, 1938, pp. 393–6, considered the School Boards with their generous franchise open to all ratepayers "one of the factors . . . which contributed much to making the pressure for the democratisation of local government irresistible." The success of the London School Board over its wide area of jurisdiction, in particular, became a favourite argument of those who demanded "the setting up of a Municipality of Greater London."

[3] Municipal Corporations Act, 1882, further cleared the ground by consolidating the Act of 1835 and succeeding amending statutes.

[4] Technical Instruction Act, 1889 (52 & 3 Vict., c.76).

[5] Education Act, 1902 (2 Edw. vii, c.42).

the first place, establish one authority for education, technical, secondary, and primary, possessed of powers which may enable it to provide for the adequate training of teachers, and for welding higher technical and higher secondary education on to the university system . . . this one authority, being as it is responsible for a heavy cost to the ratepayers, should be the rating authority of the district."[1]

This consummation was clearly in Arnold's mind when he added as a footnote to his plea for municipal re-organisation the following paragraph: "We have in England 655 unions and about 12,000 parishes; but our communes or municipal centres, ought at the French rate to be about 20,000 in number. Nor is this number, perhaps, more than is required in order to supply a proper basis for the national organisation of our elementary schools. A municipal organisation being once given, the object should be to withdraw the existing elementary schools from their present management, and to reconstitute them on a municipal basis. This is not the proper place to enter into details as to the manner in which such a withdrawal is to be effected; I will remark only that all reforms which stop short of such a withdrawal and reconstitution are and must be mere patchwork."[2]

Arnold's regard for the State as an agent of the nation's high reason led him to think of government as a directive force, and his regard for equality conduced to his concept of its educational system as an organic unity.

To revert to his criticism of the London School Board: the second reason that he gave for its unpractical administration was the fact of its treating elementary education in isolation not only from the rest of municipal finance but from other levels of education. "Elsewhere this sense of scale and proportion is practically taught by the conjunction of secondary and superior instruction, as public services, with elementary instruction. The three have to be in some measure co-ordered, and this teaches scale and proportion."[3] It was the doctrine of seeing life steadily

[1] Quoted by A. Redford, *The History of Local Government in Manchester*, vol. iii, p. 158.
[2] *Schools and Universities*, pp. 274-5, n.
[3] Marvin, ed., pp. 197-8. Cf. *Century Magazine*, 1886, p. 898, "that superiority (of German primary schools) is due to a more direct and simple cause. That cause has powerfully affected and benefited popular education in Germany for a long time past, and is now showing its power for good in France also. It has expression well given to it in the Constitution of Zurich, which declares that 'there shall be an organische Verbindung, an organic connection between all the schools of the Canton, from the lowest to the highest.' It is this connection, this vital connection of popular with higher instruction which produces its superiority."

and seeing it whole applied to educational administration. This pointed to the second grave weakness to which all the proposed schemes were prone. In each case there was a provision that the local government education committees, whilst distributing the ratepayers' money, should have no power to interfere with the management of any schools other than those that they themselves founded, except that there should be a "conscience clause" generally applicable to all denominational schools. It was this question of the powers of management that Kay-Shuttleworth in 1861 had shown to be the chief cause of the failure of the various proposals to win any widespread acceptance. Arnold's solution was the wholesale transference of management to the State in the form of the local government authorities. In this he had the Zeitgeist and the future on his side. But the 1870 solution did not go so far. It separated new local government schools from existing schools and gave full control only over the former to the local government educational authorities.

The schemes proposed from 1850 to 1870, and the Elementary Education Act of 1870 were, in fact, not schemes of national education at all. By Arnold's test of adequacy they fell far short of making sufficient provision for the educational requirements of the nation.

Some, of course, were applicable only to municipal boroughs, but even those of wider scope made no attempt to take the education of the nation as a whole into consideration. With the exception of Campbell's proposal they took into consideration only the education of those who attended schools of a type that might come within the purview of the Committee of Council. What of the "residuum" below, who could afford no fees and who found some schooling in Ragged Schools, or, as vagrants or criminals, were dispatched to Industrial and Reformatory schools, or the vast numbers who never saw the inside of any school? And above the labouring classes, with their elementary schools at 1d. to 9d. per week, the middle classes were unaffected by the legislative proposals concerning "national education". Nor were these legislators concerned with secondary or further education of any kind. Arnold and a few choice spirits such as Morell might have the vision to see the problem of education as a whole, but many years were to pass before their conception of an "organic" system of education was to be generally accepted in England. Before it could be accepted its corollary of government as a suggestive or directive force had to become more current. The Select Committee of 1865 had already been tentatively inclined to this view,[1] foreshadowing the growth of collectivist thought during the remainder of the century. This growth and what Dicey calsl "The Existence of Patent Facts which impress upon ordinary Englishmen the Interdependence of Private and Public Interest,"[2] led to an increasing willingness to look for direction and co-ordination of effort through governmental agency.

How far Arnold would have liked to see this trend develop it is not possible to determine. Had he been living in the 1940's it is possible that his voice would have been raised in warning against too great devotion to collectivism. His tendency always was to be a little "agin the government", that is to say, against established practice, with the object of shaking his contemporaries out of a possible lapse into complacency. On the other hand, he proclaimed also the need to move with the times, and who at the present day could deny that collectivism was the very essence of the Zeigeist?

At all events, for the educational situation in his own period, Arnold was on the side of those who advocated an increase of State influence, exercised in such a way as to give both an orderly and a comprehensive provision in accordance with the best ideas that the leading educationalists of the country could put forward. To Arnold it was clear at that juncture, as he pointed out in his concluding words on Italian education, "that a government's duty in education is not to fear and flatter ignorance, prejudice, and obstructiveness, but *comprendere, e insinuare nello spirito publico, che una buona organizzazione degli studi, e la grandezza intellettuale di una nazione, sono i più saldi fondamenti della potenza degli stati e della vera e ordinata libertà dei popoli.*"[3]

---

[1] *Vide supra,* p. 96.

[2] A. V. Dicey, *Law and Opinion in England,* pp. liii–iv.

[3] *Schools and Universities,* p. 150, "to understand and to make the public consciousness realise that a good organisation of studies and a high intellectual development in a nation, are the most substantial foundations of the power of states, and of the real and orderly freedom of peoples."

CHAPTER VI

FREE, SECULAR, AND COMPULSORY

"And we are here as on a darkling plain
Swept with confused alarms of struggle and flight,
Where ignorant armies dash by night."
—M. Arnold, *Dover Beach*, ll. 35–37.

WHEN the Australian colonies were faced with the problem of providing a national education they found in their educational situation factors very similar to those at work in England at the same time. The English legislature passed the Act of 1870, and, ever subsequently, has scarcely seen a session in which some measure was not proposed for the purpose of patching or extending that enactment. The Australian colonies on the other hand, without exception, cut the Gordian knot. Between 1871 and 1885 each State independently established a system of State schools designed not to "fill up gaps" but to supersede existing provision by an education that should be "free, secular, and compulsory". By one determined and inexorable move each State brought to a close years of denominational bickering and inadequate educational provision, resolving at one and the same time the questions of school attendance, school fees, and religious instruction.

The juxtaposition of these three questions in each of the definitive Education Acts of the Australian States was one of the clearest demonstrations of their intimate connection with the problem of establishing some form of national education. In England the same connection was apparent in the debates that led up to the 1870 Act and in the disputes which followed. Was there a necessary connection between them? That is to say, was it necessary for a national education to be secular, and also compulsory? Could it become compulsory if it remained denominational? And, if made compulsory, must it also be made free at least within the age limits of compulsion?

Forster's Act did not decide these questions. But, then, neither did it furnish England with a national education. It was distinctly an Elementary Education Act, solely for the children of the labouring classes. It was thus intended to cover only the field that was already within the purview of the Committee of Council.

The Act was conceived in the spirit of the Newcastle Commission, for "our object", said Forster, "is to complete the present voluntary system, to fill up gaps, sparing the public money where it can be done without, procuring as much as we can the assistance of the parents, and welcoming as much as we rightly can the co-operation and aid of those benevolent men who desire to assist their neighbours."[1]

The country was thus pledged to supply schools either by voluntary effort or through local school boards wherever there was a deficiency of provision for children of the labouring classes, but there was no guarantee that these schools would be filled. The Marquess of Townshend had tried unavailingly in a short Bill in 1869 to introduce universal compulsory education, but his lead was not followed by the 1870 Act. Instead, the principle of "permissive compulsion" was adopted, whereby it was left to each school board to decide whether it would enforce attendance in its own area within the age limits of 5–13 years, provided that children between 10 and 13 years of age might obtain exemption from attendance on being certified by Her Majesty's Inspectors to have reached a specified standard of attainment.[2]

Against this arrangement, Professor Fawcett, the "Member for India" and celebrated follower of J. S. Mill, protested on the ground that, "The question of compulsion involved a great principle, and it appeared to him that the Government could not compel every parent to educate his child if an optional and permissive character were given to this part of the measure." It was the place of parliament to decide for the whole country because it was a question of "a great principle of policy and legislation".[3]

This was fully in accord with the views expressed by Forster in supporting the bills introduced by Bruce in 1868 and 1869. But in his memorandum on education, submitted at the end of 1869, which formed the basis of the subsequent Act, Forster confessed to a modification of his opinions to accord with the practical situation. He still favoured compulsory attendance but felt that responsibility for its enforcement should be a matter for the local boards who were in a position to know the feelings and requirements of the inhabitants of their district.[4]

With this approach Arnold was in sympathy. As early as 1853

[1] *Parliamentary Debates*, 1870, cxcix, 443–4.
[2] The Elementary Education Act, 1870, 33 & 34 Vict., c.75 §74.
[3] *Parliamentary Debates*, 1870, cxcix, 482.
[4] Wemyss Reid, op. cit., pp. 446, 466, 469.

he had stated "it is my firm conviction, that education will never, any more than vaccination, become universal in this country, until it is made compulsory."[1] The idea of compulsory education, by 1867, was becoming "a familiar idea with those who are interested in schools," and it would not be difficult, Arnold thought, to pass a law making education compulsory, but "the difficult thing would be to work such a law after we had got it."[2] Taking into account existing economic conditions, "a law of direct compulsion on the parent and child would therefore, probably, be every day violated in practice."[3] This situation was well demonstrated in the Swiss canton of Vaud. There compulsory education was the law of the land,—but with what result? School attendance had actually decreased over the decade preceding Arnold's visit in 1859, caused, according to the official cantonal report, "by the introduction into the Canton of different branches of industry, which give employment to the children in their neighbourhood, who are thus drawn off from school. Under these circumstances *the Council of Public Instruction has great difficulty in reconciling the consideration due to the wants of poor families with the demands of the law.*" "What I say is," concluded Arnold, "that the making it compulsory by law has not there added one iota to its prosperity".[4]

What then are the principles governing effective compulsion? He reported in 1867 that "it may be broadly said, that in all the civilised states of Continental Europe education is compulsory except in France and Holland."[5] This led him on to a brief excursus on his favourite topic of what might be called the indivisibility of education, the need for an organic conception of it. "But the English friends of compulsory education, in their turn, will do well to inform themselves how far on the Continent compulsory education extends, and the conditions under which alone the working classes, if they respect themselves, can submit to its application. In the view of the English friends of compulsory education, the educated and intelligent middle and upper classes amongst us are to confer the boon of compulsory education upon the ignorant lower class, which needs it while they do not. But, on the Continent, instruction is obligatory for lower, middle, and upper class alike. I doubt whether our educated and intelligent

---

[1] Marvin, ed., *General Report* (1853), p. 23.
[2] id. (1867), p. 117.
[3] id. (1869), p. 138.
[4] *Popular Education*, p. 185.
[5] *Schools and Universities*, p. xvi.

classes are at all prepared for this. I have an acquaintance in easy circumstances, of distinguished connections, living in a fashionable part of London, who, like many other people, deals rather easily with his son's schooling. Sometimes the boy is at school, then for months together he is away from school, and taught, so far as he is taught, by his father and mother at home. He is not the least an invalid, but it pleases his father and mother to bring him up in this manner. Now I imagine no English friends of compulsory education dream of dealing with such a defaulter as this, and certainly his father, who perhaps is himself a friend of compulsory education for the working classes, would be astounded to find his education of his own son interfered with. But if my worthy acquaintance lived in Switzerland or Germany, he would be dealt with as follows." Arnold then described the procedure in those countries for compelling all parents to comply with the law, and concluded: "In some continental States he would be liable, in case of repeated infraction of the school-law, to be deprived of his parental rights, and to have the care of his son transferred to guardians named by the State. It is indeed terrible to think of the consternation and wrath of our educated and intelligent classes under a discipline like this; and I should not like to be the man to try and impose it on them. But I assure them most emphatically,—and if they study the experience of the Continent they will convince themselves of the truth of what I say,—that only on these conditions of its equal and universal application is any law of compulsory education possible."[1]

The first condition for making effective a law of compulsory education was that it should be equitable, by applying to all children irrespective of their status in society.

Again, as he looked at compulsory education in practice on the continent he found that where education was most prosperous, there it was also compulsory. "The compulsoriness is, in general, found to go along with the prosperity, though it cannot be said to cause it; but the same high value among a people for education which leads to its prospering among them, leads also in general to its being made compulsory."[1] A similar situation exists with religion. If a man's religion is vital, it will lead him to impose rules of conduct upon himself. "Above all, it will make a newly-awakened sinner do this; and England, . . . I must take leave

[1] id., pp. xvii–xix. Cf. *Friendship's Garland*, Letter vii, for a similar argument in lighter vein.
[2] id., pp. xvi–xvii.

to regard in educational matters, as a newly-awakened sinner."[1]

The second principle of effective compulsion, therefore, was the existence in the country of an enthusiasm for education with an educational conscience impressed with the necessity of providing the country with an adequate education. Arnold there had hit upon a sound principle of jurisprudence, whose truth has been amply illustrated throughout the history of English educational legislation, that the effective implementation of an enactment depends upon the degree of its acceptance by the public as necessary or desirable. The 1870 Act concurred in this judgment by deciding that compulsory attendance should be imposed only in the areas where the population were likely to accept it. Permissive compulsion was to be used as an educative agency inducing the more reluctant areas to join eventually in implementing universal compulsion throughout the whole country.

The development of such a desirable educational conscience, however, depended upon more than mere good example and enlightened enthusiasm. It had in it also an important economic factor. Forster in introducing his Act pointed out to the House that the principle of compulsion in education had long been accepted. "I would first remind the House that we have already admitted the principle of compulsion; we have admitted it in the Short Time Acts."[2]   Its extension, however, to elementary education in general involved a consideration of whether, in actual fact, a large number of parents could dispense with the earnings of their children of compulsory school age. Shaftesbury was so deeply impressed with the importance of this factor that he strove to have the compulsory age limits altered from 5–13, to 4–10 years. "The extent", he said, "to which persons in London depended on the labour of their children their Lordships would scarcely be aware of, and it was impossible that a man could maintain wife and family on 9/– or 10/– a week, unless he was assisted by such labour."[3] And he was able to secure an amendment granting exemption, on a certificate from Her Majesty's Inspectors, to children over 10 years of age who reached a prescribed standard.

Arnold, therefore, also pointed out that a third basic prerequisite for an effective law of compulsory attendance in England

---

[1] id., p. xvii.

[2] *Parliamentary Debates*, 1870, cxcix, 459.

[3] *Parliamentary Debates*, 1870, cciii, 1188. *Vide* also J. L. and B. Hammond, *Lord Shaftesbury*, Penguin Books, 1939, p. 236.

was a higher standard of living. "The gradual rise in their wealth and comfort is the only obligation which can be safely relied on to draw such people to school. What Government can do, is to provide sufficient and proper schools to receive them as they arrive."[1]

In dealing with the question of compulsory education Arnold was not concerned to examine or justify the principle of compulsion. He was of the opinion that education should be universal. He thought it could not become universal until it became compulsory. He was therefore concerned simply to indicate the bases upon which the successful implementing of compulsory education must depend.

These conditions were gradually fulfilled during the thirty years remaining to the century after the 1870 Act. A steady rise in real wages was supplemented by an increasing interest in education that accompanied the extension of the parliamentary franchise, and the scope of compulsory education was accordingly widened.[2]

[1] *Popular Education*, p. 154.
[2] L. C. A. Knowles, op. cit., pp. 168–9 reproduces tables from *Dictionary of Political Economy*, ed. Palgrave, 1908, to illustrate the progress of real wages in the second half of the nineteenth century.

	Nominal Wages	Prices	Real Wages
1852–1870 ..	Rising fast	Rising	Rising considerably in the whole period.
1870–1873 ..	Rising very fast	Rising fast	Rising fast.
1873–1879 ..	Falling fast	Falling fast	Rising fast.
1879–1887 ..	Nearly stationary	Falling	Rising
1887–1892 ..	Rising	Rising and falling	Rising
1892–1897 ..	Nearly stationary	Falling	Rising
1897–1900 ..	Rising fast	Rising	Rising
1900–1914 ..	Falling a little	Falling and rising	Stationary

Using an index number (1900-1904=100) the position is illustrated as follows:

	Nominal Wages	Real Wages		Nominal Wages	Real Wages
1850–54	55	50	1880–84	77	65
1855–59	60	50	1885–89	79	75
1860–64	62	50	1890–94	87	85
1865–69	67	55	1895–99	92	95
1870–74	78	60	1900–04	100	100
1875–79	80	65			

Whereas Forster's Act had permitted compulsion in school board areas only,[1] Sandon's Act of 1876 introduced a form of indirect compulsion for school board areas and, by creating new school authorities called School Attendance Committees, made it possible to enforce attendance in the parts of the country not reached by school boards. This act placed upon the statute book for the first time the principle, that the Act of 1944 continues to maintain, that it is "the duty of the parent" to see that his child receives an adequate education.[2] By 1880 it had become possible to dispense with a tentative form of compulsion, and Mundella's short act of that year made it obligatory for all local authorities to make by-laws to enforce attendance in accordance with the provisions of the Act of 1870.[3] The Acts of 1893 and 1899 raised the minimum age for complete or partial exemption from 10 through 11 to 12 years, and in 1900 the statutory age limits became 5–14, where they remained for the next four decades.[4] In 1918, by the Fisher Act, all exemptions from attendance within the statutory limits were abolished,[5] and, finally, the Act of 1944 made provision for raising the school leaving age initially to 15 and subsequently to 16 years.[6]

This steady progress towards raising the school leaving age and tightening up exemptions from compulsory attendance laws furnishes a good illustration of the slow improvement in educational conscience aided by increased economic security that Arnold saw were its necessary preliminaries. The changed wording of the provision for compulsory attendance in the Act of 1944:

"It shall be the duty of the parent of every child of compulsory school age to cause him to receive efficient full-time education suitable to his age, ability and aptitude. . . ."[7]

taken in comparison with that of the Act of 1876:

"It shall be the duty of the parent of every child to cause

---

[1] The Elementary Education Act, 1870 (33 & 34 Vict., c.75) § 74.
[2] The Elementary Education Act, 1876 (39 & 40 Vict., c.79) § 4. "Indirect" compulsion was applied by forbidding the employment of children under 10 or of those over 10 who had not received a certificate of due attendance or exemption through proficiency.
[3] The Elementary Education Act, 1880 (43 & 44 Vict., c.23) § 2.
[4] The Elementary Education (School Attendance) Act, 1893 (56 & 57 Vict., c.51) § 1. Elementary Education (School Attendance) Act (1893) Amendment Act, 1899 (62 & 63 Vict., c.13) § 1. Elementary Education Act, 1900 (63 & 64 Vict., c.53) § 6.
[5] Education Act, 1918 (8 & 9 Geo. 5, c.39) § 8, "no exemption from attendance from school shall be granted to any child between the age of 5 and 14 years,"
[6] Education Act, 1944 (7 & 8 Geo. 6, c.31) § 35.
[7] § 36.

such child to receive efficient elementary instruction in reading, writing, and arithmetic . . ."[1] is a measure of the advance that has been made in 75 years towards a conception of education, consonant with Arnold's thoughts, that would apply with equal validity to children of every class.

By the Act of 1944, for the first time, also, compulsory attendance became universal directly by statute without intervening local authority by-laws. At length, then, Professor Fawcett's desire was granted. It had in practice been fulfilled in 1880 when the State committed itself so far as to require local bodies to make appropriate by-laws; but the additional token, direct, decision on compulsion, and the acceptance of full responsibility for the principle was not made by the central government until 1944.

The question of compulsory education had seemed to Charles Kingsley in 1869 to be "the first question of the moment". "Twenty-seven years' experience as a parish clergyman" had shown him its necessity.[2] But was it possible without at the same time making education free? For many years he had opposed free education,[3] but after examining the condition of Birmingham where so many children "were kept from school simply by the poverty of their parents", he was inclined to think that compulsory and gratuitous education must go hand in hand. Furthermore, until education was free, parents would persist in regarding it as "an article which they may buy, or not, as they see fit, like beer or fine clothes, or any luxury." The only way to put education in its proper position as a social necessity was to take it out of the merchandise class by making it compulsory and free. "The only method to make them understand that educating their children is an indefeasible duty, which, as citizens they owe to the State itself, is for them to be taxed, by the State itself and for the State to say—There is your money's worth in the school. We ask no more of you; but your children shall go to school, or you shall be punished by law."[3]

Such an opinion had increased in popularity ever since the time when Fox had introduced his Secular Bill in 1850 with tentative provision for the establishment of free schools. Most sub-

---

[1] § 4.
[2] C. Kingsley, *The Address on Education* read before the National Association for the Promotion of Social Science at Bristol, on the 1st October, 1869, London, 1869, p. 10.
[3] id., p. 11.
[4] ibid.

sequent proposals had included some provision for dispensing with school fees in various circumstances. At the same time, however, a social distinction had been growing up and gradually hardening between the schools for the children of parents who could afford to pay fees, and of those who could not. For the former, National or British schools or some similar schools were provided, for the latter the Ragged schools. The managers of the former were unwilling to admit Ragged children and raised their standards to exclude them.[1] The Committee of Council in 1857 decided to assist them, but made it a condition of the payment of their grant that such schools should retain and display the title of Ragged School.[2] They duly recorded, in the following year, that "a distinction has established itself between the schools which are entered on payment of fees, ranging from 1d. to 6d. per week, by the children of independent labourers and artisans, and the schools which receive the children of a more dependent and neglected class".[3] In short, to be receiving a free education, branded a child as a criminal or a vagrant, or a pauper, or near-pauper in attendance at a reformatory, industrial, workhouse or ragged school.

Arnold saw no necessary connection between compulsory and gratuitous education. He dismissed the contention with a brief remark. "As to gratuitous schooling, which is supposed to follow necessarily upon compulsory schooling, I will only remark that in Prussia, where schooling is compulsory, and really compulsory, there is no primary school which does not levy a school fee, though a low one."[4] His experience on the Continent showed him that there was a diversity of opinion upon the question, but the majority of his informants held that the poor "value little what they pay nothing for".[5] With this view Arnold concurred. "It has so often been said that people value more highly, and use more respectfully, what they pay a price for, that one is almost ashamed to repeat it. But the advocates of free education seem never to have heard or at least considered it".[6] This was Arnold's final and considered opinion, expressed in one of his latest reports.

[1] *Parliamentary Papers*, 1861, vii, 395, *Select Committee Report on the Education of Destitute and Neglected Children*, Q.121, 2229.
[2] id., Appendix No. 4, pp. 222–3, quoting Minute of Committee of Council, 31st December, 1857.
[3] id., Appendix No. 4, pp. 223–4, quoting Report of Committee of Council, 1858–9, pp. xxxiii ff.
[4] Marvin, ed., *General Report* (1869), pp. 138–9.
[5] *Popular Education*, p. 130 n.
[6] Marvin, ed., *General Report* (1882), p. 220.

He admitted that, in a certain number of cases, free schools and free places would be an economic necessity, but he hoped "that school boards will not discontinue the school fee generally, and that where it is now too low, and less than parents can fairly pay, they will raise it."[1] He was impressed with the pleasure shown by children in a Westminster voluntary school who had secured a better supply of stationery as the result of paying an extra 1d. fee. "I could not help reflecting how wholesome this kind of pleasure is, and how it is quite lost in board schools where the gratuitous distribution of stationery is the rule. And as with stationery, so with the rest of what is furnished at school."[2] Although he showed in other places[3] that the education that was provided for a low fee or gratuitously was actually of little worth, he did not draw the conclusion that the recipients of such education were merely assessing it at its rightful value, and that had they received gratuitously the same education that others paid 6d. or 9d. for, they might have valued it accordingly.

He spent some time in analysing the effect of different rates of fees. In his earliest report, for the year 1852, he drew attention to what the select committee of 1861 also pointed out, that school fees "generally exclude the children of the very poor" from the Wesleyan schools where the rate varied from 2d. to 8d. per week.[4] He was inclined to the opinion that the rate should be lowered to "extend their sphere of usefulness."[5] In the following year he repeated the fact that these fees separated the education of the children of small farmers, small tradesmen, and skilled mechanics from that "of the lowest class, of the class found in ragged schools," and that contact with the latter was objected to by the former who desired "to see their school grow more and more 'respectable'".[6] This tended to the establishment of other schools charging fees at the higher level of the range, 4d. and 6d., and led to additional stratification. Arnold showed the conveniences to these schools of having "the better and more instructed class of children frequenting" them, and the greater intelligence of their parents, with consequently greater disposition, as well as greater means, to keep them longer at school."[7] But high fees also led

[1] id., p. 221.
[2] ibid.
[3] E.g. *Popular Education*, p. 130.
[4] Marvin, ed., *General Report*, 1852, p. 3.
[5] id., p. 4.
[6] id. (1853), p. 20.
[7] id. (1852), p. 4.

to a greater disposition on the part of parents to interfere. There spoke the son of the headmaster of Rugby, especially when he suggested that this was an inconvenience from which all private schools suffered. As a teacher's salary in the elementary schools, with which Arnold was dealing, was "principally or entirely derived from the school pence, he was forced to curry favour with the parents of his pupils to the decided diminution of his independence, and the undermining of his discipline over the children of this lower middle class whose children, he felt, were the most indulged of all classes in the country."[1]

No doubt arguing along the lines which Arnold accepted, that one values only what one pays for, some managers concluded that the higher the fee charged the more desirable would their school be considered. Arnold disagreed, by pointing out that the high school fee acted as a deterrent, simply because it could not be afforded, and added "it is not the high school fee that is the attraction, but it is the high reputation of the school which makes the poor willing to pay a high school fee."[2] He appears here to have refuted his own argument for the retention of school fees in schools. He held that they should be paid because people valued more highly what they paid a price for; but the argument above against high school fees rested on the assumption that people valued what they saw to be worthwhile. How far the sale rather than the gift of a thing might seem to make it more worthwhile was quite a matter of conjecture, at least as far as education was concerned. For no one had yet managed to present an equivalent educational article to both fee and non-fee payers.

Arnold's adherence to the principle of fee-paying was hardly consistent with his general advocacy of equality. There his chief plea was for the reduction of stratification throughout society, yet, on his own analysis, school fees, whose retention he favoured, tended not only to perpetuate existing stratification, but even to multiply it still further.

The Act of 1870 endorsed Arnold's opinions. Forster in introducing his Bill stated the government's objection to providing free education, on grounds similar to Arnold's argument, but added also as a main reason, the undesirable additional financial burden that the government would thereby incur. "Shall we give up the school fees? . . . I say at once that the Government are not

[1] id., p. 5.
[2] id. (1853), p. 22; (1867), p. 118.

prepared to do it. If we did so the sacrifice would be enormous. The parents paid in school fees last year about £420,000. If this scheme works, as I have said we hope it will work, it will very soon cover the country, and that £420,000 per annum would have to be doubled or even trebled. Nor would it stop there. This would apply to the elementary education chiefly of the working classes. The middle classes would step in—and say "There must be free education also for us, and that free education must not be confined to elementary schools". The illustration and example, so often quoted, of America would be quoted again, and we should be told that in the New England States education is free not only in the elementary schools, but free also up to the very highest education of the State. The cost would be such as really might well alarm my right honourable Friend the Chancellor of the Exchequer. . . . We do not give up the school fees, and indeed we keep to the present proportions—namely, of about one-third raised from the parents, one-third out of the public taxes, and one-third out of local funds. Where the local funds are not raised by voluntary subscription the rates will come into action."[1]

It appears, however, that the Zeitgeist in this matter was misjudged by both Arnold and Forster. By the Act of 1870 a school board was not permitted to admit a child to school without payment of a fee, although it was impowered to remit fees from time to time for short periods for those who could not afford to pay, and could also pay the fees of children attending a voluntary school where there was no board school available. By the 1876 Act poor parents were required to apply to the Guardians for the payment of fees.[2] Fifteen years later the Act of 1891 abolished all school fees in board schools where they had previously amounted to 10/– or less per annum, and in all board schools, established subsequent to the Act, for children over three and under 15 years of age.[3] School boards were also given freedom to admit children without payment of fee, and were not required to investigate

[1] *Parliamentary Debates*, 1870, cxcix, 454–5. Forster did not think the local rate "will nearly amount to 3d. in the pound".
[2] § 10. Forster in introducing his 1870 Bill (*Parliamentary Debates*, 1870, cxcix, 452) expressly stated that he wished to dissociate elementary education from pauper connections. His successors, however, in this act, forged an official connection whose taint was subsequently hard to eliminate.
[3] The Elementary Education Act, 1891 (54 & 55 Vict., c.56), § 2. A fee grant was to be paid by the Education Department in lieu of the children's fees where fees were in excess of 10/–, the fees to be charged in future to be only the amount of the excess.

whether the parents' circumstances necessitated it. A memorandum by the Education Department, May 1893, stated that "every father and mother in England and Wales has a right to free education, without payment or charge of any kind, for his or her children between the age of 3 and 15. The right to free education is not a concession to poverty, but is common to all classes alike." Nevertheless it was still permissible for public elementary schools to charge fees until the Fisher Act of 1918 summarily abolished them.[1] In secondary schools the "free place" system had enabled a considerable number of children to continue their education at a reduced cost, but it was not until 1944 that all education was pronounced to be free when provided by a local education authority irrespective of its level.[2]

Towards the end of 1867, Lord John Russell put forward in parliament four resolutions on education, of which the first affirmed: "That in the opinion of this House the Education of the working classes in England and Wales ought to be extended and improved: Every child has a moral right to the Blessings of Education and it is the duty of the State to guard and maintain that Right. In the opinion of this House the Diffusion of knowledge ought not to be hindered by Religious Differences; nor should the early Employment of the young in Labour be allowed to deprive them of Education."[3] The two hindrances to elementary education there specifically mentioned were religious differences and early employment. The latter was dealt with by the mechanism of compulsory attendance laws, but the former was a rather more involved and provocative problem.

As soon as there was wind that an Education Bill was to be sponsored by the government in the 1870 session all the feelings of religious scrupulousness, sectarian rivalry, and anti-denominationalism, that had lain dormant throughout the country since the educational contest of the early 50s, were re-aroused and organised on an even more imposing scale.

It was in vain that the Vice-President affirmed that, "It (the religious difficulty) is a most formidable difficulty in Parliament, but a very small one as between the parent of the child and the schoolmaster, and still smaller between the schoolmaster and the

---

[1] § 26.
[2] § 61.
[3] *Parliamentary Debates*, 1867, cxc, 478.

child."[1] In this he was supported by a future Vice-President, Mundella, who said that "he had never regarded the religious difficulty as being of any considerable magnitude, because he believed that the people of this country generally desired that their children should receive religious teaching, and in support of that proposition he might state that a very able man belonging to the working classes had told him that the religious difficulty had been made for and not by the lower classes."[2] Despite such statements, the religious question, more than any other consideration, was the one which occasioned the greatest strife both within and without parliament during the stormy passage of the 1870 Act and the years of contention which ensued. Each of the bills that had been presented during the 50s and 60s had shown that the issue was present in the back of each proposer's mind by the various conscience clauses that found their way into the bills, and when the official government measure was introduced, Disraeli proclaimed the obvious truth when he asked, "what was the chief provision of that measure?" and himself answered: "A provision which delegated to School Boards the power and privilege of deciding upon the religious education of the scholars."[3]

Educational agitation was somewhat re-aligned since the early 50s, and had hardened into two parties differing upon the three questions of compulsion, school fees, and religious instruction. Upon the former two the difference was intellectual and logical, upon the latter, the religious question, passionate and seemingly irreconcilable.

The earlier two Manchester parties, the secularists, to which Forster had adhered, and the denominationalists, had coalesced to form eventually the Manchester Education Bill Committee. Their sympathies were with the new organisation[4] which sprang suddenly into being, Minerva-like, militant and vigorous, as the

[1] *Parliamentary Debates*, 1870, ccii, 580. Dr. Hook, who as Vicar of Leeds had made a name for himself during the educational controversies of the 40s, wrote to Forster, with whom he was on very friendly terms, in 1870, expressing a similar opinion. "The truth is", he said, "I have always regarded the religious questions as merely a political squabble". Wemyss Reid, op. cit., vol. i, p. 496.
[2] id., 1870, cxcix, 477.
[3] id., 1870, ccii, 286.
[4] The relationship is explained in F. Adams, *History of the Elementary School Contest in England*, Chapman & Hall, London, 1882, p. 194. *Vide* also *Report of the First General Meeting of the National Education League* held at Birmingham on Tuesday and Wednesday, 12th and 13th October, 1869, published Birmingham, 1869. Francis Adams was the secretary of the National Education League, and wrote an exhaustive and somewhat partial history devoted chiefly to the educational struggle from 1869 to 1877, the period of the League's existence.

National Education League with its headquarters in Birmingham, under the leadership of George Dixon the local M.P., and a young and rising radical, Joseph Chamberlain. Within a few months of its foundation the League had established branches in most of the principal towns of England, and, its historian relates, "its progress was unexampled in the history of public organisations."[1]

Its aim was succintly set out on the back leaves of every publication and pamphlet which it sponsored:

OBJECT

The establishment of a system which shall secure the Education of every Child in the Country.

MEANS

1. Local Authorities shall be compelled by law to see that sufficient School Accommodation is provided for every Child in their district.
2. The cost of founding and maintaining such Schools as may be required shall be provided out of local Rates supplemented by Government Grants.
3. All Schools aided by Local Rates shall be under the management of Local Authorities and subject to Government Inspection.
4. All Schools aided by Local Rates shall be Unsectarian.
5. To all Schools aided by Local Rates admission shall be free.
6. School Accommodation being provided, the State or the Local Authorities shall have power to compel the attendance of Children of suitable age not otherwise receiving education.

The League's attitude upon the religious question was perhaps best expressed by Joseph Chamberlain who, as head of the executive committee, "was chiefly responsible in originating and conducting its policy in the country."[2] On the occasion of a deputation to No. 10 Downing Street, where Gladstone was supported by both the Lord President, Earl de Grey and Ripon, and the Vice-President W. E. Forster, in the midst of the debates on the Education Bill, Chamberlain said: "We object, sir, to the permissive recognition of great principles; we ask that the Government should decide those principles for the whole country. . . with reference to this permissive sectarianism, the Town Councils object to it, and regret the importation of a new element causing their election to turn upon religious opinion, and not upon personal fitness. . . . The Dissenters object to this measure, which they conceive will hand over the education of this country

[1] Adams, op. cit., p. 203.
[2] Adams, op. cit., p. 205.

to the Church of England entirely in many parts of the Kingdom, especially in agricultural districts; . . . . Further, we consider that this Conscience Clause which is contained in the proposed Bill, or any Conscience Clause, will be absolutely unsatisfactory. . . . we say that a Conscience Clause of any kind does not touch the hardship of which Dissenters complain—that the minority will in many districts be taxed to pay for the support of schools which are part of the machinery for perpetuating doctrines to which they have a conscientious objection."[1] Later, when pressed by Gladstone to be more explicit about the League's views on the religious question, Chamberlain stated that in a bill prepared on behalf of the League there was the clause: "that in the national rate schools no creed, catechism, or tenet peculiar to any sect shall be taught in any national rate school, but the School Board shall have power to grant the use of the school rooms out of school hours for the giving of religious instruction, provided that no undue preference be given to one or more sects to the exclusion of others." The school board could also permit the reading of the scriptures at a set time so that children, whose parents objected, could be withdrawn. However, said Chamberlain, "there is a very strong feeling amongst the members of the League that for that clause should be substituted one requiring that secular instruction *alone* should be given in the schools which are aided by the rates." (Applause.)[2]

The Rev. F. Barham Zincke, Chaplain-in-Ordinary to the Queen, explained at the inaugural meeting of the League the reasons that had led to this decision.

"Our present denominational, and, as it is called, voluntary system—but it would be nearer to the truth to call it eleemosynary,—has, after a long and fair trial, left us in this position. We believe it has failed because it is denominational and eleemosynary. Such a system does not aim at educating the nation, and could not succeed were it to aim at doing it. But as it has been tried, and found wanting, and as we are fully persuaded that it can never accomplish what is needed, we are driven to the conclusion that nothing can do the work except a public system; and we hold that nothing else will befit the dignity of a free, and, very properly, a proud people. A public system, of course, can only

[2] *Verbatim Report of the proceedings of a Deputation*, etc., Wednesday, 9th March, 1870, published Birmingham for the National Education League, 1870, p. 13.
[2] id., p. 28.

be supported by public funds, and therefore must be unsectarian; for everyone who contributes either towards the local rates, or the general taxation of the country, will have grounds for insisting, that his contributions shall not be used for the purpose of teaching what he conscientiously objects to."[1]

It is easy to see that such a statement could be taken as a determination to do away with denominational schools, and it was so taken by the band of people who formed themselves into the National Educational Union. The aims of this new body were outlined by Edward Baines who presided jointly with the Bishop of Ripon over a meeting at Leeds at the end of 1869. The presence of these two men on the same platform was significant of the new trend of events. Baines had announced in 1867 the long-postponed decision of the Congregational Board to seek aid for its schools from the Committee of Council[2] and Matthew Arnold had been selected to make the first inspection of the Congregational Training College at Homerton in 1868. His report reads curiously like that of a naturalist examining for the first time some little known animal and explaining its characteristics to a curious and expectant world.[3]   At the meeting of 1869 Baines, hitherto the most dissentient of the dissenters, joined hands with the representative of the Established Church in defence of denominationalism in education. It was, for Baines, still a defence of the voluntary principle though he recognised that voluntaryism needed State support.

In his speech at Leeds, Baines outlined the programme of the Union as that of "securing the primary education of every child, by judiciously supplementing the present denominational system of national education."[4]   To him there was "one fact of vital consequence" stated in the report of the Duke of Newcastle's Commission, namely, that of 1,675,158 scholars in public schools, no less than 1,549,312 are in "schools supported by religious denominations", only 43,098 in "schools not specially connected with religious denominations". Hence the Union declared for the development of a national system which should be essentially an extension of the existing situation, bolstered up with a more stringent scheme of indirect compulsion through the Factory Acts

---

[1] *Report of the First General Meeting*, op. cit., p. 155.
[2] *Parliamentary Debates*, 1867, cxc, 489.
[3] Marvin, ed., pp. 256 ff.
[4] *Authorised Report of the Educational Conference held at Leeds*, 8th December, 1869, Longmans, for the National Education Union, London, 1869, p. 3.

and the short-time system.[1] Direct compulsion was to be used only for the children "of the vagrant and out-door pauper class".[2] Fees were to be retained, and also the usual grants from the consolidated fund. This programme would "give equal liberty, and equal State support to religious schools—asking from the State (what indeed has already been promised) impartial aid to all, and solely in proportion to the ascertained results of their secular teaching". This scheme, of course, "would require from all denominational schools a conscience clause". Where there was a deficiency of provision, existing schools should be supplemented "by such additional means as Parliament may decide . . ." perhaps by new schools on the rates "which schools must necessarily be unsectarian."[3]

In retrospect the announced programme of the League and the Union appeared to differ but little on the vexed religious problem. Neither proposed to interfere with the conduct of existing schools which should continue under the safeguard of a conscience clause, and both proposed that new schools or, indeed, any schools that should be aided by local rates should be unsectarian. This was a term never authoritatively defined by either side. In practice, according to Francis Adams, it "was Bible reading or not, at the option of the ratepayers".[4] Even this could be held to be somewhat sectarian, and, in any case, satisfied very few of the contestants.

The real distinction between the League and Union was simply in a matter of emphasis. To the Union the essential provision of elementary education was through denominational schools, which might be supplemented, but without even a remote suspicion of their being superseded, by publicly provided schools. To the League the school of the future was an unsectarian board school.

The Act of 1870, therefore, with its policy of only "filling the gaps" by board schools was rather more to the taste of the members of the Union, and it was one of their leaders, Cowper-Temple, first Vice-President of the Committee of Council, who secured the acceptance of an amendment with respect to the

[1] A comprehensive analysis of the relation of the Factory Acts to education is to be found in A. H. Robson, *The Education of Children Engaged in Industry*, 1833–76, Kegan Paul, London, 1931.
[2] *Authorised Report*, op. cit., p. 72.
[3] id., p. 12.
[4] F. Adams, op. cit., p. 202.

conduct of board schools that "No religious catechism or religious formulary which is distinctive of any particular denomination shall be taught in the school."[1] This clause took the place of the Government's original proposal that each school board should have the power to determine what religious instruction was to be given in its schools, subject to a conscience clause, and that they should have the power also of assisting existing schools out of the rates.

The League view, expressed when the original proposals became known, was to press for amendment along the lines that "No creed, catechism, or tenet peculiar to any sect to be taught in schools under the management of School Boards, or receiving grants from local rates. In all other schools receiving Government aid the religious teaching to be at distinct times, either before or after ordinary school business, and provision to be made that attendance at such religious teaching should not be compulsory, and that there should be no disability for non-attendance."[2] After the Government determination to exclude voluntary schools from rate-aid, and to control the religious instruction of rate-aided board schools by the Cowper-Temple clause, H. Richard, Member for Merthyr and later member of the Cross Commission on the Elementary Education Acts, 1886, proposed an amendment that religious instruction should be provided by voluntary effort, and not out of the public funds. This point was productive of the longest and most acrimonious debate of any section of the Bill.[3] The League decided to support Richard's amendment, and a third influential body, the Central Non-conformist Committee, led by Rev. R. W. Dale, a prominent dissenter of Birmingham, with whom Matthew Arnold crossed swords, joined in the campaign. This committee, originally

---

[1] This celebrated clause was § 14 (2).

[2] F. Adams, op. cit., pp. 214–5.

[3] Richard stated, "the present system might be described as a measure for making the education of the people of England universally and for ever denominational," *Parliamentary Debates*, 1870, ccii, 497. *The Times* of 18th June, 1870, p. 9, b, in a leader, confirmed Richard's view with what was to prove a mistaken prophesy. "The present condition of the Education Question is simply vexatious. . . . The Bill as now resettled contemplates two modes of National or quasi-National Education. . . . Can it be doubted which of the two will outbid the other in the struggle for existence? The denominational school will appear under a double advantage. Half the cost of maintenance being refunded by the State, in addition to subscriptions, it can offer Education at a cheaper rate, and it will be freed from the apparent odium of adding to the local Rates. . . . We are landed, therefore, in this wonderful conclusion— The agitation of the last two or three months has been one continued protest against the spread of denominational education, and the Bill as amended and re-amended promises to assist what the voice of the nation rejects."

formed to watch the progress of the 1870 Bill, was kept alive for several years, and by electing Joseph Chamberlain as its chairman became closely identified with the policy of the League especially in regard to the agitation that centred round Clause 25 of the Act, in the six years subsequent to its passage. This clause, permitting the payment by school boards of fees for children whose parents could not afford them, at "any public elementary school" should have been dropped or amended when the clause authorising assistance to voluntary schools by school boards was dropped from the original bill. By definition "public elementary school" meant any school subject to inspection by the Committee of Council and complying with the requirements of section 7 of the 1870 Act. This, of course, included all the denominational schools in receipt of parliamentary grant. It meant, therefore, that in accordance with this clause any school board, so willing, could pay portion of its school rate to denominational schools. The amount so paid in the year 1872 was only £5,072, but it was "the key to a position" just as "were Hampden's twenty shillings".[1] John Morley, who was to the forefront in the controversy, wrote, "The fortress to be stormed is sectarianism in education. . . . The whole system is only vulnerable at present through the Twenty Fifth clause."[2]

This controversy eventually drove the League to give up its unsectarian position, and adopt in 1872 a policy of secularism.[3]

One of the most earnest opponents of the government's policy throughout these years was Edward Miall who was at that time Forster's colleague in the representation of Bradford. He declined to join the League but was active on the Nonconformist Committee.[4]

The other anti-government veteran of the earlier struggle, Archdeacon Denison, continued during the 60s to oppose the introduction of Conscience Clauses but, of course, on grounds diametrically opposite to those put forward by the League. He recognised the futility of his struggle, however, and retired from

---

[1] J. Morley, *The Struggle for National Education*, Chapman & Hall, London, 1873, pp. 8–9. The controversy was described in detail by Morley who provides the best comprehensive statement of the arguments of the League on all phases of the educational question. *Vide* also F. Adams, op. cit., Chaps. V-IX. Concerning Cl. 25, "a caustic onlooker observed that it was the smallest ditch in which two great political armies ever engaged in civil war" (J. Morley, *Life of Gladstone*, ii, p. 309).

[2] Morley, op. cit., p. 10. Morley here gives also a full statement of R. W. Dale's views on the matter.

[3] F. Adams, op, cit., pp. 277 ff.

[4] Wemyss Reid, op. cit., pp. 496, 505, 522, 539 ff, indicated the difficulties that Miall caused in Forster's own electorate.

the field after a last despairing effort at a meeting "for the maintenance of Church Education at Willis's Rooms" in 1868.[1]

Into the political arena, on the "religious problem", Matthew Arnold did not care to enter. But he was able to make known the direction in which his sympathies lay.

He was clear in his mind that religious instruction should be an integral part of the work of the elementary school.

In a preface to his 1886 Report on Elementary Education abroad, published by the Education Reform League under the auspices of Toynbee Hall, Arnold addressed himself specifically to the working classes. He made three points. First, the users of this popular school "should arrive at clear and just notions of what they want their own school to be, and should seek to get it made this. At present their school is not this, but is rather what the political and governing classes establishing a school for the benefit of the working classes, think that such a school ought to be." Secondly that popular schools are "far too little formative and humanising." And, thirdly, that religious instruction which politicians making or administering the popular school seek to exclude as embarrassing, if not futile, is a formative influence, an element of culture of the very highest value, and more indispensable in the popular school than in any other. "Political pressure tends to exclude this element of culture; clerical pressure tends to give it a false character. The interest of the people is to get a true character imparted to it, and to have it firmly planted, with this character in the popular school."[2]

His reference to religious instruction as "more indispensable in the public school than in any other" might seem to be approximating to a view of religion as an "opium of the people". And when he is found also quoting with approval Goethe's, "He who has art and science has religion. He who has not art and science, let him have religion",[3] this tendency in his thought would seem to be confirmed. It was not, however, his intention to have religion regarded as a device for securing a placid and obedient populace, nor as some sort of consolation prize. He regarded it as a main ingredient of culture, and a vital element of life that purported to be human.

[1] *Notes of My Life,* pp. 329, 338. In 1865, he issued a pamphlet containing "17 reasons against the 'Conscience Clause', any one of them conclusive by itself."

[2] *Special Report on Elementary Education in Germany, Switzerland, and France.* Published by Education Reform League, Toynbee Hall, 1888, Preface.

[3] *Century Magazine*, 1886, xix, p. 894. Arnold mentioned that it was the great classical scholar, Mommsen, who, in conversation, drew his attention to the full quotation.

Arnold's religious ideas were given to the world mainly in three short volumes, *S. Paul and Protestantism*, 1870, *Literature and Dogma*, 1873, and *God and the Bible*, 1875, all three being reprints of articles appearing in *The Cornhill Magazine* and *The Contemporary Review* from 1869 to 1875. Central both in time and importance was his *Literature and Dogma*. Through this work, and his slightly earlier *Culture and Anarchy* he made his mark in the contemporary world as a man whose opinions were worthy of careful consideration, and, if a trifle unusual, perhaps might really be a foretaste, as they claimed to be, of what the Zeitgeist had in store for a rather puzzled England.

It was during these years that Arnold first began to feel that he was really exercising an influence, and that he was a power to be reckoned with on the contemporary scene. In mid-1868 he wrote, "certainly I am struck to find what hold among these younger men what I write has taken."[1] From this time onwards Arnold's letters are full of his being at parties among the leading literary and political figures of the day, having his own ideas discussed among them, and feeling himself to be in some degree a formative influence. From this time, too, his catch-phrases became current in literature and conversation. In 1874 he wrote how he "took up the Blackwood article on School Board Religion, and found the Jews spoken of as a people who, with all their faults, had yet had so near a sense of 'the Eternal Power that makes for righteousness', and then that the Bible had the merit of putting such a mass of people in contact with so much 'of the best that has been thought and said in the world' . . . It will more and more become evident how entirely religious is the work I have done in *Literature and Dogma*. . . . I am amused to see Strahan's handbill stuck in all the magazines and book-stalls announcing Gladstone and me as his two attractions this month . . . the thing is, I gradually produce a real effect, and the public acquires a kind of obscure interest in me as this gets to be perceived."[2] Gladstone might not have been greatly pleased to have figured

---

[1] Russell, op. cit., i, p. 394, Letter to his Mother, 29th June, 1868.

[2] id., ii, 117, Letter to his sister "Fan", 2nd October, 1874. In December 1870 (id., ii, pp. 46–7), he wrote that he had had an interview with the Income Tax Commissioners at Edgware who had assessed his profits at £1,000 a year " 'on the plea that I was a most distinguished literary man, my works were mentioned everywhere and I must have a wide circulation.' 'You see before you, gentlemen,' I said, 'what you have often heard of, *an unpopular author*' . . . The assessment was finally cut down to £200 a year, and I told them I should have to write more articles to prevent my being the loser by submitting to even that assessment, upon which the Chairman politely said, 'Then the public will have reason to be much obliged to us'."

on the same handbill as Arnold, but he read him just the same, though he preferred "rank unbelief" to Arnold's irritating "patronage of a Christianity fashioned by himself".[1] Even the philosopher, F. H. Bradley, felt obliged to devote several pages of his *Ethical Studies* in 1876 to a contemptuous refutation of Arnold's views on religion and morality,[2] and Rev. J. L. Davies in *The Contemporary Review*, analysing Arnold's *Literature and Dogma*, thought that "the creed which he here expounds and commends has a good claim to be regarded as one of the three or four leading 'Gospels' of this speculative age."[3]

Arnold's interest in religion had never flagged from the youthful days when he had listened to Newman at S. Mary's and had turned the pages of the *Bhagavadgita*; but, other than his poems, he did not publish anything on the subject until he wrote a critical article on Bishop Colenso's "The Pentateuch and Book of Joshua critically Examined", in 1863.[4] In 1867 he relinquished his 10 years' tenure of the Oxford Chair of Poetry and for the next 10 years his writing was almost entirely devoted to some aspect of religion. This is the period that the great critic Saintsbury refers to as "in the wilderness", but for Arnold himself, the man who thought of poetry as a "criticism of life", it was a period of interesting and intensive exploration of contemporary society and its needs, and the means of showing himself as a moral force making for the betterment of that society in true accord with his Rugbeian upbringing.

While other liberals applauded Colenso's application of modern scholarship to the Old Testament, Arnold disapproved on the ground that it was ill-advised to undermine established tradition without setting something in its place.[5] Works such as that of Colenso could only be unsettling, and would tend to increase that fragmentariness of life against which Arnold constantly struggled. Especially was this the case among the artisan class, among whom the Bible had long been the most prominent literary guide.

[1] J. Morley, *The Life of William Ewart Gladstone*, iii, p. 520.
[2] F. H. Bradley, *Ethical Studies*, pp. 315–319.
[3] J. L. Davies, "Mr. Matthew Arnold's New Religion of the Bible", *The Contemporary Review*, May 1873, vol. xxi, pp. 842–66.
[4] "The Bishop and the Philosopher," *Macmillan's Magazine*, January 1863, vol. vii, No. 39, pp. 241–56.
[5] Cf. *Literature and Dogma*, p. 8. "To be convinced, therefore, that our current theology is false, is not necessarily a reason for publishing that reason. The theology may be false, and yet one may do more harm in attacking it than by keeping silence and waiting. To judge rightly the time and its conditions is the great thing. . . .'

After the Reform Act of 1867 the ideas of this class became of vital importance. Robert Lowe, who had fought brilliantly against the Act, after its passing, revised his opinions on education, and did all in his power "to prevail on our future masters to learn their letters."[1] Arnold's most popular contribution to this campaign was his attempt to recast current notions about Christianity into a form that would not confuse and dishearten the working classes as Colenso's work might, but which would provide them with a surer basis for belief than that provided by existing sects.

"It is unquestionable", said Mr. Davies, "that religion is greatly neglected by the common people; and it is true also, that in all classes, in proportion to the spread of the modern sceptical spirit, there is a disposition to demand new and satisfying proofs of what they are called upon to believe."[2]

"*The masses*", said Arnold, "are losing the Bible and its religion." At the Renascence many people of cultivation and wit lost their religious beliefs, now it is the masses. Of the seriousness of this he was profoundly convinced. "When our philosophical Liberal friends say, that by universal suffrage, public meetings, Church-disestablishment, marrying one's deceased wife's sister, secular schools, industrial development, man can very well live; and that if he studies the writings, say of Mr. Herbert Spencer into the bargain, he will be perfect, he 'will have in modern and congenial language the truisms common to all systems of morality', and the Bible is become quite old-fashioned and superfluous for him;—when our philosophical friends now say this, the masses, far from checking them, are disposed to applaud them to the echo. Yet assuredly, of conduct, which is more than three-fourths of human life, the Bible, whatever people may thus think and say, is the great inspirer; so that from the great inspirer of more than three-fourths of human life the masses of our society seem now to be cutting themselves off. This promises, certainly, if it does not already constitute, a very unsettled condition of things. And the cause of it lies in the Bible being made to depend on a story, or set of asserted facts, which it is impossible to verify; and which hard-headed people, therefore, treat as either an imposture, or a fairy-tale that discredits all which is found in connection with it."[3]

---

[1] *Vide supra*, p. 64. It was upon the basis of a plan prepared by Lowe, that Forster prepared his first draft of the 1870 Elementary Education Act (Wemyss Reid, op. cit., i, pp. 465–6).
[2] Davies, op. cit., p. 845.
[3] *Literature and Dogma*, pp. 290–91.

Arnold, accordingly, proceeded to jettison from Christianity all belief in miracle and prophesy, all metaphysical speculation, the divinity of Christ, the Trinity, redemption, resurrection, everything, in fact, that pertained to theology. This was "Aberglaube", the "extra-belief", that had battened itself on to the simple truths of the Bible narrative which a sensitive study by one versed in the intricacies of language and the niceties of literary style can readily discern. The Aberglaube is scientific jargon, but "the language of the Bible, then, is literary not scientific language; language *thrown out* at an object of consciousness not fully grasped, which inspired emotion."[1]

What we need to retain, and indeed the only thing that hardheaded practical artisans would wish to retain of the Bible, is whatever can be shown to be verifiable in experience. Now we cannot find "a personal First cause, the moral and intelligent Governor of the universe" in our experience. What we do find in our experience is a "Power not ourselves that makes for righteousness". How may we *verify* this?—"we may answer at once: 'How? why as you verify that fire burns,—by experience! It *is* so; try it! you *can* try it; every case of conduct, of that which is more than three-fourths of your own life and of the life of all mankind, will prove it to you!' It is this sense of righteousness, and the power not ourselves, that we may study with profit in the Old Testament—'and *therefore* study your Bible and learn to obey this'."[2]

To this concept, the New Testament added the idea of ἐπιείκεια, sweet-reasonableness, which is a combination of "the method of inwardness, and the secret of self-renouncement working in and through (an) element of mildness",[3] the characteristic grace of Jesus Christ. This is "the method and secret by which alone righteousness is possible". If you doubt it you can verify it from experience. "It *is* so! Try and you will find it to be so! Try all the ways to righteousness you can think of, and you will find that no way brings you to it except the way of Jesus, but this way does bring it to you!"[4]

[1] id., p. 70.
[2] id., p. 304. Bradley pertinently said (op. cit., p. 318 n.), "We hear the word 'verifiable' from Mr. Arnold pretty often. What is to verify? Has Mr. Arnold put 'such a tyro's question' to himself?" Arnold's religious views are comprehensively explained and analysed in L. Trilling, *Matthew Arnold*, pp. 209–15, and 297–368.
[3] id., p. 233.
[4] id., p. 313. Apropos of Arnold's generous use of exclamation marks, Davies (op. cit., p. 847) remarked, "The appropriate symbol for *religion* in any new system of hieroglyphics devised from Mr. Arnold's point of view would be a (!)."

This then is Arnold's religion, *"morality touched by emotion"* [1] freed of all contact with cosmological schemata, and concerning itself with what to every artisan is obviously three-fourths of life,— conduct. "The very power of religion . . . lies in its bringing *emotion* to bear on our rules of conduct, and thus making us care for them so much, consider them so deeply and reverentially, that we surmount the great practical difficulty of acting in obedience to them, and follow them heartily and easily." [2] Therein consists religion's great humanising power. For the essence of human life, of humanity, lies in the power of "steadying oneself . . . making order in the chaos of one's impressions" which is the basis of morality which is built upon "the notion of a whole self as opposed to a partial self, a best self to an inferior self, to a momentary self a permanent self requiring the restraint of impulses a man would naturally have indulged." [3] To understand this in the sense of possessing it and being animated by it was the great gift of the people for whom the Bible was written. Such a religion, then, uplifts and animates—"to one who knows what conduct is, it is a joy to be alive; and the *not ourselves*, which by bringing forth for us righteousness makes our happiness, working just in the same sense, brings forth this glorious world to be righteous in." [4]

Arnold's concept of religion was what he chose to call Evangelical, which, he explained, should be regarded after the fashion of the denomination called "Evangelisch" in Germany. It "means simply the man who goes to the New Testament, and to the Old Testament as seen and applied from the point of view under which the New Testament teaches us to see and apply it, for his religion, in contradistinction to the man who goes to any other authority for it—the authority of the Church, of tradition, of the Pope." [5] In Germany State-aided schools were divided into Evangelical schools and Catholic schools, and it was a division which Arnold

---

[1] id., p. 47. Bradley's criticism (op. cit., p. 315) is: "loose phrases of this sort may suggest to the reader what he knows already without their help, but, properly speaking, they *say* nothing. *All* morality is, in one sense or another 'touched by emotion'. Most emotions, high or low, can go with and 'touch' morality; and the moment we leave our phrase-making, and begin to reflect, we see that all that is meant is that morality 'touched' by *religious* emotion is religious; and so, as answer to the question, What is religion? all that we have said is, 'It is religion when with morality you have— religion.' I do not think we learn a very great deal from this."
[2] *Literature and Dogma*, p. 118.
[3] id., p. 51.
[4] id., p. 62.
[5] Marvin, ed., *Report on the Wesleyan Training College*, 1868, pp. 263-4.

thought could with profit be adopted also in England.[1] The essence of religious teaching in the elementary schools "of so great fruitfulness and importance" should consist in "the thorough study and appropriation of the Bible, both in itself and in all the course of its relations with human history." "In my opinion, they are the best friends of popular education, as well as the best construers of the word Evangelical, who, however attached to their own particular Church or confession, yet can recognise this fruitfulness and importance most fully, and who show the greatest largeness of mind in giving effect to their sense of it."[2]

He thus would have no truck with the Secularists. Religion was too important an educational influence to be thrust out of the ordinary school programme by political intrigue or sectarian dissention. His religious concepts would have fitted admirably into a school programme under the Cowper-Temple clause, but he nowhere expressed an opinion on that compromise. He thought "William's Bill will do very well",[3] but the remark was made before the Cowper-Temple amendment was proposed.

Arnold's solution to the difficulties occasioned by separate denominational schools was simply the re-union of all Protestant denominations with the established Church. This presumably would be the new Evangelical Church of England.

He became notorious during the late 60s and 70s for his attacks upon Dissenters. He showed in *S. Paul and Protestantism* how they were misguided in their doctrines, he discoursed in *Culture and Anarchy* upon their narrowness, combativeness, and lack of highmindedness, and in *Literature and Dogma* he preached the futility of arguments about doctrinal differences. During the passage of the Act of 1870 when Dixon of the Birmingham League moved for its rejection, he went to hear the debate, and wrote: "the Nonconformists by their violence have done themselves harm, but besides this the opening mind of the nation is against them and their narrowness and violences and to this I am glad to think I have contributed. . . . Their alliance with the Freethinking party, the junction as I have called it between Miallism and Millism does not do them any good either: it is too unnatural, and the real aims of the two allies are too different."[4]

[1] id., *Report on the Training College of the Congregational Board of Education at Homerton,* 1868, p. 257.
[2] id., *Report on the Wesleyan Training College,* 1868, pp. 264-5.
[3] Russell, ed., ii, p. 27, Letter to his Mother, 25th February, 1870.
[4] Unpublished letter in the possession of Miss D. Ward, to his Mother, undated (1870).

These criticisms, Mr. Dale, the Birmingham Congregationalist leader, analysed at length, and concluded: "Mr. Arnold's representations of us are too much like the engravings in some of the cheap illustrated papers. The blocks are kept ready for all emergencies. A few slight touches will make them available for a railway accident in France or a similar catastrophe in America, for a yacht race at New York or at the Isle of Wight, for the 'Derby' or for the 'Grand Prix' at Paris. He has not given us descriptions of the characteristic vices of Nonconformity—perhaps I could assist him with a few confidential hints about these if he wishes to try his hand at this work again,—he has only amused us with a collection of clever but unfinished sketches of faults and follies common to men of all churches and creeds."[1]   Arnold, however, was not perturbed by such amused disdain. He continued to administer his correctives with rather less sweet reasonableness and unction than might have been expected of the foremost devotee of culture.

He saw in Dissent, amongst other things, a continuous violation of that national solidarity and unity which he so much desired. Dissent and *laissez-faire* were allied both mentally and materially. They were nurtured on competition not co-operation, on a spirit of combativeness instead of renunciation and sweet reasonableness along which lay the true path of development for humanity. On the very next evening after he had lectured to a Birmingham audience upon the latter sentiment as the essence of Christianity,[2] the same hall was used for a meeting of the National Education League. His reflections upon the League's work were written in a letter to his mother: "The League have a meeting to-night in the very Masonic Hall where I lectured. I should like to have been there. It is curious how agreeable to them is an agitation such as that they are getting up about school fees. So dull are their lives, and so narrow is their natural circle, that these agitations are stimulating and refreshing to them in the highest degree; and that is really one reason why a movement of the kind is so vital and so hard to meet. The Liberal party being what it is, and English public life being what it is, if the clergy and the denominational schools make the slightest blunder, or give the

---

[1] R. W. Dale, "Mr. Matthew Arnold and the Nonconformists", *The Contemporary Review*, July, 1870, p. 571.
[2] "A Persian Passion Play", published in the *Cornhill Magazine*, December 1871, and reprinted in *Essays in Criticism*, 1st Series.

least opening to the enemy, they are lost. If the clergy are exceptionally judicious and reasonable, and if untoward accidents do not occur, it may be possible to make head against the Millite and Miallite coalition. But things in England being what they are, I am glad to work indirectly by literature rather than directly by politics."[1]

The League's leaders he described later at some length in an address to the London clergy, of which the theme was, "Mr. Dale is really a pugilist, a brilliant pugilist. He has his arena down at Birmingham, where he does his practice with Mr. Chamberlain, and Mr. Jesse Collings, and the rest of his band; and then from time to time he comes up to the metropolis, to London, and gives a public exhibition here of his skill. . . . The essence of religion is grace and peace. And though, no doubt, Mr. Dale cultivates grace and peace at other times when he is not busy with his anti-Church practice, yet his cultivation of grace and peace can be none the better, and must naturally be something the worse, for the time and energy given to his pugilistic interludes."[2]

To Arnold, the Dissenters represented a distressing trend towards fragmentation and the banal. He had shown the advantages of a national Academy, and of a State which might represent the best self of the nation, and in somewhat of the same light he viewed the Established Church. It was "*a great national society for the promotion of goodness.*"[3] As such it should have the nation's support through which it could steadily rise, itself, and uplift the nation with it, towards the ultimate goal of perfection. If one strove to know oneself, to find the inner clue of life it would be found in our moral being which unites us to the universal order, in harmony with the law of nature and the law of God.[4] This was the essence of Arnold's religious exposition in *Literature and Dogma*, it must also be the central thought of the national society for the promotion of goodness, and as such is capable of comprehending within it all men of good-will to work together, not separated by the non-essential theological differences which they now magnify, but co-operating to secure that "the national Church would grow more vigorously towards a higher stage of

[1] Russell, ed., ii, pp. 66–7, Letter to his Mother, 17th October, 1871.
[2] "The Church of England" address to the London clergy at Sion College, 1876 reprinted in *Last Essays on Church and Religion*, pp. 185–6.
[3] id., p. 156.
[4] *S. Paul and Protestantism*, p. 109.

insight into religious truth, and consequently towards a greater perfection of practice."[1]

Renan said, "the future will belong to that party which can get hold of the popular classes and elevate them."[2] So long as the Established Church is felt to be an appendage of the landed gentry and the propertied classes, it will not have the confidence of the popular classes and the future will not belong to it.[3] But such an attitude is not an inherent part of the Christian religion. The Church does not find an obsequiousness to propertied classes advocated in the Bible. "The truth is, the Bible enjoins endless self-sacrifice all round."[4]

"No one can overlook or deny the immense labours and sacrifices of the clergy for the improvement of the condition of the popular, the working classes:—for their schools, for instance, and for their physical well-being in countless ways. But this is not enough without a positive sympathy with popular ideals."[5] Current religious teaching by the Church turns mostly upon matters of catechism and formulary. Along such a path there is no future. There must be a return to the simplicity and vigour of the primitive gospel which preached "the establishment on earth of God's Kingdom . . . by the establishment on earth of God's righteousness. . . . And the establishment of the Kingdom does imply an immense renovation and transformation of our actual state of things;—that is certain. This, then, which is the ideal of the popular classes, of the multitude everywhere, is a legitimate ideal".[6]

The Church of England "cannot, I think, stand secure unless it has the sympathy of the popular classes. And it cannot have the sympathy of the popular classes unless it is right on this head. But, if it is right on this head, it may, I feel convinced, flourish and be strong with their sympathy, and with that of the nation in general".[7]

[1] "Puritanism and the Church of England," p. 6, printed in *S. Paul and Protestantism*. Mrs. Humphrey Ward (*A Writer's Reminiscences*, p. 235) wrote: "My uncle (Matthew Arnold) was a Modernist long before his time. In *Literature and Dogma* he threw out in detail much of the argument suggested in *Robert Elsmere*, but to the end of his life he was a contented member of the Anglican Church, so far as attendances at her services were concerned, and belief in her mission of 'edification' to the English people. He had little sympathy with people who 'went out'."

[2] *The Church of England*, p. 169.

[3] id., p. 163.

[4] id., p. 164.

[5] id., p. 170.

[6] id., p. 173.

[7] id., pp. 174-5.

Just as the means of salvation for the Church lay through a rediscovery and re-interpretation of the Bible, so too the regenerating work of the Church so far as it could be exercised in schools lay also through an intelligent use of the Bible.

Arnold was never tired of arguing that England required a system of public schools, "not schools which the clergyman, or the squire or the mill-owner, calls 'my school',"[1] but a school resting upon some form of State organisation. This to many people, such as both the adherents of the League and the Union, meant undenominational or secular schools. But Arnold's continental experience did not confirm this. "Many people in England seem to have a notion that a State System of education must of necessity be undenominational and secular. So far is this from being the case, that in all the countries to which the present work relates,—France, Italy, Germany and Switzerland,—there is a State system of education, and that system is both denominational and religious. Only the different denominations are not suffered to persecute one another."[2] He reported favourably upon its working, especially in Germany where it is seen "how little the religious difficulty practically exists",[3] and in Switzerland where "there is no unfair dealing, no proselytising, no complaint."[4] On the other hand he found that the undenominational system of Holland had given much satisfaction, though, in view of recent alterations (in 1857), only two years before his report, he was uncertain whether it would continue successfully.[5]

In his earliest report on Popular Education abroad he seemed inclined to favour a denominational principle for schools: "the great majority of mankind—the undevout, the indifferent, the sceptical—have a deep-seated feeling that religion ought to be blended with the instruction of their children, even though it is never blended with their own lives. They have a feeling equally deep-seated, that no religion has ever yet been impressively and effectively conveyed to ordinary minds, except under the conditions of a dogmatic shape and positive formularies. The State must not forget this in legislating for public education".[6]

[1] *Schools and Universities*, p. 274.
[2] id., p. 241 n. *Vide supra*, pp. 137–8 for Zincke's and Baines' opinions that a public system must of necessity be unsectarian.
[3] id., p. 218.
[4] *Special Report, etc.*, 1886, p. 8.
[5] *Popular Education*, pp. 211–19.
[6] *Popular Education*, p. 220.

It is possible that Arnold may have wished to modify such a statement, later in life, had he been called upon to make a definite pronouncement. He spoke in 1868 of "the main current of civilisation" carrying Italians away from clerical towards public and lay schools.[1] But that did not necessarily imply a change in his viewpoint. *Literature and Dogma* and his associated writings were rather anti-denominational but he adhered to the end to his approval of denominational instruction in Germany[2] and Switzerland. For the "Morale Civique" that, under the Ferry Laws, had replaced religion in French schools, he had nothing but contempt. "I thought it worth nothing."[3] It was ineffectual and futile. [4] But Arnold had great difficulty in distinguishing between moral and religious instruction when pressed in giving evidence before the Cross Commission.

"What I want to arrive at," asked Mr. Molloy, "is, how, in the consideration of the question by you as an inspector, you would define the difference between moral and religious teaching; where would you draw the line?"

"Surely that you do or do not" Arnold replied, "introduce, in teaching morals, the religious sanctions that are generally supposed, and that in common teaching are generally made, to accompany them,"[5]

Luckily for Arnold, Mr. Molloy was no Bradley.

In Arnold's view, mere moral instruction missed the mark by failing to enlist as aider and abettor to the moral system the great joy-giving force of religion that can make conduct or morality both effective and a delight. It is certain, then, that, whatever may be decided about denomenational teaching within a public system, there must be least be religious teaching in the schools. The State's duty towards religion in education he thus summed up: "The power which has to govern men, must not omit to take account of one of the most powerful motors of men's nature, their religious feeling. It is vain to tell the State that it is of no religion; it is more true to say that the State is of the religion of all its citizens, without the fanaticism of any. It is most of the religion of the majority, in the sense that it justly establishes this the most

[1] *Schools and Universities*, p. 149.
[2] Evidence before Cross Commission (1886), First Report, QQ.6094–6105. Arnold, however, thought that "the dogmatic side is pressed too much" in Germany.
[3] id., Q.5801.
[4] id., Q.6095.
[5] id., Q.6070.

widely. It deals with all, indeed, as an authority, not as a partisan;
it deals with all lesser bodies contained in itself as possessing a
higher reason than any one of them (for if it has not this, what
right has it to govern?); it allows no one religious body to persecute
another; it allows none to be irrational at the public expense; it
even reserves to itself the right of judging what religious differences
are vital and important, and demand a separate establishment;—
but it does not attempt to exclude religion from a sphere which
naturally belongs to it; it does not command religion to forgo,
before it may enter this sphere, the modes of operation which are
essential to it; it does not attempt to impose on the masses an
eclecticism which may be possible for a few superior minds. It
avails itself, to supply a regular known demand of common
human nature, of a regular known machinery."[1]

Of the religious teaching thus firmly settled in the nation's
schools the essence is a right treatment of the Bible. As far as he
could see from his inspection, and he was never called upon to
inspect any religious teaching,[2] the teaching of the Bible left
much to be desired in existing schools.[3] What an effective Bible
study might consist of, he suggested in his General Report for 1869.
"Let them make the main outlines of Bible history, and the getting
by heart a selection of the finest Psalms, the most interesting
passages from the historical and prophetical books of the Old
Testament, and the chief parables, discourses, and exhortations
of the New, a part of the regular school work."

The Bible was for the child in the elementary school almost his
only contact with poetry and philosophy. What an opportunity
therefore was lost if good use was not made of the literary qualities
of the Bible.[4] Arnold would have approved of a recent attempt to
present "The Bible designed to be read as Literature", although
he would have abhorred the extensive rearrangement and re-
translation that the editor has felt to be necessary.[5]

The method of treating a selected passage was illustrated by

[1] *Popular Education*, pp. 220–1.
[2] Evidence before Cross Commission, Q.6106.
[3] Marvin, ed., *General Report* (1869), pp. 139 ff.
[4] id., *Report on Wesleyan College* (1868), pp. 262–3. He suggested also that, "the
enemies of catechism have perhaps never considered how a catechism is for a child
in an elementary school his only contact with metaphysics; it is possible to have
too much metaphysics, but some contact with them is to every active mind suggestive and valuable." But perhaps this was merely a thought "thrown out" without much previous consideration.
[5] In his Introduction to *Isaiah of Jerusalem in the Authorised English Version* which he
published in 1883, Arnold outlined the main principles of editorship for such a work.

Arnold's *A Bible Reading for Schools*, chapters 40–66 of Isaiah, which he edited and published in 1872. It was designed specifically for use in elementary schools, in particular, in the board schools, where the use of the Bible when permitted had to fulfil the conditions of the Cowper-Temple clause.[1]

Such efforts were not a very comprehensive treatment of religion, but they were laying a foundation from which much, one day, might come.

"Some will say that what we propose is but a small use to put the Bible to; yet it is that on which all higher use of the Bible is to be built, and its adoption is the only chance for saving the one elevating and inspiring element in the scanty instruction of our primary schools from being sacrificed to a politico-religious difficulty. There was no Greek school in which Homer was not read; cannot our popular schools, with their narrow range and their jejune alimentation in secular literature, do as much for the Bible as the Greek schools did for Homer?"[2]

---

[1] In his chapter on "Schools" in *The Reign of Queen Victoria*, T. H. Ward, ed., 1886, p. 263, Arnold wrote his final opinion: "I have always thought that the Biblical instruction which the school boards have adopted, with some improvement, from the old British schools, was the religious instruction fittest on the whole to meet the desires of the population of this country and do them good." He thought "the special religious instruction of Church of England schools" to be "not, in my opinion, their best and most attractive feature."

[2] Marvin, ed., *General Report* (1869), p. 140.

EDUCATION ACTS, 1850–70

Youthful Offenders (Reformatory Schools) Act, 1854, 17 & 18 Vict., c.86 (to be inspected by Inspector of Prisons under Home Secretary, for children under 16 years, cost to be paid by Treasury and parents).

The Education of Pauper Children Act, 1855, 18 & 19 Vict., c.34 (Guardians may lend poor parents money to pay for education of children).

Parliamentary Grant for Education Act, 1855, 18 & 19 Vict., c.131 (Building Grants from Committee of Council must have the consent of Home Secretary to be valid).

Industrial Schools Act, 1857, 20 & 21 Vict., c.48 (for the improvement and extension of Industrial Schools for Vagrant Children 7–14 years—to be inspected and approved by Committee of Council).

Reformatory Schools Act, 1857, 20 & 21 Vict., c.55 (to be approved by Home Secretary).

The Endowed Schools Act, 1860, 23 & 24 Vict., c.11 (Children of other denominations may be admitted).

The Industrial Schools (Amendment of 1857) Act, 1860, 23 & 24 Vict., c.108 (Transferred powers from Committee of Council to Home Secretary).

The Industrial Schools Act, 1861, 24 & 25 Vict., c.113 (Consolidating Act).

The Education of Pauper Children Act, 1862, 25 & 26 Vict., c.43 (Guardians may send and pay for children at Voluntary School which must be open to an inspector appointed by Poor Law Board, cannot compel attendance beyond age of 14 years).

The Public Schools Act, 1864, 27 & 28 Vict., c.92 (Preparatory to 1868 Act, cf. 1868 Endowed Schools Act).

The Reformatory Schools Act, 1866, 29 & 30 Vict., c.117 (Consolidating Act, Reformatory Schools, for the better training of youthful offenders under 16 years, to be inspected by an Inspector of Prisons under the Home Secretary).

The Industrial Schools Act, 1866, 29 & 30 Vict., c.118 (Consolidating Act, Industrial Schools where Industrial Training is provided and children are wholly kept up to the age of 14, being sent there by a Magistrate—inspected by the Inspector of Prisons under Home Secretary).

The Endowed Schools Act, 1868, 31 & 32 Vict., c.32 (preparatory to 1869 Act, making appointments in Endowed Schools provisional on the terms of the later act).

The Public Schools Act, 1868, 31 & 32 Vict., c.118 (Commissioners appointed).

The Endowed Schools Act, 1869, 32 & 33 Vict., c.56 (Commissioners appointed).

The Public Schools Act, 1869, 32 & 33 Vict., c.58 (Amending Public Schools Act, 1868, 31 & 32 Vict., c.118).

The Elementary Education Act, 1870, 33 & 34 Vict., c.75.

The Public Schools Act, 1870, 33 & 34 Vict., c.84 (Amending Public Schools Act, 1868, 31 & 32 Vict., c.118).

ELEMENTARY EDUCATION BILLS PRESENTED 1850–70

Promotion of Secular Education Bill. *P.P.* (Bills) 1850, ii, 461. W. J. Fox.

Promotion of Education (Cities and Boroughs) Bill. *P.P.* 1852–3, iii, 235. Lord J. Russell.

Promotion of Education Bill. *P.P.* 1854–5, ii, 235. Lord John Russell.

Promotion of Education Bill. *P.P.* 1854–5, ii, 245. J. Pakington.

Free Schools Bill. *P.P.* 1854–5, ii, 461. Milner Gibson.

School Grants, Security for Application Bill. 1854–5, vi, 71.

The Borough Education Bill. *P.P.* 1857 (Sess. 1), i, 95. J. Pakington.

The Education of the Poorer Classes Bill. *P.P.* 1867, ii, 683. H. A. Bruce.

The Elementary Education Bill. *P.P.* 1867–8, ii, 359. H. A. Bruce.

Regulation of Distribution of Sums for Elementary Education Bill. *H. of L.* 1868, iv, 227. Duke of Marlborough.

Further Provision for the Education of Children Bill. *H. of L.* 1868–9, iv, 479. Lord Townshend.

The Borough Education Bill. *H. of L.* 1868–9, iv, 473. Lord Campbell.

The Borough Education Bill. *H. of L.* 1870, iv, 153. Lord Campbell.

The Elementary Education Bill. *P.P.* 1870, i, 505. W. E. Forster.

CHAPTER VII

EDUCATION AND CULTURE

"We are on our way to what the late Duke of Wellington, with his strong sagacity, foresaw and admirably described as 'a revolution by due course of law' . . . . Great changes there must be, for a revolution cannot accomplish itself without great changes; yet order there must be, for without order a revolution cannot accomplish itself by due course of law."—M. Arnold, *Culture and Anarchy*, p. 97.

"Take from the past all that is good and beautiful. Shape your ideal therewith and build your future in this ideal."—Paul Kruger, quoted by His Majesty King George VI, at Pretoria, March 30th, 1947.

THE decade of which the year 1870 was the centre formed a watershed in Victorian history. From the death of Palmerston and of Cobden in 1865 to the onset of the Great Depression in 1873, Victorian England was in a state of more than usual tension.

Politically and socially it was a time of revolt, with even a suggestion of revolution, if the dismantling of the Hyde Park railings and the riots of 1866–7 were to be taken as an expression of widespread uneasiness. The basis of political representation was considerably altered by the "leap in the dark" of 1867. Although the suffrage was extended only from 5 per cent to 9 per cent of the population,[1] the doubling of the electorate thus brought about, was sufficient to disturb the thoughts and policies of contemporary politicians, and initially, at least, to give an advantage to the Liberal party. Thus the Reform Act of 1867 set off a long train of army reform, civil service reform, reform of the law-courts, housing, public health and educational reform. The enfranchisement of the town artisans stimulated too the formation of groups that would secure their direct representation in Parliament. From this, side by side with a new radicalism led by Bradlaugh, Dilke, and Chamberlain that was trying to force a programme of advanced social reform on the Liberal party, arose the Labour Representation League whose candidates became the first Labour

[1] G. D. H. Cole, *British Working Class Politics*, 1832–1914, Routledge, London, 1946, pp. 4–6. The vast extension that remained to come can be realised from the fact that after the 1928 Act the percentage of the total population enfranchised had risen to 67 per cent.

M.P.'s in 1874.[1] Concurrently, the other vast body of unrepresented individuals in the community, the women of England, were bestirring themselves vigorously. J. S. Mill's manifesto, "The Subjection of Women", appeared in 1869. In the next year they began to infiltrate into the clerical staff of the telegraph office, and, in 1872, Mrs. Senior was admitted to one of the higher grades of the civil service as a poor law inspector. In the meantime, Octavia Hill was startling the readers of *Macmillan's* with her views on housing reform. Emily Davies and Ann Clough were organising women's university education at Cambridge, the Girls' Public Day School Company had been inaugurated in London, and women were exercising their vote, after 1869, in municipal elections,[2] and in elections for the new school boards which the Elementary Education Act of 1870 had set up. Truly it appeared as if Keats' "milk white lamb that bleats for man's protection" was tiring of her pretended shelter, and like Ibsen's Nora[3] was determined to force her way into the light and add her quota to the ferment that agitated and worried the middle decade of the Victorian era.

At the same time, with the passing of Cobden, the heydey of *laissez-faire* seemed also to be coming to a close, and the rising tide of collectivism was becoming more and more apparent with the increase of municipal trading, the wider spread of the co-operative movement after the foundation of the Co-operative Wholesale Society in 1862, and the increasing force of the trade union movement signalised by the first Trades Union Congress of 1868 and the legislation of the 70s that arose out of the Royal Commission on trade societies which reported in 1869.[4]

Economically, the fact that England had reached a cross-roads was brought home to industrialists by the Paris Exposition of 1867 where they saw themselves, for the first time surpassed in many fields by higher quality production from continental competitors. Soon, too, agriculturists were faced by the ruin that stared with the disastrous harvests of 1875 and was completed by the flood of cheap grain pouring in from the new wheat lands in American and the overseas colonies, opened up by the boom in

[1] id., pp. 261–2. Burt, returned for Morpeth, retained his seat without a break until 1918.
[2] Adamson, op. cit., p. 325.
[3] "The Doll's House" was published in 1879.
[4] *Vide* R. C. K. Ensor, *England,* 1870–1914, Clarendon Press, Oxford, 1936, pp. 113 ff., 131–4. Cf. Dicey, op. cit., pp. 245 ff, "combination has gradually become the soul of modern commercial systems".

railway development to which British investment and her steel export trade had largely contributed. To some extent forced on her by the economic exigencies of the period, imperialism, scorned by the recent advocates of *laissez-faire*, began to raise its head. The Royal Colonial Institute, with the motto, "United Empire", came into being in 1868, and, with the retirement of Frederic Rogers from the Permanent Under-Secretaryship of the colonies in 1871, official policy immediately changed to a steady forward movement that, in the following year, had the approval of Disraeli, hitherto of the opinion that "these wretched colonies . . . are a millstone round our necks."[1] The new trend was confirmed in 1875 by the spectacular purchase of the Khedive's Suez Canal shares, and in the following year by the Queen's acceptance of the new title of Empress of India.

Accompanying these shifts in the political and economic fields, various changes of social fashion made themselves apparent at the same period. Games, such as Association and Rugby football emerged as popular sports and spectacles, their rise paralleling the increasing articulateness of the newly-enfranchised classes.[2] These games suited the suburban dweller and the rising professional class too who had not the facilities, even if they had the inclination, for the traditional fishing and hunting pastimes of the aristocracy. Emphasis was increasingly placed upon the professional, not merely in sport but also in every walk of life, so that by 1870 the middle-class professional man, whose career lay in the civil service, the administrative sides of business and industry, law, medicine, engineering, or higher journalism, had become a lasting and characteristic phenomenon of English society.

Such, in outline, were the chief ingredients making for change in the political, social, and economic matrix of the 60s and 70s: the beginnings of a conversion of English government into democracy, and of the English people into a literate and self-possessed population, the threat to English industrial predominance and agricultural prosperity by overseas competitors, and finally, the beginning of a new orientation towards her colonial possessions.

---

[1] Monypenny and Buckle, *Life of Disraeli*, i, 1201. His Crystal Palace speech, 24th June, 1872, was a turning point in Conservative party policy. A. B. Keith, *Responsible Government in the Dominions*, Clarendon Press, Oxford, 1928, ii, 1154–9, analyses English opinion on imperial questions during his period.
[2] The first international soccer match, England *v.* Scotland, was played in 1872. The English Rugby Union was founded in 1871.

Any one of such trends might by itself have been enough to heighten considerably the elements of change and instability already developed in Victorian society. Occurring as they did, together they precipitated a cultural crisis of the first magnitude. For the new mobility and challenge to established principle and way of life, which each of these factors produced, was added to the cultural ferment already caused among established religious belief. The conflict of opinion had increased since the publication of Darwin's *Origin of Species* in 1859 and Huxley's vindication of the claims of science, in his famous 1860 debate, with Bishop Wilberforce. In a society which "was one of the most religious that the world has known",[1] the challenges of agnosticism in the hands of influential exponents such as Huxley and Morley, and, what, to many, were its inevitable consequences, militant freethought of Bradlaugh's type, or hedonistic free-living exemplified in the activities of the heir to the throne, were a confusion and bouleversement of the existing cultural pattern with a deranging and unnerving prospect.

Such a serious view of the situation was taken by Matthew Arnold. He had from his earliest years been impressed by the possible danger of a vulgarisation and fragmentation of English society consequent upon its new-found mobility. And when in 1867 he retired from the Chair of Poetry at Oxford where he had first fully experienced the joys of being regarded in matters of literary criticism as a man of weight whose utterances were worth the serious consideration of the thinking public, he determined to remain upon the public platform by devoting himself to an analysis of, and prescription for, the current cultural crisis. The manner in which his mind was working was indicated in a short passage at the conclusion to *Culture and Anarchy*. "Through the length and breadth of our nation a sense,—vague and obscure as yet,—of weariness with the old organisations, of desire for this transformation, works and grows . . . the centre of the movement is not in the House of Commons. It is in the fermenting mind of the nation; and his is for the next twenty years the real influence who can address himself to this."[2] Such an influence Arnold felt he might well be. He had already announced that poetry was a "criticism of life", and, in his final Oxford lecture,

---

[1] Ensor, op. cit., p. 137. This was the period, 1870–85, in which the Revised Version of the Bible was produced.
[2] *Culture and Anarchy*, ed. J. D. Wilson, p. 211.

"Sweetness and Light", had outlined his opinion of the most pressing defect of current life. Accordingly, in the years immediately following, he developed his theory of culture in a series of articles, which gained wide popularity, in the pages of the *Cornhill Magazine*, and which he put together and published as a separate volume entitled *Culture and Anarchy* in 1869, supplementing them by a shorter series of ironically humorous sketches in the *Pall Mall Gazette* which were published in 1870 as *Friendship's Garland*.

Arnold summarised his view of the role of culture in society in his Preface to *Culture and Anarchy*, as follows: "the whole scope of this essay is to recommend culture as the great help out of our present difficulties, culture being a pursuit of our total perfection by means of getting to know, on all the matters which most concern us, the best that has been thought and said in the world; and through this knowledge, turning a stream of fresh and free thought upon our stock notions and habits, which we now follow staunchly but mechanically vainly imagining that there is a virtue in following them staunchly which makes up for the mischief of following them mechanically. This and this alone is the scope of the following essay." [1]

In this short statement there are three points worthy of particular notice.

First, the aim of culture is total perfection; secondly, culture is an activity not a mere body of knowledge; and thirdly, culture is an instrument of social amelioration.

It is evident from this that Arnold's conception of culture was of a rather special kind. It is common to think of culture in one of two senses, either as the body of habits or specialised knowledge that distinguishes a person of special refinement or literary accomplishment, or, in the language of anthropologists, as the behaviour pattern which distinguishes one civilisation from another. [2]

Neither of these concepts fits Arnold's view of culture which is both wider than the first and narrower than the second.

[1] id., p. 6.
[2] R. M. McIver, *Society*, Farrar & Rinehart, New York, 1944, pp. 272-3, adopts a position midway between these two concepts, contrasting civilisation "the whole mechanisation and organisation" by which we control the conditions of our life, with culture which consists of "values, styles, of emotional attachments, of intellectual adventures". Civilisation is the utilitarian aspect of life, whilst culture refers to the things which are desired for their own sakes. This according to McIver is a more serviceable usage for sociologists than the more extensive one current among anthropologists.

First, his view of culture as having for its object our total perfection, at once takes it far beyond its limitation to some particular kind of accomplishment, probably literary and dilettante, to the pursuit of "a harmonious expansion of *all* the powers which make the beauty and worth of human nature."[1] He acknowledged that "a notion of something bookish, pedantic, and futile has got itself more or less connected with the word culture"[2] and he thought literary study to be an important aid to cultural development but: "If a man without books or reading nothing but his newspapers, gets nevertheless a fresh and free play of the best thoughts upon his stock notions and habits, he has got culture".[3] It says much for Arnold's own fresh and free play of intellect that a man of his studious habits and literary propensity could thus confess that the coveted goal could be reached by other paths outside his own special interests. The narrower view of culture offended Arnold's passion for social equality.[4] It was a disruptive force in society, not the harmonising, beneficial agent that he wished his own interpretation to be. "The culture which is supposed to plume itself on a smattering of Greek and Latin is a culture which is begotten by nothing so intellectual as curiosity; it is valued either out of sheer vanity and ignorance, or else as an engine of social and class distinction, separating its holder, like a badge or titles, from other people who have not got it. No serious man would call this *culture*, or attach any value to it, as culture, at all."[5] He was concerned not with upholding any traditional view attaching to the word "culture" but with his particular idea of "the unum necessarium or one thing needful,"[6] in contemporary society, which he designated by the name "culture". "We will not stickle for a name, and the name of culture one might easily give up, if only those who decry the frivolous and pedantic sort of culture, but wish at bottom for the same thing as we do, would be careful on their part, not, in disparaging and discrediting the false culture, to unwittingly disparage and discredit, among a people with little natural reverence for it, the true also. But what we are concerned for is the thing, not the name; and the thing, call it by what name we

---

[1] *Culture and Anarchy*, p. 48.
[2] id., p. 6.
[3] id., pp. 6–7.
[4] *Vide supra*, pp. 83 ff.
[5] *Culture and Anarchy*, p. 43.
[6] This is the main point of his chapter in *Culture and Anarchy*, entitled "Porro unum est necessarium"

will, is simply the enabling ourselves, whether by reading, observing, or thinking, to come as near as we can to the firm intelligible law of things, and thus to get a basis for a less confused action and a more complete perfection than we have at present.[1]

He had always been impressed with the need for seeing things as they really are, of pressing on through the external trappings to the essence of things.[2] So, therefore, when he came to analyse culture as "a study of perfection", he found one part of it to be "the sheer desire to see things as they are . . . the scientific passion for pure knowledge."[3] This he summed up in Montesquieu's words "To render an intelligent being more intelligent."[4] But to this there was also a corollary, the more important part of the pursuit of perfection, which he hit off in the words of Bishop Wilson: "To make reason and the will of God prevail."[5] This second part he described also as "the passion of doing good", and "the noble aspiration to leave the world better and happier than we found it". To achieve perfection, therefore, it is necessary to consider carefully and disinterestedly the circumstances of our time in the light of the best experience that the world has made available, and, then, to act for the improvement of the current situation so that our actions are governed and made effective by the most worthy considerations. The great aim of culture, "the aim of setting ourselves to ascertain what perfection is and to make it prevail",[6] is similar to that of religion. For the essence

---

[1] *Culture and Anarchy*, p. 163. Arnold, fastidious master of prose style that he was, was betrayed in his anxiety to make this point clear even to the extent of splitting an infinitive to do so! One is reminded of a remark of Sir Leo Cussen, one of the original draughtsmen of the Australian Commonwealth Constitution, that such was the panel's anxiety to avoid ambiguity that they would even have split an infinitive if such a barbarism would have made their meaning clearer, but, mercifully, they were spared the ignominy of such a procedure.

[2] *Vide supra*, pp. 22 ff.

[3] *Culture and Anarchy*, pp. 44–5.

[4] id., p. 45.

[5] ibid. Wilson (1663–1755) wrote a small book entitled *Maxims* from which Arnold never tired of quoting. T. H. Huxley, with whom Arnold was on terms of intimate friendship, chaffed him on his well-known devotion to the Bishop in the following letter:

"My Dear Arnold,

"Look at Bishop Wilson on the sin of covetousness and then inspect your umbrella stand. You will see there a beautiful brown smooth-handled umbrella which is *not* your property.

"Think of what the excellent prelate would have advised and bring it with you next time you come to the club. The porter will take care of it for me.

Ever yours faithfully,
T. H. Huxley."

(L. Huxley, *Life and Letters of T. H. Huxley*, vol. i, p. 311.)

[6] *Culture and Anarchy*, p. 47.

of human perfection is placed both by religion and culture "in an *internal* condition, in the growth and predominance of our humanity proper, as distinguished from our animality."[1] Culture, however, goes beyond religion. It seeks for perfection, "through *all* the voices of human experience which have been heard upon it, of art, science, poetry, philosophy, history, as well as of religion, in order to give a greater fullness and certainty to its solution."[2] Religion tends to emphasise the moral element in human nature, while culture seeks for the harmonious development "of *all* the powers which make for the beauty and worth of human nature."[3]

Perfection, therefore, as culture sees and seeks it, is a trinity: "harmonious perfection, general perfection, and perfection which consists in becoming something rather than in having something, in an inward condition of the mind and spirit."[4]

The second peculiarity of culture is that it is essentially a process, not an abstract body of knowledge. This was strongly emphasised by Arnold: "Not a having and a resting, but a growing and a becoming is the character of perfection as culture conceives it."[5] Culture is dynamic. It cannot rest or it will atrophy; it must be for ever growing. "Culture must not fail to keep its flexibility."[6] The true value of culture lies in leading human nature to find its ideal "in making endless growth in wisdom and beauty."[7] In such manner was Arnold impressed with the mobility of his age, an era of expansion, as he called it. Culture was there aligned with the great Victorian belief in Progress; but it was no inevitable progress nor a haphazard one that Arnold preached. The spirit of growth and expansion, that no Victorian could very well ignore, was, for Arnold, the product of unremitting intellectual effort seeking not any path of advance, but always the best path, by continually weighing and examining and probing stock notions and habits in the light of changing circumstances. Culture viewed from this angle was a technique, a method of approach to problems. Thus it was that Arnold could believe that if a man of little learning could apply his mind disinterestedly and free from cant to the question in hand, seeking

[1] ibid.
[2] ibid.
[3] id., p. 48.
[4] ibid.
[5] id., p. 49.
[6] id., p. 37.
[7] *A French Eton*, pp. 116–17. Cf. *Culture and Anarchy*, p. 47.

to understand it "with constant reference to some ideal of complete human perfection and happiness",[1] he was equally entitled to be called cultured with the man who through some kind of academic training was habitually able to apply the same technique.

It was upon the third characteristic of culture, its social nature, that Arnold laid the most stress. He found that the achievement of culture's aim of total perfection met in practice with constant check from numerous powerful elements in contemporary society. To neglect the relationship of culture to these factors, therefore, was to preach a barren dilettante doctrine, suitable perhaps for Arnold the Professor of Belles Lettres but inexcusable from the lips of Arnold the Inspector of national schools for the labouring classes.

"The idea of perfection", he wrote, "as an *inward* condition of the mind and spirit is at variance with the mechanical and material civilisation in esteem with us, and nowhere, as I have said, so much in esteem, as with us. The idea of perfection as a *general* expansion of the human family is at variance with our strong individualism, our hatred of all limits to the unrestrained swing of the individual's personality, our maxim of 'every man for himself'. Above all the idea of perfection as a *harmonious* expansion of human nature is at variance with our want of flexibility, with our inaptitude for seeing more than one side of a thing, with our intense energetic absorption in the particular pursuit we happen to be following."[2]

This consideration led him into an analysis of contemporary society in which he found three classes, Barbarians, Philistines, and Populace. Throughout his career he had had ample opportunity for observing all three. As private secretary to Lord Lansdowne he had had entrée to the most exclusive circles, as inspector of Nonconformist schools over a wide area of England he had long had contact with all grades of the middle classes, and when his inspectorial district was narrowed to the precincts of London he spent a considerable time in the poorer areas of Westminster and the East End.[3] The Barbarians, England's

---

[1] *Culture and Anarchy*, p. 162.
[2] id., p. 49.
[3] *Vide supra*, p. 141, Arnold's connection with Toynbee Hall. In *The Times*, 1st December, 1884, he was reported as an honoured guest at the unveiling of a mosaic in honour of the vicar of S. Jude's Church, and at a subsequent meeting held at Toynbee Hall. On rising to speak "he was received with cheers", and he recalled his long contact with and interest in what he called "the behind-the-scenes" of English civilization.

aristocracy, he had dealt with at length elsewhere, notably in his 1859 pamphlet on the Italian Question. They were characterised by a want of ideas, and a lack of flexibility. They might have sweetness but they lacked a light at a time "when light is our great requisite" and they were therefore "inadequate to our needs".[1] The middle-classes took their nickname from the "strong, dogged, unenlightened opponent of the chosen people, the people of light."[2] These Philistines lacked both sweetness and light, and were characterised by self-satisfaction, perversity, and an energetic adherence to the doctrine of self-reliance. The Populace was the vast residuum "of the working class which, raw and half-developed, has long lain half-hidden amidst its poverty and squalor, and is now issuing from its hiding place to assert an Englishman's heaven-born privilege of doing as he likes and is beginning to perplex us by marching where it likes, meeting where it likes, bawling what it likes, breaking what it likes."[3] This new democratic force "which is now superseding our old middle-class Liberalism"[4] might tend in one of three directions. They might follow Mr. Bright, in self-satisfaction at their power and achievements into a Philistinism akin to that of the middle-classes; they might turn, under the influence of Comtists such as Frederic Harrison into Jacobinism, the expression of "violent indignation with the past"[5] and an attempt to build society anew by some rational and abstract system, or they might try the path of culture. Culture does not work by the method of Mr. Bright or Mr. Harrison. "It does not try to teach down to the level of inferior classes; it does not try to win them for this or that sect of its own, with ready-made judgments and watchwords. It seeks to do away with classes; to make all men live in an atmosphere of sweetness and light, where they may use ideas, as it uses them itself, freely,—nourished and not bound by them.

"This is the *social* idea; and the men of culture are the true apostles of equality. The great men of culture are those who have had a passion for diffusing, for making prevail, for carrying from

[1] *Culture and Anarchy*, p. 83.
[2] *Essays in Criticism*, I, pp. 162–3, where Arnold first used the term in his essay on Heine. He may have picked it up from his favourite author Goethe, who used the word "philister" frequently in his conversations with Eckermann; pp. 114, 246, 318, 353, 370, 456, 545. "Philister" appears to have been a term of contempt applied by German students to a townsman who was not a member of the university.
[3] *Culture and Anarchy*, p. 105.
[4] id., p. 64.
[5] id., p. 66.

one end of society to the other, the best knowledge, the best
ideas of their time; who have laboured to divest knowledge of
all that was harsh, uncouth, difficult, abstract, professional,
exclusive; to humanise it, to make it efficient outside the
clique of the cultivated and learned, yet still remaining the
best knowledge and thought of the time, and a true source,
therefore, of sweetness and light."[1] Culture looked forward to
the time when the Barbarians, Philistines, and Populace should
cease to be. Culture in a society did not consist of all the attitudes,
habits, and institutions of the society, but it did need to take
them into account as the field in which it did its work of elevation.
A mind not oriented towards a course of social usefulness was,
however fine or well-informed, still not a cultured mind. This was
the lesson which Arnold had learnt in early manhood when he
turned from Obermann to the Bhagavadgita.[2] And it was a
doctrine which illuminated everything he wrote whether in the
sphere of literary criticism, or religion, or political philosophy,
or education.

Arnold's man of culture might be regarded as one who showed
an educated and responsible approach to social living, shot
through with a touch of idealism. But how was education to
secure the spread of such men and such attitudes throughout
society? On closer examination he found that the tripartite
division of Barbarians, Philistines, and Populace, though a reasonable generalisation, was subject to many modifications. Within
each of these classes there were to be found a certain number of
"aliens", "persons who are mainly led, not by their class spirit,
but by a general *humane* spirit, by the love of human perfection."[3]
This body of persons, he spoke of in his later American address
"Numbers", as the "remnant". In the necessary transformation
of society it is this remnant's task "to reform the State in order to
save it, to preserve it by changing it."[4] English society was on
the point of plunging into an experiment in mass government,
wherein the majority, never, in any government, noted for its
enlightenment, was likely to be fickle and unsound. It is certainly

---

[1] id., p. 70.
[2] *Vide supra*, pp. 27 ff.
[3] *Culture and Anarchy*, p. 109.
[4] *Discourses in America*, pp. 22–3. The term "remnant" was derived from Arnold's
study of Isaiah: "Though thy people of Israel be as the sand of the sea, only a remnant
of them shall return," Isa. x, 21. Plato's "There is but a very small remnant of honest
followers of wisdom, . . . and who can see, moreover, the madness of the multitude . . ." was used to support Arnold's argument.

better "that the body of the people, with all its faults, should act for itself, and control its own affairs," than that some "so-called superior class" should do it for them.[1] But if democracy is not to degenerate into ochlocracy, the state must see to it that facilities are available for the preservation and expansion of the "remnant". It is upon the extent to which the remnant can keep its own spirit alive, and leaven and elevate its surrounding society that the possibility of raising that society towards culture's ideal of total perfection depends. The provision of an environment suited to the encouragement of the "remnant", and of an attitude in society favourable to the increase of its influence was a fundamental educational task for the time. Any shortcoming in this regard would lead to the steady degeneration of civilisation, for "the failure to mind whatsoever things are elevated must impair with an inexorable fatality the life of the nation."[2]

Arnold's exposition of culture did not pass unchallenged. One of the most prominent of his contemporary critics was Frederic Harrison, a doughty opponent concerning whose championship of the lower classes Arnold wrote in his *Friendship's Garland* series, in April 1867, just prior to the passage of the Reform Bill: "My elevated position in Grub Street, Sir, where I sit commercing with the stars, commands a view of a certain spacious back yard; and in that back yard, Sir, I tell you confidently that I saw the other day with my own eyes that powerful young publicist, Mr. Frederic Harrison, in full evening costume furbishing up a guillotine."[3] Harrison retaliated in the same vein in "Culture: A Dialogue" published six months later in the *Fortnightly*. His grounds of criticism were chiefly two. First, Arnold's exposition was based on no "definite logical process . . . either from history, or from consciousness, or from experiment, or the like."[4] Culture disdained such processes, on its own author's confession, and appeared as some aerial, unsubstantial concept whose terms would not stand up to a moment's logical analysis. It spoke of

[1] *Discourses in America*, p. 7.
[2] id., p. 27. The great Barnum was so impressed by Arnold's address that he resolved forthwith to become one of the "remnant", and invited the apostle of culture to his home at Bridgeport, an invitation which Arnold accepted (Trilling, op. cit., p. 400).
[3] *Friendship's Garland*, p. 58.
[4] *The Fortnightly Magazine*, vol. ii, New Series, 1867, p. 608. This was written in the style of Arnold's *Friendship's Garland* using Arnold's Arminius von Thunder-Ten-Tronckh as the principal character. Arnold wrote that it was "in parts so amusing that I laughed till I cried" (Russell, ed., i, p. 372, Letter to Lady de Rothschild, 30th October, 1867).

"the *best* principles, the *best* ideas, the *best* knowledge:—the perfect! the ideal! the complete!

"But how does it recognise these . . . if it has neither system, method, nor logic?"[1] Secondly, admitting that culture's objects might be admirable, what sort of help did Arnold give towards attaining them?

"And now, then, how do you get it? It is very good to tell me how beautiful this is; but if a physician tells me only what a beautiful thing good health is, how happy and strong it makes those who possess it, and omits to tell me how I can gain health, or says only, be healthy, desire, seek after health I call him no physician, but a quack. So if I describe in words a very admirable state of the soul, it matters little what I call it. I might say this beautiful godlike state is such and such, and I call it fiddlestick, or sauerkraut, or the like; but what am I profited unless I learn how this same fiddlestick, or sauerkraut or culture (call it as you please), comes to a man?"[2]

This criticism was in fact very pertinent. Arnold's exposition in *Culture and Anarchy* made much of the "free play of intelligence" upon contemporary society and its problems without giving much indication of what conclusions might be expected to result from such an operation. The practical educational implications of his doctrine were to be found, not in *Culture and Anarchy*, but scattered mainly throughout his General Reports and Special Reports. What they were may best be seen by examining his thoughts in three particular fields of education, viz. on a liberal education, and on the system of payment by results, and on middle class education.

[1] id., p. 609.
[2] id., p. 606.

CHAPTER VIII

SCIENCE AND CULTURE

"Vision is the necessary antecedent to control and to direction".—A. N. Whitehead, *The Aims of Education*, p. 91.

ARNOLD was completing "Schools and Universities on the
Continent", his report for the Taunton Commission, at the same
time that he was undertaking the articles for the *Cornhill* that
became *Culture and Anarchy*, and the sketches in the *Pall Mall
Gazette* that appeared eventually as *Friendship's Garland*. There
was therefore to be found in his report the same feeling and the
same argument that appears throughout the other two works,
and the former deserves a closer attention than has hitherto been
its lot, as a practical expression of the theory of the latter in a
field in which Arnold had had a long experience.

It was produced at a critical period in the development of the
curriculum. The controversy between the advocates of science
and the old guard of the classics was at its height. Most of his
remarks were therefore directed to this question.

"The aim and office of instruction, say many people, is to make
a man a good citizen, or a good Christian, or a gentleman; or it
is to fit him to get on in the world, or it is to enable him to do
his duty in that state of life to which he is called. It is none of
these, and the modern spirit more and more discerns it to be
none of these. These are at best secondary and indirect aims of
instruction; its prime direct aim is to enable a man *to know
himself and the world*. Such knowledge is the only sure basis for
action, and this basis it is the true aim and office of instruction
to supply."[1]

This formative knowledge which is to be acquired is thus of
two parts, knowledge of man and his works, and knowledge of
nature and her works. The humanists have perceived the
importance of the former, the realists the latter. It is important
to realise that the claims of both sides are right, and that one
without the other is lop-sided and incomplete.

Arnold then attempted to justify his position by a brief
psychological excursion. Fortunately he was not fond of such a

[1] *Schools and Universities*, p. 258.

proceeding, for on the rare occasions on which he indulged in psychological generalisations the result was neither profound nor even important to his general argument. On this occasion he attempted as Plato had done before and the Norwood report was subsequently to attempt, to divide the capacities of mankind into a number of psychological classes. Arnold, unmindful of the Platonic trinity, but perhaps influenced by the author of *Iolanthe* who had recently served for several years in the education office,[1] chose two, to accord with his division of knowledge into that of the human spirit, and of the works of nature. "Every man," he said, "is born with aptitudes which give him access to vital and formative knowledge by one of these roads."[2] "Great and complete spirits" have all the aptitudes for both roads, but these cases are rare. The task for educationalists is to grasp the fact that both types of aptitudes lead to vital knowledge, and it is therefore necessary for each individual to "get his access to intellectual life and vital knowledge" through a single aptitude, or group of aptitudes, "and it is by effectually directing these aptitudes on definite points of the circle, that he will really obtain his comprehension of the whole."[3] Arnold, in fitting his curriculum to the capacities of his pupils, adopted one of the leading principles of curriculum making, but in doing so he showed a little less sophistication than one expects from his present-day successors. The typology of the Norwood Report, for example, is based not on capacity for studying a particular kind of knowledge but on the method by which that knowledge is approached. And the curriculum is accordingly varied to meet the requirements of the different types of approach. Much of the factual material is found to be common, but in practice, according to the Committee, there is also to be found a difference, between the various types, in the actual subjects studied. Arnold found his different types of mind to depend not on the method by which they learn but on the material which they tend to learn most readily. The conclusions, in both cases, were rather similar, and had Arnold survived until the present day, he would no doubt have endorsed the Norwood approach.

Both the humanists and the realists suffered from inadequately recognising the claims of the other side, but the loss on the side

[1] *Iolanthe*, however, was not published until 1882.
[2] *Schools and Universities*, p. 258.
[3] id., p. 259.

of the realists was probably the greater. "For the study of letters is the study of the operation of human force, of human freedom and activity; the study of nature is the study of the operation of non-human forces, of human limitation and passivity. The contemplation of human force and activity tends naturally to heighten our own force and activity; the contemplation of human limits and passivity tends rather to check it." Arnold's argument was a curiously partial one. It assumes that the study of human activity is on the whole inspiring, whilst the study of natural forces is for the most part depressing.

He had admitted in his early 1853 Preface that some human productions, for example, his own "Empedocles on Etna", tended to depress rather than elevate. It is evident, therefore, that contemplation of them would not inspire and heighten one's own force. His contention, then, must be amended to read that the contemplation of inspiring human activity is inspiring. Similarly, it is obvious that at least in certain circumstances, natural forces inspire various individuals, such as a Newton, or a Sophocles, or a Gauguin, rather than depress them. All that Arnold has really said, therefore, is that inspiring things tend to inspire, and depressing things tend to depress—which is not a particularly important contribution to the philosophy of education. He neglects furthermore the individual characteristics of the student, he omits the inspirational effect that may come from the contemplation of human activity that results from the study and control of natural forces, and he draws a distinction between human and natural force that it is impossible to sustain.

Although his case for the superiority of the humanities is far from convincing, he did show in a fine examination of the classics what contribution they could be expected to make to the development of culture.

Alterthumswissenschaft, the science of antiquity, "affords for this purpose an unsurpassed source of light and stimulus".[1] As at present taught, with the greatest stress on philology and grammar, it may be a gateway to culture for a few rare spirits such as Wolf, but for the majority of students it means a loss of the really valuable elements in the pursuit of mere preliminaries. This was true of classical teaching on the Continent also, where it formed the staple of secondary instruction. In Italy it appeared that the nadir had been reached. There the Superior Council of

---

[1] *Schools and Universities*, p. 258.

Public Instruction had recently made a survey and had written: "What fruits do we obtain from our classical studies at present? After a youth has spent seven or eight years in the study of Latin, five or six in that of Greek, is he in a condition to read with pleasure and without effort a Latin author, to write correctly a short piece of Latin prose, to make out by himself one of the easiest Greek authors? The Latin compositions which the Council have had before them, the entrance examinations at the University . . . , the accounts we have received from the inspectors . . . , afford convincing proof that Latin is neither studied nor liked by our youth, and that there is a notable going back in the knowledge of it in the last twenty-five years. What shall we say of Greek? The study of Greek in our schools leads to such scanty result, our young men, the moment they leave school, forget so utterly all the little Greek they have ever learned, that it is impossible not to consider as lost the time and labour which pupils and masters have spent on it."[1] When such or something similar is likely to be the result of so much effort and school-time spent on the classics, what possible justification could there be for continuing with such teaching? Very little, thought the British Association for the Advancement of Science who declared that the time had come when "it should, we think, be frankly acknowledged, and indeed few are found to deny it, that an exclusively classical education, however well it may operate in the case of the very few who distinguish themselves in the curriculum, fails deplorably for the majority of minds."[2] To Arnold, however, the fact that the bad teaching of the classics led to much educational waste was an argument not for their abolition but for their reform. "School instruction in letters and *Alterthumswissenschaft* has almost to be created anew."[3] Under the new dispensation, Greek and Latin would be taught as literature and not as a philological discipline, though there was still room for a careful study of elementary Latin grammar which with an elementary treatise of arithmetic and geometry would constitute

---

[1] *Schools and Universities*, p. 125.

[2] *On the Best Means for Promoting Scientific Education in Schools*, British Association for the Advancement of Science, Murray, London, p. 11.

[3] *Schools and Universities*, p. 262. The reviewer of this volume in the *Contemporary Review*, November 1868, was much annoyed by Arnold's apparent preference for anything that was not English, and inquired apropos Arnold's continual use of *Alterthumswissenschaft* whether he thought that there was no English equivalent for it. Cf. H. Spencer's hostility to Arnold's seeming anti-patriotic bias, *Sociology*, pp. 216 ff.

"a universally imposed preparatory discipline for procuring exact habits of mind". "By keeping within these strict limits, absolute exactness of knowledge—the habit which is here our professed aim—might be far better attained than it is at present."[1]

The important business, however, is to gain a knowledge of Greek and Latin literature as *literature*. This is the only way "to learn and catch some *power* of antiquity." And what might one expect in acquiring this power? "Dignity and a high spirit . . . the love of the things of the mind, the flexibility, the spiritual moderation" that our present-day society so strongly needs.[2]

Arnold's finest plea on behalf of classical literature was made in his inaugural lecture "On the Modern Element in Literature". He published it for the first time in 1869 with the express purpose of giving "some notion of the Hellenic spirit and its works, and of their significance in the history of the evolution of the human spirit in general . . . ."[3] In it he showed how classical literature possessed a relevance to the current social situation and an elevating influence that made it the finest instrument of education for the culture that he defined in *Culture and Anarchy*.

The Modern age stands peculiarly in need of an intellectual deliverance. This demand arises from the extraordinary complexity of present-day life with its vast multitude of facts requiring comprehension. The confusion that results from a partial grasp of the immense and moving spectacle bids fair to make life unintelligible and lead us to despair, depression, and ennui. Our need, therefore, is, above all, "to enter into the possession of the general ideas which are the law of this vast multitude of facts."[4] He who grasps these ideas, and adequately comprehends his age, has achieved the intellectual deliverance so sorely needed. Evidently other ages that have developed similarly and made a similar demand will be the most interesting, the most instructive, and most modern to us. But not all such ages have produced literary records adequate to their other achievements. When we find the conjunction of "a significant, a highly-developed, a culminating epoch, on the one hand,—a comprehensive, a commensurate, an adequate literature, on the other",[5] there will we find "what will most enlighten us, most contribute to our intellec-

---

[1] *Schools and Universities*, p. 263.
[2] id., pp. 264–5.
[3] *Essays by Matthew Arnold*, Oxford Edition, O.U.P., 1914, p. 454.
[4] id., p. 456.
[5] id., p. 457.

tual deliverance".[1] It was the merit of the Athens of the fifth century B.C. to fulfil these conditions. There we find an era of civil security, and toleration, with the multiplicity of the conveniences of life, the formation of taste, the capacity for refined pursuits and the supreme characteristic of all, the intellectual maturity of man himself manifested by a critical spirit which judges not by prejudice or caprice but by the rule of reason that searches always after a rational arrangement and appreciation of facts. To strengthen his contention, Arnold compared the age of Pericles with the Elizabethan age, to the detriment of the latter whose Raleigh was naive in comparison with Thucydides, and whose taste was flamboyant when set against the temperance of Attic culture. And furthermore we find there, too, in its literature an adequate interpretation of the age. "Now, the peculiar characteristic of the highest literature—the poetry—of the fifth century in Greece before the Christian era, is its *adequacy*; the peculiar characteristic of the poetry of Sophocles is its consummate, its unrivalled *adequacy*; that it represents the highly-developed human nature of that age—human nature developed in a number of directions, politically, socially, religiously, morally developed—in its completest and most harmonious development in all these directions; while there is shed over this poetry the charm of that noble serenity which always accompanies true insight."[2] So, too, in Pindar, Aeschylus, and Aristophanes do we find this same adequacy of representation.

This is the spirit of Hellenism, "an unclouded clearness of mind, an unimpeded play of thought" bent upon seeing things as they really are, and not being led astray to rest "in this or that intimation of it, however capital."[3] The great period of Rome, that of Cicero, Caesar, and Augustus, was a vaster, fuller period than that of Pericles and it is, therefore, also interesting to us, but its Lucretius, its Vergil, its Horace lacked the grandeur and comprehension of their Greek predecessors. That age is therefore of less educative value to the present generation.

The conclusion which would naturally arise from this analysis would seem to be that Greek should be preferred to Latin in school programmes, and that it should be taught as literature in such a way as to fulfil its function of elevating, instructing, and

[1] id., p. 458.
[2] id., p. 464.
[3] *Culture and Anarchy*, p. 132.

providing modern society with the clue to its intellectual deliverance. Arnold, however, did not venture to suggest the first conclusion. It was Latin that he recommended as a suitable study for a few picked, older children in elementary schools, and looked forward to the time when it might even be adopted "as part of the regular instruction in the upper classes of all elementary schools."[1] The possession of a second language as an object of reference and comparison had a stimulating effect upon a child's mind. Arnold did not explain the manner in which a second language was to be used as an object of reference and comparison, nor the way in which its stimulating effect acted. Latin was the language chosen for this purpose because it was "the foundation of modern European languages" and "is the best of all languages to learn grammar by."[2]

What the elementary school pupil required was only "the vocabulary, to some extent, of a second language, and that language one which is at the bottom of a great deal of modern life and modern language."[3] This seems all rather pointless, and the sort of "object of comparison" that the mere vocabulary of a second language would provide seems scarcely worth the time and energy that would be put into the accomplishment. A language is primarily a vehicle of thought, and, as Arnold had already been at pains to point out, is to be valued as an educational instrument in the degree that it embodies worth while thought, and to the extent that its learner is able to appreciate this. The study of the thoughts and aspirations of another country or another age can be of stimulating effect as "an object of reference and comparison". But this consummation was expressly excluded in Arnold's reflections upon elementary school Latin. "It should by no means be taught as in our classical schools; far less time should be spent on the grammatical framework, and classical literature should be left quite out of view."[4] This is an amazing statement to come from one who advocated the teaching of *Alterthumswissenschaft* for the insight that it gave to the mind of Greece and Rome. His plan was "to disregard classical Latin entirely", and use as a textbook, selections from "the Latin Bible, the Vulgate".[5] Now, though Jerome's latinity lacks much of the barbarity of his con-

[1] Marvin, ed., op. cit., *General Report for* 1872, p. 148; (1880) p. 210; (1874) pp. 162–3.
[2] id., (1872) p. 149.
[3] id., (1872) p. 150.
[4] id., (1872) p. 149.
[5] ibid.

temporaries, he could not be regarded as an example of, or even an introduction to "the best that has been thought and said" in the ancient world. And the plan of using the Vulgate as a text would convey nothing at all of the thought of ancient Rome. Arnold, in fact, in this suggestion entirely jettisoned his former arguments on behalf of classical studies. His elementary school Latin was in truth no Latin at all, and scarcely even a language, but a collection of Latin words strung together not to convey any idea of the thought of the cl assical world, but as a basis for the better understanding of the English language—an aim which hardly justifies elaborate entanglement in the apparatus of a foreign tongue.

He saw, too, considerable value in Greek and Latin prose and verse composition and thought that Latin composition should be preferred to Greek, "superior though the Greek literature be to Latin", for "the power of the Latin classic is in *character* that of the Greek is in *beauty*" and "character is capable of being taught, learnt, assimilated; beauty hardly."[1] Such remarks are, of course, quite irreconcilable with his previous magnificent analysis of Hellenism. The strength of Hellenism he had shown lay in the clarity and comprehensiveness of its thought that reflected the balanced maturity and seriousness of life in the Periclean age. Over Vergil there rested "an ineffable melancholy", over Lucretius "a moody gloom", whilst Horace, the third of his representative Roman writers, was "a sceptical man of the world", lacking the Sophoclean note of high seriousness.[2] Where, then, in Latin literature was the power of character that surpassed that of the Greeks? He nowhere attempted to analyse his concept of beauty, and it is not possible to estimate whether it was capable of being taught or not; but in what was teachable, in his view, character, the superiority appeared rather to lie with Greek. The explanation of his preference for Latin composition appears to lie partly in the fact that it was more commonly preferred, in all the European countries of his acquaintance, to Greek, and partly in his leaning towards a theory of formal training that was more commonly connected with the more popular practice of Latin composition. He did not express himself at any length upon this doctrine, but from time to time he used expressions, and justified various practices in a way that suggested that some unexamined

[1] *Schools and Universities*, pp. 264–5.
[2] *Essays by Matthew Arnold*, Oxford Edition, pp. 471–2.

notion of formal training was part of the apparatus of his mind.
He quoted with approval and without examination, for example,
the opinion of a distinguished Swiss who "told me he could trace
in the educated class of Frenchmen a precision of mind distinctly
due to the sound and close mathematical training of their
schools."[1] And he accepted the testimony of Dr. Jäger and "the
chief school authorities in France and Germany" concerning the
reasons for the superiority of classical pupils over Realschule
pupils. "He declared that the boys in the corresponding forms of
the classical school beat the Realschule boys in matters which
both do alike, such as history, geography, the mother-tongue, and
even French, though to French the Realschule boys devote so far
more time than their comrades of the classical school. The
reason for this, Dr. Jäger affirms, is that the classical training
strengthens a boy's mind so much more."[2] He appears not to
have inquired into the relative capacities of the "real" and
classical pupils, nor, at this stage, to have connected his earlier
remarks, that both in France and Germany teachers of "real"
subjects were less esteemed and less well paid than their classical
counterparts, with the inferior performances of their pupils.
Later, however, he somewhat made amends by stating that he
thought the comparative failure of the Realschuler resulted from
the inferiority of his teaching, and that "a clever Realschuler,
who has gone properly through the general grounding of the
lower classes, is likely to develop the greater taste for the humani-

[1] *Schools and Universities*, p. 86. The main tenets of the doctrine of formal discipline
have been well stated by Thorndike: "The common view is that the words accuracy,
quickness, discrimination, memory, observation, attention, concentration, judgment,
reasoning, etc., stand for some real and elementary abilities which are the same no
matter what material they work upon; that these elemental abilities are altered by
special discipline to a large extent; that they retain those alterations when turned to
other fields; that thus in a more or less mysterious way learning to do one thing well
will make one do better things that in concrete appearance have absolutely no
community with it" (E. L. Thorndike, *Educational Psychology*, 1903, p. 84).
The modern view of the subject is summed up by C. Burt (*Formal Training, British
Association Report*, Bristol, 1930): "Transfer of improvement occurs only when there
are *common usable elements*, shared both by the activity in which the results of the training reappear. The 'common elements' may be elements of (i) material, (ii) method,
(iii) ideal; they are most 'usable' when they are conscious. A common element is
more likely to be usable if the learner becomes clearly conscious of its nature and of
its general applicability; active or deliberate transfer is far more effective and frequent
than passive, automatic or unintentional transfer. This seems especially true when
the common element is an element of method rather than of material, an ideal rather
than a piece of information."
Both these statements are taken from *Report of the Consultative Committee on Secondary
Education (Spens Report)*, H.M.S.O., 1939, Appendix v (H. R. Hamley, pp. 439–40,
446–7).
[2] *Schools and Universities*, p. 221.

ties the more he is suffered to follow his 'real' studies without let or stint."[1] Arnold did not regard one form of study as being especially productive of a particular habit of mind; he saw the necessity for giving some help in the process of transfer, for, in his remarks on the teaching of Latin grammar with an insistence on absolute exactness of knowledge for the development of a habit of exactness, he concluded: "But it is well to insist, besides, that all knowledge may and should, when we have got fit teachers for it, be so taught as to promote exact habits of mind; and we are not to take leave of these when we pass beyond our introductory discipline."[2]

The second conclusion, mentioned above, that the classics should be taught primarily as literature, Arnold made of supreme importance.[3] It was the way by which the vast majority of pupils could be brought into vital contact with the spirit and power of the Greek and Roman mind which is the great end of the study of *Alterthumswissenschaft*. By cutting down grammar and composition, a far greater quantity of the classics could be read and their study would become more interesting and worthy of the name of the humanities. It was in appreciating this fact that German schools showed their superiority to English secondary schools, "in their far broader notion of treating, even in their schools, the ancient authors as *literature*, and conceiving the place and significance of an author in his country's literature, and in that of the world. In this way the student's interest in Greek and Latin becomes much more vital, and the hold of these languages upon him is much more likely to be permanent."[4] The same thing applied to modern languages. "It is as literature, and as opening fresh roads into knowledge, that the modern foreign languages, like the ancient, are truly school business; and far more ought to be done with them, on this view of their use, than has ever been done yet."[5] There was a tendency in teaching modern languages to lay more stress upon speaking ability than upon any other aspect of teaching. This was a diversion from the true educational path, just as excessive devotion to grammar was also in the case of the ancient languages. It was a preferring of a commercial theory of education to the liberal one; "not culture

[1] id., p. 269.
[2] id., p. 263.
[3] *Vide supra*, p. 175–6.
[4] *Schools and Universities*, p. 210.
[5] id., p. 268.

and training of the mind, but what will be of immediate palpable utility in some practical calling."[1]

For elementary school pupils French had a commercial value, and such was a valid reason for considering its admission to the school curriculum. But it also had an educational value both as a second language, and also by reason of "its precision and lucidity."[2] It was important to see that the cultural aspect was not overshadowed by the commercial. The criterion of method and of curriculum construction lay in the realisation that "the true aim of schools and instruction is to develop the powers of our mind and to give us access to vital knowledge."[3]

Through the teaching of English this aim could probably be most fruitfully realised. "We have still to make the mother tongue and its literature a part of the school course,"[4] he said of English secondary education, and he looked forward to the time when it would play an important part in the secondary school curriculum. It was, however, to elementary school teaching of English that most of his remarks were directed on the subject. In his very first year as an inspector he was impressed by the want of taste, and the poor comprehension of the meaning of a plain passage of prose or poetry, displayed by the pick of the elementary school pupils, the pupil-teachers. "I have been much struck in examining them towards the close of their apprenticeship, when they are generally at least eighteen years old, with the utter disproportion between the great amount of positive information and the low degree of mental culture and intelligence which they exhibit."[5] This is a theme to which Arnold constantly returned. In a letter soon after taking up his duties as H.M.I. in 1851 he looked forward to the civilising influence that the schools would have on the next generation of the lower classes who might be expected to hold most of the political power of the country.[6] Sixteen years later, by 1867, political power had passed in a much greater degree to the working classes, and the democratisation of England was under way. But had the schools exercised a

---

[1] id., p. 221. Cf. p. 267. The clear distinction was made in Germany where "it may wound an Englishman's vanity to find 'that French is obligatory and is referred to as the Culture-Sprache, learnt for the purpose of the mind and spirit,' whilst English, the Handel-Sprache, is optional and is 'learnt for mere material and business purposes' " (id., p. 45).

[2] Marvin, ed., *General Report for* 1878, pp. 185–6.

[3] *Schools and Universities*, p. 267.

[4] id., p. 266.

[5] Marvin, ed., *General Report for* 1852, p. 16.

[6] *Vide supra*, p. 18, Russell, ed., Letter to his Wife, 15th October, 1851, p.

sufficiently civilising influence? He had defined civilisation as the humanisation of man in society.[1] The rising classes had increased their stock of positive knowledge, but had they gained in the qualities of tolerance, understanding and critical detachment, that make men truly human? Arnold was more than doubtful. Towards the end of his career, he wrote that the popular school was "far too little formative and *humanizing*"[2] and in the year of his retirement, 1886, he said: "In popular education at present 'the common and average thing' is the ability to read, write, and calculate, and the possession of a certain amount of what is called useful knowledge. That is what, in progressive nations, we nowadays expect the whole population to attain, and what they do attain. If we ask for the educative result of this, we shall find it to be, in the main, that the whole population learns to read the newspapers, is formed by the newspapers. That is what modern popular education really leads up to, and many of us are apt to congratulate ourselves when this result has been achieved, and to think that here we have indeed a triumph of progress and civilisation."[3] Arnold feared a swing of the English public towards "American vulgarity". The absence, in England, of any arbiter of taste such as the French Academy, of any national centre of excellence that a central educational authority might provide, contributed to the general lack of enlightenment: "by all means we are encouraged to keep our natural taste for the bathos unimpaired".[4] And the great moulders of the nation's taste, the newspapers, either pander to the lower, the sensation-loving nature of the populace, through the flamboyance of a Sala and his fellow young lions of the *Daily Telegraph*, or they tell us, like *The Times*, or *Daily News* that we must accept things as they are and trust to the effluxion of time to effect some improvement in them.[5] In either case we are left with our natural taste for the bathos still unimpaired.

How then did Arnold think the problem ought to be handled? It was for him an important task of the elementary schools, a

[1] *Vide supra*, pp. 83–4.
[2] *Special Report on Elementary Education*, published by Education Reform League, Toynbee Hall, 1888, Preface.
[3] *Century Magazine*, 1886, "Common Schools Abroad", p. 891.
[4] *Culture and Anarchy*, p. 110.
[5] id., pp. 8, 120 ff. G. A. Sala, celebrated reporter of the period, comes in for many caustic remarks in *Friendship's Garland*. Arnold has "A Young Lion", a disciple of Sala, refer to "the divine madness of our new style—the style we have formed upon Sala", p. 108. Arnold was referred to by the *Daily Telegraph* as "a high priest of the kid-glove persuasion" (p. 33).

contribution that they must make in the mounting cultural crisis. The best effect was likely to be produced by an improved teaching of English.

First, English grammar, though, like Latin grammar, the least important aspect of the subject, was not to be neglected but improved. It had been much objected to both for the insufficiency of the provision for it, and for its uselessness, and some inspectors discouraged it. "But," wrote Arnold in 1861, "I confess that I should be very sorry if this study should be discontinued, or should be suffered to decline".[1] And he advanced two main reasons for his opinion. The study of "a subject-matter which is *exact*" should counteract the tendency to verbiage apparent among ill-informed minds. To accomplish this, however, the teaching of grammar must be confined to exact processes. Too much of the rationale of grammar was taught, and not enough insistence was put by teachers upon learning a simple rule and applying it with common sense.[2] Pupil-teacher candidates learn by heart long passages about the classification of pronouns, and the "meta-physics of mood and tense", and write correspondingly woolly thoughts about grammatical constructions, whereas with a simpli-fied teaching of a few essential laws, as laws and not as theorems, a sounder basis would be laid for greater exactitude in the use and understanding of the English language.[3] Grammar, in the second place, should be used even from the lower standards upward as an exercise in simple logic, "Affording . . . the means of opening the child's understanding a little, and of planting the beginnings of clear and accurate thinking".[4] Both Arnold's reasons were admirable, if intelligently applied, but both tended towards a mechanical formal training which Arnold appeared to suggest when he referred to grammar as "more effective than arithmetic as a logical training, because it operates with concretes, or words, instead of with abstracts or figures."[5]

The second and most important feature of English teaching was the need for the study of English literature. "What is comprised under the word literature is in itself the greatest power available in education; of this power it is not too much to say that in our elementary schools at present no use is made at all."[6] This

[1] Marvin, ed., (1861) p. 85.
[2] id., pp. 85–6.
[3] id., p. 85, (1874) p. 162.
[4] id., (1878) p. 192.
[5] id., (1880) p. 213.
[6] id., (1871) p. 143.

realisation appeared to come home to Arnold particularly after the passing of the 1870 Elementary Education Act which increased the spread of elementary educational facilities and at the same time severed governmental connection with religious instruction in schools. It was during these years that he suggested the treatment of the Bible as literature and its careful use as a source of elevation and inspiration. In his treatment of literature he showed how a direct application of his concept of culture should be made. The pursuit of our total perfection through our getting to know the best which has been thought and said in the world, should be carried out in school work by attention to the best models of classical English poetry suitable for the age and attainments of the pupils. "That the poetry chosen should have real beauties of expression and feeling, that these beauties should be such as the children's hearts and minds can lay hold of, and that a distinct point or centre of beauty and interest should occur within the limits of the passage learnt, all these are conditions to be insisted upon".[1] Thus some of Scott and Mrs. Hemans[2] was suitable for inclusion, whilst longer extracts from Shakespeare, because of the lack of a distinct centre of beauty and interest within a suitably small compass, might prove to be not so suitable, though, generally, the greater poets were to be preferred. The literature of Arnold's choice, was, as might be expected, poetry, for poetry was formative in a way that no other study could be. Arnold's remarks at this point become rather mystical. Poetry has "the precious power of acting by itself and in a way managed by nature, not through the instrumentality of that somewhat terrible character, the scientific educator."[3] "Good poetry does indeed tend to form the soul and character; it tends to beget a love of beauty and of truth in alliance together, it suggests, however indirectly, high and noble principles of action, and it inspires the emotion so helpful in making principles operative. Hence its extreme importance to all of us; but in our elementary schools its importance seems to me to be at present quite extraordinary."[4] In making such assertions Arnold appears to have let his enthusiasm for his own craft temporarily master his better judgment. He was undoubtedly right to insist that the best

[1] id., (1880) p. 202.
[2] Mrs. Hemans (1792–1835) wrote *Casabianca*, *The Better Land*, and *The Homes of England*, from which comes the quotation "The stately homes of England".
[3] Marvin, ed., (1878) pp. 186–7.
[4] id., (1880) pp. 200–1.

poetry is the right poetry to study. All educators from Plato to
Sir Richard Livingstone in our own day would agree upon the
principle of employing the "first-rate", and becoming familiar
with acknowledged masterpieces, as a sound educational method.
The question of what is a masterpiece in poetry is rather a matter
of literary criticism, and to this topic Arnold devoted much of his
critical work. It does not follow, however, that a piece of first-
rate literary craftsmanship is necessarily a suitable educational
vehicle, a fact that Plato had long ago pointed out. And though
a poetical masterpiece should under most circumstances be a
source of inspiration to a poet who aspires to improve his work,
it is not necessarily an inspiration towards the improvement of
other persons whose interests and aptitudes lie in other directions.
Good poetry may beget, as Arnold said, a love of beauty; but
there is no justification for believing that that love of beauty is a
love of beauty in general. It is more likely to be simply a love of
beautiful poetry. How good poetry can beget a love of truth
Arnold did not attempt to explain. From the fact that it has a
peculiarly emotional appeal it might equally be contended that
good poetry is sometimes inimical to a rational consideration of
the facts with which it deals. The duty of being true to ourselves,
and of learning to see things as they really are, which is an important element of Arnold's doctrine of culture, as it was also of
Plato's, implies rather a search for truth freed from its emotional
trappings. In drawing attention to the importance of studying
good poetry Arnold, however, did a service to contemporary
education. His insistence led, at least in his own inspectorial
districts, to an improvement in "the recitation exercise" to which
he attached great value.[1] Learning by heart, suitable passages
of poetry, was in fact the central prop of his study of English
literature. The Revised Code of 1862 instituted this exercise as
part of the syllabus for pupil-teachers, and it was one of the few
regulations of that Code for which Arnold had a good word to
say.[2] There was no further provision for it, however, until
English literature was made a "specific subject in 1871 for the
study of elementary school pupils in the upper three standards,
consisting of children usually over 11 years. Again, Arnold gave
this extension an immediate welcome. " 'Recitation' is the special
subject which produces at present, so far as I can observe, most

[1] id., (1878) p. 186; (1880) p. 204; (1870) p. 267.
[2] Revised Code § 88; Marvin, ed., (1861) p. 88.

good." [1] The rather quaintly worded syllabus of English literature "as it is too ambitiously called", [2] consisted of:

"1st year: One hundred lines of poetry, got by heart, with knowledge of meaning and allusions. Writing a letter on a simple subject.

"2nd year: Two hundred lines of poetry, not before brought up, repeated; with knowledge of meaning and allusions. Writing a paraphrase of a passage of easy prose.

"3rd year: Three hundred lines of poetry, not before brought up, repeated; with knowledge of meaning and allusions. Writing a letter or statement, the heads of the topics to be given by the Inspector." [3]

During the period from 1872 to 1883, when English became compulsory if any "class" subject for standards II–VI was taken, the percentage of children presented in the subject to the total of scholars on the register rose from about .5 to approximately 3 per cent. [4] Arnold held that the passages for recitation should be thoroughly understood by the pupils, should be a means of extending their vocabulary, and a source of lively pleasure to them. [5] The formative influence that he expected from such work he undoubtedly over-estimated, for he rather tended to lose sight of the wider field to which the study of the best that has been thought and said in the world is applicable. He regarded literature, and poetry in particular, as the humanising element in the curriculum, whilst the remaining subjects were the "knowledges". Despite his argument in *Culture and Anarchy* that culture could be approached from many different sides [6] he could not reach the conception that the best that had been thought and said in all the other spheres of human activity might also be as humanising as literature and capable of an equally significant contribution to our growth towards general perfection. He was, on several occasions, struck by the fact that non-literary pursuits seemed to arouse and perhaps elevate some pupils. It rather puzzled him, but did not lead him to question the primacy of literary studies.

---

[1] Marvin, ed., (1872) p. 147.
[2] id., (1880) p. 200.
[3] Quoted in C. Birchenough, *History of Elementary Education*, p. 319.
[4] Calculation based on the returns recorded in *Special Reports on Educational Subjects* 1896–7, art. I "Public Elementary Education in England and Wales, 1870–1895", M. E. Sadler and J. W. Edwards, pp. 64–5. For "specific" and "class" subjects *vide infra*, pp. 221–2.
[5] Marvin, ed., (1880) p. 205; (1882) p. 229.
[6] *Vide supra*, p. 162.

His contemplation of the problem finally produced the following conclusions:

"I had occasion to remark which I have remarked so often, how musical and physical science seem each of them to *awaken* young men of the class to which these students belong; to be capable of 'striking the electric chain' in them, in a way in which no other part of their instruction can. No doubt it is because of this capacity that the civilising power of music has always been famed so highly; for instruction civilises a raw nature only so far as it delights and enkindles it. Perhaps it will be found that physical science has, for such natures something of a similar power, and that we may well make more use of both agents than we do at present. Undoubtedly no refining influence is more powerful than that of literary culture, but this influence seems to need in the recipient a certain refinement of nature at the outset in order to make itself felt; and with this previous refinement music and physical science appear able to dispense." [1]

The conflict between the advocates of the humanities and those of the sciences, that reached one of its crises in the mid-decade of the Victorian era, was no new phenomenon in educational history. It had been a fruitful source of controversy between the school of Isocrates and that of Plato, it had worried the Christian Fathers of the third century, and perturbed the thinkers and educators of the Renascence, and, in eighteenth century Germany, with the increasing popularity of "real" studies and the proselytising genius of Basedow and his followers, had taken up a position in the forefront of educational discussion from which it was seldom afterwards absent. In nineteenth-century England the controversy became one of considerable moment when Herbert Spencer, the great popularist, published his essay, "What Knowledge is of Most Worth" in 1859. "Its leading thesis", he said, "that the teaching of the classics should give place to the teaching of science, was regarded by nine out of ten people as monstrous." [2] And so it may have been, but his forceful, eminently readable, argument compelled them to consider their opinion carefully, and take thought whether there might not be a place in the school curriculum, a little more exalted than had hitherto been its lot, for the rising natural sciences, proclaimed by so doughty a champion. "To the question we set out with—what knowledge is of most

[1] id., (1861) pp. 250–1.
[2] H. Spencer, *Autobiography*, vol. ii, p. 36.

worth?—the uniform reply is—Science. This is the verdict on all counts. For direct self-preservation, or the maintenance of life and health, the all-important knowledge is—Science. For that indirect self-preservation which we call gaining a livelihood, the knowledge of greatest value is—Science. For the due discharge of parental functions, the proper guidance is to be found only in—Science. For that interpretation of national life, past and present, without which the citizen cannot rightly regulate his conduct, the indispensable key is—Science. Alike for the most perfect production and present enjoyment of art in all its forms, the needful preparation is still—Science, and for purposes of discipline—intellectual, moral, religious—the most efficient study is, once more—Science. . . . we find that the study of Science, in its most comprehensive meaning, is the best preparation for all these orders of activity." [1] It was of no avail to point out that Spencer had so extended the range of the word "Science" as to make it virtually meaningless. He had at least used the word "Science", had signalised its every appearance with capital letters, and had unmistakably contrasted it with the study of "extinct languages". Moreover, Spencer's challenge had caught a rising tide of interest in scientific achievement. The Great Exhibition was not long over, and the Prince Consort, its prime mover, had been zealous to use the prestige of his position to maintain and stimulate a wider interest in science. The Science and Art Department had been united to the Education Department three years later. Industry was becoming aware of, and more and more vociferous about the need for scientific training. And finally, in the year of Spencer's essay, Darwin published his book of the century, *The Origin of Species*.

From that year onward for the next two or three decades the protagonists of the humanities and the sciences ranged themselves in opposing order with their supporters in varying degrees of devotion on either side of the somewhat nebulous dividing line between the two. The full history of the controversy has yet to be written. It is intended here only to outline sufficient of it to display Matthew Arnold's place in the field, and indicate the relevance of his thought upon the subject. If the classicists be regarded as the right wing, and the scientists, as befits a radical movement, the left, then Dr. Moberly, Headmaster of Winchester, may be regarded as occupying the extreme right, and Herbert

[1] *Herbert Spencer on Education*, ed. F. A. Cavenagh, C.U.P., 1932, pp. 58–9.

Spencer the extreme left. Robert Lowe was midway to the left, and clustered round the centre were the 1867 Essayists on a Liberal Education, and the scientists Tyndall and Huxley a little to the left, with John Stuart Mill and Matthew Arnold a little to the right of centre.

The position of those who, like Dr. Moberly, could see no fault in the traditional teaching of the classics, and would not modify the importance of their place in the curriculum was summarised in his evidence before the Clarendon Commission. Winchester, said the Headmaster, was not accustomed to move very much.[1] "Classical learning is the inheritance of all former ages. Combined with its allied subjects of philology, history, etc., it puts a person into the possession of the inherited wisdom of all ages."[2] "All classical learning tells on a man's speech; it tells on a man's writing; it tells on a man's thoughts; and though the particular facts go, they leave behind a certain residuum of power."[3] On the other hand, the scientific studies are in their callow youth: "these sciences, the greater part of them, are not above 70 years old",[4] and "I hardly know what their value is; . . . as a matter of education and training of the mind, which is our particular duty as instructors, I do not feel the value of them."[5] "An amateur of science is the better for knowing the elements of it, and every man of liberal education is the better for not being ignorant of any thing; but compared with other things a scientific fact, either as conveyed by a lecturer, or as reproduced in an examination, is a fact which produces nothing in a boy's mind. It is simply a barren fact, which he remembers or does not remember for a time, and which after a few years becomes confused with other facts and is forgotten. It leads to nothing. It does not germinate, it is a perfectly unfruitful fact."[6]

Moberly was taken severely to task by J. M. Wilson who contributed an essay, "On Teaching Natural Science in Schools", to F. W. Farrar's collection, *Essays on a Liberal Education*, which

---

[1] *Parliamentary Papers*, 1864, xxi, pp. 333 ff, *Report on Revenues and Management of certain Colleges and Schools* (Clarendon Commission), vol. iii, pp. 331 ff for Moberly's evidence. Moberly was Headmaster of Winchester from 1835 to 1869 before becoming Bishop of Salisbury. Matthew Arnold had been under his care during the one year, 1836, when he was at Winchester.
[2] id., Q.512.
[3] id., Q.509.
[4] id., Q.510.
[5] id., Q.506.
[6] id., Q.494. Moberly expanded these thoughts in a pamphlet "Five short letters to Sir William Heathcote, on the Studies and Discipline of Public Schools," Rivingtons, London, 1861, *vide* especially Letters II and III.

appeared in 1867. These were, by reason of the subsequent eminence of their authors and the comprehensiveness and cogency of their arguments, in the event, the most significant contribution made to the controversy. Farrar introduced his volume with the statement: "The principles and methods of Liberal Education are at the present time undergoing considerable discussion, and it cannot be otherwise than useful to direct general attention to the changes already in progress, and to other reforms which have become either imperative or desirable."[1] The main burden of the volume was an attack upon the existing predominance and methods of classical education. In this there were many points of similarity with the criticism of Arnold who acknowledged his sympathy with a lecture given by Farrar earlier in the year foreshadowing the arguments elaborated in the volume of essays.[2] Of them all Sidgwick's essay the most carefully reasoned. He examined all the stock defences of the classics and showed that for most students they had no practical significance, that they were a wasteful means of improving English expression or of learning modern languages, that almost their entire benefit could be obtained through the study of translations, and, finally, that, though the mental gymnastic involved in learning the classics might be of the highest importance, the onus of proving that the practice involved in learning "the things which it is distinctly understood are to be forgotten" was superior to that involved in "the process of teaching useful knowledge", still devolved upon the advocates of the former.[3] The brief for increased study of the natural sciences

[1] F. W. Farrar, ed., *Essays on a Liberal Education*, Macmillan, London, 1867, p. v. Farrar taught for a year at Marlborough, fifteen years at Harrow, and six years as Headmaster of Marlborough before becoming Archdeacon of Westminster in 1883, and eventually Dean of Canterbury. While at Harrow he wrote *Eric or Little by Little*. The other eight contributors were: C. S. Parker, "On the History of Classical Education", Liberal M.P. and author of the Lives of Sir Robert Peel (1891–99), and Sir James Graham (1907). H. Sidgwick, "The Theory of Classical Education" (1838–1900), philosopher, and professor at Cambridge. J. Seeley, "Liberal Education in Universities" (1834–95), then professor of Latin, University College, London, later professor of modern history at Cambridge, published two celebrated books, *Ecce Homo* (1865), and *The Expansion of England* (1883). E. E. Bowen, "On Teaching by means of Grammar", master at Harrow, composed the song "Forty Years On". J. M. Wilson, "On Teaching Natural Science in Schools". Headmaster of Clifton (1879–90). J. W. Hales, "The Teaching of English", Fellow of Christ's College, Cambridge. W. Johnson (Cory), "On the Education of the Reasoning Faculties" (1823–92), master at Eton, and well-known poet. R. Monckton Milnes (Lord Houghton), "On the Present Social Results of Classical Education", Liberal M.P. and author.

[2] *Schools and Universities*, p. 266 n.

[3] *Essays on a Liberal Education*, pp. 81 ff. The views of most of the essayists are summarised in E. C. Mack, *Public Schools and British Opinion since 1860*, Columbia University Press, New York, 1941, pp. 61 ff; J. W. Adamson, op. cit., pp. 309 ff; and R. L. Archer, *Secondary Education in the Nineteenth Century*, C.U.P., 1921, pp. 141 ff.

rested chiefly with Wilson who argued that scientific knowledge was a necessary ingredient of a liberal education. Like Arnold, he made the distinction of knowledge of man and knowledge of nature, and contended that the second was an essential which could be supplied only by a more generous supplementing of the humanities by an extended study of science. He also lent support to Sidgwick's argument by showing that the sciences could be as effective a vehicle of formal training as the classics.[1]

In the following year the report of the British Association for the Advancement of Science, "On the Best Means for Promoting Scientific Education in Schools", 1868, conveniently summarised the reasons for urging the inclusion of science courses in secondary schools as follows:

"As providing the best discipline in observation and collection of facts, in the combination of inductive with deductive reasoning, and in accuracy both of thought and language.

"Because it is found in practice to remedy some of the defects of the ordinary school education, many boys, on whom the ordinary school studies produce very slight effect, are stimulated and improved by instruction in science; and it is found to be a most valuable element in the education of those who show special aptitude for literary culture.

"Because the methods and results of Science have so profoundly affected all the philosophical thought of the age, that an educated man is under a very great disadvantage if he is unacquainted with them.

"Because very great intellectual pleasure is derived in after life from even a moderate acquaintance with Science.

"On grounds of practical utility as materially affecting the present position and future progress of civilisation."[2]

These reasonably sober statements and essays advocating the enlargement of the concept of a liberal education by a closer attention to the claims of science, were supplemented by a rhetorical outburst, towards the end of 1867, from the lips of the

---

[1] id., pp. 264 ff. *The Times*, 6th February, 1868, p. 4, rather over-excitedly referred to the book as "a Manifesto of the anti-classicists".

[2] *On the Best Means for Promoting Scientific Education in Schools*, p. 10. The Report was drawn up by Rev. F. W. Farrar, G. Griffith, Professor Huxley, Professor Tyndall and J. M. Wilson. It (p. 13) made a distinction between scientific information and scientific training both of which were important. The first needed a course or courses providing the simple facts of the main sciences, the second required the thorough study of one science of which physics, chemistry, and botany were considered the most suitable from which to make a choice.

enfant terrible of English education, Robert Lowe. One of the finest classical scholars of his age, he poured scorn upon contemporary methods of teaching the classics.[1] "Learning the language is a joke compared with learning the grammar. The grammar is one thing, and the language another. I agree with the German wit, Heine, who said—'How fortunate the Romans were that they had not to learn the Latin grammar, because if they had done so they never would have had time to conquer the world.' But learning the language easily is apparently not what the schoolmasters want. Because it is said 'You must discipline the mind', therefore a boy is put through torture of elaborate grammars,[2] which he is forced to learn by heart, and every syllable of which he forgets before he is twenty years of age. There seems something like a worship of inutility in this matter; . . . It is an idea that a thing cannot be good discipline for the mind unless it be something that is utterly useless in future life. Now, I do not think so."[3] So far Lowe and Arnold would have been in agreement, though Arnold would have deprecated the forceful language of the other as, indeed, he deprecated almost everything that Lowe said and stood for.[4] Lowe, however, went considerably further. He established four rules "of the new science of ponderation" for weighing the value of respective subjects in the curriculum. First, as we live in a universe of things and not of words, "the knowledge of things is more important than the knowledge of words". Secondly, it is more important to know what is true than what is false. It is for example more important to know the history of England than the mythologies of Greece and Rome. Thirdly, as we cannot teach people everything, "it is more important that we should teach them practical things than speculative things."

[1] L. Campbell, Professor of Greek at S. Andrews, in an address *The End of Liberal Education*, 3rd November, 1868, Edmonston & Douglas, Edinburgh, p. 16, referred to Lowe's address as follows, "The periodical reaction against classical studies seems to have again set in. Their partial or entire abolition was advocated about a twelve month since, in a well-known speech, on grounds which tell almost equally against every form of liberal education."

[2] Kennedy's *Latin Primer* which has remained the standard grammar in many schools down to the present day, had just been published. Lowe (*vide* n. 4, p. 31) makes a contemptuous reference to its "abstruser rules of grammar".

[3] R. Lowe, *Primary and Classical Education*, an address before the Philosophical Institution of Edinburgh on Friday, 1st November, 1867, Edmonston & Douglas, Edinburgh, 1867, p. 18.

[4] Arnold noted with disapproval Lowe's "preachment about the Universities not giving enough of their prizes to reward natural science" at a dinner given by the Geological Society which Arnold attended at Huxley's invitation. Russell, ed., i, p. 389, Letter to his Mother, 22nd February, 1868.

And, fourthly, "if we must choose in these matters, the present is more important to us than the past."[1]

Applying these criteria to the existing classical pabulum, he considered that it was a rather narrow view of education which confined it mainly to the acquisition of a language. Language is the vehicle of thought and is not valuable for its own sake but for the sake of the thought and knowledge conveyed by it. If language is to be an important part of education, then surely it should be the language we are most concerned with "and I must be permitted to say that in my science of ponderation I think English has a prior claim over Latin and Greek".[2] Similarly, the preference given to ancient history is a misdirected one. For by the study of the classical languages and ancient history our thought is directed to a past which lacks the leading characteristic of the modern age, "that principle of representation which has made it possible in some degree to reconcile the existence of a large country with the existence of a certain amount of freedom."[3] It lacks also "the idea of progress". "Now it is no small fault of the modern system of education that it withholds that conception, the key of modern society—that is, not to look at things as stationary, but to look at the human race as, like a glacier, always advancing, always going from good to better, from better to worse, as the case may be—an endless change and development that never ceases, although we may not be able to mark it every day."[4]

Lowe summed up his position by saying: "After all, gentlemen, education is a preparation for actual life, and I ask you—though no doubt the memory is sharpened and the faculties are exercised by these studies in some degree—whether they really in any degree fulfil that condition". And again, "Education does not communicate to us knowledge, and, . . . it does not communicate to us the means of obtaining knowledge, and . . . it does not communicate to us the means of communicating knowledge".[5] He did not examine carefully what should replace the *Alterthumswissenschaft*, but he indicated in general terms, that, to be in accord with the principles of the science of ponderation, it should

---

[1] id., pp. 14–15.
[2] id., p. 17.
[3] id., p. 21.
[4] id., pp. 22–3. Lowe had evidently forgotten Heracleitus' πάντα ῥεῖ, οὐδὲν μένει.
[5] id., pp. 26–7.

take account of English and modern European literature, modern history, the recent developments of physical science, geology, botany, and dependent on them "All those noble studies and speculations which are the glory and distinction and lifeblood of the time in which we live".[1]

Lowe was thus approximating both in style and ideas to Spencer's position, but he modified the latter's almost exclusively scientific prescription by admitting modern literature and history to his curriculum. The same current, however, drew them both irresistibly on, the need to keep abreast of the contemporary world; and the Zeitgeist, for them, was heavily charged with the scientific spirit.

With this approach Arnold had great sympathy. He, too, from his earliest years, had been a devotee of the Zeitgeist. Spencer's aim, for education, of "perfection" or "complete living", was none other than the aim of Arnold's "culture": general and harmonious perfection. The Zeitgeist had read the same lecture to them both about the current temptations of fragmentariness and the need for holding firm to the clue which would show them the way to appreciate experience as a comprehensible whole. But on the means of achieving this, the message of the Zeitgeist had not been equally distinct to both. It had impressed upon them both the growing strength of science, but to one the impression of this strength was overwhelming, whilst the other found it rather as a stimulating and increasing supplement to a long-established literary tradition. "The main current of modern civilisation", Arnold reflected after inspecting Italian schools, was not only away from religiously controlled schools towards public and lay schools, but it was also showing an aversion to the old classical

---

[1] id., p. 27. Lowe's severest critic was H. H. Almond, celebrated Headmaster of Loretto, who was moved to write a pamphlet, *Mr. Lowe's educational theories examined from a practical point of view*, Edmonston & Douglas, Edinburgh, 1868, His point of view was that of a formal disciplinarian, convinced of the value of a persevering study of Latin grammar and Latin composition in preference to English, though prepared to admit that the sciences ought to have a larger share of the curriculum than was their lot, and that the English classics ought to be more read in the schools—"Sometimes when boys are tired with a hard run and a football match . . .; sometimes a spare quarter hour when a regular lesson has been quickly got over, may be utilised in this way" (p. 21). He wrote of Lowe's intellectual gin-palaces of which "their glitter and their tinsel even now lure many to send their children to imbibe the deleterious concoctions of their projectors, who have not waited for Mr. Lowe's telling that there is a demand for their wares, and do not need Mr. Lowe's encouragement to degrade an almost sacred profession by pandering to popular ignorance bolstered up by educated twaddle" (pp. 27–8). He referred also to "what I can only call an infuriated essay by Mr. Farrar".

studies and a "strong preference for studies which are scientific'
modern, and positive."[1]
Arnold found the clearest trend of the modern spirit in the
actions and views of M. Duruy, French Minister of Education, in
his reorganisation of secondary education, and they made a deep
impression on him. Victor Duruy was a well-known historian, a
classical scholar of note, and a teacher of some experience before
he was appointed Minister of Education by Napoleon the Third
in 1863. He was, therefore, a man of the type who might reasonably be expected to impress Arnold, and when, to his other
virtues, he added the charm of "a most flattering reception"[2] in
Arnold's honour during his tour of inspection, the latter was
captivated, and impressed by the opinions that the eminent
scholar had formed.

"Conservons précieusement ces nobles études qui ont fait la
France moderne et son glorieux génie; mais aussi suivons le
monde du côté où il marche", ran the text of Duruy's 1863
"Instructions to the Rectors".[3] He saw that the new social and
economic condition of France required an education suited to the
new situation, and he therefore proposed a dual system of
secondary education: "l'un classique, pour les carrières dites
libérales, l'autre professionnel, pour les carrières de l'industrie,
du commerce et de l'agriculture." And in order to counteract
the inevitable prejudice against these new studies, they must be
united under the same administration in the same secondary
schools, where he hoped to see living "sous la même discipline,
dans une égale communauté de goûts et de sentiments, des
enfants d'Origine et de destination différentes."[4] Duruy's sentiments were consonant with Arnold's arguments for social equality
and his desire for a just representation of both the humanities and
sciences. Unfortunately, the French Minister's professions were
not matched by his actions, for the result of his adherence to the
"modern spirit" was the institution of the "enseignement secondaire spécial", a pale shadow and, at times, a caricature of Victor
Duruy's grand thoughts.[5] This was a four year course, designed
to be complete in every year, to cope with the expectation that

[1] *Schools and Universities*, p. 150.
[2] Russell, ed., i, p. 257, Letter to his Wife, 13th April, 1865.
[3] Quoted in F. Vial, *Trois Siècles d'Histoire de l'Enseignement Secondaire*, Delagrave,
Paris, 1936, p. 220, from L'Administration de l'Instruction Publique de 1860 à 1869,
Ministère de S. E. M. Duruy, pp. 33 ff.
[4] id., p. 225.
[5] id., p. 226.

large numbers would not complete it, and taught by a separate group of teachers trained in a distinct Ecole Normale, much inferior to the celebrated institution of the Rue d'Ulm, and graded at a lower salary. The course of studies was, French, history, geography, mathematics, physics, mechanics, chemistry, natural history, drawing, accountancy, moral and religious instruction, and a selection from music, gymnastics, foreign languages, and common information about government, industrial and rural economy, and health. The last subject Arnold found particularly interesting and novel. It was in fact the type of work that the secularists, Combe and William Ellis, had for the past two decades been successfully undertaking in their schools.

Duruy's scheme seemed important to Arnold because it was a concrete embodiment of the modern spirit put into practice by a responsible educationalist. It might not succeed at first, but eventually, something along similar lines, was bound to come into vogue. It served to confirm him in his contention that a modern liberal education required both the study of man and the study of nature, the humanities and the sciences; though the former might be of greater importance, there was need at the present juncture to insist upon an increased study of the sciences. "The intellectual insufficiency of the humanities, conceived as the one access to vital knowledge, is perhaps at the present moment yet more striking than their power of practical stimulation."[1] "To say that the fruit of the classics in the boys who study them, is greater than the fruit of the natural sciences" was merely to say that the realists were but recently in the field and had not yet organised their teaching so well; but when the sciences "have as recognised a place in public instruction as Latin and Greek they will be as well taught."[2] Meanwhile it behoved educational thinkers to make clear to the public mind the important position that the modern spirit required for the sciences.

For this task there was no lack of candidates of varying shades of opinion. There can be no doubt that Arnold's adherence to the cause was of considerable importance. It cannot be estimated in terms of actual subjects added to the curriculum or any immediate change in emphasis. He showed rather how it was possible for an intelligent and respected man of literary upbringing and renown to become persuaded of the inadequacy of such a

[1] *Schools and Universities*, p. 260.
[2] id., pp. 260–1.

discipline, and to feel the need, in existing circumstances, to supplement it by the study of the sciences. Arnold was no scientist, nor even a mathematician—he spoke of having to learn his elementary arithmetic after he became an inspector.[1] He had, therefore no vested interest to subserve in advocating the cause of science, and his influence was, therefore, the more effective with those who, of similar taste and education, were, after all, the men who, as departmental administrators or headmasters, had the determining voice in the curriculum of schools.

Arnold's slight brush with his friend T. H. Huxley on the question of science and culture produced from him a lecture which he regarded as "in general my doctrine on Studies as well as I can frame it."[2]

Huxley, since his first eloquent plea, on behalf of biology, in 1854,[3] had been a leader in the movement for increased attention to the sciences in education. In his speech "A Liberal Education: and Where to Find It" made in 1868, at the height of the controversy, he made his well-known comparison of human life with a game of chess where "the chess-board is the world, the pieces are the phenomena of the universe, the rules of the game are what we call the laws of Nature."[4] Education he held to be the learning of the rules of "this mighty game",[5] and a liberal education to be one "which has not only prepared a man to escape the great evils of disobedience to natural laws, but has trained him to appreciate and to seize upon the rewards which Nature scatters with as free a hand as her penalties."[6] How could one attain such a liberal education? Not, assuredly, by means of the stunted, narrow provision then offered in elementary schools, nor even through the classical training of secondary schools. His satirical remarks upon current teaching of the classics are perhaps the most effective that have ever been produced. He could, he maintained, from his own specialty, "get up an osteological primer so arid, so pedantic in its terminology, so altogether distasteful to the youthful mind, as to beat the recent famous production of the headmasters out of the field in all these excellencies.[7] Next,

---

[1] *First Report of Cross Commission* 1886, C.4863, Q.5838.
[2] Russell, ed., ii, p. 218. Letter to Mrs. Forster, 5th October, 1883.
[3] "On the Educational Value of the Natural History Sciences", printed in *Science and Education*, collected essays, vol. iii, by T. H. Huxley, pp. 38–64.
[4] *Science and Education*, p. 82.
[5] id., p. 83.
[6] id., p. 86. This definition he expanded in the next paragraph into his celebrated and slightly rhetorical version of a liberally educated man.
[7] This is a dig at Kennedy's *Latin Grammar, vide supra*, p. 191.

I could exercise my boys upon easy fossils, and bring out all their powers of memory and all their ingenuity in the application of my osteo-grammatical rules to the interpretation, or construing, of those fragments. To those who had reached the higher classes, I might supply odd bones to be built up into animals, giving great honour and reward to him who succeeded in fabricating monsters most entirely in accordance with the rules. That would answer to verse-making and essay-writing in the dead languages. . . .

"But it will be said that I am forgetting the beauty and the human interest which appertain to classical studies. To this I reply that it is only a very strong man who can appreciate the charms of a landscape as he is toiling up a steep hill, along a bad road. . . . The ordinary schoolboy is precisely in this case. He finds Parnassus uncommonly steep, and there is no chance of his having much time or inclination to look about him till he gets to the top. And nine times out of ten he does not get to the top."[1]

In his address, twelve years later, at the opening of Mason College, the forerunner of the University of Birmingham, Huxley gave his most constructive contribution to the subject. It was in this address, entitled "Science and Culture", that he paid tribute to Arnold's influence, and then proceeded to criticise what he took to be the implication of some of Arnold's well-known phrases.

The narrow view of culture, said Huxley, that was held by "a great majority of educated Englishmen, was that it was the perquisite of those who had 'learned Latin and Greek, however little', whilst one who was versed in other branches of knowledge was a 'more or less respectable specialist, not admissible into the cultured caste'."[2]

This, however, he acknowledged, was not Arnold's view. "I am too well acquainted with the generous catholicity of spirit, the true sympathy with scientific thought, which pervades the chief apostle of culture to identify him with these opinions."[3] Yet it was possible to cull from his writings "sentences which lend them some support."

"Mr. Arnold tells us that the meaning of culture is 'to know the best that has been thought and said in the world.' It is the criticism of life contained in literature." And Arnold also had

[1] *Science and Education.* pp. 99–100.
[2] id., pp. 141–2.
[3] id., p. 142.

said Europe might be regarded as one great confederation with a common outfit of a knowledge of Greek, Roman and Eastern antiquity, and of one another, and that "that modern nation will in the intellectual and spiritual sphere make the most progress, which most thoroughly carries out this programme." Therein, thought Huxley, were contained two propositions: that a criticism of life was the essence of culture, and that "literature contains the materials which suffice for the construction of such a criticism." With the first he agreed, against the second he vehemently protested.[1]

Culture meant more than learning or technical skill; it implied the possession of an ideal and the habit of critically estimating the value of things by it. Thus a criticism of life could rightly be considered the essence of culture; but literature alone was not competent to provide sufficient knowledge of life and its possibilities for the establishment of an adequate standard of value. Without physical science such a standard would be maimed and insufficient. "I should say that an Army, without weapons of precision and with no particular base of operations, might more hopefully enter upon a campaign on the Rhine than a man devoid of a knowledge of what physical science has done in the last century, upon a criticism of life."[2]

An exclusively literary education may have been a suitable road to culture in the past, but as "the distinctive character of our own times lies in the vast and constantly increasing part which is played by natural knowledge" our whole theory of life is so influenced by this new factor that a lively part of our criticism of life, the essence of culture, must be based upon a scientific education.[3] Indeed, we should misinterpret even the Greeks if we did not appreciate in them their "free employment of reason, in accordance with scientific method."[4]

Huxley was careful to show, however, that he was no Spencer. He did not wish to "depreciate the value of classical education properly undertaken, nor the importance of genuine literary education. Intellectual culture could not be complete without it, and in the present confusion of scientific studies, it probably offered the best path to culture for the majority of students, provided that its deficiences were made up by an adequate study

[1] id., p. 143.
[2] id., p. 144.
[3] id., p. 149.
[4] id., p. 152.

of science. Similarly, for those whose aptitudes lay especially along scientific lines, it was necessary, to avoid lop-sidedness, to go to the study of literature, not necessarily classical nor even foreign, but at least the literature of his own tongue, English literature which contains 'models of every kind of literary excellence'."[1]

Arnold was moved to reply in his Rede Lecture at Cambridge in 1882, entitled "Literature and Science". For this performance he had "a crowded audience."[2] and was so pleased with the reception that he had the lecture printed in the *Nineteenth Century*, and, with appropriate alterations, made it one of the three lectures of his repertoire on his first tour of America in the following year. There it proved to be a popular favourite. "There is a perfect craze in New England for hearing it" he said, where "everyone is full of the education question, and of the contest between letters and science more particularly."[3] He even delivered it in French in Quebec, and on his return held an audience of more than two thousand at Dundee in rapt attention with the self-same lecture.[4]

In it, Arnold had no difficulty in showing that Huxley had not fully comprehended his concept of culture. To know "the best that had been thought and said" meant, according to Huxley, knowing literature, and by literature he meant belles-lettres, a superficial humanism, the opposite of science or true knowledge.[5] But, Arnold pointed out, knowing belles-lettres was very far from knowing the best that had been thought and said in the world. His phrase was meant to include a knowledge of the life and genius of the people studied, "and what they were and did in the world; what we get from them, and what is its value . . ."[6] and it must certainly also include "what in modern times has been thought and said by the great observers and knowers of nature."[7] There was therefore really "no question between Professor Huxley and me as to whether knowing the great results of the modern scientific study of nature is not required as a part of our culture, as well as knowing the products of literature and art."[8]

[1] id., pp. 153–4.
[2] Russell, ed., ii, p. 200, Letter to Grant Duff, 29th July, 1882.
[3] id., ii, p. 232, Letter to Miss Arnold, 27th November, 1883; ii, p. 236, Letter to C. J. Leaf, 6th December, 1883, cf. ii, p. 233; 241.
[4] id., ii, p. 265, Letter to M. Fontanès, 2nd April, 1884; ii, p. 269, Letter to his Son (R. P. Arnold), 28th October, 1884.
[5] "Literature and Science" in *Discourses in America*, pp. 86, 90.
[6] id., p. 88.
[7] id., p. 94.
[8] id., p. 95.

Where Arnold, however, did part company with many of the advocates of the scientific cause was on this contention that in the general pursuit of culture, physical science should be "the staple of education for the bulk of mankind."[1] Huxley made no such claim as this, but he did say that "for the purpose of attaining real culture, an exclusively scientific education is at least as effectual as an exclusively literary education."[2] With this Arnold did not quarrel, but neither did he approve. He was content to point out the vital issue upon which scientific learning fell short. For him the powers which go to the building up of human life were four: "the power of conduct, the power of intellect and knowledge, the power of beauty, and the power of social life and manners."[3] One might observe further that the generality of mankind had a tendency to relate the knowledge acquired through the power of intellect and knowledge to our sense for conduct and our sense for beauty.

"We experience, as we go on learning and knowing,—the vast majority of us experience,—the need of relating what we have learnt and known to the sense which we have in us for conduct, to the sense which we have in us for beauty."[4]

Now, however much we pursue scientific studies we remain with them in the sphere of knowledge only. We may acquire interesting facts, and we may build from them important general conceptions of the universe that Professor Huxley has rightly pointed out to be of vast importance, "but still it will be *knowledge* only which they give us; knowledge not put for us into relation with our sense for conduct, our sense for beauty, and touched with emotion by being so put; not thus put for us, and therefore, to the majority of mankind, after a certain while, unsatisfying, wearying."[5]

This is the crux of Arnold's argument, and the central feature of his educational thought. It is human beings that we are educating, and our aim must therefore be to make them more perfect as human beings. When he inspected schools he looked to see what humanising influence was being exerted by the teachers and the curriculum, when he pondered the problems of educational administration he sought to devise more effective means of

---

[1] ibid.
[2] id., p. 98.
[3] id., p. 101, cf. *supra,* p. 84.
[4] id., p. 105.
[5] id., p. 112.

spreading the influence of "civilisation" which meant "the
humanisation of man in society",[1] and when he toured the schools
of foreign countries he found he had written again and again in
his notes: "the children human".[2] In the humanising process
which is education, the acquisition of knowledge was important,
but the vital functions of the educator were moral and aesthetic;
it is the "instinct for conduct" and the "instinct for beauty" that
are characteristic of humanity, and form the core which demands
to be related to all our other experience and knowledge. "Education lays hold upon us, in fact, by satisfying this demand."[3] And
it is the great function of humane letters to be the principal agents
of this synthesising process. They have the power, as "poetry and
eloquence", to engage the emotions, and in some way, incompre-
hensible to Arnold, to exert an influence upon the senses of conduct and beauty.[4] Moreover, as the discoveries of modern science
change the pattern of man's existence, enlarge the boundaries of
his knowledge, and reconstruct the framework of his thinking,
the importance of humane letters in education, becomes not less,
but all the greater. They have an ever-increasing task of relating
the new movements to man's sense of conduct and beauty. They
are the integrating force constantly endeavouring to humanise
science. "They have a fortifying, and elevating, and quickening,
and suggestive power, capable of wonderfully helping us to relate
the results of modern science to our need for conduct, our need
for beauty. . . .

"And the more that men's minds are cleared, the more that the
results of science are frankly accepted, the more that poetry and
eloquence come to be received and studied as what in truth they
really are,—the criticism of life by gifted men, alive and active
with extraordinary power at an unusual number of points;—so
much the more will the value of humane letters, and of art also,
which is an utterance having a like kind of power with theirs, be
felt and acknowledged and their place in education be secured."[5]
Arnold's advocacy of natural philosophy, or Natur-kunde, as he
called it, as a compulsory subject in elementary schools well
illustrated his position. It was a "blot", he thought that the

[1] *Vide supra*, p. 13–4. *Irish Essays*, "The Future of Liberalism," p. 108.
[2] *Special Report on Elementary Education in Germany, Switzerland, and France*, 1886,
C.4752, p. 14.
[3] *Literature and Science*, p. 115.
[4] id., p. 119 ff. Arnold used the terms "power", "sense", "instinct" for conduct,
etc., throughout his lecture with no sense of distinction between them.
[5] id., pp. 123–4.

ordinary class programme made no provision against ignorance of the system of nature.[1] Some simple instruction in the facts and laws of nature given in a single comprehensive properly proportioned course ought to be required for all who pass through the country's elementary schools.[2] But such provision must not be made at the expense of the study of literature. As the claims of technical education, and the voices of the advocates of scientific instruction grew more insistent, Arnold foresaw an increasing pressure to substitute natural science for literature. It was true that the teaching of science appeared to be more immediately useful in the improvement of health and living conditions, and for the maintenance of England's threatened leadership of the industrial world, but without the power that letters exert there would be no corresponding development in humanity, no growth towards greater human understanding and perfection.

"To have the power of using, which is the thing wished, these data of natural science, a man must, in general, have first been in some measure '*moralised*'; and for moralising him it will not be found easy, I think, to dispense with those old agents, letters, poetry, religion. So let not our teachers be led to imagine, whatever they may hear and see of the call for natural science, that their literary cultivation is unimportant. The fruitful use of natural science itself depends, in a very great degree, on having effected in the whole man, by means of letters, a rise in what the political economists call the *standard of life*."[3]

[1] Marvin, ed. *General Report for the Year* 1878, p. 183.
[2] id. (1876), pp. 169–70.
[3] id. (1876), p. 178.

CHAPTER IX

CULTURE AND THE REVISED CODE

"The weakness is in the unawakened and uninformed minds
of the majority of our school children."—M. Arnold, *General
Report for the Year* 1874, Marvin ed., p. 155.

ARNOLD'S doctrine of culture had its best-known practical
expression, during his lifetime, in his unwearied opposition to
the system of Payment by Results that came into being ten years
after his appointment to the inspectorate, remained in vogue for
the rest of his career, and was not finally superseded until some
ten years after his death.

The parliamentary grant for education had been distributed
since 1839 in accordance with Minutes agreed upon and added to
from time to time by the Committee of the Privy Council on
Education. Since 1852 it had been the practice to lay fresh
minutes on the tables of the Houses of Parliament a sufficient
time before they were called upon to vote the estimates,[1] and,
subsequently, by the Elementary Education Act of 1870, it was
enacted that a minute should not be "deemed to be in force until
it has lain for not less than one month on the table of both Houses
of Parliament."[2] It was not until 1855, however, that the minutes
were collected in one body and issued in chronological order in a
Parliamentary Paper.[3]

[1] *Parliamentary Debates*, 3rd ser., 1862, clxv, 253.
[2] § 97.
[3] A thorough history of the work of the Committee of Council on Education, and
in particular, of the Payment by Results scheme, has yet to be written. The various
codes and the chief minutes relating to them, with the most important underlined,
are to be found in *Parliamentary Papers* as follows:
Minutes arranged in Chronological order, with marginal headings of subjects;
     1854–5, xli, 191.
Consolidation of Minutes and Regulations; 1857–8, xlvi, 157.
Minutes of Committee of Council reduced into form of Code; 1860, liii, 275.
Revised Code; 1861, xlviii, 365—1862, xli, 115.
     Changes proposed; ib., 163.
     Minutes confirming alterations announced in Parliament, 13th February and
     28th March, 1862, ib., 167.
Revised Code; 1864, xliv, 501.
     Supplementary Rules; 1867–8, liii, 89.
Revised Code; 1868–9, xlvii, 227.
Revised Code (1870); 1870, liv, 243.
Minute establishing new code; 1871, lv, 303.

This may be considered to be the first code. The piecemeal publication of minutes, however, continued in the ensuing years, interrupted only by an abstract of them published in 1858, until Robert Lowe ordered a fresh codification in 1860, which dispensed with chronological order and arranged the regulations in force under appropriate subject headings. This code was issued just prior to the publication of the report of the Newcastle Commission, which had been sitting since 1858 to consider and assess the results of parliamentary encouragement to elementary education over the past two and a half decades, and it cleared the ground in preparation for a revision consequent upon the Commission's recommendations. In July 1861 the Revised Code first made its appearance, being tabled at the very end of the parliamentary session. As a result of public remonstrance during the recess it was modified, and, again revised after parliamentary criticism, was finally adopted, in May, as the "Revised Code of Minutes and Regulations of the Committee of the Privy Council on Education, 1862."[1]

The dependence of the Revised Code upon the report of the Newcastle Commissioners was made clear in the speech of the Vice-President, Robert Lowe, in introducing the first revised version of the original Revised Code on February 13th, 1862. "Lord Granville and myself felt that we could not sit still in the face of that Report, without showing the House and the country that we had done all in our power to remedy that state of things."[2] He pointed out that the Commissioners had found fault with the

New Code; 1872, xlvi, 291.
New Code; 1873, lii, 75—1874, li, 241—1875, lviii, 1.
New Code; 1875, lviii, 37.
New Code; 1876, lix, 1—1877, lxvii, 1.
New Code; 1878, lx, 177; with statement of modifications since 1873, ib., 217 (Education Code of 1878).
New Code; 1878-9, with Appendix of new articles, and articles modified, lvii, 95.

New Code; of 1880; 1880, liv, 71.	New Code; of 1890; 1890, lv, 423.
1881; 1881, lxxii, 165.	1891; 1890-1, lxi, 141.
1882; 1882, l, 511.	1892; 1892, lx, 1.
1883; 1883, lii, 59.	1893; 1893-4, lxviii, 1.
1884; 1884, lxi, 125.	1894; 1894, lxvi, 1.
1885; 1884-5, lxi, 33.	1895; 1895, lxxvi, 1.
1886; 1886, li, 43.	1896; 1896, lxiv, 1.
1887; 1887, lxv, 1.	1897; 1897, lxviii, 1.
1888; 1888, lxxviii, 51.	1898; 1898, lxix, 705.
1889; 1889, lix, 31.	1899; 1899, lxxiv, 731.

[1] It is published in full as an appendix to Matthew Arnold's *Reports on Elementary Schools*, ed. F. S. Marvin.
[2] *Parliamentary Debates*, clxv, 205. Lord Granville was Lord President of the Privy Council.

existing system on four chief grounds. It was partial, in that the foundation of elementary schools depended upon the wealth and public spirit of the inhabitants of particular districts, to the consequent educational neglect of many poorer and more needy districts. This situation was inappropriate in any system that purported to be a national one, but it was irremediable so long as the government continued its educational subsidies on the present system. Further, however, it was partial, in that, on the commissioners' estimate, only one-ninth of the children in schools which the grants of the Privy Council were intended to assist "get the benefit of a really good education."[1] This was a defect that it should be possible to remedy by a recasting of the grant system. The second great fault alluded to by the commissioners was the complexity of the system. The department paid capitation grants on attendance, grants to the certificated teachers as augmentation of their salaries in accordance with the class they obtained in their certificate examinations, grants for teaching drawing, Welsh, and Gaelic, and, lastly, grants to pupil-teachers. In consequence, the department was in direct correspondence with almost 40,000 persons on the question of salary payments, and about another 10,000 managers concerning grants and all manner of questions relating to their schools. These grants, it was recommended by the commissioners, should be swept aside, and replaced by a capitation grant from the central government payable on the basis of a scholar's attendance at school and another grant payable out of county rates upon the examination of pupils.[2] The Committee of Council, however, could not endorse the principle of local rating, and had decided upon a single grant from the central government payable upon the results of the examination of individual children. It appeared, moreover, to the Commissioners that the means of testing the efficiency of schools was rather loose. They had found that the schools "have not yet succeeded in educating to any considerable extent the bulk of the children who have passed through them,"[3] but the inspectorate continued to report that the teaching was generally excellent, and to make vague statements about the "tone", the "general efficiency", or "the general impression on the whole" of the schools under their care. Such impressionistic

---

[1] *Parliamentary Debates*, 1862, clxv, 198.
[2] *Vide supra*, pp. 109 ff.
[3] *Parliamentary Debates*, 1862, clxv, 202.

reports were clearly an inadequate guarantee of the proper employment of public money. Finally, it seemed also that this public money was being distributed in excess, to the detriment of voluntary contributions. Lowe announced, therefore: "after a review of the evils of an inadequate quantum of teaching, a loose test of efficiency, far too expensive machinery, and a decline of the voluntary spirit, we came to the conclusion that the Commissioners were right in recommending that a system of annual grants with these defects should be swept away, and a simpler one substituted in its place."[1]

Insinuating itself all through his speeches in the several debates on the Revised Code was a constant plea for the necessity of reducing expenditure. It appears, therefore, that although the report of the Newcastle Commission was the immediate pretext which startled the Committee of Council into undertaking a revision of the manner of their connection with elementary education, the real genesis of the Revised Code lay in the current demand for retrenchment. England's finances were still on a war-time footing dependent largely upon the inflated income tax that had been built up during the Crimean War. This, Gladstone, as Chancellor of the Exchequer, had promised to abolish, but had so far succeeded in reducing it only from 10d. to 9d. His constant cry, therefore, was the need for economy in government departments, and out of his apparent inability to effect it the opposition made much capital.[2] The terms of reference of the Newcastle Commission, "to consider and report what measures, if any, are required for the extension of sound and cheap elementary instruction" had reflected a growing anxiety concerning the mounting expenditure of the Committee of Council; and when the Commissioners had reported that it seemed possible that the present estimate of some £800,000 would, at no far distant date, under the existing method of management, grow to about two and a half million pounds, it was widely felt that the time for retrenchment was really due.

---

[1] id., 214. In his previous speech (11th July, 1861) on the estimates he had summed up the Commissioners' criticisms as: "First, the great expense of the present system; secondly the defective instruction given under it, thirdly, its complexity, and fourthly, its inability to remote rural districts and the lower parts of towns" (clxiv, 721).

[2] Monypenny and Buckle, ii, p. 30. Gladstone's efforts to economise became the more insistent as he had to find additional money to finance a fresh campaign of military preparedness occasioned by the war with China, and by several French scares. Out of the latter came the Volunteer Movement of which Arnold was an enthusiastic member.

Lowe made it quite clear that the Committee of Council had no intention of improving the quality of education in the schools with which it was concerned, it did not "profess to give those children an education that will raise them above their station and business in life,"[1] it desired simply to fix "a *minimum* of education, not a *maximum*."[2] To this end he would see that a great many schools which under the existing system received more than was right, and the great many teachers who had established what they thought was a vested interest in past governmental subsidy, "a sort of golden bond,"[3] would have their pretensions rudely shattered. The Committee wished to confine its total grant to schools to £500,000, equivalent to 10s. per pupil, estimating that, when the Revised Code came into operation on the 31st March, 1863, there would be an average attendance of one million children.[4] It was Lowe's duty to see that this money was not frittered away, but that the public should "get value for its money" in the most tangible fashion possible.[5] "So," he concluded, "taking denominational education based on religion as the basis of our plan, we are about to substitute for the vague and indefinite test which now exists, a definite, clear, and precise test, so that the public may know exactly what consideration they get for their money."[6] "I cannot promise the House that this system will be an economical one, and I cannot promise that it will be an efficient one, but I can promise that it shall be either one or the other. If it is not cheap it shall be efficient; if it is not efficient it shall be cheap."[7]

Lowe, of course, had the support of the Lord President, Earl Granville, who opposed any concessions which might "tend to diminish its economy and weaken the effect of the stimulus which we wished to apply to that elementary instruction."[8] With these sentiments the former Lord President, Lord Lansdowne, and C. B. Adderley, Lowe's predecessor both concurred.[9]

But the most important influence, along with the Vice-

[1] *Parliamentary Debates*, 1862, clxv, 238.
[2] id., 237. Cf. "We want not better schools, but to make them work harder" (id., 215).
[3] id., 211.
[4] id., 206–8. 10/–a head was the estimate of the Newcastle Commission of a sufficient subsidy to secure efficient teaching.
[5] id., 230.
[6] id., 242.
[7] id., 229.
[8] id., 1862, clxvi, 756.
[9] id., 756, 175.

President, in framing the revised code, appears to have been Ralph Lingen, the Permanent Secretary of the Education Department in whom Lowe found "a congenial spirit".[1] Lingen who had secured Arnold's initial appointment to the inspectorate remained Arnold's friend, despite his dictatorial manners which made him "rather a bore" and despite the important part which he played in framing and implementing the Revised Code. It is interesting to note that Lingen was eventually promoted in 1869 to the Permanent Secretaryship of the Treasury where he was reunited with Lowe the then Chancellor of the Exchequer in Gladstone's first ministry. It was said that in that post "Mr. Lowe highly prized Lingen's power of saying 'No', with an emphasis and determination which repelled the most obstinate and the most ingenious of petitioners".[2] Both were men of brilliant academic attainments and a legal training, who abhorred administrative untidiness and longed to see their work based logically with Benthamite purity and simplicity, upon a few clear principles.[3]

Arnold described their partnership in inaugurating Payment by Results as follows: "The Vice-President of the Education Department in 1861 was Lord Sherbrooke, then Mr. Lowe, an acute and brilliant man to whom pretentiousness with unsoundness was very distasteful and contemptible. The permanent secretary was one of the best and most faithful of public servants, the present Lord Lingen, who saw with apprehension the growth of school grants with the complication attending them, and was also inclined to doubt whether Government had not sufficiently done its work, and the schools might not now be trusted to go alone. These powerful officials seized upon the statements and proposals of the Commissioners, and produced, as a consequence of them, the Revised Code. But they went far beyond the Commissioners."[4]

The essential change effected by the Revised Code was to make the payment of grants to schools by the central authority dependent upon a combination of inspection and individual examination of pupils in reading, writing, and arithmetic, instead of relying upon an inspector's report on the conduct of the school

[1] *The Times*, 24th July, 1905, p. 8, a, b, obituary notice on Lord Lingen.
[2] *The Times*, id., b.
[3] Dicey, op. cit., p. 165, refers to Lowe as one of the "rigid utilitarians", and (p. 253) as "the last of the genuine Benthamites".
[4] T. H. Ward, ed., op. cit., pp. 258-9.

in general. This was no startling innovation. The pupil-teacher system, inaugurated by the Minutes of 1846, was based upon a scheme of payment by results whereby, not only the stipends of pupil-teachers and the masters and mistresses who instructed them, depended upon their successful performance in an annual examination, but even the grants paid to normal schools for their further training were distributed in the same manner.[1] Three years after Lingen had entered office he had issued a Minute dated the 2nd April, 1853, making it a condition of the payment of school grants to rural schools "that three-fourths of those above seven and under nine years of age: three-fourths of those above nine and under eleven: and three-fourths above eleven and under thirteen respectively pass such an examination before Her Majesty's inspector or assistant inspector as shall be set forth in a separate Minute of details." The explanatory circular of the following August addressed to the Inspectorate required examinations to be held only of the pupils of two divisions, those between nine and eleven, and those over eleven years of age. The examination, for example, of the lower division was to test how many were able:

(a) To read simple narratives with intelligence.
(b) To work from dictation a sum in simple subtraction, multiplication, or division correctly.
(c) To write on a slate from dictation, with correct spelling, a simple sentence twice read to them, first consecutively, and then by one word at a time.[2]

This early attempt at a scheme of partial payment by results lacked the definiteness of the later one, and remained a dead letter. But four years later the principle was applied in a prize-giving scheme adopted by the Art Section, and two years later, on an experimental scale by the Science Section of the Department of Science and Art.[3] And in a circular of the 30th September,

[1] Marvin, ed., pp. 281, 291, 294. Appendix C, Minutes by the Committee of Council on Education, dated 25th August, and 21st December, 1846.
[2] Marvin, ed., op. cit., pp. 302 ff; Minutes 1852–3, pp. 14 ff.; *vide supra*, p. 58 n.
[3] D. H. Thomas, *The Development of Technical Education in England*, 1851–89, Ph.D. Thesis, London, 1940, p. 74. A. P. Martin, *Life of Lord Sherbrooke*, ii, p. 220. *Fourth Report of the Department of Science and Art, Parliamentary Papers*, 1857 (Sess. 2), xx, 15; 5th Report, 1857–8,xxiv, 240. This report quotes Dr. Playfair's report: "The most healthy mode of doing this (encouraging local schools of Science) would appear to be by paying for the results of teaching in the way of small rewards to the taught and more considerable rewards to the teacher, or to the institutions which secure the services of competent teachers. This system will be tried on a small scale by way of experiment in some of the schools during the present year. . . ."

1857, Their Lordships asked the inspectors in all their examinations "to lay the greatest possible stress upon the ability of the children to read, write, and work sums in such a manner as will really enable them to employ those attainments in the practical business of life."[1] As has already been mentioned, the Commissioners favoured a scheme of payment by results, and the Committee of Council adopted their recommendation.

The method by which the twin framers of the Revised Code proceeded is indicated in a subsequent letter written by Lowe to Lingen. "As I understand the case," wrote Lowe, "you and I viewed the three Rs not only or primarily as the exact amount of instruction which ought to be given, but as an amount of knowledge which could be ascertained thoroughly by examination, and upon which we could safely base the Parliamentary grant. It was more a financial than a literary preference. Had there been any other branch of useful knowledge, the possession of which could have been ascertained with equal precision, there was nothing to prevent its admission. But there was not."[2]

No sooner was the first version of the Revised Code announced in July 1861, than it aroused a storm of protest. Petitions flowed in to the House of Commons and the House of Lords, meetings of teachers and other interested parties were held in various parts of the country, and letters, pamphlets, and resolutions were rained upon the heads of all members of parliament. Lowe pictured himself, in a speech when parliament resumed, as sitting during the recess by ever-increasing piles of broad sheets, newspapers, remonstrances, magazine articles, and pamphlets, the volume of which he had never previously encountered. It is a little surprising to find, therefore, that despite this work of protest expressed by the general public who were interested in education, opposition to the Revised Code within parliament was not very strenuous.[3] A substantial amendment was secured in the terms of government grants to schools, but the basic principle of payment by results was not seriously challenged and appeared to be acquiesced in by almost every speaker during the debates.

---

[1] Minutes 1857–8, p. 25, Instructions to Inspectors. Extract from Circular Letter to H.M.I.'s, dated 30th September, 1857.

[2] A. P. Martin, op. cit., ii, p. 217. Letter dated 17th March, 1882.

[3] The debates on the questions, recorded in *Hansard*, have very little spirit. The leader writer of the *Daily News* (29th March, 1862) referred to the House as "fatigued and bored". "Very few members have spoken, the prevailing desire being to get a troublesome matter over as soon as possible, but the arguments have immensely preponderated in favour of the Revised Code".

The most powerful and important pamphlet that appeared early in the controversy was a "Letter to Earl Granville, K.C., on The Revised Code" by the veteran educator and godparent of the existing system, Sir James Kay-Shuttleworth.[1] Arnold remarked, "Shuttleworth has just published a most important pamphlet . . . it sells like wildfire."[2] It examined the new proposals in great detail, vigorously argued their fallacies, and foretold the mechanisation of teaching, contraction of school studies, and impoverishment of the teaching profession that would ensue.

Arnold decided to follow Kay-Shuttleworth's lead. His view of the latter's pamphlet he expressed as follows: "For readers already familiar with the subject, for school-managers, school-teachers, school inspectors, it is admirable: for the general reader it is somewhat too copious."[3]

His aim, therefore, was to provide a general examination of the Revised Code not with the meticulous attention to detail of Kay-Shuttleworth's Letter but on broad principles, summing up the controversy in a way suitable to the needs of the intelligent public. He therefore contributed to *Fraser's Magazine* in March 1862, a somewhat lengthy article entitled "The Twice-Revised Code". This was also printed separately as a pamphlet and had a wide distribution.

"I hope," he wrote to his mother, "I have supplied a readable popular statement of the case against them which will take hold and do good. Lady de Rothschild writes me word that she is making Disraeli read it who wants just such a brief to speak from: and Shuttleworth and his Anti-Code Committee think it may be so useful that they have asked me to get leave from the editor for them to reprint it for distribution to Members of Parliament."[4] Three weeks later he "had just heard from Shuttleworth that my paper is reprinted and that he had sent me twenty copies, and a copy to every Member of each House of Parliament."[5]

At the beginning of his article, Arnold stated his aim. "For those . . . who desire only to know the essential facts of the case, so

[1] The Letter, dated 4th November, 1861, was published by Smith, Elder & Co., London, 1861, and was reprinted in the following year in *Four Periods of Public Examination as reviewed in* 1832–1839–1846–1862 *in papers by Sir James Kay-Shuttleworth, Bart.,* Longmans, London, 1862, pp. 574–638.

[2] Russell, ed., Letter to his Mother, 13th November, 1861, i, p. 150.

[3] "The Twice-Revised Code", *Fraser's Magazine*, vol. lxv, March 1862, p. 347.

[4] Russell, ed., Letter to his Mother, 5th March, 1862, i, p. 161.

id., 24th March, 1862, i, p. 167.

as to be able to form an opinion upon it a simpler statement (than Kay-Shuttleworth's) is required,—a statement dealing less with the details of the subject and more with its *rationale*. Such a statement we here propose to attempt."[1]

He endeavoured to show: "1. What it is that the Revised Code will actually do; 2. Why its authors are trying to do this; 3. What is the merit of the design in itself, and what, moreover, is the prospect of its accomplishing what it intends."[2]

The Revised Code would actually succeed in reducing considerably existing State grants for education, and should therefore also have the effect of reducing State influence in education much to the delight of the Voluntaryists. "The secretary who drew up the new Code should have been Mr. Miall; the vice-president who defended it should have been Mr. Baines."[3] And the justification for such a procedure? It lay in a concept of the State's role in education that could be summed up in pseudo-Benthamite phraseology as: "The duty of a State in public education is, when clearly defined, to obtain the greatest possible quantity of reading, writing, and arithmetic for the greatest number."[4] The State has hitherto been concerned with "paying for discipline, for civilisation, for religious and moral training, for a superior instruction to clever and forward children."[5] In this it was acting outside its rightful sphere and it must in future give up such pretensions of civilising its citizens to ensure that, by a system of prize-giving called "payment by results", they concentrate solely upon reading, writing, and arithmetic. The twin principles, then, upon which the Revised Code was based were *"payment by results"*, and *"the lowering the standard of popular education"*.[6] A third principle has also been added, that of "the *extending more widely the area and benefit* of popular education." In respect to this principle, it must be admitted that the existing system left untouched many necessitous areas in the country, but it was not too much to ask the supporters of the Revised Code how their system would improve the situation. It appeared, on the face of it, that the new system would not redistribute educational energies and facilities throughout the country, but

---

[1] *Fraser's Magazine*, lxv, 1862, p. 347.
[2] ibid.
[3] id., p. 348.
[4] ibid.
[5] ibid.
[6] id., p. 349.

would simply reduce them all round. The principles of the new Code therefore remain as above, *"reduction* and a *prize scheme."* [1]

We come then to consider what are its merits and what its prospects. It was claimed that, under the new dispensation, the criticism of the Newcastle Commissioners, that the lower grades were being neglected in favour of a few extra accomplishments for the members of the upper grades, would be remedied. Arnold acknowledged the great want of literacy in the schools, but claimed that the neglect of the pupils in the lower grades was vastly exaggerated. In later life he went so far as to say that "I have always thought that the Commissioners, finding in the state of the junior classes and of the elementary matters of instruction a point easy to be made and strikingly effective, naturally made it with some excess of energy and pressed it too hard." [2] The main difficulty was not the teachers' preference for the subjects of the upper grades but simply the shortness of school life. This was borne out a few years later when the Committee of Council asked its inspectors in 1866 and 1867 to report upon the chief difficulties of current education. The consensus of opinion was that "the two great hindrances to education" were irregular attendance and the early age at which pupils leave school. [3] Given a school life of only two or three years, often of erratic attendance, a low standard of literacy was not to be wondered at. To this Arnold added also "the utter want of care for books and knowledge in the homes from which the majority of them come forth, to which the great majority of them return." [4] If the schools were examined not from the point of view of how much reading, writing, and arithmetic their pupils could be formally instructed in, but how much they had humanised and advanced the children of the labouring classes in civilisation, one would have a fairer measure of their worth.

This was the important feature of Arnold's argument. He looked upon the schools as centres of culture, civilising influences for the elevation of the lower classes towards the general perfection at which culture aimed. The government's grant in aid should, therefore, be "given to a school not as a mere machine for teaching reading, writing, and arithmetic, but as a living whole with

[1] id., p. 350.
[2] T. A. Ward, ed., op. cit., p. 260.
[3] Minutes (1867), pp. 114, 175–7, 238–9; (1867–8) pp. 85–6, 95, 210, 243.
[4] *Fraser's Magazine*, lxv, 1862, p. 353.

complex functions, religious, moral, and intellectual."[1] By concentrating upon machinery the government fell into the typical middle class fault of tinkering with the superficial aspects of a subject without taking the trouble to think the problem through, get to the fundamental principles, and act accordingly. Hence, also, the other merit urged for this "reduction and prize-scheme" policy, that, at last, the State by paying on results of the 3 Rs only would resume its real function in education, was based upon a short-sighted misconception.

Here, Arnold showed once more how his doctrine of culture and his doctrine of the State were to be combined. Patrick Cumin, an old friend of Arnold's, who later became Permanent Secretary to the Education Department, had alleged that the lower classes were not interested in anything but the rudiments of education, and that the higher instruction given was merely a conceit of the teachers; but he was undoubtedly wrong. For the lower classes, though their efforts were often misguided, were profoundly interested in raising themselves through education, and this effort deserved the assistance and, what was more important, the direction of the State. In this there was a distinct line of cleavage between Arnold and the advocates of the Revised Code. The latter still held a view of the function of the State as little removed from that of a policeman. Its interference was to be carefully checked wherever possible, and in education it should be confined to ensuring that only a necessary minimum of instruction was meted out. Arnold, on the other hand, saw it as the embodiment of the collective wisdom of the nation which should use its influence to raise its people's standards even higher and higher. It was a directing, elevating force. And, through its servants, the best that had been thought and said could be brought to contribute to the growth of culture among its people. It was therefore calamitous to confine its ministrations to rewarding success in teaching the rudiments only. "Other matters, really of vital importance to the state—the humanising of that multitude of children where home-training is defective, . . . the forming of those habits of order, discipline, and neatness" and "the discipline, efficiency and general character of schools,"[2] which must become secondary under the principles of the Revised Code, were more truly the educative concern of the State. With the new scheme

[1] id., p. 354.
[2] id., p. 357.

"under the specious plea of simplifying and giving greater liberty of action to managers," "something *vital* in the connection established between the State and the lower classes by the old system"[1] would be lost.

"For it withdraws from popular education, so far as it can, all serious guidance, all initiatory direction by the State; it makes the action of the State upon this as mechanical, as little dynamical, as possible."[2]

Arnold's criticism was being directed at the Code when it still contained the proposal to pay the whole educational grant on the basis of individual examination in the 3 Rs after a favourable report in general by the inspector. It was obvious that the proviso of a general report from the inspector would be nugatory, and that the real business, on which he would also inevitably base his report, would be the examination festival. Arnold contended that the State would really be better served by adhering to its old policy of making a *"grant for maintenance"*, rather than a distribution of prize-money on the basis of an inspector's report that the "discipline, efficiency, and general character" of a school were satisfactory.[3] He was hopeful but not confident that the Revised Code would be rejected. "The friends of the Revised Code were numerous, resolute and powerful." Mr. Lowe, *The Times* "which naturally upholds Mr. Lowe", the *Daily News*, the friends of economy at any price, the "selfish vulgar of the upper classes", the "clever and fastidious" would all be gratified by the triumph of the Revised Code.[4] Nevertheless during the session of parliament which opened in February 1862 at which Arnold directed his manifesto, the Code was so far modified as to make one-third of the grant dependent upon the attendance of pupils subject to inspection of the type which Arnold advocated. This modification was directly due to Spencer Walpole[5] who put forward a set of Resolutions which Lowe eventually, in large part, accepted. Walpole was supported chiefly by Arnold's brother-in-law, W. E. Forster, and there can be little doubt that this first successful onslaught on the Revised Code was very largely the

[1] id., p. 360.
[2] ibid.
[3] id., p. 356.
[4] id., p. 365.
[5] Walpole (1806–98) Conservative M.P. was three times Home Secretary and is chiefly remembered for his undistinguished handling of the Hyde Park Reform League Meetings in 1867. This episode is featured several times in Arnold's *Culture and Anarchy*.

fruit of Arnold's agitation. On the very day on which Walpole's Resolutions were presented there appeared in the *Daily News* a letter signed "A Lover of Light". This, full of his usual "vivacities", was Arnold's attempt to set the question of examinations in a more proper light. He was replying to Lord Overstone,[1] who had declared that he had progressed far more rapidly under the tuition of Blomfield, later to become Bishop of London, who submitted him constantly to examination, than he had in his earlier schooling at Eton. Arnold pointed out that the use of an examination as a stimulus was good policy, and that was what Blomfield had done with the young Overstone. "No doubt Lord Overstone got on better the more Bishop Blomfield examined him. But the question is—Is it a good thing to make the scholar's success in his examination the sole measure of the payment of those who educate him? If Lord Overstone's father had proposed to Bishop Blomfield to make his son's performance in an examination at the end of the year the basis for fixing what he should pay for that year's schooling, and proposed this before the Bishop could know the admirable talents which Lord Overstone, under his care, was to develop, would the excellent tutor have 'willingly submitted'? If he did not submit, ought he to have submitted? Would his 'shrinking' from this test have implied that there was 'something unsound' even in that tuition which has made Lord Overstone what we see him? Would the Bishop have deserved all the deprecatory sarcasm of Mr. Lowe, all the exquisite amenities of *The Times*, for shrinking from it?

"For this is all that the managers of schools are doing!"[2]

Forster told Arnold that he thought this letter "one of the most telling and useful strokes in the whole contest."[3] Certainly, in the debate the same evening Forster modelled much of his speech on the lines of Arnold's letter, whilst Walpole, whether or not he was influenced by "The Twice Revised Code", put the most stress, in his opening remarks, upon its main argument that as the chief function of the elementary schools was to civilise their neighbourhood, "how, in the name of common sense, can the Government set up a scheme which takes away all provision for

---

[1] S. J. Loyd, first Baron Overstone (1796–1883) was a leading banker and one of the wealthiest men in England.

[2] *Daily News*, 25th March, 1862. Lowe's eventual acceptance of most of Walpole's proposals, the following Saturday, was characterised by the *Daily News* as a "humiliating capitulation", 29th March, 1862.

[3] Russell, ed., *Letter to his Wife*, 30th March, 1862, p. 169.

the due encouragement of that object, and distributes the education grants for totally different purposes?"[1] The upshot of the week's debates and agitation was that the Revised Code was modified in three particulars. A third of the grant, instead of none at all, was to depend solely upon a pupil's attendance and the favourable report of the inspector. Children were not to be grouped by age but by educational standards for the purpose of being presented for examination and, thirdly, although the Committee of Council would in future have no responsibility for the stipends of pupil-teachers, those apprenticed before the 30th June, 1862, who were to have been summarily cut off, were guaranteed their maintenance until the end of their apprenticeship.

The compromise could not, of course, satisfy Arnold who considered that it still left "a great deal to be done. That it is as good as it is, is in great measure due to William (Forster), his earnestness, his thorough knowledge of the subject, and the courage which his reputation for honesty gave to other Liberals to follow him in opposing the Code."[2]

The critical parts of the Revised Code appeared in Chapter 2, Part 1, Section i, and read as follows:

"40. The managers of schools may claim at the end of each year, defined by Article 17:—

(a) The sum of 4s. per scholar according to the average number in attendance throughout the year at *the morning and afternoon* meetings of their school, and 2s. 6d. per scholar according to the average number in attendance throughout the year at *the evening meetings* of their school.

(b) For every scholar who has attended more than 200 morning or afternoon meetings of their school:—

   (1) If more than six years of age 8s., subject to examination (Article 48).

   (2) If under six years of age 6s. 6d., subject to a report by the inspector that such children are instructed suitably to their age, and in a manner not to interfere with the instruction of the older children.

(c) For every scholar who has attended more than 24 evening meetings of their school 5s., subject to examination (Article 48).

44. Every scholar attending more than 200 times in the

[1] *Parliamentary Debates*, clxvi, 34.
[2] Russell, ed., Letter to his Wife, 30th March, 1862, i, p. 169.

morning or afternoon, for whom 8s. is claimed, forfeits 2s. 8d. for failure to satisfy the inspector in reading, 2s. 8d. in writing, and 2s. 8d. in arithmetic (Article 48).

45. Every scholar attending more than twenty-four times in the evening for whom 5s. is claimed, forfeits 1s. 8d. for failure to satisfy the inspector in reading, 1s. 8d. in writing, and 1s. 8d. in arithmetic (Article 48).

46. Every scholar for whom the grants dependent upon examination are claimed must be examined according to one of the following standards, and must not be presented for examination a second time according to the same or a lower standard.

47. Under any Half Time Act, 100 attendances qualify scholars for the grant:—
  (a) Upon examination.
  (b) Without examination, after they have passed according to the highest standard, but continue to attend school under the Act.

48	Standard I	Standard II	Standard III
Reading	Narrative in monosyllables.	One of the Narratives next in order after monosyllables in an elementary reading book used in the school.	A short paragraph from an elementary reading book used in the school.
Writing	Form on blackboard or slate, from dictation, letters, capital and small, manuscript.	Copy in manuscript character a line of print.	A sentence from the same paragraph, slowly read once, and then dictated in single words.
Arithmetic	Form on blackboard or slate, from dictation, figures up to 20; name at sight figures up to 20; add and subtract figures up to 10 orally, from examples on blackboard.	A sum in simple addition or subtraction, and the multiplication table.	A sum in any simple rule as far as short division (inclusive).

48	Standard IV	Standard V	Standard VI
Reading	A short paragraph from a more advanced reading book used in the school.	A few lines of poetry from a reading book used in the first class of the school.	A short ordinary paragraph in a newspaper or other modern narrative.

| Writing | A sentence slowly dictated once by a few words at a time, from the same book, but not from the paragraph read. | A sentence slowly dictated once, by a few words at a time, from a reading book used in the first class of the school. | Another short ordinary paragraph in a newspaper, or other narrative, slowly dictated once by a few words at a time. |
| Arithmetic | A sum in compound rules (money). | A sum in compound rules (common weights and measures). | A sum in practice or bills of parcels. |

49. The grant may either be withheld altogether or reduced for causes arising out of the state of the school.

50. The inspector does not proceed to examine scholars in reading, writing, and arithmetic for the grant, until he has first ascertained that the state of the school does not require it to be withheld.

51. The grant is withheld altogether:—

(a) If the school be not held in a building certified by the inspector to be healthy, properly lighted, drained, and ventilated, supplied with offices, and containing in the principal school-room at least 80 cubical feet of internal space for each child in average attendance.

(b) If the principal teacher be not duly certificated (Article 67), and duly paid. . . .

(c) If the girls in the school be not taught plain needlework as part of the ordinary course of instruction.

(d) If the registers be not kept with sufficient accuracy to warrant confidence in the returns. . . ."

The approximate ages at which "the several standards are intended to be passed" were given in a report of 1868[1] as:

Years between	6 & 7	7 & 8	8 & 9	9 & 10	10 & 11	11 & 12
Standards ..	I	II	III	IV	V	VI

Thus was the Revised Code launched in 1862. It is not difficult to see how it came into being. It was conceived in an ungenerous view of the function of the State in National Education, born of utilitarian precision out of post-war financial stringency, and

[1] *Minutes of Committee of Council*, 1868–9, p. xxi.

delivered, amid the bystanders' protests, by the grimmest most unrelenting attendants that any child of English education has ever had to encounter. The birth was undoubtedly Caesarian.

If the establishment of Payment by Results is not surprising, its continuance over three decades is a little more difficult to account for.

Fundamentally it was probably attributable to an unwillingness of the central government to accept a wholehearted responsibility for directing and planning national education. It was willing to admit an interest but only to the extent of seeing that elementary schools conformed at least to certain minima that the central authority felt should be incorporated in their programmes. Although the trend towards collectivism and a social service state was growing throughout this period, the time had not yet arrived when the State could be regarded as the educator of the nation. It had to await the development of other machinery. Arnold put the same point a little differently when he wrote that "the State has an interest in the primary school as a *civilising agent*, even prior to its interest in it as an *instructing agent*. When this is once clearly seen nothing can resist it, and it is fatal to the new Code. If we can get this clearly established in this discussion a great point will have been gained for the future dealings of the State with education, and I shall hope to see State-control reach in our time our middle and upper schools."[1]

The acceptance of an extension of the sphere of State educational responsibility, however, had to await the emergence of local machinery to deal with the new concept. It is noticeable that with the development of school boards, and a more coherent local government system in the counties, the system of payment by results was steadily broken up. By the turn of the century it had passed out of existence at the same time as the central government was busy recognising the ability of local government authorities to assume satisfactorily the direction of the State's educational service.[2]

---

[1] Russell, ed., Letter to his Mother, 5th March, 1862, i, p. 162.
[2] Arnold in evidence before the Cross Commission in 1886 alluded further to this view.
Q.6141. "You seemed to think that if the principle of payment by results were abolished you would throw the provision of the means upon some local bodies?"—"I should".
Q.6142. "Do you think that in England in the localities there is a sufficient faith in education to make that a safe experiment?"—"There is no machinery at present; you have to make your local government. That England is in an absolutely chaotic state as to local government everybody is agreed; but if the country was covered with municipalities like Germany, or America, you might require what was necessary."

Arnold's above remarks, however, implied more than the need for adequate State machinery upon which acceptance of fuller educational responsibility largely depended. They drew attention also to the need for an enlarged concept of the role of education. The thirty years following the adoption of the Revised Code saw just such an enlargement, to which Arnold himself made no mean contribution. The needs of an industrial economy and the growing popularity of science increasingly showed the inadequacy of confining elementary education to instruction in the 3 Rs. But, above all, the system of Payment by Results was rendered untenable, by the growing consciousness that as the "poorest he that is in England" was politically the equal of the "greatest he", the life he had to live and his education should also be equally human.

The Revised Code, however, was not without its redeeming features. It retained the requirement that schools eligible for grant must be under the care of a certificated teacher, and its authors resisted an amendment in committee proposing the abolition of this condition. It did also lay emphasis upon individuals as distinct from classes, so that greater attention was probably paid to the requirements of individual pupils, within the very narrow limits presented, than ever before. These limits were extended from time to time as the administration became more enlightened.

Four chief modifications were made. Careful analysis during the early years of the working of the Revised Code showed the Committee of Council that whereas they had thought that the younger pupils had been neglected in favour of the older ones, now the pendulum had swung the other way. "The Revised Code has tended, at least temporarily, to discourage attention to the higher branches of elementary instruction—geography, grammar, and history."[1] Accordingly, in 1867, extra grants were offered to schools which taught one or more "specific" subjects beyond the 3 Rs.

In 1871, following Forster's Elementary Education Act, a New Code was instituted. To Arnold's disappointment, Forster did not fulfil the early promise that his 1862 speeches betokened. He wrote fifteen years later: "The false direction given by the Revised Code to teaching Mr. Forster did not correct; 'payment by results' he left as he found it. I doubt whether he even took its faults and fallacies into his mind at all."[2] The 1871 Code first

[1] *Minutes of Committee of Council*, 1865-6, p. xiii.
[2] T. H. Ward, ed., op. cit., p. 265.

made a special grant for each individual pupil passing in a "specific" subject. These subjects were restricted to the upper standards IV—VI, and might be "geography, history, grammar, algebra, geometry, political economy, languages, or *any* definite subject of instruction. . . ."[1]

The next major expansion took place in 1875 with the introduction of "class" subjects. Four shillings per pupil was to be paid if the classes, from standard II—VI, were to pass a creditable examination in any two subjects out of grammar, history, elementary geography, and plain needlework. This was a substantial inroad upon the principle of individual examination which had been the basis of the system of payment by results, and Arnold hailed it joyfully. "The introduction of class subjects has been of great benefit. . . . The spread of interest in education was already doing much to re-awaken and re-invigorate our schools, bound in a narrow routine and dispirited as many of them certainly were. The introduction of the class subjects of grammar, geography, and history, has also done much in the same direction, and will do more."[2]

In 1882 the new Vice-President, A. J. Mundella, made extensive alterations. A seventh standard was added, and the number of "specific" subjects was greatly increased, while English was made a compulsory "class" subject. But, most important of all, the grant made in future on the basis of average attendance was increased, and was to be supplemented by a Merit Grant which gave the inspectors the discretionary power of adding to the grant, earned by individual examination, a bonus based on their assessment of the quality of the teaching and the general conduct of the school.

Following on the recommendations of the Cross Commission, the New Code of 1890 trebled the grant paid on average attendance, and abolished the original, Revised Code payment on the results of examination in the three Rs. This marked the virtual abandonment of the system. Its overthrow was completed by a series of Minutes between 1895 and 1897 which swept away the remaining payments on individual examination in "specific" subjects.[3]

---

[1] *Parliamentary Papers*, 1871, lv, 321, Schedule iv.
[2] Marvin, ed., (*General Report for 1876*), pp. 167–8.
[3] A detailed summary of the development of the elementary school curriculum and the changes in the Codes is given in *Special Reports on Educational Subjects*, 1896–7, chap. I, by M. E. Sadler and J. W. Edwards, pp. 33–45, 56–70, H.M.S.O., 1897.

When Arnold published his first criticism of the Revised Code, he was a little apprehensive as to its possible effect upon his career in the Education Department. It had become known in the office, though he wrote anonymously, that he was writing against the Code, and even his former chief, Lord Lansdowne, appeared to be a little cool. "I don't think, however, they can eject me," Arnold wrote to his wife, "though they can and perhaps will, make my place uncomfortable."[1] He was eventually completely reassured by Forster's opinion that the department "cannot touch me", and by an amiable dinner party with the Lingens after the Revised Code had received parliamentary revision and approval.[2]

His apprehension on that occasion, however, was not sufficient to prevent his continuing to oppose official policy, and his campaign went on biennially in his General Reports. In the Preface to his reports on Schools and Universities on the Continent, he was able to insert some critical remarks also, but he admitted that the "part of it, where I touch on the Revised Code, needed very delicate handling."[3] He was not always so tactful, however, and his reports were sometimes so outspoken that they were returned for revision and one, for 1862, was suppressed.[4] This was concerned chiefly with the evils of having to give notice of inspection to schools, necessitated by the introduction of the Revised Code. He considered that it was impossible thereby to obtain a true idea of the normal working of a school. It was true that the giving of notice, and thus time for preparation, would make inspectorial visits equally fair to all schools, "but if it is a Government's object to learn, through its Inspectors, the condition of aided schools, as it really is, it can be no great satisfaction to it to know that it gets an equally false impression of that of all of them."[5]

In his evidence before the Select Committee on Education with respect to the Reports of Her Majesty's Inspectors of Schools,

---

[1] Russell, ed., Letter to his Wife, 28th March, 1862, i, p. 168.

[2] id., Letter to his Wife, 30th March, 1862, i, p. 169; to his Mother, 28th June, 1862, p. 172.

[3] id., Letter to his Mother, 16th November, 1867, i, p. 376.

[4] Parliamentary Papers, 1864, ix, 94. Report on Education (Inspectors' Reports), App. A, p. 4. The Report is there printed in full. It does not appear in either of the collections of Arnold's Reports made by Sandford (1889) and Marvin (1908). His report for the year 1861 was printed only in part, but Arnold destroyed the remainder of the mss. so that it was not possible to reproduce it with the 1862 Report in the above Parliamentary Papers. His letter (dated 25th June, 1864) describing its fate may be read in Parliamentary Papers, 1864, ix, 115, ib., App. B, p. 25.

[5] Parliamentary Papers, 1864, ix, 95, ib., App. A, p. 5.

in 1864, Arnold stated that his 1862 report had been returned
unmarked to him requesting his alteration of it on the ground
that it did not conform to the inspectors' instructions. "I sent it
back", he went on, "saying that I did not see in what way it did
not conform to the instructions, but if it were pointed out to me
that in any way it did not conform to the instructions, I would
alter it. I heard no more of it; it was suppressed."[1] His previous
report for 1861, had contained references to fresh information he
had just received from France on the teaching of the 3 Rs which
tended to show that the proposed method of the Revised Code
for dealing with backwardness in these subjects was "not the best
way of mending them."[2] This matter would have appeared in
his report just at the time when the Revised Code was under
consideration in Parliament. Arnold said that "as it bore upon
matters that were being discussed here at the time about instruction, and the relations of schools to Government and to local
bodies, I thought it was extremely interesting."[3] So apparently
also did Lingen, who marked the offending passage, sent it with a
minute, for perusal by Robert Lowe, and returned it to Arnold
for deletion on the ground that he had already had a report on
French education printed at public expense and could not expect
to have further information on the same subject printed at further
expense in his general report!

Throughout his reports there were three main lines along
which he directed his criticism of the Revised Code; its effect
upon the pupils, its effect upon inspection, and its effect upon
teacher-training.

On his return from the Continent in 1867 he was called upon
to produce his first general report for four years. In it he recorded
his melancholy impression of the change that had taken place.
"I find in them, in general, if I compare them with their former
selves, a deadness, a slackness, and a discouragement which are
not the signs and accompaniments of progress. If I compare them
with the schools of the Continent I find in them a lack of intelligent
life much more striking now than it was when I returned from
the Continent in 1859.

"This change is certainly to be attributed to the school legislation of 1862."[4]

[1] id., Q.585.
[2] id., Q.592.
[3] id., Q.593.
[4] Marvin, ed., (1867) pp. 102–3.

"In a country", he continued, "where everyone is prone to rely too much on mechanical processes, and too little on intelligence, a change in the Education Department's regulations, which by making two-thirds of the Government grant depend upon a mechanical examination, inevitably gives a mechanical turn to the school teaching, a mechanical turn to the inspection, is and must be trying to the intellectual life of a school."[1] In this respect the introduction of "specific" subjects in 1867 was no improvement, for they were to be examined on the same mechanical plan. "The Minute though it is meant to give relief to sufferers under the Revised Code, is a stupendous specimen of the intricate, overlaboured, and puzzling regulations of our office."[2] "It attempts to lay down, to the very letter, the requirements which shall be satisfied in order to earn grants. The teacher, in consequence, is led to think, not about teaching his subject, but about managing to hit those requirements."[3] The study of "specific" subjects had been intended to broaden out the grasp of the elder children, but by tying it closely into the scheme of payment by results, the enrichment that it effected was almost negligible. Of this situation Arnold gave several examples. "A child who has never heard of Paris or Edinburgh, will tell you measurements of England in length and breadth, and square mileages till his tongue is tired. I have known a class, presented in English history, to take the period from Caesar's landing to the Norman Conquest, and to be acquainted in much detail with the Roman invasion of Anglesey; but Carnarvon, on the coast opposite Anglesey, being mentioned, they neither knew what Prince of Wales was born there, nor to whom the title of Prince of Wales belonged."[4] This sort of result indicated a narrowness of instruction and sterility that were as far removed from the really pressing task of elementary education as could be imagined. As instruments of elevation, as a means of civilising the lower classes in a critical period of English history, as a vital factor in fitting those classes to play the all-important part to which they would surely one day be called, existing elementary schools were a failure. "The animation of mind, the multiplying of ideas, the promptness to connect, in the thoughts, one thing with another, and to illustrate one thing by another, are what are wanted; just

[1] id., (1867) pp. 112–3.
[2] Russell, ed., Letter to his Mother, 2nd March, 1867, i, p. 353.
[3] Marvin, ed., (1869), p. 129.
[4] id., (1869) p. 130.

what *letters*, as they are called, are supposed to communicate."[1] Hence Arnold's advocacy of grammar and English literature in elementary schools, and his attempt to insist on intelligent reading in the schools of his district. He was glad when one effect of the Revised Code appeared to be the marketing of improved text-books for elementary reading. "At last the compilers of these works seem beginning to understand that the right way of teaching a little boy to read is not by setting him to read such sentences as these (I quote from school works till lately much in vogue): 'the crocodile is viviparous,' 'quicksilver, antimony, calamine, zinc, etc., are metals, . . .' Reading books are now published which reject all such trash as the above, and contain nothing but what has really some fitness for reaching the end which reading books were meant to reach."[2] But the use made of such books in pursuance of the letter of the Revised Code went far to destroy their value. The same book was read over and over again, and the children were examined on it alone with the result that they could read the necessary sentence or two from it quite fluently but they could read no other book. "The circle of the children's reading has thus been narrowed and impoverished all the year for the sake of a *result* at the end of it, and the *result* is an illusion."[3]

Such were the outspoken comments which Arnold recorded as his impressions of the cramping effect of the Revised Code upon the general conduct of schools. It comes then as rather a shock to find that he did not object to the principle of Payment by Results. He did not wish to see the system abolished, but only modified. "No one questions the advantage of an individual grant-rewarded examination, or that the Newcastle Commissioners did well in suggesting it, or that the Education Department did well in giving effect to this suggestion; . . . the real question is whether we have not somewhat overdone this sort of examination by attaching to it so overwhelming an importance; and whether some improved mode of combining it with the old inspection might not be hit on."[4] He accordingly suggested a triple division of the grant, an attendance grant, as already in

---

[1] id., (1874) p. 156.
[2] id., (1863) pp. 97-8.
[3] id., (1869) p. 126. Concerning similar effects in arithmetic, Arnold quoted a colleague's report: "Unless a vigorous effort is made to infuse more intelligence into its teaching, *Government arithmetic* will soon be known as a modification of the science peculiar to inspected schools, and remarkable chiefly for its meagreness and sterility" (p. 128).
[4] id., (1869) p. 132.

operation, of 4/–, an elementary examination grant reduced to
6/–, and a higher instruction grant of 3/–, making in all 13/–
instead of the existing 12/–. On this plan the grant on the results
of individual examination would form less than half the total
instead of two-thirds, and the merits of pre-Revised Code inspection would be restored, for the higher instruction grant was to
depend upon four things, an adequate staffing ratio of pupil-
teachers, and the opinion of the inspector, that the school is taught
with "intelligence", that a "proper extent" is given to the instruction, and that the work is done "in good form and style."[1] This
suggestion was, in fact, an anticipation of the Merit Grant
instituted in Mundella's code of 1882. His proposal, nevertheless,
did embody a retention of payment by results, even if it was in a
reduced form, and it is very difficult to reconcile this with his
criticisms. In the same passage he said, "Certainly, if a man
wants a certificate, or a diploma, or honours, of you, you must
fix just what he shall get them for, which is by no means of the
same extent as a liberal education. . . . But, at any rate, to
make a narrowing system of test examinations govern the whole
inspection of our primary schools, when we have before us not
individuals wanting a diploma from us, but organisations wanting
to be guided by us into the best way of learning and teaching, seems
like saddling ourselves with a confessed cause of imperfection un-
necessarily."[2] This was quite sound, and in accordance with his more
general reflections upon culture and the guiding influence of the
State. But to suggest a reduction rather than an abolition of the current practice was to countenance still the very principle of payment
by results that he considered vicious. He seems to have been led
astray through his desire to retain the individual examination of
pupils as a stimulus to teaching; and, as individual examination
was the established technique of the system of payment by results,
he appears temporarily at least, to have identified the two. Now,
it is perfectly possible, though difficult, to devise examinations
that shall stimulate without formalising education,[3] but the same
tests cannot be equally valid as a stimulus to teaching and as a
measure for the assessment of a teacher's salary. For the first
should be essentially mobile and suited to individual requirements,
whilst the second, for fairness' sake, must be based upon a rigid,
well-announced standard.

[1] id., (1869), pp. 136–7.
[2] id., (1869) p. 134.
[3] *Vide* D. A. T. Gasking, *Examinations and the Aims of Education*, Melb. Univ. Press 1945, for an excellent examination of this question.

In his final comprehensive statement on elementary education Arnold somewhat made amends for the suggestions of his 1869 Report. He gave evidence, lasting for two days, in 1886, before the Cross Commission which was then enquiring into the working of the Elementary Education Acts. Frederick Temple, a member of the Commission, then Bishop of London, later Archbishop of Canterbury, and formerly himself one of Her Majesty's Inspectors of Schools and Headmaster of Rugby, questioned Arnold closely concerning his views on payment by results. He pointed out that though Arnold had, in earlier evidence, expressed disapproval of the system, and had objected even to "class" and "specific" subjects since a grant was still made to depend on them, he had yet suggested that a payments by results examination for the original three lower standards only would have been a suitable introduction in 1862 instead of the more drastic Revised Code. This, thought Temple, was hardly a logical position. Arnold, however, explained that he had taken up that viewpoint because "at the time, with the tastes of England" it "might have been a good thing."[1] His present inclination concerning standards and examinations based on them was to "sweep them all away together, and prescribe the work for each class so many hours in each subject, to approve the books, and to have the teachers better trained."[2] When pressed further, he agreed with Bishop Temple that the examinations set were not of the right character and that his objection was not to individual examinations but the payment of grant on the result of a pupil's examination.[3] When asked what guarantee he would require to justify a government grant, he suggested that the most suitable procedure would be to provide a school with "the funds necessary for keeping it properly found and properly staffed without prizes and grants of money besides,"[4] and if as a result of a careful examination by the inspector, the teaching was found to be faulty, to penalise not the school by a reduction of grant but the teacher by removal or demotion. "No fine, but capital punishment?" one of the Commissoners appropriately suggested.[5] The stimulus to teaching by "fear of dismissal on the part of the teacher", in which Arnold acquiesced, seems, just as unhappily, part of a Free Trade policy

[1] *First Report of the Royal Commission on the Elementary Education Acts*, 1886, c.4863, Q.5825.
[2] id., Q.5833.
[3] id., QQ.5845, 6044.
[4] id; Q.6080.
[5] id., Q.5971–5974.

in education as was the original scheme of payment by results devised by that great advocate of free trade, Robert Lowe. Arnold's evidence before the Commission was in many ways not a very happy experience, although their final recommendations accorded well with his views.

He was examined also at length as to his views on inspection. He had been in many ways a peculiar inspector. He had been one of the earliest laymen to take up the work and he had always been regarded as something of, if not quite an oddity, at least a person to be regarded in a different light from the remainder of his colleagues. Thus, he was sent off on three occasions to examine educational systems on the Continent, and was regarded as somewhat of an authority in the field of comparative education. Most of his evidence, in fact, before the Cross Commission turned upon comparisons between English and Continental practices. He was able to disavow openly the current English system and yet retain his position, and even attain promotion to the newly created Senior Inspector's rank in 1870.[1] He acknowledged that he was

[1] The following is a summary of the changes in Arnold's Inspectorial Districts:
1852.   "The midland district in which these schools are situated is a new district, formed in 1851"—for British Wesleyan and other Non-Conformist Schools, included the English countries of Lincoln, Notts, Derby, Stafford, Salop, Hereford, Worcester, Warwick, Leicester, Rutland, Northampton, Gloucester, and Monmouth together with all of North Wales except Flintshire and Derbyshire, and all of South Wales.
1853.   Gloucester, Hereford, Worcester, Monmouthshire, and South Wales withdrawn.   Middlesex, Hertford, Bedford, Essex, Huntingdon, Cambridge, Suffolk, Norfolk added.
1854.   4 counties in North Wales and 7 North Midland and Eastern counties withdrawn. Kent, Sussex, Bucks, Oxford, and Worcester added. Many of the schools of his district were in London.
1855.   The title of the district became "Midland Metropolitan and S. Eastern Division of England".
1856.   Arnold referred to the extent to which his district had changed by speaking of South Staffordshire as "the nucleus of my original district but which forms nearly the remotest portion of my present district, the centre of which is London".
1857.   The district originally "extended from Milford Haven to the Humber" now consists of Middlesex, Kent, Essex, Hertford, Buckingham, Oxford and Berks.
1867.   District restricted to Middlesex, Herts, Essex, Suffolk and Norfolk.
1869.   Lost the counties of Suffolk and Norfolk, and gained Bucks.
1871.   Reduced to the Metropolitan district only of Westminster with Hendon, and Barnet and Edmonton districts of Middlesex, also designated one of the eight new Senior Inspectors with general responsibility for Essex, Middlesex, and London districts north of the Thames.
1875.   Lost the districts of Hendon and Barnet.
1879.   Lost Edmonton.
1883.   Retained Westminster and was made Senior Inspector for the whole Metropolitan District consisting of the District of the London School Board, Middlesex (extra-metropolitan), and Essex.
1884.   Title changed to Chief Inspector, lost part of Essex. England and Wales in this year was divided into 10 Chief Inspectorates.
1886.   Retired.

out of sympathy with most of his colleagues, but he was not greatly concerned about it. "I have never had any great sympathy from the other inspectors, I think, in my disapprobation of the code."[1] He was, however, on intimate terms with the heads of the Education Department. Lingen had been his tutor and remained his friend, though quite uninfluenced by his views. Sandford his successor was closer to Arnold who had once written him a glowing testimonial when he had applied for the Chair of Greek at Edinburgh.[2] Cumin, who followed Sandford was again a University colleague of Arnold's. Of the vice-presidents, Arnold was, of course, on most familiar terms with his brother-in-law, W. E. Forster. A. J. Mundella was another with whom he had a close acquaintanceship, and it was he who regretted that his subordinate's official duties might interfere with the production of more poety which he exhorted Arnold to continue writing.[3] How far Arnold's ideas were eventually reflected, as a result of this personal contact, in official policy, it is impossible to determine. He wrote from time to time of the influence that he was able to wield at the office; he was, for example, consulted by H. A. Bruce as to the personnel of the Taunton Commission, but generally he did not specify what his consultations were concerned with.[4]

As an inspector, a colleague, Sneyd-Kynnersley, did not rate him very highly. He "was—to put it in most courteous terms— more efficient on the literary side."[5] This was evidently because it was not Arnold's habit to follow in meticulous detail the routine of inspection, and examination such as may be found set out in D. R. Fearon's manual on School Inspection that that worthy inspector produced in 1876.[6] Arnold's tendency was rather more towards a style that the following somewhat exaggerated story reveals. "Mr. Arnold inspects our school in Westminster," a

[1] First Report of Cross Commission, 1886, Q.5822.

[2] F. R. J. Sandford, Testimonials in favour of F. R. Sandford (a candidate for the Greek Chair in the University of Edinburgh), Edinburgh, 1852.

[3] Russell, ed., Letter to his Wife, 16th September, 1880, ii, p. 176.

[4] id., in letters of 15th September to his Sister and to his Wife, ii, 174–5, Arnold wrote when holidaying in Switzerland with Sir Francis Sandford and A. J. Mundella, that the latter had "asked me a great deal about the policy which the office should follow, and I had an opportunity of urging upon him several things which I think important". "He is very anxious to do right and I think I have more chance of having influence with him than with any Vice-President we have had". Vide also Appendix for letters of Arnold to Mundella. His contact with Bruce was mentioned in Letters to his sisters Fan, August 1864, i, p. 238, and Jane, 3rd January, 1865, i, p. 244, vide infra, Appendix, p. 285.

[5] E. M. Sneyd-Kynnersley, H.M.I., Macmillan, London, 1913, p. 156.

[6] D. R. Fearon, School Inspection, Macmillan, London, 1876.

London school manager said to me. "Of course we are much honoured, and the managers make a point of attending to meet him. He arrives in the course of the morning; shakes hands with the managers and teachers; and talks very pleasantly for a few minutes; then he walks through the classes between the desks, looking over the children's shoulders at some exercises, and so makes his way to the door, and we see him no more."[1] The same author remarks that "Arnold's other mission in the world of education was to supply the Office with amusement", and illustrated this penchant by an anecdote concerning Arnold's travelling expenses. When he held the two districts of Westminster and Edmonton he was expected to remain overnight at Edmonton, if his inspection there lasted for two successive days, or at least not to charge to the office his fare for the journey home and back. "Being a poet, of course, he returned home, and charged his fare every day. 'The Knight of the Blue Pencil', as he called his enemy, sharpened his blue pencil, and wrote—'Mr. M. Arnold, H.M.I. Why not stay at Edmonton?' and the great man plaintively replied: 'How can you expect me to stay at Edmonton, when John Gilpin couldn't?' The account was passed."[2]

It is evident, however, that though Arnold may have affected a casualness and perhaps sometimes a disdain, to the impression of which his use of a monocle may have contributed, he was nevertheless an effective inspector. An anonymous contributor to the *Cornhill* writing in 1899 wrote, "He became the teachers' and children's friend, and though many a droll anecdote of his casual methods of marking and taking stock of his schools still goes the rounds, and though, as he frankly confessed on the occasion we refer to (his address at Westminster on his retirement), he was a very unpunctual inspector, none of his colleagues had a shrewder sense of what was wanting in each school he visited, or could reckon it up more readily. For the general body of elementary school teachers he thus acquired an honest respect and liking. . . ."[3] Arnold's assistant inspector, Thomas Healing, who as a "white-haired boy", had his apprenticeship as a pupil-teacher arranged by Arnold,[4] wrote that he had acted as an inspiration on many a young teacher to the study of letters and

[1] Sneyd-Kynnersley, op. cit., p. 157.
[2] id., p. 158.
[3] *Cornhill Magazine*, February 1899, art. "The Humours of School Inspection", anon.
[4] *The Times*, 13th November, 1886, p. 5, e.

the undertaking of a London degree for their own improvement, and the eventual benefit of the children. "His usefulness as an Inspector . . . lay very much in his success in bringing some tincture of letters into the curriculum of the Elementary School."[1] One of the finest of inspectors, J. G. Fitch, who owed his appointment to Arnold's favourable report and personal intervention with the then Lord-President, Earl Granville,[2] gave it as his opinion that "indirectly, his fine taste, his gracious and kindly manner, his honest and generous recognition of any new form of excellence which he observed, all tended to raise the aims and tone of the teachers with whom he came in contact, and to encourage in them self-respect and respect for their work."[3] And, though he had small part in arranging any details of educational administration, "when questions of principle were involved, he was frequently consulted, and we who were his colleagues received from him at times very weighty and practical suggestions."[4]

To a man of this type of approach the introduction of the Revised Code with its insistence on minutiæ was a serious inroad into the proper functions of the inspectorate. He made this one of the key points of his criticisms from the very beginning, in "The Twice Revised Code".

If one of the main drawbacks of the system of payment by results was the loss of the directing and elevating function of the State, it was apparent that the functions of its educational representatives, Her Majesty's Inspectors, would be changed also. "It turns the inspectors into a set of registering clerks with a mass of minute details to tabulate, such a mass as must, in Sir James Shuttleworth's words 'necessarily withdraw their attention from the religious and general instruction, and from the moral features of the school'."[5]

The essential function of an inspector was to act as the directing agent of the enlightened State. Their's was no niggardly function of checking over log-books, and adding or subtracting two and eightpences from school budgets. They were to mark out the lines of advance, to inspire, and lead their educational cohorts

[1] J. G. Fitch, *Thomas and Matthew Arnold*, Heineman, London, 1904, pp. 174–5.
[2] A. L. Lilley, *Sir Joshua Fitch*, Arnold, London, 1906, p. 22; Marvin, ed., op. cit., p. 241.
[3] Fitch, op. cit., p. 171.
[4] id., p. 177. But for a very adverse opinion by an ex-pupil under his inspection, *vide* J. G. Legge, *The Rising Tide*, pp. 76–7.
[5] *Fraser's Magazine*, lxv, 1862, p. 360.

ever forward in the general advance. Such a vision seemed to be set at naught by the Revised Code. "It is as if the generals of an army,—for the inspectors have been the veritable generals of the educational army,—were to have their duties limited to inspecting the men's cartouch-boxes. The organisation of the army is faulty: —inspect the cartouch-boxes! The camp is ill-drained, the men are ill-hutted, there is danger of fever and sickness. Never mind; inspect the cartouch-boxes! But the whole discipline is out of order, and needs instant reformation;—no matter; inspect the cartouch-boxes! But the army is beginning a general movement, and that movement is a false one; it is moving to the left when it should be moving to the right: It is going to a disaster! That is not your business; inspect, inspect the cartouch-boxes!" [1]

Under their existing organisation the inspectors were, it seemed, not equal to the task Arnold would have them perform. It was the inspectors before appointment, not the children, whom the Vice-President should really examine. [2] The great Dutch educator, Van den Ende, had said, "Take care how you choose your inspectors; they are men whom you ought to look for with a lantern in your hand." [3] And his inspectors had been not only carefully selected, but also trained for their tasks with equal care. In England, on the other hand, they had been simply "able and promising university men" selected without any consideration as to their familiarity with school work and submitted to only a desultory training. [4] At the present time, Arnold wrote in 1862, there were sixty of them all independent and with salaries like inspectors-general, but "not chosen with the care with which inspectors-general should be chosen." [5] They should be reduced in number to 10 or 15 inspectors in chief, supervising large areas of England, and having under them local officials who could do any necessary examining work. In this way the State could be assured of a select body of first-rate men, whose influence in their districts would be an inspiration, and whose voice, because of their smaller number, could be effectively heard at headquarters. This was the current practice in Holland which Arnold had lately been investigating and it fitted neatly also into his scheme of provincial

[1] ibid.
[2] id., p. 358.
[3] *Popular Education*, p. 199.
[4] *First Report of Cross Commission*, QQ. 5187–90. J. Leese, *The History and Character of Educational Inspection in England*, Ph.D. Thesis, London, 1934, has examined at length the practice of selection of H.M.I.'s.
[5] *Fraser's Magazine*, lxv, 1862, p. 362.

administration which he proposed six years later in his report on Schools and Universities on the Continent.[1] The institution of the rank of Senior Inspector in 1871, and later that of Chief Inspector, answered somewhat to Arnold's conception. The Senior Inspectors were severally responsible for the supervision of ordinary inspectors over the, at first, eight districts into which England and Wales were divided. But though in time the larger Local Educational Authorities appointed their own inspectors these did not become subordinate to Her Majesty's Inspectors nor did Arnold's proposal of employing local men outside the inspectorate as examiners gain any acceptance. From his continental experience he put forward a further suggestion in 1871 that the new class of Senior Inspectors might form a team, together with the inspectors of training schools, for advising their Lordships on the matter of "studies and books" in elementary schools.[2] Such a Code Committee, as it was called, was later instituted, but Arnold was never a member of it.[3]

In an early General Report (1854) he had laid stress upon the fact that the primary duty of Her Majesty's Inspectors was to report faithfully to Their Lordships what they had found to be the actual state of the schools. "Inspection exists for the sake of finding out and reporting the truth, and for this above all."[4] As his experience increased and he realised more fully the possibilities that lay in the future development of elementary education, he began to stress rather the stimulating and directing function of the inspectorate. It was this position that he had reached when he wrote his pamphlet against the Revised Code, and it was in the same strain that he compiled his first report on the working of the Code in 1863. He drew a distinction between "the old inspection" and the "new". Both tested and promoted the discipline and material arrangements of the schools with somewhat the same care, but "considered as an agency for testing and promoting the intellectual force of schools" there appeared to be a great difference.[5] The new examination seeks to discover whether the pupils have reached certain minima and since it does not go beyond them it becomes an inadequate means of testing the real attainments and the intellectual life of the pupils.

---

[1] *Vide supra*, pp. 110–11.
[2] Marvin, ed., (1871) p. 144.
[3] *First Report of Cross Committee*, Q.6256.
[4] Marvin, ed., (1854) p. 30.
[5] id., (1863) p. 91.

On the other hand, "the whole school felt, under the old system, that the prime aim and object of the Inspector's visit was, after insuring the fulfilment of certain sanitary and disciplinary conditions, to test and quicken the intellectual life of the school. The scholar's thoughts were directed to this object, the teacher's thoughts were directed to it, the Inspector's thoughts were directed to it. The scholars and teacher co-operated therefore with the Inspector in doing their best to reach it; they were anxious for his judgment . . . after he was gone; at present the centre of interest for the school when the inspector visits it is changed. Scholars and teacher have their thoughts directed straight upon the new examination, which will bring, they know, such important benefit to the school, if it goes well, and bring it such important loss if it goes ill. On the examination day they have not minds for anything else." [1]

Arnold had here hit upon the essential problem in inspection. In modern terminology, it is the differentiation of the functions of a supervisor and an inspector, where a supervisor is concerned with the sympathetic study of a teacher's problems and the improvement, by stimulus and advice, of the level of instruction, whilst the inspector has the task of checking achievement in order to grade a teacher for purposes of salary and promotion. [2] In some countries the two functions are combined in the one officer, but, as Arnold had speedily recognised, they are incompatible. Inspection inevitably overrides supervision. The institution of payment by results changed the role of Her Majesty's Inspectors from that of supervisor to that of inspector. This, in itself, need not have been a cause of complaint, if some other provision had

[1] id., p. 94-5.
[2] A sound analysis of this problem may be found in J. F. Cramer, *Australian Schools through American Eyes*, Aust. Council for Ed. Res., Melb. U.P., 1936, chap III, and I. L. Kandel, *Types of Administration*. Kandel's description of the function of a modern inspector could very well have been written by Matthew Arnold. "The inspector should exercise a double role—he should, on the one hand be the local representative of the Education Department, and, on the other, he should be the organizer and leader of education in his area. This means that he must be in a position to come into closer and more frequent contacts with the public in his district in order to develop a public opinion favourable to educational progress and reform. It means, further, that more of his time should be devoted to helping the teachers of his district, to promote opportunities for further professional study by teachers, and to serve as an educational leader by collecting and disseminating the best ideas in educational theory and especially in educational practice. These functions an inspector cannot exercise when he has in the main opportunities of seeing teachers only once a year and then primarily for the purposes of classification, and when the remainder of his time is taken up in travel, in clerical work, and in some places in the marking of examination papers." *Impressions of Australian Education*, A.C.E.R., 1938, pp. 12-13.

been made for supervision. Unfortunately it was not. And English education was largely deprived for three decades of such quickening, elevating power as had been available to it from 1839 to 1862. Foreseeing this and being very apprehensive as to its results, Arnold made a plea to the managers of schools to try to find some "mode of stimulus to their schools" which would supply the deficiency,[1] but there is little evidence to show that they were able to effect much. It may be said, therefore, that by turning its inspectors into little more than financial agents of the government, the Education Department committed England, during a vital, formative period, to a system devoid of educational leadership, or at least devoid of persons whose specific function was recognised to be that of leadership. The vast multiplication of school places[2] and educational facilities that ensued upon the Elementary Education Act of 1870 was not only, in the absence of a Minister of Education, without "a centre where we can fix the responsibility," but also, in the changed conception of inspection, without a body of enlightened educators whose prime duty was to provide a cultural leadership which would convert a grinding mechanical pursuit of minimum results into an adventurous quest of the nation's general perfection, "turning a stream of fresh and free thought upon our stock notions and habits, which we now follow staunchly but mechanically, vainly imagining that there is a virtue in following them staunchly which makes up for the mischief of following them mechanically."[3]

Of similar importance in Arnold's estimation, for the future of English education, was the effect that payment by results was likely to have upon the supply and the quality of the teaching profession. Since the Minutes of 1864 the elementary school teachers had been very largely recruited from the ranks of apprenticed pupil teachers whom Arnold regarded as "the sinews of English primary instruction."[4] At the first hint of proposals that might, in any way, impair the pupil teaching system,

[1] Marvin, ed. (1863), p. 96.
[2] Between 1870 and 1895 the number of public elementary day schools rose from 8,798 to 19,739, and the number of pupils in average attendance from 1,231,434 to 4,325,131 (*Special Reports on Educational Subjects*, 1896–7. M. E. Sadler, p. 6).
[3] *Culture and Anarchy*, p. 6. In view of the function of the inspectorate under the Revised Code, Arnold was in favour of admitting ex-elementary teachers to the rank of inspector, but because of their limited opportunities of higher education he did not consider that they were suitable for the higher posts of Chief Inspectors. *First Report of Cross Commission*, QQ.5087–88, 5189–94, 5574–77. Cf. *Popular Education*, pp. 121, 153.
[4] *Popular Education*, p. 108.

Arnold rose in defence with an impassioned plea which he submitted in his report to the Newcastle Commissioners. "Pupil-teachers—the conception, for England, of the founder of English popular education, of the administrator whose conceptions have been as fruitful as his services were unworthily maligned, of Sir James Shuttleworth. In naming them I pause to implore all friends of education to use their best efforts to preserve this institution to us unimpaired. Let them entreat ministerial economy to respect a pensioner who has repaid the outlay upon him a thousand times; let them entreat the Privy Council Office to propose to sacrifice some less precious victim. Forms less multiplied, examinations less elaborate, inspectors of a lower grade—let all these reductions be endured rather than that the number of pupil-teachers should be lessened."[1] Nevertheless one of the first noticeable effects of the Revised Code was a decline in the pupil-teacher system. Already for some years previous to 1862 there had been a falling off in the number of recruits due to the improved prospects offered by occupations outside the teaching profession,[2] but the decline was accelerated by the institution of payments by results. Arnold set out the details in his Report for 1867. "The rate of pupil-teachers to scholars in our elementary schools was, in 1861, one pupil-teacher for every thirty-six scholars; in 1866 it was only one pupil-teacher for every fifty-four scholars. Throughout all the training colleges only 1,478 candidates presented themselves for admission last Christmas, whereas 2,513 candidates presented themselves in 1862. Yet the number of schools recruiting their teachers from this source had risen from 6,258 in 1861 to 8,303 in 1866, and the average population of such schools from 919,935 to 1,082,055."[3] The Committee of Council had been forced by the facts of the situation to authorise a ratio of 1 pupil-teacher for 90 scholars in place of the former ratio of 1 to 50.[4] Not only was there a decline in numbers, there was also a decline in quality. "The performance of the reduced number of candidates is weaker and more inaccurate than was the performance of the larger numbers six years ago."[5] What concerned Arnold most, however, was not the contemplation of

---

[1] id., p. 109.
[2] Marvin, ed., (1857), p. 68.
[3] id., (1867), p. 104.
[4] R. W. Rich, *The Training of Teachers in England and Wales during the Nineteenth Century*, C.U.P., 1933, p. 186.
[5] Marvin, ed., (1867) p. 104.

such statistics, but the reflections that were called forth by what was the obvious reason for the decline. "The main obstacle to their steady recruitment and good training" was "the indifference of the principal teacher to seeking them out, taking pains with them, and inspiring them with a zeal for their calling."[1] The affliction besetting pupil-teachers was but one instance of the blight that had settled upon the whole teaching profession. Its members were discouraged and apathetic. Teaching was no longer a calling to attract men of spirit and ambition. Whereas, earlier, the teachers had been encouraged to regard themselves as fellow crusaders with the Committee of Council and had had their connection with that national body cemented by direct subsidy, since the introduction of the Revised Code they had been snubbed for their pretensions to the status of public servant, and severed from all connection with the central government which dealt only with the managers of schools. Their efforts furthermore were directed not to the constant improvement and enrichment of their own and their pupil's work, but to a circumscribed and uninspiring round of instruction. This was a heavy blow for English education, for upon the quality of its teachers more than upon any other factor, depended its future prospects.[2] Arnold was constantly solicitous for the general improvement of the teachers with whom he was in contact. It was among teachers that he detected the greatest desire "for a better culture" and he "gladly seized every opportunity" to encourage this wholesome aspiration. He specially welcomed "the wise liberality" of the London University in making its degrees widely accessible, and induced many of his teachers to study for them.[3] With his eye always on the ultimate task of forwarding the nation's culture, he saw, in the continuing efforts of the teachers to improve themselves, a gradual seeping down of culture through pupil-teacher and assistant into the whole life of the schools, the best, and surest way to that long-range goal. That was why, despite his affection for the pupil-teacher system, he was prepared to see it superseded when, at the end of his career, he was able to welcome "a higher order of teaching" which "has come in and will come in more and more". Pupil-teachers were ceasing to be adequate to the higher requirements of the age and had therefore to give way to the new developments in teaching training, notably to the day

[1] id., (1867), p. 110.
[2] *First Report of Cross Commission*, QQ.5962–63.
[3] Marvin, ed., (1863) p. 101; (1874) p. 164.

training colleges whose students were of greater maturity and were able to assimilate a wider culture.[1] He hoped that the new institutions might be provided by the State, and if the country was ever organised into provincial divisions that each province would organise its own system of training colleges.[2]

It was his same feeling for the ultimate elevation and progress of the nation's culture that led him to praise every effort to infuse students with a more liberal outlook and "*general culture*", that he found, in particular at the Borough Road Training College under J. G. Fitch.[3] Hence also his indifference to pedagogical doctrines and methods even when backed by the eminent authority of Pestalozzi.[4] It is doubtful if he ever read any works of educational philosophy; at least, he certainly did not spend much time in perusing them.[5] He thought that such doctrines might be excellent, and so might the methods be that depended on them, but "the practical application alone tests this, and often and often a method thus tested reveals unsuspected weaknesses. . . . The best thing for a teacher to do is surely to put before himself in the utmost simplicity the problem he has to solve."[6]

Arnold seldom commented on specific pedagogical methods in use, to him they were "machinery" just as pupil-teachers; managerial details, and even the subjects of the curriculum were

[1] *First Report of Cross Commission*, QQ.5098, 5160, 5232, 5284, 5615–26.
[2] id., QQ.5616–17. Arnold would surely have welcomed the McNair Report recommendation for establishing Area Training Authorities.
[3] Marvin, ed., (*Training College Reports*, 1855), p. 241.
[4] id., (1878) p. 189.
[5] Arnold kept in his Notebooks extensive lists of the books he intended to read and those he had actually read each year. In the published selections of his Notebooks there is no mention of any educational classics. The complete edition of the Notebooks, edited by H. F. Lowry, has not yet appeared.
[6] Marvin, ed., (1878) pp. 189–90. He did not favour the development of a training college as simply a centre of professional education following upon a general secondary or university education. "I think the training college would be a very curious thing with no real teaching in it, and nothing but a talking about educational principles". (*First Report of Cross Commission*, Q.5401).
   Current manuals in use in training colleges, as mentioned in *Committee of Council Reports* were:
      Currie's *Manual of Early and Infant Training*.
      Currie's *Principles of Common School Education*.
      Dunn's *Principles of Teaching*.
      J. Gill's *School Management*.
      T. Morrison's *School Management*.
      Stow's *Training System*.
      Symons' *School Economy*.
      T. Tate's *Philosophy of Education*.
      Unwin's *Primary School*.
   Arnold was impressed by the teaching of "Paedogogy" in Germany and thought it might with advantage be extended in England but thought its most useful part was "the history of education and the biography of educators". (*Schools and Universities*, p. 188 n; *First Report of Cross Commission*, Q.5395.)

"machinery", subordinate to the leading purpose of the schools.[1]
They were all of value but they were not the matters upon which
he thought it essential to insist. His mind conceived the function
of the elementary schools in their broad cultural setting and he
was concerned with the details of their conduct only in so far as
they conduced to the realisation of the broad purpose of elementary education. To him the teacher's purpose was clear, and
simple. He had to instruct children between the ages of four and
thirteen. "He has, so far as secular instruction goes, to give to
those children the power of reading, of writing, and (according
to the good old phrase) of casting accounts. He has to give them
some knowledge of the world in which they find themselves, and
what happens and has happened in it. . . . He has to do as
much towards opening their mind, and opening their soul and
imagination, as is possible to be done with a number of children
of their age and in their state of preparation and home surround-
ings."[1] It is a task which few people have found as simple as
Arnold appeared to think it to be. But his two pieces of advice to
teachers in executing the task were as sound as any to be found
in educational textbooks:

"My word for all teachers of elementary schools who will listen
to me therefore is: *simplify*. Put before yourselves as simply as
possible the problem which you have to solve; simplify, as much
as you are at present allowed to simplify them, your means for
solving it, and seek to be allowed to simplify them yet more."[3]
It was an important part of his own philosophy of life.

To this he also added: "Whatever introduces any sort of creative
activity to relieve the passive reception of knowledge is valuable.
. . . But governing the teacher's whole design of instruction in
these knowledges should be the aim of calling forth, by some means
or other, in every pupil a sense of pleasurable activity and of
creation; he should resist being made a mere ladder with
'information'."[4]

It is this sense of creation that is the really important human
element in education. This belief of his animated all his writing
on the humanities, and had been long since expressed in a different
context in his celebrated essay on the Function of Criticism at
the Present Time: "to have the sense of creative activity is the

[1] Cf. *Special Report on Elementary Education in Germany, Switzerland and France*, 1886,
c.4752, p. 25.
[2] Marvin, ed., (1878) p. 190.
[3] id., (1878) pp. 192–3.
[4] id., (1882) pp. 228–9.

CULTURE AND THE REVISED CODE 241

greatest happiness and the greatest proof of being alive."[1]
Arnold's twin principles are of permanent value. The second
is unexceptionable, the first, sound but dangerous. In the process
of continual simplification there is a danger of rejecting the vital
for the more tangible. It is fatally easy to gloss over complicated
issues with sweeping generalisations, and produce a satisfying
masterpiece of logical simplicity. Arnold's own essays of literary
criticism are chiefly criticised on this very score. It is the fault of
many modern definitions of education, and it was the essential
fault also of the Revised Code. Its authors conceived of education
as too simple and uncomplicated a process. For them it meant
simply the acquirement of a degree of literacy necessary for a
certain station in life. Hence they were able to produce a simple
mechanical pattern of education in accordance with this aim.
The Committee of Council became the Board of Directors for the
Education Department Ltd., Manager, R. Lignen Esq., paying
on a commission basis, with a standardised system of bookkeeping
in all its branches, producing a very limited type of product and
quite without a Sales Promotion department. It tackled its
problem from the wrong end. Instead of examining the children
and paying for a minimal result, it would, as Arnold pointed out,
have had a much better guarantee of excellence if it had devoted
the time, energy, and expense involved in such examinations to
the training of its teachers. After it had been in operation for a
few years, in the late 60s there was an abortive move to simplify
it further by eliminating the condition requiring a certificated
teacher in grant earning schools. It was contended that the
government was concerned only with results and therefore if
results could be produced there was surely no adequate reason
for any concern with the means by which they were obtained.
This to Arnold was the supreme travesty of education. The
quality of teacher training had greatly fallen off, but it still
remained the main hope for raising the cultural level of the
elementary schools. He illustrated the sounder attitude to the
question by the example of Prussia. "So well do the Prussian
authorities know how insufficient an instrument for their object,—
that of promoting the national culture and filling the professions
with fit men,—is the bare examination-test; so averse are they to
cram; so clearly do they perceive that what forms a youth, and
what he should in all ways be induced to acquire, is the orderly
development of his faculties under good and trained teaching."[2]

[1] *Essays in Criticism*, 1st Series, p. 40.   [2] *Schools and Universities*, p. 182.

Fortunately, the ill-starred assault on the certification of teachers came to naught; but Arnold's other opinions concerning payment by results did not win such a ready acceptance. It was not until the year of his death, 1888, two years after his retirement, that his opposition to the Code was vindicated by the findings of the Cross Commission and then in a curious way. The majority report, of two-thirds of the Commission, in their main finding, adopted substantially the position that Arnold had taken up when he wrote his General Report for the year 1869.[1]

"But", they said, "after weighing all the evidence laid before us, tending to show the evils which arise from the present method of payment by results, we are convinced that the distribution of the Parliamentary grant cannot be wholly freed from its present dependence on the results of examination without the risk of incurring graver evils than those which it is sought to cure. . . . Nevertheless we are unanimously of the opinion that the present system of 'payment by results' is carried too far and is too rigidly applied, and that it ought to be modified and relaxed in the interests equally of the scholars, of the teachers, and of education itself."[2] And furthermore, "that individual examination should be treated not as a means of individually assessing grants, but merely as testing the general progress of all the scholars."[3] In a dissenting view, Lord Norton, who as C. B. Adderley, had been Vice-President of the Committee of Council, justly pointed out that this latter was a remark inconsistent with the proposal to retain payment by results which he thought should be "entirely abandoned".[4]

The minority, a more alert and forward-looking group, rejected the Arnold of 1869, and reached the same sort of conclusions that the retiring chief inspector had given in evidence before them in 1886. They thought payment by results "far from being a satisfactory method of securing efficiency", and to be "forced upon the country by the irresponsible and isolated character of the management of the majority of our schools." This, finally, could be eliminated only by a comprehensive and responsible "organisation of our school system under local representative authorities."[5]

---

[1] *vide supra*, pp. 226–7.
[2] *Parliamentary Papers*, 1888, xxxv, 220–1 : Final Report, pp. 244–45.
[3] Final Report, 221.
[4] Final Report, 225.
[5] Final Report, 249.

CHAPTER X

MIDDLE CLASS EDUCATION

"If there is one need more crying than another, it is the need of the English middle class to be rescued from a defective type of religion, a narrow range of intellect and knowledge, a stunted sense of beauty, a low standard of manners. And what could do so much to deliver them and to render them happier, as to give them proper education, public education, to bring them up on the first plane; to make them a class homogeneous, intelligent, civilised?"—Matthew Arnold, *Mixed Essays*, "Porro unum est necessarium", pp. 178-9.

BECAUSE he was not called upon to write official reports about it, Arnold did not examine secondary education in the same detail as elementary education but he nevertheless regarded a proper provision of it as the one matter in education that most needed agitation. Elementary education had already been taken in hand by the government at the time when he became interested in it, and he thought the importance of its extension was realised. There were many urgent problems connected with its improvement and diffusion, but at least the movement was under way. The elevation of the lower classes was a distant prospect but it could, at any rate, be seen slowly coming into more and more definite focus. "Even so long as twenty years ago", he wrote in 1879, "popular education was already launched. I was myself continually a witness of the progress it was making; I could see that the cause of popular education was safe."[1] On the other hand it seemed that the vital importance of the organisation of secondary instruction was far from receiving due recognition. The term secondary itself had not yet come into general use, and Arnold was keen to see it more widely adopted. On his return from his inspection of continental elementary education in 1859, he requested the Newcastle Commission "to say to the Government, Regard the necessities of a not distant future, *and organise your secondary instruction*."[2] A few years later he congratulated M. E. Grant Duff on his introduction of the word into a parlia-

[1] *Irish Essays*, "Ecce, Convertimur ad Gentes", p. 86. This first appeared in the *Fortnightly Review*, February 1879.
[2] *Popular Education*, p. 77, cf. id., p. 74; *Schools and Universities*, p. 296 *et passim*; *A French Eton*, pp. 4-5.

mentary resolution: "I am glad you have employed and given official stamp to that useful word *secondary*."[1] Arnold gave it no formal definition. He found the term in use on the Continent, particularly in France, to describe instruction above the elementary level and below that of institutions of University standing, and he made a similar use of it in his own writings. He did not restrict "secondary" to the grammar school education that the Board of Education Regulations for Secondary Schools, first issued in 1904, made the customary significance of the term, until both the Hadow (1926)[2] and Spens (1938)[3] Committee Reports protested against such undue restriction, and led on eventually to its first statutory definition by the Education Act, 1944, as "full-time education suitable to the requirements of senior pupils," a senior pupil being "a person who has attained the age of twelve years but has not attained the age of nineteen years".[4] Arnold, in conformity with his desire to see a coherent and comprehensively organised system of education, spoke frequently of its three parts as primary, secondary, and superior, a designation which has recently also been reflected in the Education Act, 1944, which declared that "the Statutory system of public education shall be organised in three progressive stages to be known as primary education, secondary education, and further education."[5]

Arnold, however, did regard secondary education as catering for the requirements of social classes different from those who attended the primary or elementary schools. It was the sphere of the upper and middle classes. However much it was desirable that the lower classes should proceed beyond the elementary grades, it was undeniable that secondary instruction was in Arnold's period largely confined to the higher strata of society. And it was to the improvement of it as an instrument for their benefit that Arnold devoted his efforts. It was not the well-known Public Schools, despite his father's influence upon them, that chiefly interested him. He had a fairly high opinion of them. M. de Talleyrand had "truly said that the education of the great

---

[1] Russell, ed., Letter to M. E. Grant Duff, M.P., 24th May, 1864, i, p. 233.
[2] *The Education of the Adolescent* (1926), pp. 93–9.
[3] *Secondary Education* (Grammar Schools and Technical High Schools) (1938), pp. 66–7, 314–5.
[4] Education Act, 1944 (7 & 8 Geo. 6, Ch. 31), § 8; § 114 (1).
[5] id., § 7. On one occasion (*Mixed Essays*, "Porro unum est necessarium", p. 174) he professed dissatisfaction with the term "secondary". "Perhaps *secondary* is a bad word to use, because it is equivocal. Intermediate is a better". He, however, continued to use the former term.

English public schools was the best in the world. He added to be sure, that even this was detestable. But allowing it all its merits, how small a portion of the population does it embrace!"[1]

Institutions such as the Public Schools and the great Universities "have formed the upper class of this country—a class with many faults, with many shortcomings, but imbued, on the whole, and mainly through these influences, with a high magnanimous governing spirit, which has long enabled them to rule, not ignobly, this great country."[2] Accordingly "no wise man will desire to see root-and-branch work made with schools like Eton and Harrow, or see them diverted from the function which they at present discharge, and, on the whole, usefully."[3] Thus, they might be considered well-fitted for this purpose, but that purpose was a very limited one, and did not embrace the vital tasks of secondary education. That their high-souled magnanimous product was not always advantageous to the nation he was also well aware. In an obituary notice to an Eton boy killed in the first Boer War, he wrote concerning the Duke of Wellington's famous remark: "Alas! disasters have been prepared in those playing-fields as well as victories; disasters due to inadequate mental training—to want of application of knowledge, intelligence, lucidity. The Eton playing-fields have their charms, notwithstanding."[4] He was himself charmed there to give an address to the Eton Literary Society, and spoke, in the home of the Barbarians, in typical style, upon the great lack among Barbarians of εὐτραπέλια which he translated "Flexibility". Thus though he was interested in, and prepared to admire the finer qualities of the Public School system he thought it did not bear much upon the main problems of secondary education and that with changing social circumstances it would not long remain intact. "That school system is a close and narrow one; that order of things is changing, and will surely pass away. Vain are endeavours to keep it fixed for ever, impotent are regrets for it; it will pass away. The concern for the future in secondary education lay elsewhere."[5] "But, for the champions of the true

---

[1] *Popular Education*, pp. 74-5.
[2] *A French Eton*, pp. 66-7.
[3] id., pp. 71-2.
[4] *The Fortnightly Review*, "An Eton Boy", June, 1882, p. 684.
[5] id., p. 696. Dr. Moberly, *Five Short Letters to Sir William Heathcote;* Letter I, pp. 13-14, defines a Public School as: "in my judgment the perfect idea of an English Public School is that of a School of sufficient size, possessed of endowment and constitution so well established as to secure it from the caprices of Masters, Trustees,

cause of secondary instruction, for those interested in the thorough improvement of this most important concern, the centre of interest is not there."[1]

It was the multitude of lesser schools which catered in an inadequate way for the middle classes that needed the greatest attention. "Our middle classes are nearly the worst educated in the world,"[2] and, "the schools for this class . . . are the worst of the kind anywhere"[3] were sentiments Arnold was never tired of uttering. His interest in these schools arose from his over-riding sense of the importance of the middle classes, and of the patent defects which they showed. "The master-thought by which my politics are governed is . . . this,—the thought of the bad civilisation of the English middle class."[4]

"The great work to be done in this country," thought Arnold, "and at this hour, is not with the lower class, but with the middle; a work of raising its whole level of civilisation, and, in order to do this, of transforming the British Puritan."[5]

The past lay with the aristocracy, the indeterminate future with the lower classes, but the present was in the hands of the middle classes whose influence on the lower classes would also be of importance for the future. Both friends and enemies of the middle class, and Arnold considered himself among the discriminating section of the former, were agreed that it had "risen into such preponderating importance of late years, and now returns the House of Commons, dictates the policy of Ministers, makes the newspapers speak with its voice, and in short governs the country."[6]

The middle class had steadily increased in importance since the time of the First Reform Act of 1832 when Brougham had

Proprietors, and the like—in which the dead languages and their literature form the staple of the instruction given; but, above all, where certain of the most trustworthy boys are empowered to exercise some real authority among their school fellows, for the purpose of order, morality, and protection, without being called upon or expected to report continually to the Masters every act that they repress, or every secret they know. Where this system is in full and long established operation, so that a complete traditional usage bounds and checks every liability to abuse to which it may be subject, and the superintendence of watchful Masters allows it to proceed freely and naturally, curbing it when need be, but at other times giving it free scope to produce its own effects, there we may, I think, acknowledge that the English Public School system is in full, and probably in beneficial operation."

[1] id., p. 5.
[2] *Popular Education*, p. 75.
[3] *Irish Essays*, "The Future of Liberalism", p. 115.
[4] id., p. 102.
[5] *Mixed Essays*, "Irish Catholicism and British Liberalism", p. 141.
[6] *The Study of Celtic Literature*, "My Countrymen", p. 198.

even then hailed them as "the wealth and intelligence of the country, the glory of the British name", and "the genuine depositories of sober, rational, intelligent, and honest English feeling."[1] To the manufacturers and industrialists had been added the vast scores of workers in the multiplying commercial concerns of the Victorian world dependent as never before upon accountancy.[2] The professional section of the middle class was also increasing apace, and its influence was reflected in improved administrative techniques and in the growth of a body of professional middle class administrators who steadily displaced the aristocracy from a controlling position in the civil service. "The gibe that government by the middle class meant government by small shopkeepers had already lost its force. The essential fact lay in the control of technical knowledge by the professional members of the middle class; there was no longer any need of aristocratic direction, and, unless they joined the professional classes, the upper class had little or nothing to contribute to the management of the common affairs of a highly organised society."[3]

This middle class ranging from humble shop assistants to important bankers and industrial magnates was rather amorphous and diffuse in character. Arnold recognised the difficulty of defining its limits and declared that "to prevent ambiguity and confusion, I always have adopted an educational test, and by the middle class I understand those who are brought up at establishments which are more or less like Salem House, and by educators who are more or less like Mr. Creakle. And the great mass of the middle part of our community, the part which comes between those who labour with their hands, on the one side, and people of fortune on the other, is brought up at establishments of the kind, although there is a certain portion broken off at the top which is educated at better."[4] Sir John Coleridge, father of Arnold's Balliol contemporary, John Duke Coleridge, in two letters to the *Guardian* on 18th and 25th November, 1863, outlined the groups, for whom he thought secondary education to be inadequately provided, as "the clergy of moderate or contracted incomes, officers of the navy and army, medical men, solicitors, and gentry of large family and small means", and separated from them a

[1] *Brougham's Speeches*, ii, pp. 617, 600.
[2] *Early Victorian England*, ed. G. M. Young, i, p. 181.
[3] E. L. Woodward, *The Age of Reform, 1815–1870*, p. 600.
[4] *Irish Essays*, "The Incompatibles", pp. 45–6.

group also of tenant-farmers, small-landowners, and retail trades-men. With this line of demarcation Arnold could not agree. He preferred to group them all together and to add also "the manu-facturers" whom Coleridge had omitted.[1] He did not attempt, however, any more formal examination of the constitution of this class to whose elevation and improvement he gave much thought, and whom he made the subject of much exhortation over the three decades from the time of his report on Popular Education for the Newcastle Commission until his death in 1888.

He considered the middle class sufficiently homogeneous to have certain well-defined characteristics and deficiencies, that he spared no pains to point out. In his most striking analysis he chose two public figures as the mean and the excess respectively of the middle class. Thomas Bazley, chairman of the Manchester Chamber of Commerce, a leading supporter of the National Public School Association for secular education at Manchester in the early 50s, and, at the time of Arnold's writing, in 1868, M.P. for Manchester, was "the happy mean of the middle class." This leading cotton-spinner and free-trader summed up the middle class, "its spirit and its works". His "memorable words" upon the occasion when there was some agitation for improved middle-class education that "he did not think that class need excite the sympathy either of the legislature or the public",[2] were truly representative of the state of self-satisfaction which was a leading middle class characteristic. To this one should add the features of middle class civilisation that became clear when the activities of a representative man of "the excess", Rev. W. Cattle, were examined. Mr. Cattle was a dissenting minister who had taken the chair at a meeting in Birmingham addressed by a violently anti-Roman Catholic agitator, and "speaking in the midst of an irritated population of Catholics", had "with his zeal without knowledge" endeavoured to stir up strife "which neither he nor anyone else could easily compose".[3] In him one saw an example of that noble self-reliance upon which the middle classes prided themselves. What it could lead to had already been demonstrated by the action of "another middle-class man, Alderman Wilson, Alderman of the City of London and Colonel of the City of London Militia," who had led his militia through the London

[1] *A French Eton*, p. 48.
[2] *Culture and Anarchy*, p. 90.
[3] id., pp. 91–2.

streets and when the London roughs robbed and beat the bystanders who had gathered to see him pass, refused to let his
troops interfere on the ground that they might have had their
rifles taken from them and used against them by the roughs.
This was a characteristic example of the middle classes' "distrust
of themselves as an adequate centre of authority."[1] "What light
have we," they say, "beyond a free-born Englishman's impulse
to do as he likes, which could justify us in preventing, at the cost
of bloodshed, other free-born Englishmen from doing as they
like, and robbing and beating us as much as they please."[2]
Perhaps the most outstanding representative of all was Lord
Palmerston whom the great mouth-piece of the middle-class, *The
Times*, described as "the best type of our age and country", "the
interpreter of the wishes of that great middle class of this country
which supplies the mind, the will, and the power requisite for all
the great and good things that have to be done, and therefore
acknowledged by a whole people as their best impersonation!"[3]
Taking his career from 1830 to his death in 1865, wrote Arnold,
"there cannot be a shadow of doubt . . . that he found England
the first power in the world's estimation, and that he leaves her
the third, after France and the United States."[4] It was under his
leadership that England embarked upon a policy of energetic
but unintelligent blustering in all the Chancelleries of Europe,
making her middle class government a thing of contempt in the
eyes of foreign rulers which culminated in her ridiculous posturing
over the Schleswig-Holstein question. "It was the strong middle
part which showered abuse and threats on Germany for mis-
handling Denmark; and when Germany gruffly answered, *Come
and stop us*, slapped its pockets, and vowed that it never had the
slightest intention of pushing matters so far as this."[5]

In such a manner did Arnold seek to drive home to his public
what he considered the outstanding characteristics of the middle
class.   First there was its bustling energy ever seeking to act
according to the light it had got hold of without first finding out
whether it was the best light.   To this he gave the name of
Hebraism, contrasting it with Hellenism which seeks to see the
thing as it really is. With such a defect of intelligence went a

[1] id., p. 93.
[2] id., pp. 92-3.
[3] *My Countrymen*, pp. 199-200.
[4] id., p. 200.
[5] id., p. 201

defect of delicacy of perception or taste[1] that could permit approval of the Corinthian style of G. A. Sala's newspaper articles, and could even get up an agitation for the rescinding of the law prohibiting marriage with a deceased wife's sister.[2] Associated with and contributing to these deficiencies was a defective religion of which people such as Mr. Cattle were leading exponents. The core of the middle class was Nonconformist, and they took eagerly to catch words such as the Dissidence of Dissent, and The Protestantism of the Protestant Religion.[3] The obstinate determination which this engendered, to stand fast in an unattractive Hebraistic religion, and not to seek to sweeten their behaviour by looking for fresh ideas and enlarging their intellectual horizons, earned for them the sobriquet of Philistines. "For *Philistine* gives the notion of something particularly stiff-necked and perverse in the resistance to light and its children; and therein it specially suits our middle class, who not only do not pursue sweetness and light, but who even prefer to them that sort of machinery of business, chapels, tea-meetings, and addresses from Mr. Murphy and the Rev. W. Cattle, which makes up the dismal and illiberal life on which I have so often touched."[4] Arnold's most telling description of how hum-drum middle class existence could become occurs in his essay "My Countrymen" that he wrote as a forerunner to *Friendship's Garland.* "Your middle-class man thinks it the highest pitch of development and civilisation when his letters are carried twelve times a day from Islington to Camberwell, and from Camberwell to Islington, and if railway trains run to and fro between them every quarter of an hour. He thinks it nothing that the trains only carry him from an illiberal, dismal life at Islington to an illiberal, dismal life at Camberwell; and the letters only tell him that such is the life there."[5] That such a dismal civilisation should exist was bad enough, but that it should be a source of satisfaction to the middle classes argued a grave cultural defect on their part. When Arnold heard the glowing

---

[1] *Culture and Anarchy*, p. 182.
[2] The Corinthian style "has glitter without warmth, rapidity without ease, effectiveness without charm," *Essays in Criticism*, 1st Series, pp. 75–6, where it was considered characteristic of Kinglake's *Invasion of the Crimea.* The hardy parliamentary annual Bill for permitting Marriage with a Deceased Wife's Sister was a favourite topic for Arnold's "vivacities". *Vide Friendship's Garland*, pp. 62 ff; *Culture and Anarchy*, pp. 180 ff.
[3] J. H. Clapham (Young, ed., op. cit., i, pp. 243–4) lends support to Arnold's view: "seriousness, few amusements, religion and work were the hallmarks of the middle class in the new towns, where all that was not labour was middle-class."
[4] *Culture and Anarchy*, p. 102. Mr. Murphy was the agitator at whose Birmingham meeting Mr. Cattle presided. Cf. *supra*, pp. 148 ff.
[5] *My Countrymen*, p. 213.

utterances of Robert Lowe upon the achievements of the middle
class, or the encomium such as that passed upon them by a Congregationalist minster in the Crosby Hall lectures: "There is more
religion, morality, soundness of character, and social happiness
among the middle classes of British society, than in any other
country. They are the strength of the Commonwealth, the source
and spring of our industry, genius, commerce, science and prosperity",[1] he could agree with much in the sentiments expressed,
but he also wanted to know what was the good of this constant
reiteration of self-praise. Did it not tend to blind the middle classes
to their very considerable short-comings? And was not just such a
spiritual pride one of their gravest dangers? One steeped in Greek
literature knew the Greek fear of ὕβρις, and the nemesis which
awaited an overweening self-satisfaction. It seemed that the middle
classes of Victorian England might not be immune from such
dangers, and that unless some transformation took place their pre-
eminence was a source of weakness to the country. A class with a
defective religion, a defective taste, a defective intelligence, full of self-
reliance, and self-satisfaction at its own achievements was hardly the
kind to take a place at the head of contemporary civilisation and
be regarded as an object for the emulation of the less fortunate.

Arminius, Arnold's forthright character in *Friendship's Garland*,
as he took his final leave of England wrote his farewell message
to the middle classes: "I do exhort your Philistine middle class,
which is now England, to get, as I say 'Geist', to search and
not rest till it sees things more as they really are, and how little
of a power over things as they really are is its money-making, or
its unrestricted independence, or its newspaper publicity, or its
Dissent, or any of the things with which it is now most taken. . . .
My dear friend, I have told you our German programme,—*the
elevation of a whole people through culture.* That need not be your
English programme, but surely you may have some better programme than this your present one,—*the beatification of a whole
people through clap-trap.*

"And now, my dear friend, it is time for me to go, and to what
fate I go I know not; but this I know, that your country, where
I have lived so long and seen so much, is on its way either to a
great transformation or to a great disaster."[2]

Two things, which could be turned to advantage, stood out

---

[1] *Crosby Hall Lectures*, p. 240, chap. VII, "The Educational Condition of the People
of England: and the Position of Nonconformists in Relation to its Advancement",
Rev. R. Ainslie.

[2] *Friendship's Garland*, pp. 81–2.

when one examined the contemporary middle class. First there was amongst it a considerable intellectual ferment. An energetic mental curiosity was apparent in "that immense literature of the day which we see surging up all round us" and of which the middle classes were the great readers. Hardly a word of such literature, it was true, would reach the future, but its existence was at least a sign of the mental ferment of that class. What were the possibilities of that movement? "Will it conduct the middle class to a high and commanding pitch of culture and intelligence? That depends on the sensibility which the middle class has for *perfection*; that depends on its power to *transform itself*."[1] The second possible source of strength lay in the religion of the middle class, "a source of vitality, energy, and persistent vigour."[2] From it, they had gained an undeniable strength of character. But though it provided such a source of strength, it had by no means brought them to perfection; "nay by the rigid mould in which it has cast their spirit, it has kept them back from perfection. The most that can be said of it is, that it has supplied a stable basis on which to build perfection; it has given them character, though it has not given them culture."[3]

What the middle class required therefore was the re-direction of its intellectual impulses and the supplementing of its religious force in a way that would ensure its continued growth towards perfection.

The middle class, in short, must be transformed.

This was Arnold's great mission in life. Sprung of the middle class himself,[4] fully conversant with and at times painfully aware of its shortcomings, able to stand aside and above it to point out its imperfections, he yet never lost faith in it and ever had its best interests at heart. Even after two decades of seemingly fruitless exhortation he was able to write: "The Puritan middle class, with all its faults, is still the best stuff in this nation. Some have hated

---

[1] *A French Eton*, p. 114.   [2] id., p. 116.   [3] id., p. 116.
[4] The son even of a Philistine, according to Swinburne, in an elaborate review of his poetry, *The Fortnightly Review*, October, 1867.

In June 1864 he sent to W. E. Gladstone *A French Eton*, and in a covering letter wrote: "in a now twelve years' acquaintance with British schools all over the country and with their promoters, I have perhaps had more than common opportunities for studying the English middle class—and particularly one of its strongest and most characteristic parts—the Protestant Dissenters" (British Museum, Add MSS. 44403, f. 107, *Gladstone Papers*). {W. H. G. Armitage, art. "Matthew Arnold and W. E. Gladstone: Some New Letters," *University of Toronto Quarterly*, vol. xviii, no. 3, April 1949, reproduces most of the correspondence between Arnold and Gladstone preserved in the Gladstone Papers of the British Museum.

and persecuted it, many have flattered and derided it—flattered it that while they deride it they may use it; I have believed in it. It is the best stuff in this nation, and in its success is our best hope for the future. But to succeed it must be transformed."[1]

How then was it to be transformed? Arnold had no complete solution for the problem, but he was of the opinion that at least the most powerful agent of its transformation lay through its formal educational establishment. It was "not a panacea by any means, not all-sufficient, not capable of working miracles of change in a moment, but yet a remedy sure to do good; the first and simplest and most natural remedy to apply, although it is left singularly out of sight, and thought, and mention."[2] In 1878, he still complained that his policy was unappreciated: "For some twenty years I have been full of this thought, and have striven to make the British public share it with me; but quite vainly. At this hour, in Mr. Gladstone's programme of the twenty-two engagements of the Liberal Party, there is not a word of middle-class education".[3] Again, seven years later, in another General Election, he counselled his Liberal friend, A. J. Mundella that there was "a good opening now to speak of middle class education—and nobody takes it."[4]

Arnold opened his campaign for better middle-class education with a short reference to its desirability in his report on foreign schools in 1859.[5] In 1863–4, he produced a comprehensive statement of his views in "A French Eton" which came out in three parts in *Macmillan's Magazine*. This he followed by extensive contributions containing many references to middle-class education in the *Cornhill Magazine* and *Pall Mall Gazette*, *My Countrymen* in February 1866, a series of letters between March 1866 and November 1870 which were subsequently published as *Friendship's Garland*, and the articles between July 1867 and August 1868 which he published as *Culture and Anarchy*. In the meantime an extensive examination of the continental situation, *Schools and Universities on the Continent*, came out in 1868. There was then an interval of several years while he was chiefly occupied in writing upon religion. In July 1878 he resumed his task with "Irish

---

[1] *Mixed Essays*, "Irish Catholicism and British Liberalism," p. 142, first published in *The Fortnightly Review*, July 1878.
[2] *Irish Essays*, "An Unregarded Irish Grievance," p. 61.
[3] *Mixed Essays*, "Porro unum est necessarium", p. 144.
[4] *Vide infra*, Appendix, p. 3, Letter dated 14th October, 1885.
[5] *Vide supra*, p. 243.

Catholicism and British Liberalism" in *The Fortnightly Review*, and, in the following November, in the same periodical, he rather glumly summed up his previous arguments and efforts for middle-class education in "Porro unum est necessarium". The *Fortnightly* was again his mouthpiece in the February of 1879 when he published an address to the Ipswich Working Men's College entitled "Ecce convertimur ad gentes". Four essays in *The Nineteenth Century* followed: "The Future of Liberalism" July 1880, "The Incompatibles" in two parts in April and June 1881, and "An Unregarded Irish Grievance", in August 1881,[1] the latter of which was his last eloquent plea for the renovation of the middle classes through a reform of their schools. These he supplemented by several short paragraphs in his General Reports for the years 1878 and 1882. A final general review of the situation appeared in Arnold's article on "Schools" in T. H. Ward's *Reign of Queen Victoria*, which was published in 1887.

In the first period of his activities, during the 60s, he considered "A French Eton" to be his chief contribution. Concerning Part III of this, he wrote to his mother: "I have written to my own mind, nothing better."[2] It was one of the key works in the prevailing campaign for the overhaul of English secondary education. There had recently been a rapid growth of interest in this topic starting from the time when Nathaniel Woodard published his pamphlet "A Plea for the Middle Class" in 1848, founded an educational society, and established three flourishing secondary schools in various parts of Surrey. His founding zeal was matched by a sudden outcrop of new proprietary schools for the upper middle class that appeared in the early 60s, of which Clifton, Malvern, and Haileybury, all founded in 1862, were the outstanding examples. In particular, at this juncture, the establishment of the Oxford and Cambridge Local Examinations in 1858 set many people thinking more seriously about the state of secondary schools, and middle class education in general. *The Guardian*, of 11th November, 1863, had an editorial on the subject in which it saw the only means of improvement to be the extension of the Local Examination system in an attempt to draw all grammar schools within its orbit and thereby establish a recognised standard of achievement for them. It hoped that the upper

---

[1] The essay published subsequently as "An Unregarded Irish Grievance," in *Irish Essays* appeared in *The Fortnightly* as "Irish Grammar Schools".
[2] Russell, ed., Letter to his Mother, 29th April, 1864, i, p. 231.

and lower strata of the middle class would pool their common educational resources but thought that that could not be expected at the present juncture. "The exclusiveness of English character—quite as great in the lower as in the higher strata of social life—forbids the combination of this (classical) instruction with that which would be suitable to persons engaged in humbler pursuits. A town of a few thousand inhabitants requires its grammar-school, its commercial academy, and its National School, and seems to separate these three institutions one from another with as much jealousy as could be displayed in guarding the barriers of an ancient aristocracy from democratic assault. The division is perhaps neither liberal nor economical: much more might be effected by a combination of resources at least in the higher departments of educational work. But people will not have it so. . . ." By this time the Clarendon Commission, appointed to inquire into the conduct of the nine great Public Schools, was sitting, and it was natural to think of rounding off the labours of the recent series of Royal Commissions on the two ancient universities (1850–52), on elementary education (1858–61), and on the public schools (1861–64) by a further comprehensive investigation into "the education given in schools not comprised within Her Majesty's two former Commissions."[1]

In bringing about the establishment of this commission, the Taunton or Schools Inquiry Commission, in 1864, Arnold appears to have played no small part. He gave himself, earnestly, at the beginning of the year, to the task of stirring up a public conscience on the matter of middle-class education. This was the purpose of "A French Eton". Of Part II, which he composed in January, he wrote: "I really want to *persuade* on this subject."[2] He thought "it will in time produce much effect",[3] and to assist this con-summation he sent off copies to Cobden and Sir John Pakington: "Cobden because of his influence with the middle classes, Paking-ton because of his lead among the educationists." From both he received handsome acknowledgements, and also from Macmillan his publisher, who regarded it as of high importance.[4] His Part III made him "perfectly miserable with fret and worry",[5] but when completed, he regarded it as his *chef d'oeuvre*. He was not a

[1] Terms of reference of the Taunton Commission, appointed 28th December, 1864.
[2] Russell, ed., Letter to his Mother, 22nd January, 1864, i, p. 219.
[3] id., 11th February, 1864, i, p. 226.
[4] ibid; id., 2nd February, 1864, i, p. 224.
[5] id., Letter to Lady de Rothschild, 15th March, 1864, i, p. 228.

little flattered by its reception and recorded with some satisfaction that "people say it is revolutionary."[1] Three months later he had the further satisfaction of a request from H. A. Bruce, Vice-President of the Committee of Council, for his suggestions as to the personnel of a proposed commission on middle class schools and a further letter asking his advice as to its scope.[2] What Arnold's proposals were, is largely unknown. As W. E. Forster served on the commission it may be conjectured that he was on Arnold's list of suggestions, and Frederick Temple, at least, who was also appointed, was submitted by Arnold to Bruce "as a man who certainly ought to be on the Commission."[3] Arnold himself seems to have been asked to serve, or at least to have been proposed as a commissioner, and also to have been put forward as a possible secretary for the Commission.[4] He preferred, however, to be "sent abroad by the new Middle Class Schools Commission,"[5] and wrote to Lord Lyttleton, one of the leading members, suggesting an investigation of secondary education overseas. Lyttleton replied "strongly approving" of the idea[6] and Arnold duly received an invitation to become "Assistant Commissioner for Parts of the Continent of Europe."[7] His subsequent report on secondary education was an important document which appeared to carry great weight with the Commissioners, and became a favourite source of quotation and information for all interested in the reform of secondary education during the remainder of the nineteenth century.

Arnold made much of the unsatisfactory condition of middle class schools. He thought that Dickens had hit them off admirably in *David Copperfield*. Arnold read it for the first time in 1880 and wrote to J. G. Fitch: "I have this year been reading *David Copperfield* for the first time. Mr. Creakle's school at Blackheath is the type of our ordinary middle class schools, and our middle

[1] id., 10th May, 1864, i, p. 232.
[2] id., To Miss Arnold, August 1864, i, pp. 238–9.
[3] id., To Mrs. Forster (Jane), 3rd January, 1865, i, p. 244.
[4] id., To his Mother, 11th March, 1865, i, p. 251.
[5] id., To Lady de Rothschild, 14th October, 1864, i, p. 242.
[6] id., To Mrs. Forster (Jane), 3rd January, 1865, i, p. 244. Lord Lyttleton later became chief of the three commissioners of endowed schools appointed under the Endowed Schools Act, 1869.
[7] id., To his Mother, 11th March, 1865, i, p. 250. He received 6 months leave of absence from the Education Department, and left for Paris early in April 1865. His instructions are recorded in *Report of Schools Inquiry Commission*, vol. ii, Miscellaneous Papers, p. 126. The Secretary chosen for the Commission was H. J. Roby, then a master at Dulwich College, later M.P. for Eccles, and a well-known classical scholar, subsequently celebrated for his work on Roman Law.

class is satisfied that so it should be."[1] Dickens had drawn "with the hand of a master . . . a type of the teachers and trainers of its youth, a type of its places of education."[2]

The dismal academy of Salem House, with its ignorant tyrannising headmaster, underpaid ushers, its daily strife and struggle, its "alternation of boiled beef with roast beef, and boiled mutton with roast mutton; of clods of bread and butter, dog's-eared lesson books, cracked slates, tear-blotted copybooks, canings, rulerings, hair-cuttings, rainy Sundays, suet puddings and dirty atmosphere of ink surrounding all,"[3] was a common uninspiring boarding-school in which the hosts of middle class children throughout the country obtained what was called an education. Arnold did not mention that Dickens had balanced Salem House with Dr. Strong's School at Canterbury, and had painted a much more favourable picture of it. For Arnold, however, Dr. Creakle's establishment was the more typical, and in *Friendship's Garland*, he had previously invented his own counterpart to it, Lycurgus Academy. The passage in which he described the education of a peer, a clergyman, and a self-made man of the middle class who were serving as magistrates at a court visited by his censorious Prussian friend, Arminius, is one of the finest examples of his ironic wit, and deserves quotation in full. Arnold has just described the magistrates' political affiliations.

" 'That is all very well as to their politics', said Arminius, 'but I want to hear about their education and intelligence.' 'There, too, I can satisfy you,' I answered. 'Lumpington was at Eton. Hittall was on the foundation at Charterhouse, placed there by his uncle, a distinguished prelate who was one of the trustees. You know we English have no notion of your bureaucratic tyranny of treating the appointments to these great foundations as public patronage, and vesting them in a responsible minister; we vest them in independent magnates, who relieve the State of all work and responsibility, and never take a shilling of salary for their trouble. Hittall was the last of six nephews nominated to the Charterhouse by his uncle, this good prelate, who had thoroughly learnt the divine lesson that charity begins at home.' 'But I want to know what this nephew learnt', interrupted Arminius, 'and what Lord Lumpington learnt at Eton.' 'They

[1] id., Letter to J. G. Fitch, 14th October, 1880, ii, p. 184.
[2] *Irish Essays*, "The Incompatibles", p. 44.
[3] Quoted by Arnold, id., pp. 44–5, from *David Copperfield*, chap. VI *ad fin.*

followed,' said I, 'the grand, old, fortifying, classical curriculum'. 'Did they know anything when they left?' asked Arminius. 'I have seen some longs and shorts of Hittall's,' said I, 'about the Calydonian Boar, which were not bad. But you surely don't need me to tell you, Arminius, that it is rather in training and bracing the mind for future acquisition—a course of mental gymnastics we call it—than in teaching any set thing, that the classical curriculum is so valuable'. 'Were the minds of Lord Lumpington and Mr. Hittall much braced by their mental gymnastics?' inquired Arminius. 'Well,' I answered, 'during their three years at Oxford they were so much occupied with Bullingdon and hunting that there was no great opportunity to judge. But for my part I have always thought that their both getting their degree at last with flying colours, after three weeks of a famous coach for fast men, four nights without going to bed, and an incredible consumption of wet towels, strong cigars, and brandy-and-water, was one of the most astonishing feats of mental gymnastics I ever heard of.'

" 'That will do for the land and the Church,' said Arminius. 'And now let us hear about commerce.' 'You mean how was Bottles educated?' answered I. 'Here we get into another line altogether, but a very good line in its way, too. Mr. Bottles was brought up at the Lycurgus House Academy, Peckham. You are not to suppose from the name of Lycurgus that any Latin and Greek was taught in the establishment; the name only indicated the moral discipline, and the strenuous earnest character, imparted there. As to the instruction, the thoughtful educator who was principal of the Lycurgus House Academy—Archimedes Silverpump, Ph.D., you must have heard of him in Germany?— had modern views. "We must be men of our age," he used to say. "Useful knowledge, living languages, and the forming of the mind through observation and experiment, these are the fundamental articles of my educational creed." Or, as I have heard his pupil Bottles put it in his expansive moments after dinner (Bottles used to ask me to dinner till that affair of yours with him in the Reigate train): "Original man, Silverpump! fine mind! fine system! None of your antiquated rubbish—all practical work— latest discoveries in science—mind constantly kept excited—lots of interesting experiments—lights of all colours—fizz! fizz! bang! bang! That's what I call forming a man." '

" 'And pray,' cried Arminius, impatiently, 'what sort of man do you suppose this infernal quack really formed in your precious friend Mr. Bottles?' 'Well,' I replied, 'I hardly know how to answer that question. Bottles has certainly made an immense fortune; but as to Silverpump's effect on his mind, whether it was from any fault in the Lycurgus House system, whether it was that with a sturdy self-reliance thoroughly English, Bottles, ever since he quitted Silverpump, left his mind wholly to itself, his daily newspaper, and the Particular Baptist minister under whom he sate, or from whatever cause it was, certainly his mind, qua mind—' 'You need not go on,' interrupted Arminius, with a magnificent wave of his hand, 'I know what that man's mind, qua mind, is, well enough.' "[1]

The schools run by Mr. Creakle and Dr. Silverpump were the types of private venture "Educational Homes" whose advertisements could be seen in large numbers in the current issues of *The Times*, offering various inducements of a dietary, scholastic, or disciplinary nature to middle class parents, to enter their children at their establishments.[2]

There were, as Arnold admitted, schools of a more satisfactory nature, such as Marlborough which he described as "probably just now the best-taught school in England,"[3] but their fees were beyond the reach of the bulk of middle class parents in England. The majority of the children of the middle class he held were "scattered about through the numberless obscure endowed schools and 'educational homes' of this country, some of them good, many of them middling, most of them bad; but none of them great institutions, none of them invested with much consideration or dignity."[4]

This verdict was confirmed by the finding of the Taunton Commission who reported that the secondary schools "whether public or private, which are thoroughly satisfactory, are few in proportion to the need," and "that there are very many English parents who, though they are willing to pay a fair price for their children's education, yet have no suitable schools within their

[1] *Friendship's Garland*, pp. 48–51.

[2] Even some twenty-five years after Arnold had described these schools in *A French Eton*, A. H. D. Acland was able to refer, in a parliamentary debate, to the same situation and to quote an actual advertisement which sought to reduce the school's budget by a barter exchange of education for supplies from the local butcher's or grocer's shop. It read: "To Butchers and Grocers—Education—A young lady can be received in a first class and old-established school on the sea coast on reciprocal terms." *Parliamentary Debates*, Apl., 1888; cccxxv, 815. *A French Eton*, pp. 41 ff.

[3] *A French Eton*, p. 46.

[4] id., p. 60.

reach where they can be sure of efficient teaching, and that, consequently, great numbers of the youth of the middle class, and especially of its lower divisions, are insufficiently prepared for the duties of life, or for the ready and intelligent acquisition of that technical instruction the want of which is alleged to threaten such injurious consequences to some of our great industrial interests . . . there is in this country neither organisation nor supervision, nor even effective tests to distinguish the incompetent from the truly successful; and we cannot but regard this state of things as alike unjust to all good schools and schoolmasters, and discreditable and injurious to the country itself."[1]

The last sentence might well have come from the pen of Matthew Arnold for he declared the two great needs of middle class education to be, sufficiency of provision of fit schools, and sufficiency of securities for their fitness.[2] The second is provided in schools such as Eton or Harrow by the moral security of their reputation, but this is not the kind of security that can apply to schools in general. Others offer the security of outstanding head-masters such as Bradley at Marlborough or Nathanial Woodard, but this again is not a type of security that is applicable to all schools.[3] The promoters of the "Oxford and Cambridge Middle Class Examinations" had suggested them as "a very plausible security", and much good had been done by them. But they are manifestly insufficient, for they provide for the examination only of a few select pupils who can be specially coached for them by any unscrupulous master of an "educational home". What was needed was an examination of the entire working of the school, in other words, a system of competent inspection. Arnold had been impressed with the high standard of achievement and the deserved prestige of secondary schools in France. He described at length in "A French Eton" his visit to a lycée at Toulouse and a private school at Sorèze presided over by Lacordaire, the celebrated Dominican preacher.[4] What most caught his attention was the fact that the State insisted upon guarantees of competence from

---

[1] This was quoted with approval by Arnold in Ward, ed., op. cit., pp. 274–5. For a comprehensive analysis of the findings of the Taunton Commission *vide* Adamson, op. cit., pp. 258 ff.

[2] *A French Eton*, p. 53.

[3] id., pp. 44 ff. Bradley who eventually succeeded Arthur Stanley as Dean of Westminster, was the author of the evergreen *Latin Prose Composition*.

[4] The French critic Sainte-Beuve, whom Arnold much admired, has a panegyric on him in *Etudes de Lundi, Les Grands Ecrivains Français*, xix⁰ Siècle, Philosophes et Essayists, III, written in 1849.

persons proposing to engage in teaching, and of satisfactory premises and equipment from those proposing to open a school. This sort of security was lacking to English secondary education which needed "the security of competent supervision."[1] This might well be supplied by the universities. If they could organise and pay a body of inspectors to travel all over England, report on, circulate their reports to, and exercise effective control over "the four or five hundred endowed schools of the country and its unnumbered "educational homes", then Arnold could imagine no better security. University inspection had been Sir John Coleridge's suggestion,[2] and Arnold cordially agreed to it, if it should prove to be a feasible proposition; but of that he had his doubts, and hinted at his own preference. Was such an under-taking within the capabilities of an English university? "The French University could; but the French University was a depart-ment of State. If the English Universities cannot, the security of their inspection will be precarious; if they can there can be no better."[3]

But what of the other, the first requirement, a sufficiency of provision of good schools? "Granting that the Universities may give us the second, I do not see how they are to give us the first."[4] Provision in the past had been effected by endowment; but "the age of endowments is gone".[5] It is interesting to see Robert Lowe and Arnold in some sort of agreement upon this point. They both held that dependence upon endowment made for inflexi-bility, incompetence, and insufficiency of provision of secondary education.[6] Lowe strongly criticised the Taunton Commission on this head. "It is my conviction that its recommendations are founded on an erroneous assumption" that "it is on endowed schools that we must rely for the education of the middle class."[7] His strictures were based upon a misreading of the Report, for, though the Commissioners expended most of their energies on questions relating to endowed schools they did envisage secondary education as a whole, and proposed establishing a central body, an enlarged Charity Commission, under a Minister who should have the supervision of all classes of secondary school, public or

[1] id., p. 45.
[2] *Guardian*, 25th November, 1863; *A French Eton*, p. 58.
[3] *A French Eton*, p. 59.
[4] id., p. 60.
[5] id., p. 67.
[6] id., p. 67.
[7] R. Lowe, *Middle Class Education*, Endowment or Free Trade, pp. 3, 4

private, with the exception of the great Public Schools. The central authority would act through provincial authorities, an inspectorate, and a Council of Examinations which should set school standards and issue certificates to teachers. Such a widespread scheme, however, was not in fact implemented, and Lowe's criticisms were quite apposite to the actual result of the Commission. For out of the mountainous report of twenty-one volumes, there eventually emerged the mouse of the Endowed Schools Act, 1869, which set up a commission of three to take in hand only the arrangement of schemes for the better application of existing endowments. This, to Lowe, was perpetuating a great evil. He thought that it was a necessary tendency of endowments "to be injurious to education, by putting to sleep the diligence of teachers—by bribing parents to accept inferior teaching at a cheaper rate—by discouraging healthy private enterprise—and by fostering an undue adherence to obsolete subjects and methods of instruction."[1] His remedy was an increased dose of free trade, by sweeping endowments aside and allowing free play to the establishment of private venture schools which by the law of supply and demand would soon be established in sufficient quantity throughout the land. Arnold, while agreeing with Lowe, that endowed schools would not, however reformed, entirely supply the deficiency of secondary school provision, had a very different solution. He looked for the provision of schools of a public and national character. Only in this manner could the middle class be assured of *"respected* schools as well as *inspected* ones."[2]

He outlined what he would consider a satisfactory scheme.

"What should be had in view is to constitute, in every county, at least one great centre of secondary instruction, with low charges, with a security of inspection, and with a public character. These institutions should bear some such title as that of *Royal Schools*, and should derive their support, mainly, of course, from school-fees, but partly, also from endowments—their own, or these appropriated to them—and partly from scholarships supplied by public grants."[3] The direction of this "public and coherent organisation" should be in the hands of local bodies, "with a power of supervision by an impartial central authority".[4] Though it did not suggest quite the same details, the Taunton

[1] id., pp. 13–14.
[2] *A French Eton*, p. 61.
[3] id., pp. 70–71.
[4] id., p. 73, *Mixed Essays*, "Porro unum est necessarium", pp. 172–5:

Commission once more gave support to Arnold's views by endorsing his principle of public supervision:

"There is no public inspector to investigate the educational condition of a school by examination of the scholars, no public board to give advice on educational difficulties, no public rewards given directly to promote educational progress except those distributed by the Science and Art Department, hardly a single mastership in the gift of the Crown, not a single payment from the central government to the support of a secondary school, not a single certificate of capacity for teaching given by public authority professedly to teachers in schools above the primary schools. In any of these senses there is no public school and no public education for the middle and upper classes. The State might give test, stimulus, advice, dignity; it withholds them all."[1]

The organisation of a coherent system on a national scale which Arnold desired would not only secure adequate provision of secondary schools, but it would also confer upon the middle class an even greater boon. "Its greatest boon to the offspring of these classes would be its giving them great, honourable, public institutions for their nurture—institutions conveying to the spirit, at the time of life when the spirit is most penetrable, the salutary influences of greatness, honour, and nationality—influences which expand the soul, liberalise the mind, dignify the character."[2]

This then was the best way for transforming the middle classes—by bringing their secondary schools into an effective connection with the State. In place of the hole-in-corner educational homes and academies, there were to be reorganised and supervised by public officers a sufficiency of guaranteed, well-organised and honourable schools for the requirements of all the middle classes.

Eton and the like were schools of dignity and reputation which conferred a sense of belonging to an honourable and uplifting institution upon those who attended them. But they could cater only for the upper classes and a mere fragment of the top of the middle classes. In order to perform for the rest of the middle classes somewhat the same enlarging and liberalising function it was necessary to make their education a matter of public establishment. Other countries had done so; why should not England too? Arnold here once more invoked the Zeitgeist. It was the

[1] Quoted by Arnold, Ward, ed., op. cit., p. 270; *Schools Inquiry Commission*, vi, p. 107.
[2] *A French Eton*, p. 66.

modern tendency to dispense with a jumbled and defective
establishment that stemmed from the Middle Ages, and to replace
it by one which made provision for the actual state of affairs with
"institutions formed by modern society, with modern modes of
operation, to meet modern wants."[1]

"M. Gambetta is the son, I am told, of a tradesman at Cahors,
and he was brought up in the lycée of Cahors; a school not so
delightful and historic as Eton, certainly, but with a status as
honourable as that of Eton, and with a teaching on the whole as
good. In what kind of schools are the tradesmen in England and
Ireland brought up? They are brought up in the worst and most
ignoble secondary schools in Western Europe. . . . For the great
bulk of our middle class . . . the school provision is miserably
inadequate.

"It can only become adequate by being treated as a public
service, as a service for which the State, the nation in its
collective and corporate character, is responsible."[2]

There was some feeling that State-aided education was State-
tainted education. This had been a view commonly expressed
concerning popular-education and its implication was "that in
education given, wholly, or in part, by the State, there is something eleemosynary, pauperising, degrading."[3] Such an opinion
rested upon an inadequate idea of a citizen's relation to the State.
It is not that of a dependent to a parental benefactor, "it is that
of a member in a partnership to the whole firm." They are all
partners striving in association towards the perfection of living
which culture has as its goal. "Towards this great final design of
their connection, they apply the aids which co-operative association can give them". Therefore instead of being tainted and
degraded by making use of a public organisation of schools a
member of the middle class would be "wisely and usefully turning
his associated condition to the best account."[4]

This solution was not readily accepted and acted upon because
the upper class does not care to see such an improvement and the
middle class, in its self-satisfaction, does not realise what it is
missing: "the upper class among us does not wish to be disturbed
in its preponderance, or the middle class in its vulgarity."[5]

[1] id., p. 68.
[2] *Irish Essays*, "An Unregarded Irish Grievance", p. 70; *vide supra*, pp. 79–80,
where this proposition is related to his general considerations on the State.
[3] id., pp. 70–1; *A French Eton*, p. 79.
[4] *A French Eton*, pp. 79–80.
[5] "An Unregarded Irish Grievance," p. 71.

What sort of transformation did Arnold expect to see from his desired reform of middle class education?

Two main results he thought could be achieved beneficial to English civilisation.

First, he looked for a greater homogeniety of the middle classes. He was ready to paint the general characteristics of the middle class on a broad canvas, its earnestness and self-reliance, its defective intelligence and religion, its want of sweetness and light, but he recognised at the same time the extensive divisions that existed within its ranks. The *Guardian* had briefly pointed out the stratification and the resulting division among secondary schools. The Taunton Commissioners had made much of the same factor. "Much of our evidence", they reported, "tends to show that social distinctions in education cannot at present be altogether ignored." [1] And they maintained throughout their report a threefold division of middle-class schools: those with a leaving age of 18–19 years for the children of well-to-do parents contemplating a university education, second grade schools with a leaving age of about 16 years for those of more straightened means of the lower professional class aiming at lower civil service posts, the lesser positions in the legal or medical professions, the army or civil engineering, and schools of the third grade with a leaving age of about 14 years catering for the children of small tenant farmers, small tradesmen, and superior artisans. [2] Arnold was more concerned at a further division that affected the middle class. This was the circumstance that the professional part of the middle class had its education on a different plane from the rest. They were brought up with the upper classes and tended to defer to their views and take their cast of thought. Thus the professional classes were separated out by education from the commercial and industrial classes with whom they should be on a social level. "So we have amongst us the spectacle of a middle class cut in two in a way unexampled anywhere else; of a professional class brought up on the first plane, with fine and governing qualities, but without the idea of science; while that immense business class, which is becoming so important a power in all countries, on which the future so much depends, and which in the leading schools of other countries fills so large a place, is in England brought up on the second plane, cut off from the

[1] *Report*, vol. i, p. 82.
[2] id., p. 20.

aristocracy and the professions, and without governing qualities."[1] This was not the case in France where the professional man and the business man were intellectually on a par, largely because they had passed through the same nation-wide system of secondary schools of the first plane. "The middle class of France has, in consequence, in France, a homogeneity, an extent, and an importance which it has nowhere else."[2] The French have shown clearly that it is possible for a nation to do this. And it is clear that a middle class brought up in this manner will thrive in comparison with one brought up, as in England, on the second plane. Arnold's desire for culture and his desire for equality were both combined in this plea for the elevation of the middle class through an improved provision of secondary education. A middle class brought up to be homogeneous and on the first plane would not need to defer to an aristocracy, and would not feel themselves inferior, nor would they rest content with the defective civilisation with which they were at present satisfied. With a higher education they would make higher demands upon life. As the middle classes were brought into touch with the best, so would they grow constantly in culture and in light. "Our middle class at present *cannot* take the lead which belongs to it"[3]; but, made coherent, and freed from provincialism, by a contact with a uniformly good and national system of education they would be fitted to assume their responsibilities, and to further the growth of the English nation in social equality and culture.

The second effect of an improved middle class education, followed from the first. The amelioration of English society depended for its consummation upon the civilising effect of each class of society upon the one below. This was a theme to which he returned again and again in his essays. Culture appeared to effect its growth towards perfection by raising the lower strata ever upwards towards the higher, in a general equalising and liberalising movement, but in order for this movement to take place, the upper strata must have an attracting and increasingly humanising force. This did not seem to be the case with contemporary English society. The aristocracy appeared to be concerned merely with increasing facilities for ministering to its own pleasures. Thus, "the action of such a class materialises all the

---

[1] *Schools and Universities*, pp. 276–7.
[2] *Mixed Essays*, "Porro Unum est necessarium", p. 162.
[3] *Irish Essays*, "Ecce, Convertimur ad Gentes", p. 98.

class of newly enriched people as they rise. The middle class, having above them this materialised upper class, with a wealth and luxury utterly out of their reach, with a standard of social life and manners, the offspring of that wealth and luxury, seemingly utterly out of their reach also, are inevitably thrown back too much upon themselves, and upon a defective type of civilisation. The lower class, with the upper class and its standard of life still further out of their reach, and finding nothing to attract them in the standard of life of the middle classes, are inevitably, in their turn, thrown back upon themselves, and upon a defective type of civilisation." [1] We see therefore an upper class materialised, a middle class vulgarised, and a lower class brutalised. How can we break through this vicious situation. The solution, in large part, lay in "the establishment of public schools for the middle classes." [2] "Middle-class education is a great democratic reform, of the truest, surest, safest kind." [3] "I am convinced," he wrote, "that nothing can be done effectively to raise this (lower) class except through the agency of a transformed middle class." [4] The promising ones of these "children of the future whose day has not yet dawned" [5] could rise through the agency of these middle class schools "into the class above them to the great advantage of society". [6] But, important as such isolated climbing might be, the influence of a "transformed middle class" would be more extensive still. They would in general exercise an attracting force upon the lower classes inspiring them to rise out of their present "brutalised" condition, humanising them and making them eventually fit to assume that high destiny over the nation's fortunes that they would one day be called to. "This obscure embryo, only just beginning to move, . . . this immense working class . . . will have, in a cultured, liberalised, ennobled, transformed middle class, a point towards which it may hopefully work a goal towards which it may with joy direct its aspirations." [7]

[1] id., p. 88; cf. *supra*, p. 85.
[2] id., p. 93. "I mean the provision by law, throughout the country, of a supply of properly guaranteed schools, in due proportion to the estimated number of the population requiring them; schools giving secondary instruction, as it is called—that fuller and higher instruction which comes after elementary instruction—and giving it at a cost not exceeding a certain rate."
[3] id., p. 99.
[4] Russell, ed., Letter to his Mother, 2nd February, 1864, i, p. 224.
[5] *A French Eton*, p. 131.
[6] "Ecce Convertimur ad Gentes", p. 94.
[7] *A French Eton*, pp. 130–1.

He felt, therefore, that the current move towards an unrelieved technical training for aspiring members of the lower and middle classes showed evidence of a wrong approach to education. "Our educated and intelligent classes in their solicitude for our backward working class, and their alarm for our industrial pre-eminence, are beginning to cry out for technical schools for our artisans. Well-informed and distinguished people seem to think it is only necessary to have special schools of arts and trades, as they have abroad, and then we may take a clever boy from our elementary schools, perfected by the Revised Code, and put him at once into a special school." [1] But the best continental experience has shown that a pupil cannot get the best out of a special school unless he enters it after an adequate secondary preparation. "To send him straight there from the elementary school, is like sending a boy from the shell at one of our public schools to hear Professor Ritschl lecture on Latin inscriptions." [2] Furthermore, to embark upon a programme of exclusively technical education was to commit the error of Swiss education which had developed through its trade schools and its polytechnics an intelligent industrialism "but not quite intelligent enough to have cleared itself from vulgarity." [3] Through such a system pupils learn the techniques of industry and the sciences, but they do not learn science which is the "aptitude for finding their way out of a difficulty by thought and reason." [4] Industrialists were blaming the ignorance and unreasonableness of the working classes for the labour questions which were just then embarrassing them, but some intelligent people were of the opinion that the poverty of the employers' middle class education, the inferior governing qualities and their lack of science had much to do with the matter, making them incapable of "creating new relations between themselves and the working class when the old relations fail." [5] This called for a broadening of outlook, a humanising, and a flexibility which could come only from an education which took them beyond the narrow confines of their mechanical pursuits, and put them in touch with the "best that has been thought and said in the world." Such were Arnold's reflections in 1868, and at the end of his career nearly twenty years later he repeated the

[1] *Schools and Universities*, pp. xx–xxi.
[2] id., p. xxi.
[3] *Schools and Universities*, p. 254.
[4] id., p. xx.
[5] ibid.

same sentiments. "The failure, after all, and the menace to the future of our industry and commerce, lies far more in the defects of mind and training of our middle class than of our lower."[1] This situation was not to be remedied until England made for herself an organic system of education. And in such a structure the keystone was an adequate supply of properly guaranteed secondary schools for the middle classes. Their influence reached in both directions. Below them, primary education was a truncated, uninspired thing without a well-developed secondary system, and above them, the universities were similarly weak without the foundation of good secondary education on which to build. "Secondary and higher schools are closely connected with each other. Without good secondary schools you cannot have good universities; without good universities you cannot have good secondary schools."[2]

Arnold did not write a great deal about university education. He composed two short letters to John Churton Collins, one of which was published in the *Pall Mall Gazette*, on 7th January, 1887, in support of the introduction of English literature as a regular part of the university course, but deprecating any move which might lead to an undue multiplicity of subjects. Fearful as ever of fragmentariness that was akin to Americanism he distrusted the "restlessness" of university authorities, and wanted the innovation confined to "the great works of English literature in the final Examination for honours in Litera Humaniores."[3] Arnold examined continental universities in his report for the Taunton Commission in 1868, giving therein several reflections upon the aims of a university education, and finally, in an address at the opening session of the Liverpool University College in 1882, he showed their relevance to his favourite theme of middle class education.

"University education," he wrote in 1868, "is in the opinion of the best judges, the weakest part of our whole educational system, and we must not hope to improve effectually the second-

---

[1] Ward, ed., op. cit., p. 278.
[2] *The Nineteenth Century*, "A Liverpool Address", November 1882, p. 711.
[3] *Letters from Matthew Arnold to John Churton Collins*, printed for private circulation (20 copies), London, 1910. Letter I, 24th October, 1886; Letter III, 29th December, 1886, printed in *Pall Mall Gazette*, 7th January, 1887. Cf. *supra*, p. 180. J. C. Collins (1848–1908), professor of English Literature, Birmingham 1904–8, did much to encourage the study of English Literature in universities. His article in *The Quarterly Review*, October 1886, began a controversy, during which he collected the views of leading literary figures and published them in the *Pall Mall Gazette*, which was largely responsible for the foundation of a Final Honours School of English at Oxford in 1893.

ary school without doing something for the schools above it with which it has an intimate connection."[1] "It is the function of the university to develope into science the knowledge a boy brings with him from the secondary school,"[2] and "the want of the idea of science, of systematic knowledge, is, as I have said again and again, the capital want, at this moment, of English education and of English life; it is the university ,or the superior school, which ought to foster this idea."[3] This it does by enabling a student to pursue the particular line, along which his special aptitudes lead him, systematically, under first-rate instruction. But the three existing universities did nothing of the sort. Oxford and Cambridge were, as Signor Mateucci described them, hauts lycées; "and though invaluable in their way as places where the youth of the upper class prolong to a very great age, and under some very desirable influences, their school education, . . . they are still, in fact, *schools*, and do not carry education beyond the stage of general and school education."[4] "The University of London labours under a yet graver defect."[5] It was a mere board of examiners, giving no instruction at all. It should be recast, King's and University Colleges should be "co-ordered" with the University of London, and "faculties formed in connection with it, in order to give some public voice and place to superior instruction in the richest capital of the world . . . London would then really have, what it has not at present, a university."[6]

The poverty of our university education, "this entire absence of the crowning of the edifice not only tends to give us, as I have said, a want of scientific intellect in all departments, but it tends to weaken and obliterate, in the whole nation, the sense of the value and importance of human knowledge; to vulgarise us, to exaggerate our estimate, naturally excessive, of the importance of material advantages. . . ."[7]

Therefore, to the advice that he appended to his earlier report on Popular Education: "*Organise your secondary education,*" Arnold could not help "presenting myself once more to my countrymen with an increased demand '*Organise your secondary and your superior*

[1] *Schools and Universities*, p. 286.
[2] id., p. 222.
[3] id., p. 286.
[4] ibid.
[5] id., p. 287.
[6] id., p. 291.
[7] id., p. 288.

instruction."[1] Once more he repeated the necessity for a Minister of Education with a Superior Council of Public Instruction who could see things on a national scale and with an adequate sense of public responsibility. Arnold had the vision of the expansion through this agency of university facilities throughout the length and breadth of England. To maintain academic standards the new bodies brought into being would be under the aegis of one of the three established universities who alone would confer degrees, but the important matter was to "plant faculties in the eight or ten principal seats of population, and let the students follow lectures there from their own homes, or with whatever arrangements for their living they and their parents chose. It would be everything for the great seats of population to be thus made intellectual centres as well as mere places of business; for the want of this at present Liverpool and Leeds are mere overgrown provincial towns while Strasbourg and Lyons are European cities."[2]

He was therefore greatly gratified to see the creation of a University College in Liverpool, and to be invited to address the students at its opening of its second session in 1882. He rejoiced that the new institution was not a mere examining board like the London University. He valued the degrees of the London University, recommended his promising elementary teachers to study for them, and regarded the university generally with great respect, but a university of its type and function would not have had the influence upon the middle class population of a provincial city that he envisaged and thought of immense value for the future civilisation of the nation.

Far more valuable than mere examining was the function of bringing young men into personal contact with teachers of high mental gifts and high attainments, and of raising and forming the pupil by that contact. He hoped that the State might add dignity and prestige to this function by assigning some Regius Professorships to the new institution in Liverpool and to Owens College in Manchester.[3]

The presence of this new university college should be an important step forward in the growth in culture of the middle classes. It should prove a powerful agency for the spread among

[1] id., p. 296.
[2] id., p. 290.
[3] "A Liverpool Address", pp. 714–5.

them of "*lucidity*" in which they were sadly lacking. Lucidity "is the perception of the want of truth and validness of notions long current; the perception that they are no longer possible, that their time is finished and they can serve us no longer."[1] Immersed in a round of money making and manufacturing, the middle classes needed the stimulus of the scientific approach which university studies brought, they needed to see things clearly freed from clap-trap and unessentials, and to "see life whole". Fifteen years before he had urged them to "get Geist", now they had in their hands an instrument for acquiring Geist, or lucidity, as he chose to call it.

"To generate a spirit of lucidity in provincial towns and among the middle classes, bound to a life of much routine and plunged in business, is difficult. Schools and universities—universities with serious studies, with disinterested studies, universities connecting these studies the one with the other, and continuing them into the years of manhood—are in this case the best agency we can use. It may be slow, but it is sure. Such an agency you are now going to employ".[2]

And of the effect that was to be produced in this process of transformation he gave, to the students of the middle class city of Liverpool, an eloquent picture: "Money making is not enough by itself. Industry is not enough by itself. Seriousness is not enough by itself. . . . The need in man for intellect and knowledge, his desire for beauty, his instinct for society, and for pleasurable and graceful forms of society, require to have their stimulus felt also, felt and satisfied. . . . You provide by this college a direct stimulus and satisfaction to the need in human nature for intellect and knowledge. But you at the same time provide indirectly a powerful help to the desire for beauty and to the social spirit. For intellectual culture quickens the wish for a proper satisfaction to these, and if by means of this college intellectual culture becomes a power among you, without doubt it will gradually affect and transform the amusements, pleasures, society, even the aspect and architecture of Liverpool."[3]

[1] id., p. 718.
[2] id., p. 720.
[3] id., p. 717.

CHAPTER XI

MATTHEW ARNOLD AS PROPHET

"English civilisation,—the humanising, the bringing into one harmonious and truly humane life, of the whole body of English society,—that is what interests me."—M. Arnold, *Irish Essays*, "Ecce, Convertimur ad Gentes," p. 85.

IN HIS essay on the eighteenth-century poet, Thomas Gray, Arnold summed him up in four words: "He never spoke out."[1] He might equally have applied the same description to his own poetry. What he produced was small in quantity compared with the output of his leading contemporaries, and for the most part in a minor key. But in his prose works the situation was reversed. He was an indefatigable essayist, not voluminous, but reasonably copious, and certainly forthright. It is this characteristic of forthrightness that largely justifies the title of "Prophet" that has been applied to him by various writers from time to time. For prophecy is a word of two meanings: it means both to speak out, and to foretell. And in both these senses Arnold qualified for the title, but to his contemporaries at least he was more conspicuous as an outspoken critic of current social shortcomings, and an advocate of certain plain, and often reiterated, solutions.

He did not claim to be an original thinker. He claimed simply to bring common sense and a varied experience to bear on the situation, and to deliver in unambiguous terms his findings, indifferent to praise or blame, but hopeful of their eventual acceptance by the community.

There were two clear and distinct policies enunciated throughout his writings, the need for an expansion of State activities, and the need for a greater diffusion of culture.

With the decline of aristocratic government in England, the elevating and directing influence that the aristocracy once wielded should be replaced by the State, representing the "best self" of the nation, an association of all citizens formed for their mutual benefit and inspiration. The State should become the focus of national culture and a means of its further promotion. Through an expansion of the State's activities a coherence could also be given to English life that was sadly lacking, and nowhere

[1] *Essays in Criticism*, 2nd Series, p. 49.

more obviously than in the sphere of education. He therefore thought of the problem of National Education not as that of the provision of elementary instruction for the children of those who support themselves by manual labour, but as that of the development of an organic system of education throughout the country from elementary school to university. Arnold was an early and persistent advocate of the social service state, an organism which was not merely for the purpose of "holding the ring" to see fair or reasonably fair play between the various conflicting parties and interests in the community, but one which actually entered the ring "to bestow certain broad collective benefits upon the nation."[1] The most vital extension of State organisation lay in the field of local government. He could see no reasonable end to the Revised Code without the assumption of authority for education by local governing bodies,[2] nor could he, in fact, see the development of an acceptable system of National Education without the preliminary of an effective municipal organisation.[3]

The promotion of culture was the great aim of every administrative reform that Arnold favoured, just as it was the aim of all human education. His consistent devotion to this ideal led his contemporary, Sidgwick, to call him the "Prophet of Culture". Arnold saw in culture three factors.[4] It was in itself not a static body of knowledge, but an attitude of activity which would not rest content with the status quo but sought to be ever growing. The object of this growth was the attainment of perfection which was a state of things in which men should both act by the best light that they had, and see also that this light was the best that could be had. Hence the middle class, about whose education Arnold was greatly concerned, who were accustomed to act with self-satisfaction according to their best light, stood in need of a cultural transformation through which a reformed public educational system would lead them to seek assurance that the light they had was really the best that was obtainable. From this followed the third feature of culture. It was to be no hole-in-the-corner virtue that could be treasured up in private. A man of culture could not dwell in Olympian remoteness from the common affairs of life; in seeking his own elevation he sought also the elevation of the society in which his lot was cast. However well-informed his

---

[1] *Mixed Essays*, "Democracy", p. 32.
[2] *Vide supra*, p. 220.
[3] *Vide supra*, p. 106.
[4] *Vide supra*, p. 161.

mind, it could not be considered to be cultured, unless his activities were directed towards a career of social usefulness.[1] Arnold illustrated the procedure of his man of culture in his own treatment of many questions, but perhaps in none so simply and clearly as in the field of comparative education. He became interested in continental education on his first official tour in 1859 on behalf of the Newcastle Commission. His subject was elementary education but he did not rest content with his terms of reference. On his return his most impressive recommendation was his advice to English educational authorities to organise their secondary education, and he managed, on tour, to obtain material for an important series of essays in secondary education which led to his second visit in 1865 on behalf of the Taunton Commission. He returned this time with a recommendation to organise university and secondary education, and for the rest of his career he continually kept abreast of current developments, incorporating the lessons from their progress in his essays from time to time. Finally in 1886 he returned once more, eager as ever, for a further investigation of elementary education. The knowledge thus gathered he found, like many students of comparative education, interesting for its own sake, but he felt its real importance to lie in the suggestions that could be drawn from it for the improvement of education in his own country. Other investigators tended, in a spirit of national self-satisfaction to seek out the practices in which their own system was superior to that of others. The man of culture, however, tried "to treat this comparative study with proper respect, not to wrest it to the requirements of our inclinations or prejudices", and wished to appreciate the ways in which foreign ideas and practices might be superior to those of his own country. He tried "simply and seriously to find what it teaches us."[2] The study then had some social usefulness, if he could urge the adoption or modification of whatever ideas seemed transferable and beneficial. Thus Arnold was able to find inspiration in the French treatment of middle class education, and in the French High Council for Education, in the Prussian state organisation of education, in Zurich's organic integration of schools of all grades, in Swiss treatment generally of compulsory education, and in Italian and Dutch views upon religious teaching in schools.

[1] *Vide supra*, pp. 166-7.
[2] *Schools and Universities*, p. xi.

These two leading, and, for Arnold, inter-related policies of the extension of State influence, and the diffusion of culture penetrated all his work, so that there is hardly an essay that he wrote upon any topic that does not contain a reference to one or other, or both of them. For the student of education, the best exposition of them and their educational implications may be found clearly and succinctly set forth in four essays. His Preface to *Popular Education in France* written in 1861, and reprinted as "Democracy" in *Mixed Essays*, and *A French Eton*, Part III, 1864, summarise his thoughts upon the part to be played by the State in education, and its importance, in particular, for middle class education. The Preface to *Culture and Anarchy*, 1869, and his Rede Lecture "Literature and Science" delivered in 1882 and printed in *Discourses in America*,[1] set forth, in his most readable style, his doctrine of culture.

The reader of these four essays may gain from them an outline of what Arnold strove to see implemented in English education, and he may discern through them also the convictions which lay behind Arnold's various enthusiasms.

From the time when he emerged from the emotional and intellectual stress of the period of his youth, and settled into his life's work as an inspector of schools, he held and expressed several consistent ideas that form the background of all his utterances upon culture and the State in their relation to education. Of these lines of thought four were most prominent.

First came his apprehension of the spread in his own country of what he called "Americanism". He had expressed his fear of this phenomenon in one of his earliest extant letters in 1848, and it was constantly in his mind during the four decades of continuous literary output that lay before him. Americanism meant especially two things, a tendency in life towards fragmentariness, and an addiction to the banal.[2] To counteract the insidious spread of these influences was an important educational task. The antidote to fragmentariness was greater coherence of organisation by means of the State, and a change of outlook which culture could bring about. Similarly culture, with its preference for the first-rate in every field of endeavour and its contemplation of the best that has been thought and said in the world, was the chosen instrument in the campaign against banality. To Arnold, as to

---

[1] It was published also in *The Nineteenth Century*, August 1882.
[2] *Vide supra*, pp. 68 ff.

General Smuts at a later date, civilisation had struck its tents and was everywhere on the march. No longer were the old signposts visible, no longer could the old guides be trusted. Under such circumstances there was a danger of civilisation going astray for want of suitable direction, or even a danger of regression if its various elements should act independently and in opposition to one another. Arnold was thus led to lay great stress upon unity. The need for seeing a problem as a whole with all the inter-connections of its various aspects was constantly before him. Hence his great desire for a Minister of Education as a "distinct centre of responsibility" who should be able to plan for the country as a whole.

Allied to this feeling was the second characteristic of his reflec-tions, his conviction that his mission was to further the humanisa-tion of society. He was supremely interested in "civilisation" or the "humanisation of man in society". This was the essential task of education, to make a human being and human society more truly human. This was the touchstone by which school subjects and methods were to be judged. His argument for the retention of religious instruction in elementary schools was based on these grounds; and his continued opposition to the Revised Code rested on his view that it substituted a formal examination of the results of the mechanical teaching of the rudiments of literacy, for an inspection into the manner in which schools "had human-ised and advanced the children of the labouring classes in civilisation."[1] One of the important tenets of Arnold's humanism was the need for social equality. As he looked around him he found everywhere in England a "religion of inequality" barring the development of national solidarity and the opportunity for the expansion of human personality. A belief in social equality was the prerequisite of a truly national education which should characterise an enlightened society.[2] For such a society seeks the elevation of all the individuals composing it, seeks, in other words, the diffusion of culture throughout all its members. In this attitude Arnold has won the approval of subsequent leading Liberal thinkers. He regarded himself as a Liberal of the Future, and appears to have been largely justified in his self-chosen epithet. For the keynote of modern Liberal thought upon educa-tion has been the transformation of society through greater

[1] *Vide supra*, p. 213–4.
[2] *Vide supra*, p. 87.

equality of opportunity effected by a public provision of schools of all grades.

The desire to transform and elevate society was the third salient characteristic of Arnold's thought. Just as his father sought to transform Rugby and the Public School system, so Matthew sought to transform society at large by improving its educational provision. Matthew, in this, was Dr. Arnold writ large. He tended, in fact, to become more and more conscious of like-thinking with his father as he grew older. At the time when he was writing *Culture and Anarchy* he related how he felt inclined to reflect upon the tendencies of his father's work, "and to try and connect my own with them".[1] Thus in his reflections upon the State he thought he was "quite papa's son, and his continuator",[2] and in his thoughts upon the establishment of a general Evangelical Church he re-echoed his father's sentiments. Dr. Arnold's whole policy that "was founded on the principle of awakening the intellect of every individual boy",[3] his concern at the widening gap between upper and lower classes, and even his minor traits, such as his affection for German literature, his admiration for France, contempt for Lord Palmerston, and penchant for seizing upon a telling word or phrase and elaborating it at length, were all characteristics of his son. Prince Lee's[4] summary of Dr. Arnold's influence, "what I feel especially I have derived from you, a knowledge of higher aims and a desire to aim at a simpler, truer course of life and thought,"[5] might with equal validity have been written by an admirer of Matthew Arnold. Above all there ran through the lives of both father and son a missionary zeal for the transformation and elevation of society. Both were quite clear in their minds as to what was wrong with contemporary England and how it should be remedied, and both felt a compulsion to preach, the one from the pulpit, the other from the pages of a periodical, the way to the new dispensation. Thus we find that, at every turn, Matthew Arnold's writing upon education was connected with the current social situation. He was haunted at times with the thought of the "almost imminent danger of England losing immeasurably in all

---

[1] Russell, ed., op. cit., Letter to his Mother, Christmas Day, 1867, i, p. 381.
[2] id., 11th February, 1864, i, p. 226, *vide supra*, pp. 74–75.
[3] A. Whitridge, op. cit., p. 107.
[4] J. P. Lee (1804–69) taught at Rugby under Dr. Arnold, 1830–38, was appointed Headmaster of King Edward's School, Birmingham, and later became Bishop of Manchester.
[5] id., p. 100.

ways, declining into a sort of greater Holland",[1] unless the English spirit should undergo "a great transformation".[2] He felt it his destiny to do everything in his power to effect this desirable consummation, which meant essentially the conversion of the Philistines from their self-satisfied provincialism, to the pursuit of culture. Hence his unwearied advocacy of adequate secondary education for the middle classes through which the spirit of England might be transformed. Hence also his spirited plea for the study of literature in elementary schools to leaven and elevate the lower classes. His assessment of the relative claims of science and literature to a major place in the curriculum was based upon their likely social effects, and the palm was awarded to literature for its greater possibilities of humanising society and effecting an elevation in "the standard of life".[3] He was aware that mere literacy and a knowledge of natural science are not enough to ensure the development of a civilised nation.

His emphasis upon the progressive elevation of society was closely related to the fourth notable feature of his thought. This was his insistence upon "growth". He would have approved of the statement of John Dewey that "the criterion of the value of school education is the extent in which it creates a desire for continued growth, and supplies means for making the desire effective in fact."[4] Growth, however, was not a haphazard development, but a pursuit of perfection. This required flexibility of mind so that one could appreciate the way in which the modern world was moving, and adjust one's course accordingly. The Zeitgeist which indicated the current direction of civilisation's growth was an important force determining his educational opinions. He did not submit it to a very close analysis. He did not explain the mechanism of how to determine whether it was making towards the goal of perfection, or even how to determine what was the Zeitgeist itself. It was, nevertheless, a useful way of calling attention to new political and social developments, and new

---

[1] Russell, ed., op. cit., Letter to Miss Arnold, November 1865, i, p. 309.
[2] id., Letter to Mrs. Forster, 14th November, 1863, i, p. 207.
[3] *Vide supra*, pp. 202.
[4] J. Dewey, *Democracy and Education*, p. 62. Dewey gave much attention to Arnold's work and frequently quotes him with approval. In *Characters and Events*, vol. i, pp. 3–17, "Matthew Arnold and Robert Browning" (published originally in *The Andover Review*, August, 1891) he analysed Arnold's view of philosophy and in vol. ii, pp. 776 ff (published originally as "Science and the Education of Man", in *Science*, 28th January, 1910) he approved of Arnold's emphasis upon literature, but complained of his neglect of scientific method as a leading element in culture.

trends in educational thought that might require serious examination. And he saw in it also a stimulus to educators to be constantly alert to ensure that their organisation and their practices were an adequate response to the times in which they lived.

Arnold's profound sense that he was witnessing the breakdown of a culture, and that the future prospects of civilization depended upon a widespread realization of the crisis and upon the implementation of measures adequate to transform society to cope with the problems and responsibilities of a new age, led him to take an unusually comprehensive view of the role of the school in society. In his mind it should be a unifying and transforming agency, humanising those under its care, developing in them a greater flexibility and alertness to the meaning of the contemporary scene, and fostering in them an untiring zeal for the pursuit of perfection.

He was perturbed to see that English education was lacking in such aims and ideals. And where he saw the lack he drew attention to it, and offered his solution for the situation. Arnold's chief importance as an educator was that he raised, and made known, with all the influence and prestige of his literary reputation, such problems at a time when there was insufficient consciousness of them. He was very conscious of living in a transitional period in which old institutions and old values were passing away. It is to his great credit that this consciousness made him acutely aware of the need for re-examining England's educational tradition, and impelled him to proclaim to his countrymen the necessity for its transformation. In three major particulars, English education, to his mind, was making an inadequate response to the requirements of the times. It lacked responsible organisation, it lacked a due appreciation of its task as a humanising agent, and it lacked a social consciousness. Hence his persistent agitation for three things above all, the establishment of a Ministry of Education and effective local educational authorities, the reform of the Revised Code, and provision of adequate secondary education for the middle class.

Arnold was, in fact, not merely a Liberal of the Future, but an Educationalist of the Future also. "I have a profound conviction", he wrote at the conclusion of *Schools and Universities* in 1868, "that if our country is destined . . . still to live and prosper, the next quarter of a century will see a reconstruction of English education as entire as that which I have recommended in these remarks, however impossible such a reconstruction may to many now seen".[1] His prophecy was unfulfilled.[2] Arnold, however, in due course and by slow degrees, was to establish his right to the title of Prophet in the more generally accepted sense of the term. The Act of Parliament establishing a Board of Education, and the enlightened Suggestions for the Consideration of Teachers that emanated from that Board, the comprehensivere organisation initiated by the Act of 1902, and the subsequent modifications and extensions that led eventually to the transformation of education that was embodied in the Act of 1944, bear testimony to Arnold's prescience. He would assuredly have approved of the Act of 1944 as making an adequate legal provision for the education of the nation. But it is a far cry from the legal embodiment of "the collective wisdom of the nation's best self" in an Act of Parliament, to the appreciation of the transformation that it implies, and to its actual working out in practice in the spirit of sweet reasonableness and flexibility that Arnold advocated. Perhaps in many ways there is need, still, among educationalists of that great force of moral committment to the task of cultural reconstruction that Arnold felt so poignantly.

[1] *Schools and Universities*, p. 296.

[2] Twenty years later, in the year of Arnold's death, John Morley who, before the House, referred to "the disappearance of that bright ornament of his time . . . who showed constantly a very keen and luminous insight into some of the most urgent social, intellectual, and political needs of his generation and his country", and A. H. D. Acland moved a resolution inspired by Arnold's writings to draw the government's attention to the state of secondary education, and the necessity for the appointment of a Minister of Education. *Parliamentary Debates*, 3rd Series, cccxxv, 820. This was one of the opening moves in the campaign that led up to the Board of Education Act, 1899, and the Education Act of 1902.

APPENDIX A

10 Letters of Matthew Arnold to A. J. Mundella and Miss Mundella,
6th March, 1882—26th November, 1886.

Athenaeum Club,
  Pall Mall.   *March 6th* (1882)

Dear Miss Mundella,
  There is so much about education in this volume that I ought to
send it to your father—but then he is so very busy, that I send the
volume to you,—one of my very best readers,—instead. Make him
read some of the essays, and do not be frightened yourself at the ever-
recurring topic of public schools for the middle classes: think of the
"upper ten thousand" of Sheffield and their wants!
  I was very glad to have that glimpse of you on the other night,
but I wish it had been on the Riviera or at Algiers. I hope Mr.
Mundella continues to mend.
                              Ever most truly yours,
                                MATTHEW ARNOLD.

Pains Hill Cottage,
  Cobham, Surrey.   *April 25th* (1882)

My dear Miss Mundella,
  It is true we are living down here, and I accept very few invitations
in London, but I am going to give myself the pleasure of accepting
yours, and of coming to dine with you on the 17th of May.
                              Most truly yours,
                                MATTHEW ARNOLD.

Pains Hill Cottage,
  Cobham, Surrey.   *March 27th* (1883?)

My dear Miss Mundella,
  I had fully meant to call upon you to-day when I was in London,
but I have been kept close prisoner at a Conference all day long, and
I forsee that such will also be my fate to-morrow. Do let me have
one line to say how your father is going on and how Mrs. Mundella
and you yourself are. Pray say everything kind to your father and
mother for me—what a trying time you have all had! I fear these
horrid cold days keep your patient back.
                              Most sincerely yours,
                                MATTHEW ARNOLD.

Fox How,
    Ambleside. *August 4th,* 1883

Dear Mr. Mundella,

I am sure I am not wrong in attributing in great measure to your good offices the frank and full permission which I have received to take my desired leave of absence, at a moment when, from what I heard of opposition at the Treasury, I had abandoned all expectation of it. Many, many thanks for this proof of your active kindness.

I was going to write to you about Mr. Willis. When I was at Harefield I made enquiries on the spot, and from a clergyman well disposed to him. If I go to the promoters of The Memorial I shall only hear fresh charges against him, as he has undoubtedly given much offence. I think the best plan would be to send an official letter to the Memorialists, saying that a new system of control has now come into operation, and that the Department is indisposed now to go into complaints of a kind which arose before it came into operation, but which they hope it will remove. I think also Mr. Willis should be cautioned against roughness of manner and excessiveness of requirement. I am told that since the complaint he has carried myself (sic) more gently, and it is to be hoped that this improvement may continue.

I have returned the portfolio with the correspondence.

Believe me, dear Mr. Mundella,
Most truly yours,
MATTHEW ARNOLD.

Pains Hill Cottage,
    Cobham, Surrey. *October 14th,* 1885

My dear Mundella,

I am just off to Oxford to inspect the Culham Training School. There is indeed a good opening now to speak of middle class education —and nobody takes it.

Look at my Reports in the Minutes for 1878–79, p. 468—and for 1882–3, p. 225.

My Foreign Reports you know. Look also at my *Mixed Essays,* p. 143, and my *Irish Essays,* p. 129. I shall be delighted to give you either or both of these volumes, if I have not given them to you already, as I ought to have done.

To map out the ground, to determine what trust funds are properly available, and to provide buildings is what we might even now put forward as fitting to be done by the State.

I hope after Easter, when my inspecting ends, to go to France and Belgium for two or three weeks, and to ascertain three points: 1. what the literary instruction in their Training Schools now comes to: 2. whether aid to higher and secondary instruction has increased similarly to that to primary: 3. how gratuitous primary instruction—

which is new since I saw the French and Belgium schools—really works.

Ask Fearon how far it can be said with truth that middle age endowments, now diverted to secondary and higher instruction, were originally designed for *popular instruction*. I don't believe it. I don't believe the medieval founder had any notion of what we call popular instruction. To prepare all promising subjects for the clerical career was his aim.

Ever truly yours,
MATTHEW ARNOLD.

Let me have a line here about the volumes of Essays.

Pains Hill Cottage,
 Cobham, Surrey.   *November 2nd* (1885)

My dear Miss Mundella,
 I see your father is moving about: will you kindly tell me whether I could find him on Wednesday either at home or at his club, and at what time? The Government are sending me to enquire as to schools and free schooling at present in Germany, Switzerland and France— and there is no one with whom I so much wish to communicate before setting out as your father.

Most sincerely yours,
MATTHEW ARNOLD.

Athenaeum Club,
 Pall Mall, S.W.   *November 4th* (1885)
My dear Miss Mundella,
 I don't think I need telegraph to your father, as he will hear from you this afternoon. I leave England on Monday, and I rely on your kindness to let me know if I shall find him in London before that.

Most sincerely yours,
MATTHEW ARNOLD.

Cobham.   *November 6th,* 1885.

My dear Mundella,
 Your letter is most valuable: I assure you I am going with a perfectly open mind. At the present time I am against the abolition of school fees in our country; but this is not for the sake of the voluntary schools at all. I am going to Berlin first—then to Saxony; I had already determined on Chemitz because of what you have formerly said of its schools. Then I shall go to Lucerne, and of course Zurich. Do you think it really important for me to go to Bavaria, if I am pressed for time? I start on Tuesday, and must get my German and Swiss informa-

tion by Christmas; to Paris I shall go for a fortnight after the Christmas holidays.

Again let me thank you for your letter, written, too, when you had so much else to occupy you. You are doing the act of a true friend to Forster in going to Bradford.

Most sincerely yours,
MATTHEW ARNOLD.

Pains Hill Cottage,
  Cobham, Surrey. *January 3rd*, 1886

My dear Mundella,

One line to say that the Holloway Candidate is not Hastings but Hastings *Crossley*—a brother to the maker of the Otto Gas Engine, at Manchester.

I have had a note to-day from Goschen which ends with a sentence looking very much as if he were going to take office. We shall know to-morrow, I suppose. I am sure Lord Hartington's taking it would have impaired the majority; perhaps Goschen will not.

Ever cordially yours,
MATTHEW ARNOLD.

Athenaeum Club,
  Pall Mall. *November* 26th, 1886

My dear Mundella,

One line to say that the *Minister* before my mind, who knew nothing about my work, was not you, but the man who gives preferment and opportunity—the Minister in the continental sense.

Lord Ripon and Lord Aberdare both of them tried, in their time, to get opportunity given to me—but in their case, too, the politics and ignorance of the *Minister* stopped the way.

However, no one made so strenuous an effort as you did, and I must some day make public acknowledgement of it.

You are right, the permanent officials know I cared little about my performances; but all I meant to say of them was that in the routine work I had to do for them they were entirely friendly. The pension was expressly for literary and poetic performances, not educational. It is as a functionary of public education that I say I owe nothing to Governments. The recognition and opportunity which would have been useful to me they never gave me. It does not matter now; the work will be done by others, I rejoice to hear that you, for your part, mean to take it in hand. Literature is henceforth my business, if at sixty-three it is not presumptuous to speak of having still a business.

Ever most sincerely and cordially yours,
MATTHEW ARNOLD.

APPENDIX B

Excerpt from *The Modern Church*, 5th November, 1891, p. 507:—

AN UNPUBLISHED LETTER OF MATTHEW ARNOLD

In connection with the unveiling of the bust of Matthew Arnold at Westminster on Saturday, the London correspondent of *The Glasgow Herald* remarks that on one occasion the poet was requested to stand as Member of Parliament for a London constituency, but "with his customary grace" he declined. It may be interesting to the readers of *The Modern Church*, many of whom, no doubt, like the writer, often soothe their troubled brains at the limpid stream of Matthew Arnold's pure poetic inspiration, to know how gracefully and sympathetically he could decline the offer of a position of public dignity and honour. In the year 1877 a group of students at St. Andrews, who were ardent admirers of his poetry and who were grateful to him, moreover, for the side-lights he threw upon their theological studies, wished to have him as Lord Rector of the University. A party was formed to promote his candidature, meetings were held, and a reasonable prospect of success was assured. But before proceeding further I was instructed to write him to ascertain whether or not he was willing to stand. A reply came promptly by telegraph that he was not, and with the next post the following letter reached me. His supporters considered at the time, and though they are scattered far and wide now, I am sure they consider still, that literature lost something by Arnold's too scrupulous conscientiousness.

Athenaeum Club.   *November 22nd, 1877*

My Dear Sir,

I must say to you somewhat more fully than I could say by telegraph how cordially I thank you and those who acted with you for your kind wish to elect me Lord Rector of your University. It cannot but gratify a man who seeks to influence people's minds by his writings to find that he has won the attention and goodwill of a body of young men so sure to tell upon the future of our country and our national thought as are the students of the Scotch universities. But my position as school inspector disqualifies me, in my opinion, for suitably filling that of Lord Rector. A plain man of letters might quite properly fill that post of high dignity, but not, in my opinion, the holder of a very subordinate post in the public service. This is an objection in your interest; I have another in my own. The Department which I serve has always left me perfect freedom in my literary publications. In return, I consider myself bound to abstain from all appearance on the stage of public life, and your Rector, in making his address, must certainly be considered as appearing on this stage.

I have given you this frank explanation because I think it due to your kindness. Once more accept my cordial and grateful thanks to all the St. Andrews' students who supported me, and to yourself in especial as their representative, and belive me, my dear sir, most sincerely yours,

MATTHEW ARNOLD.

Andrew Miller, Esq.

BIBLIOGRAPHY

WORKS OF MATTHEW ARNOLD

A Bible-Reading for Schools. The Great Prophecy of Israel's Restoration—Isaiah, chapters 40–66, arranged and edited by M. Arnold, 1872.
Culture and Anarchy, ed. J. Dover Wilson. C.U.P. 1946.
Discourses in America. Macmillan, New York, 1906.
E. Burke, Letters, Speeches and Tracts on Irish Affairs, ed. M. Arnold. London, 1881.
England and the Italian Question. Longmans, London, 1859.
Essays in Criticism, First Series. Macmillan, London, 1891.
Essays in Criticism, Second Series. Macmillan, London, 1930.
Essays by Matthew Arnold. Oxford Edition. O.U.P., 1914.
A French Eton and *Schools and Universities in France.* Macmillan, London, 1892.
Friendship's Garland. Smith, Elder, London, 1903.
Irish Essays and Others. Smith, Elder, London, 1891.
Isaiah XL—LXVI, ed. M. Arnold, 1875.
Isaiah of Jerusalem, ed. Matthew Arnold. London, 1883.
Last Essays on Church and Religion. Smith, Elder, London, 1877.
Literature and Dogma. Nelson, London. N.D.
Matthew Arnold's Notebooks, ed. E. Wodehouse. Smith, Elder, London, 1912.
Mixed Essays. Smith, Elder, London, 1879.
On Translating Homer. Routledge, London. N.D.
On the Study of Celtic Literature and Other Essays. Everyman edition. Dent, London, 1932.
Oratio anniversaria in memoriam publicorum benefactorum Academiae Oxoniensis—habita in Theatro Sheldoniano. Spottiswood, London, 1862.
Reign of Queen Victoria, T. H. Ward, ed., vol. ii. Article "Schools", by Matthew Arnold. Smith, Elder, London, 1887.
Reports:
  Reports on Elementary Schools, 1852–1892, ed. F. Sandford. Macmillan, London, 1889.
  Reports on Elementary Schools, 1852–1882, ed. F. S. Marvin. H.M.S.O., 1908.
  Report on Higher Schools and Universities in Germany. Macmillan London, 1874.
  Schools and Universities on the Continent. Macmillan, London, 1868.
  Special Report on Certain Points Concerned with Elementary Education in Germany, Switzerland and France. Published by the Education Reform League, Toynbee Hall, 1888.

The Popular Education of France, with Notices of that of Holland and Switzerland. Longmans, London, 1861.

S. Paul and Protestantism. Smith Elder, London, 1870.

The Poetical Works of Matthew Arnold, with an Introduction by Sir A. T. Quiller-Couch. O.U.P., 1942.

The Poetry of Matthew Arnold, C. B. Tinker and H. F. Lowry. O.U.P., 1940.

Thoughts on Education Chosen from the Writings of Matthew Arnold, ed. L. Huxley. Smith Elder, London, 1912.

Letters and Works containing Letters of Matthew Arnold on Educational Topics.

Armytage, W. H. G., art. "Matthew Arnold and W. E. Gladstone: Some New Letters," *University of Toronto Quarterly,* vol. xviii, No. 3, April 1949.

Bowood Papers, one unpublished letter by M. Arnold to Lord Shelburne.

Coleridge, E. H., *Life and Correspondence of John Duke Lord Coleridge, Lord Chief Justice of England.* Heineman, London, 1904.

Collins, J. Churton, *Letters from M. Arnold to John Churton Collins.* London, 1910.

Galton, A., *Two Essays upon Matthew Arnold, with some of his Letters to the Author.* E. Matthews, London, 1897.

Galton, A., *Fifteen Letters of Matthew Arnold to A. Galton* (1886–7), published in The Century Guild Hobby Horse, April 1890.

Gladstone Papers, Twenty-two unpublished letters between Matthew Arnold and W. E. Gladstone, British Museum.

Lowry, H. F., ed., *The Letters of Matthew Arnold to Arthur Hugh Clough.* O.U.P., 1932.

Morley, E. J., ed., *Correspondence of Henry Crabb Robinson with The Wordsworth Circle,* 2 vols. Oxford, 1927.

Mundella Correspondence, Ten unpublished letters of Matthew Arnold to A. J. and Miss Mundella. University of Sheffield, Library.

Oriel College, Oxford, Library. Four unpublished letters.

Russell, G. W. E., ed., *Letters of Matthew Arnold,* 1848–88. 2 vols. Macmillan, 1895.

Sainte-Beuve, C. A., *Chateaubriand et son Groupe Littéraire sous l'Empire.* 2 vols. Garnier Frères, Paris, 1861 (contains extract of one letter of Matthew Arnold to Sainte-Beuve).

The Modern Church, 5th November, 1891, "An Unpublished Letter of Matthew Arnold to A. Miller".

Unpublished letters in the possession of Miss Dorothy Ward.

Whitridge, A., *Unpublished Letters of Matthew Arnold.* New Haven, 1923.

GENERAL BIBLIOGRAPHY

Acland, A. H. D., and Smith, H. L., ed., *Studies in Secondary Education.* Percival, London, 1892.

Adams, F., *History of the Elementary School Contest in England.* Chapman & Hall, London, 1882.

Adams, J., *The Evolution of Educational Theory.* Macmillan, London, 1928.

Adamson, J. W., *English Education,* 1789–1902. C.U.P., 1930.

Allen, B. M., *Sir Robert Morant, a Great Public Servant.* Macmillan, London, 1934.

Almond, H. H., *Mr. Lowe's Educational Theories Examined from a Practical Point of View.* Edmonston & Douglas, Edinburgh, 1868.

Archer, R. L., *Secondary Education in the Nineteenth Century.* C.U.P., 1921.

Arnold, W. D., *Oakfield or Fellowship in the East,* 2nd Edition. Ticknor & Fields, Boston, 1855.

Balfour, G., *The Educational Systems of Great Britain and Ireland.* Clarendon Press, Oxford, 1903.

Barker, E., *Political Thought in England,* 1848 to 1914. O.U.P., 1945.

Barnard, H. C., *A Short History of English Education from* 1760 to 1944. University of London Press, 1947.

Basu, A. N., *Education in Modern India.* Orient Book Coy., Calcutta, 1947.

Bhagavadgita, *The Message of the Gita,* as interpreted by Sri Aurobindo, ed. Anilbaran Roy. Allen & Unwin, London, 1938.

Birchenough, C., *History of Elementary Education in England and Wales from* 1800 to the Present Day. University Tutorial Press, London, 1938.

Bosanquet, B., *The Philosophical Theory of the State.* Macmillan, London, 1910.

Bradley, F. H., *Ethical Studies.* Clarendon Press, Oxford, 1935.

British Association for the Advancement of Science. *On the Best Means for Promoting Scientific Education in Schools.* Murray, London, 1868.

Brougham, H., *Speeches of Henry Lord Brougham,* 4 vols. Black, Edinburgh, 1838.

Brown, C. K. F., *The Church's Part in Education* 1833 to 1941. National Society, London, 1942.

Brown, E. K., *Matthew Arnold: A Study in Conflict.* University of Chicago Press, 1948.

Brubacher, J. S., *Modern Philosophies of Education.* McGraw-Hill, New York, 1939.

Bryant, A., *English Saga* (1840–1940). Collins, London, 1946.

Burke, E., *Reflections on the French Revolution.* Everyman Ed. Dent & Sons, London, 1912.

Butler, A. G., *The Three Friends: A Story of Rugby in the Forties.* H. Frowde, London, 1900.

Caird, J., *Spinoza.* Blackwood, Edinburgh, 1888.

Campbell, L., *The End of Liberal Education.* Edmonston & Douglas, Edinburgh, 1868.

Carlyle, T., *Sartor Resartus, Lectures on Heroes, Chartism, Past and Present.* Chapman & Hall, London, 1894.

Carlyle, T., *Past and Present, Latter-Day Pamphlets, etc.* The Standard Edition, vol. iii. Chapman & Hall, London, 1904.

Carlyle, T., *Shooting Niagara.* Chapman & Hall, London, 1867.

Carritt, E. F., *Ethical and Political Thinking.* Clarendon Press, Oxford, 1947.

Chambers, E. K., *Matthew Arnold: A Study.* Clarendon Press, Oxford, 1947.

Chesterton, G. K., *The Victorian Age in Literature.* Williams & Norgate, London, N.D.

Clapham, J. H., *An Economic History of Modern Britain*, 3 vols. C.U.P., 1926–38.

Clarke, F., *Education and Social Change.* The Sheldon Press, London, 1940.

Cole, G. D. H., *British Working Class Politics, 1832 to 1914.* Routledge, London, 1946.

Coleridge, E. H., *Life and Correspondence of John Duke Lord Coleridge, Lord Chief Justice of England.* W. Heineman, London, 1904.

Combe, G., *Education, Its Principles and Practice*, ed. W. Jolly. Macmillan, London, 1879.

Courtney, J. E., *Free Thinkers of the Nineteenth Century.* Chapman & Hall, London, 1920.

Craik, H., *The State in its Relation to Education.* Macmillan, London, 1914.

Cramer, J. F., *Australian Schools through American Eyes.* Australian Council for Educational Research. Melbourne University Press, 1936.

Crosby Hall Lectures on Education. John Snow, London, 1848.

Cubberley, E. P., *The History of Education.* Houghton Mifflin Co., Cambridge, Mass., 1920.

Cubberley, E. P., *Readings in the History of Education.* Houghton Mifflin Co., Cambridge, Mass., 1920.

Davis, H. W. C., *Balliol College.* Robinson & Co., London, 1899.

Dawes, R., *Remarks Occasioned by the Present Crusade Against the Educational Plan of the Committee of Council on Education.* Groombridge & Sons, London, 1850.

Dawson, W. H., *Matthew Arnold and his Relation to the Thought of our Time.* Putnam, New York, 1904.

De Montmorency, J. E. G., *The Progress of Education in England.* Knight, London, 1904.

Denison, G. A., *Notes of My Life* (1805–1878). Parker, Oxford, 1878.

Dewey, J., *Characters and Events*, 2 vols. Allen & Unwin, London, 1929.

Dewey, J., *Democracy and Education.* Macmillan, New York, 1929.

Dicey, A. V., *Lectures on the Relation Between Law and Public Opinion in England during the Nineteenth Century.* Macmillan, London, 1926.

Dickens, C., *David Copperfield.* Macmillan, London, 1925.

292 EDUCATIONAL THOUGHT AND INFLUENCE OF MATTHEW ARNOLD

Dickens, C., *Hard Times*, London, 1898.
Drinkwater, J., *The Eighteen Sixties*. C.U.P., 1932.
Durvy, J. F. W., *Manual of Education*. Heywood, Manchester, 1903.
Dyment, C., *Matthew Arnold*. Phoenix House, London, 1948.
Education Reform League, *Special Report on Elementary Education*. Toynbee Hall, 1888.
Emerson, R. W., *Works*, vol. iii. Bell & Sons, London, 1904.
Ensor, R. C. K., *England, 1870–1914*. Clarendon Press, Oxford, 1936.
Epictetus, *Moral Discourses*, ed. W. H. D. Rouse. Everyman Edition. Dent & Sons, London, 1933.
Farrar, F. W., *Essays on a Liberal Education*. Macmillan, London, 1867.
Farrar, F. W., *General Aims of the Teacher*. C.U.P., 1883.
Fearon, D. R., *School Inspection*. Macmillan, London, 1876.
Findlay, J. J., *Arnold of Rugby*. C.U.P., 1925.
Fitch, J. G., *Thomas and Matthew Arnold*. Heineman, London, 1904.
Franks, O., *Central Planning and Control in War and Peace*. London School of Economics. Longmans, 1947.
Galton, A., *Two Essays upon Matthew Arnold*. E. Matthews, London, 1898.
Garvin, J. L., *The Life of Joseph Chamberlain*. Macmillan, London, 1932.
Gasking, D. A. T., *Examinations and the Aims of Education*. Melbourne University Press, 1945.
General Education in a Free Society. Harvard University Press, Cambridge, Mass., 1945.
Gill, J., *Systems of Education, a History and Criticism of the Principles, Methods . . . Advocated by the Eminent Educationists*. London, 1876.
Goethe, J. W. von, *Wilhelm Meisters' Apprenticeship and Travels*. Trans. T. Carlyle. Chapman & Hall, London, 1890.
Graves, J., *Policy and Progress in Secondary Education, 1902–42*. Nelson, London, 1943.
Hammond, J. L., and B., *The Bleak Age*. Longmans, London, 1945.
Hammond, J. L., and B., *Lord Shaftesbury*. Penguin Books, 1939.
Harvey, C. H., *Matthew Arnold: A Critic of the Victorian Period*. Clarke & Co., London, 1931.
Hayward, A., *Lord Lansdowne*. A Biographical Sketch. 1872.
Hearnshaw, F. J. C., *The Social and Political Ideas of Some Representative Thinkers of the Victorian Age*. Harrap, London, 1933.
Hicks, J., *The Stoicism of Matthew Arnold*. University of Iowa Humanistic Studies, vol. vi, no. 1. 1942.
Hobhouse, L. T., *Liberalism*. O.U.P., 1911.
Hobhouse, L. T., *The Metaphysical Theory of the State*. Allen & Unwin, London, 1918.
Hole, J., *The Homes of the Working Classes*. Longmans, London, 1886.
Holman, H., *English National Education*. Blackie, London, 1898.
Huxley, L., *The Life and Letters of T. H. Huxley*, 2 vols. Macmillan, London, 1900.

293

Huxley, T. H., *Science and Education*. Macmillan, London, 1895.
Jennings, W. I., *Cabinet Government*. C.U.P., 1936.
Jolly, W., ed., *Education, Its Principles and Practices by G. Combe*. Macmillan, London, 1879.
Jolly, W., ed., *Ruskin on Education*. Allen, London, 1907.
Kandel, I. L., *Impressions of Australian Education*. Australian Council for Education Research, 1938.
Kay-Shuttleworth, J. P., *Memorandum on Popular Education*. Ridgway, London, 1868.
Kay-Shuttleworth, J. P., *Letter to Earl Granville on the Revised Code*. London, 1861.
Kay-Shuttleworth, J. P., *Public Education as Affected by the Minutes of the Committee of Privy Council from 1846–1852*. Longmans, London, 1853.
Kay-Shuttleworth, J. P., *Four Periods of Public Education as reviewed in 1832–1839–1846–1862 in Papers by Sir James Kay-Shuttleworth, Bart.* Longmans, London, 1862.
Keith, A. B., *Responsible Government in the Dominions*. Clarendon Press, Oxford, 1928.
Kekewich, G. W., *The Education Department and After*. Constable & Co., London, 1920.
Kendall, G., *Charles Kingsley and his Ideas*. Hutchinson, London, 1946.
Kingsley, C., *Alton Locke*, with a prefatory memoir by T. Hughes, London, 1876.
Kingsley, C., *The Address on Education read before the National Association for the Promotion of Social Science at Bristol on 1st October, 1869*. London, 1869.
Kingsmill, H., *Matthew Arnold*. Duckworth, London, 1928.
Knowles, L. C. A., *The Industrial and Commercial Revolutions of Great Britain during the Nineteenth Century*. Routledge, London, 1937.
Laski, H. J., *The Danger of Being a Gentleman*. Allen & Unwin, London, 1939.
Laski, H. J., *A Grammar of Politics*. Allen & Unwin, London, 1928.
Legge, J. G., *The Rising Tide*. Blackwell, Oxford, 1929.
Lesse, J., *History and Character of Educational Inspection*. London University Ph.D. Thesis, Education. 1934.
Lilley, A. L., *Sir Joshua Fitch*. Arnold, London, 1906.
Link, S. G., *Matthew Arnold's "Sweetness and Light" in America, 1848–1938*, unpublished Ph.D. dissertation, George Peabody College for Teachers, Nashville, Tennessee, 1938.
Low, S., and Sanders, L. C., *The History of England during the Reign of Victoria (1837–1901)*. Longmans, London, 1913.
Lowe, R., *Middle Class Education. Endowment or Free Trade*. Bush, London, 1868.
Lowe, R., *Primary and Classical Education*, Address before the Philosophical Institute of Edinburgh. Edmonston & Douglas, Edinburgh, 1867.
Lowndes, G. A. N., *The Silent Social Revolution*. O.U.P., 1941.

Lynd, H. M., *England in the Eighteen Eighties*. O.U.P., 1945.
McCallister, W. J., *The Growth of Freedom in Education*. Constable, London, 1931.
Maccoby, S., *English Radicalism*, 1853–1886. Allen & Unwin, London, 1938.
MacIver, R. M., *Society*. Farrar and Rinehart, New York, 1944.
Mack, E. C., *Public Schools and British Opinion since 1860*. Columbia University Press, New York, 1941.
Magid, H. M., *English Political Pluralism*. Columbia Studies in Philosophy, New York, 1941.
Maltby, S. E., *Manchester and the Movement for National Elementary Education*, 1800–1870. Manchester University, 1918.
Mannheim, K., *Man and Society*. Kegan Paul, London, 1942.
Martin, A. P., *Life and Letters of Viscount Sherbrooke*, 2 vols. Longmans, London, 1893.
Martin, G. H., *The Evolution of the Massachussetts Public School System*. Appleton, New York, 1904.
Martin, T., *The Life of the Prince Consort*, 5 vols. Smith Elder, London, 1875.
Mathew, D., *Acton: The Formative Years*. Eyre & Spottiswoode, London, 1946.
Meiklejohn, A., *Education Between Two Worlds*. Harper and Brothers, New York, 1942.
Miall, A., *Life of Edward Miall*. Macmillan, London, 1884.
Michaut, G., *Senancour: ses amis et ses ennemis*. Paris, 1909.
Mill, J. S., *Principles of Political Economy*. Longmans, London, 1883.
Mill, J. S., *Autobiography*. Longmans, London, 1873.
Mill, J. S., *On Liberty, and Considerations on Representative Government*, ed. R. B. McCallum. Blackwell, Oxford, 1946.
Minutes of the Committee of Council on Education.
Moberly, G., *Five Short Letters to Sir William Heathcote, on the Studies and Discipline of Public Schools*. Rivingtons, London, 1861.
Montalembert, *De L'avenir politique de L'Angleterre*. Paris, 1856.
Monypenny, W. F., and Buckle, G. E., *The Life of Benjamin Disraeli*, 2 vols. Murray, London, 1929.
Morley, J., *Life of Richard Cobden*, 2 vols. Macmillan, London, 1908.
Morley, J., *The Life of William Ewart Gladstone*, 3 vols. Macmillan, London, 1903.
Morley, J., *The Struggle for National Education*. Chapman & Hall, London, 1873.
Mowat, R. B., *The Victorian Age*. Harrap & Co., London, 1939.
Murray, R. H., *Studies in the English Social and Political Thinkers of the Nineteenth Century*. Heffer, Cambridge, 1929.
National Education League.*Report of the First General Meeting of the National Education League held at Birmingham, on Tuesday and Wednesday, 12th and 13th October*, 1869. Birmingham, 1869.
National Education League. *Verbatim Report of the proceedings of a Deputation, etc., Wednesday, 9th March, 1870*. Birmingham, for the National Education League, 1870.

National Education Union. *Authorised Report of the Educational Conference held at Leeds, 8th December,* 1869. Longmans, for the National Education Union, London, 1869.

Newman, J. H., *On the Scope and Nature of University Education.* Everyman Edition. Dent & Son, London, 1943.

Newman, J. H., *Select Discourses from the Idea of a University,* ed. M. Yardley. C.U.P., 1931.

Orrick, J. B., *Matthew Arnold and Goethe.* Publication of the English Goethe Society, New Series, vol. 4. 1928.

Parliamentary Debates ⎱ Full details are given under the appropriate
Parliamentary Papers ⎰ references.

Paul, H. W., *Matthew Arnold.* English Men of Letters Series. Macmillan, London, 1902.

Paulsen, F., *German Education, Past and Present.* T. F. Unwin, London, 1908.

Paulsen, F., *Geschichte des Gelehrten Unterrichts.* Band ii. Leipzig, 1919.

Pollard, A. F., *The Evolution of Parliament.* Longmans, London, 1926.

Pollock, F., *Spinoza, His Life and Philosophy.* Duckworth, London, 2nd edition, 1912.

Quick, R. H., *Life and Remains.* C.U.P., 1899.

Radhakrishnan, S., *Indian Philosophy,* 2 vols. Allen & Unwin, London 1923.

Radhakrishnan, S., *The Hindu View of Life.* Allen & Unwin, London, 1927.

Redford, A., *The History of Local Government in Manchester.* Longmans, London, 1940.

Reid, T. Wemyss, *Life of the Rt. Hon. W. E. Forster,* 2 vols. Chapman & Hall, London, 1888.

Reisner, E. H., *Nationalism and Education since* 1789. Macmillan, New York, 1927.

Reports:
Report of Commissioners on Popular Education in England, 1861 (*Parliamentary Papers* (House of Commons), 1861, xxi, parts i–vi) [Newcastle].

Report of Her Majesty's Commissioners on Revenues and Management of Certain Colleges, 1864 (1864, xx, xxi) [Clarendon].

Report of Commissioners on Education in Schools in England not comprised within Her Majesty's two recent Commissions on Popular Education and Public Schools, 1867–8 (1867–8, xxviii, parts i–xvii) [Taunton].

Report on Elementary Education Acts (England and Wales) [Cross].
First Report 1886 (1886, xxv).
Second ,, 1887 (1887, xxix).
Third ,, 1887 (1887, xxx).
Final ,, 1888 (1888, xxxv, xxxvii).
Appendices 1888 (1888, xxxvi).

Fourth Report of the Department of Science and Art, 1857.
Report of the Consultative Committee on the Education of the Adolescent (Hadow Report). H.M.S.O., 1927.
Report of the Consultative Committee on Secondary Education (Spens Report). H.M.S.O., 1939.
Curriculum and Examinations in Secondary Schools (Norwood Report). H.M.S.O., 1943.
Teachers and Youth Leaders (McNair Report). H.M.S.O., 1944.
Special Reports on Educational Subjects, 1896–7, ed. M. E. Sadler. H.M.S.O., 1897.
Vide also *Minutes of the Committee of Council.*
    National Education League.
    National Education Union.
    British Association for the Advancement of Science.
Rich, R. W., *The Training of Teachers in England and Wales during the Nineteenth Century.* C.U.P., 1933.
Robertson, J. M., *Modern Humanists.* Swan Sonnenschein, London, 1891.
Robson, A. H., *The Education of Children Engaged in Industry,* 1833–76. Kegan Paul, London, 1931.
Ruskin, J., *Stones of Venice,* vol. iii. George Allen, London, 1898.
Sainte-Beuve, *Chateaubriand et son Groupe Littéraire sous l'Empire,* 2 vols. Garnier Frères, Paris, 1861.
Sainte-Beuve, *Les Grands Écrivains Français,* XIXeme, Siècle, Philosophes et Essayists, III. Libraire Garnier Frères, Paris, 1930.
Saintsbury, G., *Matthew Arnold.* Blackwood, Edinburgh, 1899.
Sandford, F. R. J. (Baron Sandford), *Testimonials in favour of F. R. Sandford* (a candidate for the Greek Chair in the University of Edinburgh). Edinburgh, 1852.
Schilling, B. N., *Human Dignity and the Great Victorians.* Columbia University Press, New York, 1946.
Scott, R. P., ed., *What is Secondary Education? and other short Essays.* Rivingtons, London, 1899.
Sells, I. E., *Matthew Arnold and France.* C.U.P., 1935.
Senancour, Pivert de, *Obermann,* ed. G. Sand. Charpentier, Paris, 1882.
Senancour, Pivert de, *Obermann,* trans. A. E. Waite. London, 1903.
Senior, N. W., *Suggestions on Popular Education.* Murray, London, 1861.
Slosson, E. E., *Six Major Prophets.* Little, Brown & Co., Boston, 1917.
Smart, T. B., *The Bibliography of Matthew Arnold.* Davy & Sons, London, 1892.
Smellie, K. B., *A History of Local Government.* Allen & Unwin, London, 1946.
Smiles, S., *Self Help.* Murray, London, 1913.
Smith, Adam, *An Inquiry into the Nature and Causes of the Wealth of Nations.* Routledge, London, N.D.
Smith, F., *A History of English Elementary Education,* 1760–1902. University of London Press, 1931.

Smith, F., *The Life and Work of Sir James Kay-Shuttleworth*. Murray, London, 1923.

Smith, Goldwin, *Reminiscences*, ed. A. Haultain. Macmillan, New York, 1911.

Smith, W. O. Lester, *To Whom do Schools Belong?* Blackwell, Oxford, 1943.

Sneyd-Kynnersley, E. M., *H.M.I.* Macmillan, London, 1913.

Somervell, D. C., *English Thought in the Nineteenth Century*. Methuen, London, 1940.

Spencer, H., *An Autobiography*, 2 vols. Williams & Norgate, London, 1904.

Spencer, H., *On Education*, ed. F. A. Cavenagh. C.U.P., 1932.

Spencer, H., *Study of Sociology*. Kegan Paul, London, 1904.

Spinoza, Benedict de, *Ethics*. Trans. A. Boyle. Dent & Sons, London, 1938.

Stanley, A. P., *The Life and Correspondence of Thomas Arnold*, D.D. Ward Lock, London, 1893.

Stephen, Leslie, *The English Utilitarians*, 3 vols. Duckworth, London, 1900.

Strachey, L., *Eminent Victorians*. Chatto & Windus, London, 1938.

Tate, T., *The Philosophy of Education*, 3rd edition. Longmans, London, 1860.

Tawney, R. H., *Equality*. Allen & Unwin, London, 1931.

Thomas, D. H., *The Development of Technical Education in England*, 1851–89. Ph.D. Thesis. London, 1940.

Thring, E., *Education and School*. Cambridge and London, 1864.

Tinker, C. A., and Lowry, H. F., *The Poetry of Matthew Arnold*. O.U.P., 1940.

Tocqueville, Alexis de, *Democracy in America*, ed. H. S. Commager. O.U.P., 1946.

Trevelyan, G. M. (Mrs.), *The Life of Mrs. Humphrey Ward*. Constable, London, 1923.

Trevelyan, G. M., *British History in the Nineteenth Century* (1782–1901). Longmans, London, 1934.

Trevelyan, G. M., *Life of John Bright*. Constable, London, 1913.

Trilling, L., *Matthew Arnold*. Norton, New York, 1939.

University of Iowa Studies, *Critical Studies in Arnold, Emerson, and Newman by J. Hicks, E. E. Sandeen, A. S. Ryan*, ed. J. E. Baker. Iowa, 1942.

Vaughan, C. E. V., *Studies in the History of Political Philosophy before and after Rousseau*. Vol. ii. Manchester University Press, 1925.

Vial, F., *Trois Siècles d'Histoire de l'Enseignement Secondaire*. Delagrave, Paris, 1936.

Walker, H., *The Greater Victorian Poets*. Swan Sonnenschein, London, 1895.

Ward, Mrs. Humphry, *A Writer's Recollections*. Collins, London, 1918.

Ward, T. H., ed., *The Reign of Queen Victoria*—A Survey of Fifty Years of Progress. 2 vols. Smith Elder, London, 1887.

Webb, S., *Grants in Aid: A Criticism and a Proposal*. Longmans, London, 1920.

Whitehead, A. N., *The Aims of Education*. Williams & Norgate, London, 1946.

Whitridge, A., *Dr. Arnold of Rugby*. Constable, London, 1928.

Willoughby, L. A., *The Classical Age of German Literature, 1748 to 1805*. O.U.P., 1926.

Woods, A., *Educational Experiments in England*. Methuen, London, 1920.

Woodward, E. L., *The Age of Reform, 1815–1870*. Clarendon Press, Oxford, 1938.

Woolf, L., *After the Deluge*. L. & V. Woolf, London, 1931.

Wright, T., *The Great Unwashed*, by the Journeyman Engineer. London, 1868.

Young, G. M., ed., *Early Victorian England, 1830–1865*, 2 vols. O.U.P., 1934.

Young, G. M., ed., *Victorian England, Portrait of an Age*. O.U.P., 1944.

LIST OF PERIODICALS AND NEWSPAPERS USED

(*Details of articles are given under individual references.*)

The Academy.
The Athenaeum.
The Bookman.
The Century Magazine.
The Contemporary Review.
The Cornhill Magazine.
Daily News.
The Eclectic Review.
The Economist.
The Edinburgh Review.
The Fortnightly Magazine.
Fraser's Magazine.

The Guardian.
Macmillan's Magazine.
The Modern Church.
The Nineteenth Century.
The North American Review.
The Pall Mall Gazette.
The Quarterly Review.
Revue Anglo-Americaine.
The Times.
The Times Literary Supplement.
The Westminster Review.

INDEX

Aberdeen, Earl of, 5, 12
Aberglaube, 145
Acland, A. H. D., 259 n., 281
Acton, J., 78
Adams, F., 138
Adderley, C. B. (Lord Norton), 48 n.,
    50 n., 92 n., 207, 242
adequacy, 31, 36, 175, 264
Aeschylus, 175
Almond, H. H., 193 n.
Alterthumswissenschaft, 172 f., 179, 192
Americanism, 68 ff., 73, 181, 269, 276
Ampère, J. J. A., 70
Antonelli, Cardinal, 89
Arbuthnot-Trevelyan reform, 76
Arminius, 251, 257 ff.
aristocracy, 71 ff., 76, 84, 166, 246, 266, 273
Aristophanes, 175
Arnold, Edward P., 104
Arnold, Jane, 26 f., 32, 55 n., 69, 112
Arnold, Mary (Twining), 25
Arnold, Matthew:
    Academy, views on French, 81, 181
    adequacy, use of the term, 31, 36, 175, 264
    America, views on, 68 ff., 73
    Barbarians, on, 165 f., 245
    Bhagavadgita, influence of, 26 f., 143, 167
    Bible in schools, use of, 151, 153 f.
    Chair of Poetry, 143, 160
    classical studies, 172 ff., 191, 195 ff.
    comparative education, 229
    compulsory education, 122 ff.
    Council on education, 97 ff.
    creativity in education, on, 240 f.
    criticism, literary, 80, 160, 240-1
    Cross Commission evidence, 152,
        220 n., 228 f., 233
    culture, views on, 28, 161 ff., 199 ff.,
        213, 252, 266, 274 ff.
    dandyism in early life, 16
    democracy, on, 72 ff., 84, 166, 267
    dissent, views on, 147 ff., 248, 250 ff.
    elevation, 35, 68, 79, 236, 266, 278
    English, teaching of, 179 ff.
    Epictetus, influence of, 29 f.
    equality, 83 ff., 131, 162, 277
    Essay on Gray, 32, 273
    Establishment, views on, 149 f.
    examinations, on, 216, 241
    father's influence, 35, 278
    feels his own importance, 142 f., 160
    flexibility, on, 245 f.
    formal training, attitude on, 177 ff.
    Forster, W. E., connection with, 112 f.,
        131, 215-7, 221, 223, 230, 256
    free education, on, 129 f.
    freedom, 83, 85
    grammar, teaching of, 176 ff., 182, 226
    Hebraism, 71, 249, 250

Hellenism, 34, 175 ff., 249
humanism, 170, 186 ff., 225, 240
humanizing, 82-3, 141, 180 ff., 185-6,
    200 ff., 213 f., 277
humour, 16, 231, 233, 248, 251, 257 ff.
Inaugural Lecture, 31, 174
income tax assessment, 142 n.
inspection, opinion of, 225, 226-7,
    229 ff., 261
inspector of schools, 1, 15, 17, 165, 180,
    196, 208, 223 f., 229 ff.
liberalism, 82, 86, 227
life, vii f.
literature, teaching of, 176, 179 ff.,
    182 ff., 199 ff., 201, 226, 279
local government and education, 97,
    116, 118, 220, 262
Lowe, R., opinion regarding, 191, 208,
    215-6, 224, 250-1, 261-2
lower classes and education, 141 f.,
    150, 214, 225
lucidity, on, 272
middle class, on, 71, 79, 165 ff., 244,
    249 ff., 279, 280
Ministry of Education, views on, 88 ff.,
    97, 98 ff., 236, 271, 277, 280
modern languages, teaching of, 179 f.
Nature, on, 22, 25 f.
Newcastle Commission, 72, 99, 106,
    111, 213, 226, 237, 243, 248, 275
Obermann's influence, 22 ff., 32
opinion of teaching profession, 18
organic system of education, 118 f., 123
Oxford, 14 f., 19
Philistines, 165 ff., 250 ff., 279, vide
    also middle class
poetry, 18, 23 ff., 32 ff.
    teaching of, 183 ff.
private secretary to Lord Lansdowne,
    16 f.
reading, teaching of, 226
Rede Lecture, 199 ff.
religion, on, 142 ff., 164, 277
religious education, views on, 141 ff., 202
Revised Code, attitude towards,
    203 ff., 211 ff., 224 ff., 277, 280
Rugby, 14 f., 19
School Boards, opinion of, 116
science, teaching of, 195 ff., 270, 279
secondary education, 88, 243 f.,
    256 ff., 279, 280
simplicity, on, 239-40
Spinoza's influence, 30 ff.
State and education, 72 ff., 100, 151, 214
sweet-reasonableness, on, 145
Taunton Commission, 110 f., 255 ff.
teacher training, on, 236 ff., 241
universal education, 126
university education, on, 269 ff.